MW00643964

DISCARDED
COUNTY OF STRATHCONA
MUNICIPAL LIBRARY

FEB 1 8 1998

796.54
BRI
Bridge, Raymond.
The new complete snow
camper's guide

14313

County of Strathcona Municipal Library

THE NEW COMPLETE
SNOW
CAMPER'S
GUIDE

THE NEW COMPLETE
SNOW CAMPER'S GUIDE

4 1974 02219 9795

THE NEW COMPLETE
SNOW
CAMPER'S
GUIDE
Raymond Bridge

CHARLES SCRIBNER'S SONS · NEW YORK

County of Strathcona Municipal Library

Copyright © 1973, 1981 Raymond Bridge

Library of Congress Cataloging in Publication Data

Bridge, Raymond.
  The new complete snow camper's guide.

  Bibliography: p.
  Includes index.
  1. Snow camping.   2. Winter sports.   I. Title.
GV198.9.B74   1981   796.54   81-8854
ISBN 0-684-16842-1   AACR2

This book published simultaneously in the
United States of America and in Canada—
Copyright under the Berne Convention.

All rights reserved. No part of this book
may be reproduced in any form without the
permission of Charles Scribner's Sons.

1 3 5 7 9 11 13 15 17 19   F/C   20 18 16 14 12 10 8 6 4 2

Printed in the United States of America.

This book is dedicated to the memory of Harry Waldrop,
a lover of high places and wild waters, and a good friend.
His memory and spirit still quicken the places he loved
and the hearts of those who knew him.

Books by Raymond Bridge

America's Backpacking Book, Revised Edition
Freewheeling: The Bicycle Camping Book
The Camper's Guide to Alaska, the Yukon,
  and Northern British Columbia
Tourguide to the Rocky Mountain Wilderness
Climbing: A Guide to Mountaineering
High Peaks and Clear Roads
The Complete Guide to Kayaking
The Complete Canoeist's Guide
The Runner's Book
Bike Touring: The Sierra Club Guide to Outings on Wheels
Running Without Pain: A Guide to the Prevention and
  Treatment of Running Injuries
The New Complete Snow Camper's Guide

Contents

PREFACE to the Revised Edition   xi

INTRODUCTION   1   Why winter?   1   Getting started   3

1.   **HEADING OUT IN WINTER   7**   How to keep your body running   7   Heat loss   8   Windchill   9   Insulation   9   The shell game   12   Keeping water out   13   Getting water out   13   Getting water in   14   Hazards and emergencies   14   Equipment   15

2.   **COLD-WEATHER CLOTHING   16**   Basic clothing   17   Outer clothing   22   Dressing for the cold   28

3.   **SLEEPING WARM   30**   How much sleeping bag do you need?   30   A buyer's guide to sleeping bags   32   Innovations and special designs   40   A recommended system   42   Shopping for sleeping bags   45   Ground insulation   47   Sleeping warm   48   Caring for your sleeping bag   50

4.   **CAMPING ON SNOW   52**   Getting started   52   Shelters to carry with you   53   Snow shelters   60   Improvised shelters   70   Tools   71   Living in the snow   72   Cars   74

5.   **COOKING OUT IN THE SNOW   75**   Stoves versus fires   76   Choosing a stove   76   Cooking inside   78   Meals   80

6.   **ON THE TRAIL   86**   Planning your trip   86   Pace and conditioning   88   Carrying your gear   90   Making up the party   91   Solo trips   92   Route finding   92   Walking in winter   97   Boots   97   Care of the boots and the feet   100   Equipment   101   Along the winter trail   109   Children on the trail   111   Staying on top of the snow   112

7.   **SNOWSHOEING: WALKING ON THE DRIFTS   114**   Types of snowshoes   117   Choosing snowshoes   121   Hitches and bindings   122   Footwear   123   Getting around on snowshoes   126

8. SKIING THE WHITE WILDERNESS 129 The equipment revolution 130 Equipment recommendations 132 Touring on skis 144 Waxing your skis 145 Climbers 154 Beginning skiing technique 156 Improving your skiing 162

9. FINDING YOUR WAY 165 Learning to look 166 Maps 167 Reading the map 170 Direction finding 173 Compasses 174 Where the compass points 174 What good is direction? 176 Types of compasses 177 Systems for knowing your location 180 Map and compass 186 Keeping track of where you've been 189 Erratic compass? 192 More on compass features 193

10. STEEP SNOW: AN INTRODUCTION 196 How steep is steep? 197 Climbing aids and safety measures 198 Snowshoe tools and techniques 199 Skis on steep snow 200 Step-kicking 201 The safety factor 201 Crampons 207 A few notes on snow climbing 209

11. STORMS AND AVALANCHES 211 Weather in winter 211 Watching the weather 212 Weathering a storm 215 Camps and bivouacs in storms 216 Avalanches 221 Judging hazardous conditions 232 Crossing avalanche terrain 234 A final caution 238

12. EMERGENCIES AND ACCIDENTS 240 Staying out of trouble 241 Getting lost 242 Storms 244 Injuries and medical emergencies 245 Injuries where seconds count 247 Examining an accident victim 251 Fractures 254 Wounds 257 Special problems 258 Shock 262 Cold injuries 263 Getting the victim out 268 Risks, rescuers, and responsibility 268

13. THE WORLD OF WINTER 272 The interrelationship of things 272 Watching in winter 274 Learning what's what 276 Choosing guidebooks 278 Where to begin 279 Gadgetry 280

14. A PLEA FOR WILD PLACES 281 A defense of wilderness 284 Saving what we have 288 Wild places and open spaces 291 A final note 295

APPENDIX A: HOW TO MAKE YOUR OWN EQUIPMENT 301 From kits or from scratch 302 Getting started 303 Getting your materials 305 Design considerations 305 Cagoule 315 Rain chaps 316 Bivouac sack and sleeping bag cover 316

APPENDIX B: SELECTED READING   317   General   317
Food and cooking   318   Snowshoeing   318   Skiing   319   Finding your way   319   Storms, avalanches, and snow   319   Steep snow   320   Emergencies   320   Nature and wilderness   321
Making your own gear   322

APPENDIX C: WHERE TO BUY IT   323

APPENDIX D: CHECKLISTS OF WHAT TO TAKE   325
Emergency kit   327   Saving money on your outfit   329

INDEX   331

Preface to the Revised Edition

In working on the new edition of *The Complete Snow Camper's Guide,* I have been struck by how greatly some aspects of lightweight winter camping have changed and how little others have changed. Few parts of the original book have needed moderate revision; either they are grossly outdated or they stand quite well as they were originally written, nearly ten years ago. The reason for the discrepancy is obvious on reflection. Equipment and technique have changed, generally for the better, but the basic principles of living in the wilderness in cold weather remain pretty much the same from one year or decade to the next.

The biggest change in wilderness travel during the winter months has been its enormous increase in popularity. Only a few years ago, most of the ski tourers in the Sierra Nevada, the Rockies, or the White Mountains knew one another. They were a small group of eccentrics. Once out of view of the road or local downhill ski area, one saw few other winter travelers, and even those few usually stayed on a few prepared ski trails or followed the path to a club hut. The change in the last ten years has been enormous. The popular trailheads are now crowded, there are citizens' cross-country races every weekend, centers with networks of prepared tracks are springing up in many areas, and fashionable suits are replacing army surplus on the touring scene as they did in downhill skiing ten or fifteen years before. Anyone who did much backcountry skiing or snowshoeing a decade or more ago can't help feeling a little nostalgic, but significant benefits have derived from the boom.

The most important advances have been in the area of equipment. Lightweight skis have been developed that are strong enough to be used safely far from the nearest road. Snowshoes are now lighter and stronger. The development of Gore-tex has vastly improved the quality of winter shell clothing, albeit at a high price. Avalanche beacons have improved the ability of a small party to accomplish a rescue if they miscalculate avalanche hazards. There have been a few unfortunate changes in equipment, such as the decline in down quality, but not many.

xii THE NEW COMPLETE SNOW CAMPER'S GUIDE

Coupled with improvements in equipment have been advances in travel and camping techniques. Some of these are the result of the rediscovery and refinement of traditional skills. The revival of the telemark turn in skiing is an example. Along with the development of tough light-touring skis with metal edges, the telemark revival has made it possible for a large number of backcountry tour skiers to negotiate slopes steep enough to challenge most downhill skiers. Extensive practice at building snow shelters has given many winter travelers the ability to dispense with tents, enabling them to travel lighter and faster, covering more ground with greater enjoyment. Since snow shelters are warmer than tents, lighter sleeping bags can also be used once enough practice has been acquired.

These changes and other similar ones have opened up possibilities for the winter traveler in the backcountry. Lighter weight allows one to travel much farther and to have more fun doing it. It is far more enjoyable to ski a bowl of untracked powder with a twenty-five-pound pack than with one weighing sixty pounds. As mobility increases, many wilderness areas become accessible to the experienced winter traveler that were once very hard to reach. This additional freedom of movement makes fresh challenges possible for the expert at light-weight winter camping, and many new winter traverses of mountain ranges have become feasible, even without expeditionary tactics. More and more skiers and snowshoers are learning to pare the weight of their packs mercilessly.

The new popularity of winter travel in the backcountry has created some dangers for the unwary, however. When few people went far away from the roads in winter, inexperienced individuals were usually kept out of trouble by a natural caution and fear of the unknown. With crowds assembling at many trailheads these days and packed trails extending into the wilderness, it is much easier to get in over your head without realizing that you are in any danger at all. The winter wilderness is far less forgiving of mistakes than the same country in summer. In most parts of North America, a night spent out in the open during the warmer months may result in some discomfort, but a healthy person will usually survive even during bad weather spells in the mountains. In winter, things are quite different. A pleasant stroll can suddenly change into a survival ordeal if a few mistakes and misfortunes combine in the wrong way. The beginner needs to keep this in mind and to proceed with some caution and with proper respect for winter conditions. The pitfalls that need to be avoided are emphasized in later chapters.

In this revised edition, I have tried to take account of many improvements in equipment, in technique, and in my own understanding of snow camping so that the newcomer to winter travel in the back-country can take advantage of these developments. The summer backpacker or the experienced ski tourer who wants to start taking multiday trips should be able to learn quickly the special techniques needed for winter trekking. This book remains a basic guide for the beginner and the intermediate, however, and it is impossible to cover all the fine points that are of special interest to expert winter travelers. The nuances of telemark technique in varying snow conditions, the subtleties of ski design for expert skiers, and the sophisticated methods of avalanche prediction in the backcountry are beyond the scope of this book. In the new text I have tried to point out some of the disagreements that exist even between experts and, for those interested, I have suggested additional reading in Appendix B: Selected Reading. Basically, however, the best way to learn most of these subjects is to get out into the backcountry, leaving yourself a healthy safety margin when you make decisions. I hope this new edition of *The Complete Snow Camper's Guide* will prove useful to those who are planning trips into the incredibly beautiful world of the white wilderness.

Introduction

Custom dictates that an author owes readers some justification before asking them to delve into a book—a reasonable requirement in an age when trees and leisure are scarcer than words on wood pulp. So, why this book?

One morning a couple of years ago, I drifted slowly into wakefulness from a warmth made blissful by the contrasting cold of the air on my face. I pulled on my clothes inside my sleeping bag and crawled out of the small mountain tent, moving carefully to avoid knocking frost from the walls onto my sleeping companion.

Outside was a world so fantastically bright and new and sparkling with white light that my first reaction of exultation was replaced by a wonder that I should be allowed to be there at all. The clarity of colors—orange tent, green trees, blue sky—stood out against the snow, and above it all stood the peaks of the Sierra Nevada—the Snowy Range—renamed the Range of Light by John Muir.

The day before, we had skied to this spot in "whiteout" conditions—snow blowing so hard we could see nothing. We struggled with the tent in the wind, finally pitching it well enough to last the night, and tumbled into our sleeping bags inside. The roar of our cooking stove competed with that of the wind, and the meal completed a kind of existential sense of well-being that seems only to come with hard physical effort.

Now, the next morning, the fruits of the storm sparkled on the branches of lodgepole pines—the miracle of the Spartan, pristine, incredibly beautiful world of winter, a world born clean and new with every snowstorm.

This is a book about some of the pedestrian aspects of exploring that world—a how-to-do-it book for the beginning cold-weather wilderness traveler. It deals with the techniques of exploring the white wilderness on foot and of living there while traveling.

WHY WINTER?

The most important reason for going hiking, camping, snowshoeing, and skiing in the winter is that it is a beautiful time of year. There is a unique loveliness in the hills and woods when snow is on the ground. The obvious difficulties which often scare off the fair-season camper become happy challenges to the devotee. Advantages not immediately apparent are learned when one travels much in the cold seasons. Many areas that receive heavy snows are much easier to visit in winter than summer: Impenetrable brush is covered over with a highway of snow, and watery regions are often passable on foot only when temperatures remain below freezing.

I have a more selfish reason for visiting the woods in winter, though. Many of my favorite wilderness areas are no longer wilderness except in winter.

The great interest shown by all sorts of Americans in the outdoors and the wilderness has had the laudable effect of giving many people a taste for the magnificence of those wild places that have escaped "progress" in some degree. Unfortunately, this growing enthusiasm has also made it increasingly difficult to find those things for which many of us go to the woods in the first place—solitude or the companionship of chosen friends in an atmosphere of beauty and simplicity. For good reasons and bad, the pressure on wilderness and semi-wilderness areas has increased tremendously in the last few years. It has increased fastest in those areas that are easy to reach on weekends and during short annual vacations. Such short periods are all the time most of us have available for a wilderness experience.

For those who have discovered the fact that the wilderness can only really be experienced on its own terms there are still some ways out. Luckily, most of the highly mechanized Americans who are creating the pressure on readily accessible wilderness areas are gone after Labor Day. They depart when the first snows begin to fall and cover the beer cans with beauty.

The areas of the country that are covered by snow in the winter still offer the challenge of discovery to those willing to make some effort to learn the skills necessary to travel the winter wilds on foot. Until just a very few years ago, vast areas that are crowded in summer were rarely visited in winter at all. A hundred yards from the nearest plowed road or ski trail one entered a world where it was possible to travel for weeks, never meeting a soul. In some areas this has changed quite a bit with the advent of the snow machine, but it is still possible to experience far more of the beauty of this country on short winter trips than on much longer summer jaunts.

I have tried to present all the information that would be needed by a person with some skill in mild-weather camping who would like to try the more challenging experience of traveling on snow. It is not necessary to climb a 14,000-foot peak twenty miles from the roadhead to have a fine wilderness experience. Though this is a worthwhile endeavor, which I recommend to you when you are ready for it, a short hike and an overnight camp can be quite satisfying and valuable.

Modern lightweight wilderness camping, whatever the season, is very different from the camping done by the men who wrote many of the classics on the outdoors. Modern equipment has completely changed the techniques and possibilities of lightweight backcountry travel, but so have modern problems, pressures, and consciousness. Modern equipment makes it possible for a small woman in only reasonably good physical condition to comfortably carry an outfit that will enable her to live in luxury. An outfit with the same capacity a few years ago would have worn down a person hardened by years of packing heavy loads. At the same time, in the areas that most of us visit it is criminal in fact, if not in law, to use a lot of the old north-woods techniques of camping. The environment simply cannot stand it. The days are gone when trees could be cut for any whimsical reason with no thought for the environmental consequences. Most of the books on wilderness living that are now available are written about the kind of camping that may still be appropriate in the great wilderness areas of the north woods but is completely out of place in the California Sierra, the tableland of Katahdin, or most of the other heavily used camping areas of North America. This type of camping is based on very low population density, and that is something you have to travel a long way to find these days.

The good modern wilderness traveler still tries to travel self-sufficiently, without depending on stores, restaurants, or hotels for reasonable comfort under expected conditions or for survival in unexpected emergencies. However, you should also realize that the wilderness is fragile, and if you expect to continue enjoying it, you cannot "live off the land."

This book is a description of the techniques necessary for self-contained, low impact travel in winter, and it attempts to help fill the need for books on modern methods and equipment.

GETTING STARTED

An obvious division of the subject of winter travel is between travel techniques proper—hiking, snowshoeing, or skiing—and the methods of cold-weather camping. This is an important distinction for the beginner to make, since the two aspects can be learned separately. You can begin by camping near your home or car, or you can start by taking short ski tours or snowshoe hikes. Learning one thing at a time reduces the number of difficulties and expenses that have to be dealt with at the beginning.

The choice of the best way to start may be dictated by your inclinations and the finances, location, and equipment you already possess. If you live in snow country outside urban areas, you may be able to start snowshoeing or ski touring near your home, even on weekdays. Equipment costs are low, and you can extend your activities to overnight trips when you feel ready. Even basic camping techniques can be learned in your back yard.

On the other hand, if you have to drive one or two hundred miles to snow country, you may want to learn snow camping first. Then you will have a base of operations for touring without paying for accommodations. Summer backpacking and car-camping equipment is sometimes adaptable to winter use with the addition of some warm clothes. The dictators of fashion in civilian and military life have fortunately made it possible to get good cold-weather clothing cheaply.

However you start, winter travel is not very expensive, once you buy the equipment. Most good lightweight equipment will give years or decades of hard service. The initial investment is not exorbitant, but it's certainly not negligible for those who live on budgets like mine. Fortunately, not everything has to be bought at once. A judicious use of rental equipment, plundering of surplus stores and storage chests, careful comparison shopping in catalogs, and taking advantage of sales and second-hand equipment can greatly reduce costs and spread them out. Making some of your own equipment, either from scratch or from kits, will cut expenses even more. Once it is acquired, it costs almost nothing to keep your outfit in repair.

The beginner is faced with a choice of several ways to travel over the snow. If it isn't deep, you can simply walk, but even then you must be prepared for more snow if you go far. When the snow drifts deep, it is time to get out the webs or skis.

If you have never skied, don't try Alpine ski-touring equipment. You'll be happier with touring skis and boots or with snowshoes, either of which is easier to learn to use and allows great versatility in the terrain that can be handled. Take your pick between skis and snowshoes after reading the chapters on each. Experienced downhill skiers may want to use specialized Alpine touring gear to deal with some kinds of terrain, but they should consider the alternative of modern lightweight touring gear before automatically choosing the more familiar-looking Alpine equipment.

Novices who haven't skied and want to be able to handle mountain terrain without any intermediate fuss should get a pair of snowshoes.

You can learn to walk on them in an hour, though you may not win any races until your second weekend.

Confirmed skiers will pick the slats on any terrain. The type of equipment will depend on the country in which you'll be skiing.

The main thing is to get out in the snow. You don't need fancy equipment to start—there's a lot of it discussed in this book, but there's also advice on cutting corners. Get a five-dollar pair of army bearpaw snowshoes, dig out grandpa's heavy wool trousers, and take a walk in the woods. You'll soon be a confirmed enthusiast.

A few words are in order about the intended limitations of this book. I have made no attempt to discuss the kind of camping and travel used in deep wilderness areas on true expeditions. This book describes the methods used in the sort of camping where you carry everything necessary on your back. The increasing weight of food limits this experience to about two weeks, though caches or airdrops can be used to extend it indefinitely. Weather conditions are assumed to be those prevailing in the "temperate" regions, which can be quite severe in winter, especially in the mountains. This book does not talk about winter conditions on Mount McKinley or at the South Pole. You probably won't be going to either on your first few trips.

Mountains are the natural provinces of the winter traveler in those parts of the country where they are available. In midwinter you can walk the snows at all altitudes, but as spring arrives you'll learn to follow the beloved white stuff up into the hills and peaks. The mountains, along with their many other virtues, are the poor person's Arctic expedition. For every thousand feet of altitude gained, the climber sees a climatic change equivalent to a latitude 300 miles north. In a weekend trip to the Sierra Nevada or the Cascades, the West Coast dweller gets a taste of an Alaskan expedition. The New England mountaineer will experience Arctic conditions on the summit plateaus of Mount Washington or Katahdin. Winter lasts longer in the high country, so the white wilderness may still be found there when the lowlands are in the heat of early summer.

There is no discussion in this book of mountaineering techniques on difficult terrain. I have drawn my line at the point where a rope is necessary for safety. There is some description of the use of the ice ax and crampons on moderate slopes, but covering the techniques necessary on difficult terrain would either expand this book to twice its size or mislead the reader with a superficial treatment of a serious subject. Detailed descriptions of techniques for steep snow and ice can be found in my *Climbing: A Guide to Mountaineering*.

Finally, a note on the way the book is arranged. A great deal of emphasis has been placed on the discussion of equipment. This has been done for two reasons. The first is that one of the problems confronted immediately by the beginner is the choice of an outfit, so that more help is needed with this than some other things. My main motive is that the discussion of choosing equipment necessarily includes details about its use and the conditions that dictate a certain design. This method places an unfortunate emphasis on means rather than ends, however, as talk about equipment and technique must. The book may place undue stress on gadgets, but the reader can easily redress the balance by getting out into the woods, where people and their works take on a proper perspective.

1 | Heading Out in Winter

Traveling the wilderness in the cold seasons doesn't require any kind of supernatural physiology or masochistic desire to undergo terrible ordeals. Still, the beauty of nature at this time of year is of a much starker kind than when the flowers are in bloom, and it is well for the would-be lover to be prepared for a cold rebuff. Nature is not forgiving of foolish mistakes in the winter. It is important to know what you are about.

The cardinal rule of winter camping and travel is not to exceed your limitations. Your knowledge and skill will increase rapidly with experience, and as they do your trips will become more ambitious. The trick is not to attempt a trip until your skill and knowledge are adequate to it. All this is not meant to discourage the adventurous. Push yourself, but don't push your luck.

Winter travel and camping are fun, and they should be. It's pleasant to have a balance between larks and trips with more bite and challenge, but if you consistently exceed your abilities, you'll find winter travel a series of grim survival struggles.

HOW TO KEEP YOUR BODY RUNNING

The big difference in winter camping is, of course, that it's cold outside. The human body will only function when it is kept at the right temperature. If the temperature of the body's central core, where the vital organs are, varies a few degrees in either direction, essential functions start to deteriorate rapidly. The body has its own mechanisms for regulating its temperature, and it is important for the winter sojourner to understand them.

When the core of the body becomes too hot, circulation to the surface of the skin is increased, perspiration is excreted to produce cooling by evaporation, and there is a general inclination to avoid exercise which will produce more heat. Most people are aware of these reactions, but they don't always realize what happens in the cold. When the body's core temperature drops, a reverse process occurs: The blood

7

vessels near the surface of the skin contract, the blood supply to all
the extremities except the head is greatly reduced, and if the core temperature continues to drop, violent involuntary exercise of the muscles
occurs in the form of shivering. When you are living in cold weather,
you have to help your body to prevent excessive heat loss, since the
naked human body can't handle low temperatures by itself.

HEAT LOSS

There are several ways that your body can lose heat. "Lose" is the key
word here, since heat is a form of energy and cold is simply the
absence of heat. If you sit down on the snow in a thin pair of pants,
the cold snow absorbs energy from your nether regions; this is heat
loss by conduction. The cold wind blows air molecules against your
face which absorb more heat; this is heat loss by convection. If you
have sweated a lot climbing up a hill, the wind will also dry some of
the sweat, producing heat loss from evaporation. Finally, if you are
sitting under the black night sky you are losing some more heat by
radiation directly to the sky.

Your body tries to reduce all these forms of heat loss by allowing
the skin temperature to drop, reducing the difference between it and
the temperature of the air. Heat energy is only transferred when there
is a temperature difference, and the smaller the temperature difference, the less the heat loss will be from any of these effects. Your body
is trying to reduce the temperature difference between the skin and
the surrounding air. The way to keep your body warm is to put an
insulating layer around the body. The principle is simple: The outside
of the insulating layer remains at about the temperature of the air or
ground outside, so that little heat is transferred. The inside of the
insulating layer is the same temperature as your skin. The layer is
effective if heat passes only very slowly from the warm side of the
insulating layer (you) to the other side.

The insulating layer provided by your clothing or sleeping bag is
what prevents the heat from your body from escaping too rapidly into
the world around you. At the same time, your body continues to produce heat, using the food you eat as fuel. Some heat is always being
produced by the body at a basal metabolic rate, even when you are
sleeping. Digestion of food produces additional heat, and metabolism
of some foods produces more heat than others. Heat is also produced
as a side product when the muscles are exercising. The intelligent winter camper can use all of these principles to stay warm. Eating fats
before bed, for example, will produce extra heat throughout the night.

A working knowledge of such tricks is what separates the experienced traveler from the beginner.

A few of the first rules for winter travel follow pretty obviously from what has already been said. Heat is produced from food, so that if you want to keep warm, keep eating. Trail snacks kept in the pocket are munched on the trail throughout the day, making the period between breakfast and supper a sort of continuous lunch. Since exercise produces heat, you can keep fairly warm without much insulation while you are going up a hill, but when you stop for a rest at the top, you had better put on some clothes right away or you will get a chill.

WINDCHILL

Before going into more detail on protecting the body from the cold, it's important to talk a little more about what we mean by "cold." Everyone knows that low temperatures will rob your body of heat much faster than higher temperatures, but few people realize how important the wind is in chilling your body. Wind has just as important an effect as temperature. Thirty degrees below zero may not feel too cold if you are protected from air movement, but when a strong wind comes up it can freeze exposed flesh in short order. Wind is dangerous in cold weather. Respect it and treat it with caution.

The effects of windchill are generally measured by stating the calm-air temperature that would produce the same effect as a particular wind and temperature. A glance at the chart will show how this works. Very small amounts of air movement have considerable chilling effect because they carry away the thin layer of warmed air that builds up near the body. Increasing wind velocity has the effect of lowering temperatures until it reaches about forty miles per hour. Wind velocities higher than this produce little additional cooling effect.

The chilling produced by both wind and water will be mentioned in more detail later. Besides its direct cooling effect, wind robs certain types of insulation of their effectiveness, and this is also the danger presented by wetness. A temperature of thirty-five degrees above zero with a cold, wind-driven rain is more to be feared than a windless thirty-five below.

INSULATION

The function of the insulating layer has already been mentioned. It serves to prevent heat from escaping from the body to the cold environment. The insulator itself is almost always the same: air. Air that is held in numerous small compartments and prevented from moving around in little breezes is the most practical insulator because it weighs almost nothing and is readily available anywhere on earth. The trick is to hold it still so that convection currents cannot start moving about, carrying body heat with them. Wool sweaters, down sleeping bags, Dacron jackets, foam pads, fur coats, and Orlon blankets all serve primarily to trap a layer of air cells next to your body. The actual insulation is provided by the air, and for this reason the amount of insulation provided by the layer depends only on its thickness and on the size and immobility of the cells of air trapped by the insulation. Thickness is the important factor, but insulation with smaller trapped compartments of air that is less free to circulate will be a little warmer. Other factors—weight, color, and space-age design—are of little importance.

Protection against wind and water is also necessary in winter, but without an insulating layer it is of no use. The main principle of cold-weather clothing has already been mentioned: Thickness counts. A very tight-woven, heavy sweater is not a better insulator than a light, fuzzy one of the same thickness. The tight one may be more durable or wind resistant, but when it is worn under a windproof shell garment, the extra weight is wasted.

A second principle of insulation for cold-weather dress is the use of layers of clothing. Two medium-weight fuzzy sweaters are generally better than one heavy fuzzy sweater weighing the same amount. A layer of still air is trapped between the two sweaters and provides extra insulation. Besides, the two sweaters are more versatile. You can't put on one half of a heavy sweater. This flexibility is very important, for reasons which will be discussed in detail a bit later.

Insulating materials are many, and their advantages overlap in such a confusing hodgepodge that many week-long blizzards in high-mountain bivouacs have been whiled away with arguments over the virtues of various combinations. Some blessings and evils are undisputed, however, and these are the ones the beginner must learn. They are part of the basic knowledge of winter travel, and should be acquired early. You can take more time in developing an interesting set of prejudices.

The best insulator is northern goose down. The amount of down required to provide a given insulating layer weighs less and takes up less space when compressed and packed than any other insulator. Down is the underlining of the breasts of waterfowl, and it is distinct from feathers, which have quills. True down consists of tiny central pods, each with a myriad of filaments extending out. Down has

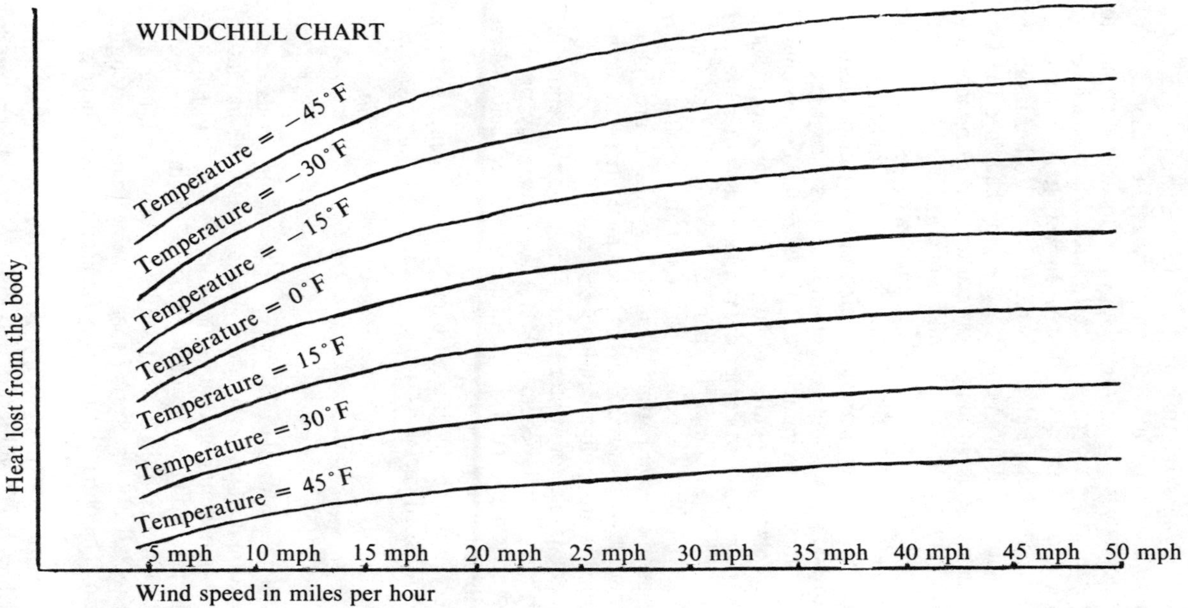

WINDCHILL CHART

Wind speed in miles per hour

Heat lost from the body

Temperature = −45° F
Temperature = −30° F
Temperature = −15° F
Temperature = 0° F
Temperature = 15° F
Temperature = 30° F
Temperature = 45° F

5 mph 10 mph 15 mph 20 mph 25 mph 30 mph 35 mph 40 mph 45 mph 50 mph

This chart shows the amount of heat lost from the body at various temperatures as the speed of the wind increases. As the curves show, increasing wind speed causes more heat to be lost, just as lower temperatures do. This effect is especially pronounced at low wind speeds—an increase from 5 to 10 mph makes a great difference, especially at very cold temperatures. At very high wind velocities, additional wind no longer has much effect. Note that improper wind-shells or sweating will make these effects even more pronounced.

numerous disadvantages, but its insulating qualities are unequaled for the traveler who must carry a lot of light, compact insulation.

Down is expensive; it has characteristics that make it expensive to work with; it cannot be woven into fabric but must be enclosed by other material, and it becomes useless when wet. It is best used in equipment where so much insulation is required that other insulators would be impractically heavy or bulky. Sleeping bags are the best example. Another use is in big down parkas for extremely cold weather. The advantages and disadvantages of down will be discussed in more detail in the chapters on clothing and sleeping gear.

Various synthetic insulators and materials made from wool have the advantage of retaining some of their insulating characteristics even when they become wet, whereas down is useless once it gets wet. Because of this important characteristic, these insulators are chosen in preference to down for a number of purposes, particularly in clothing, though they are heavier than good down, have a shorter life, and cannot be stuffed into as compact a bundle. Wool is the traditional material of this type, but it is being replaced in many applications by synthetic piles and polyester batting because the synthetics are lighter, cheaper, and hold less moisture. Specific recommendations on the use of various insulators are included in later chapters.

Cotton is undesirable for winter wear. It is not an exceptionally good insulator, and when it becomes wet it is heavy, clammy, provides no insulation, and is hard to dry. Its main use is in outer shells, where it is often combined with nylon.

Nylon is very useful for its great strength, mainly to enclose down or Dacron and for shell garments, tents, packs, and the like.

THE SHELL GAME

An extension of the principle of dressing in layers brings us to the outer shell of clothing. This layer is not generally used for insulation but consists of light, tough garments designed to be windtight and water resistant, preserving the insulation value of the inside layers. If the weather is such that rain or sleet may be encountered, it is also necessary to have a truly waterproof shell system, usually very light, to shed the rain. The outer clothing may be used over any necessary amount of insulation, and its value is incalculable. It will not eliminate the windchill factor, which simply makes low temperatures more effective at cooling, but it will insure that the insulating layers can do their work. Wind can blow through a fuzzy sweater as if it were not there. A wind shell reduces this problem.

KEEPING WATER OUT

Wet, cold weather, besides being miserable, is dangerous. Dry snow creates no real problems for the winter traveler, but wet snow, sleet, or rain can soak all your clothing and make it practically useless. A cold wind can then make short work of the strongest person unless shelter or dry clothing is found quickly. When weather like this is at all possible, you must carry water*proof* equipment, and if you are caught without it, you should find shelter before you get wet.

Standard waterproof rain gear cannot be substituted for the normal outer wear because if it is fitted tightly enough to keep out the wind, it will trap the body's own moisture inside. This will not soak insulation quite as fast as a cold rain, but in the long run it can be just as deadly. This is also the objection to most waterproof tents: if they are waterproof and tight enough to withstand winter storms, the occupants will soon drench their gear, even when there is no visible perspiration. The quantity is likely to be larger during the day. All clothing must "breathe," that is, the water vapor must be able to pass out.

Until the invention of Gore-tex, there was no material available which was reasonably waterproof and which also breathed well enough to avoid the buildup of condensation inside, especially in cold weather. Despite some problems, Gore-tex laminates provide a nearly ideal shell material for the winter traveler because they shed rain and are very windproof while permitting the escape of water vapor. Their biggest disadvantage is high price. Gore-tex is described in detail in the next chapter.

GETTING WATER OUT

Wet clothing and sleeping gear is the winter traveler's biggest problem. As long as you keep your gear dry, you can sit out almost any storm. Get it wet, and you have an emergency situation. The obvious dangers of precipitation have been discussed, but you should keep reminding yourself of the less obvious danger of perspiration. One of the reasons for the layer system is that the spaces between layers help water vapor to escape through the clothing. This will be discussed at greater length in the next chapter, but no clothing can disperse very much perspiration. When traveling in cold weather, it is essential to avoid sweating. Novices always tend to peel off a layer of clothing a bit too late, after they have already worked up a sweat. The rule is to remove a layer of clothing *before* you really get warm and start perspiring. At the same time, various means are employed to help the body get rid of unfelt perspiration through adequate ventilation, a subject that will be continued in the next chapter.

GETTING WATER IN

The importance of food intake and insulation have been discussed, but one other winter problem should be mentioned here. With snow all around, obtaining water would seem to present little problem in winter, and in one way it does not. The winter traveler never runs into the problem of water being completely unavailable, but, oddly enough, dehydration is often a problem because liquid water is often unavailable. It is a good idea to eat moderate amounts of snow throughout the day, perhaps combined with small snacks. Whenever liquid water is available, the traveler should "tank up," drinking as much as possible and filling canteens or water bottles. Observation of these rules can save fuel and time in the evening, for if thirst is not quenched during the day, the body's liquid supply will have to be taken care of then.

One reason for avoiding mild dehydration follows from its consequences in emergency situations. Dehydration aggravates the syndromes of shock and hypothermia (exposure). The body will be better able to deal with serious situations if it is kept adequately supplied with food and water throughout the day.

HAZARDS AND EMERGENCIES

It is difficult to write about the dangers of winter conditions in a way that conveys the proper perspective to the reader. One sounds either like a Pollyanna or a Cassandra. The winter wilderness is no place for the careless or foolhardy; there are quite a few dangers, and a party is required to avoid them or meet them with its own resources, without any helpful bystanders to get it out of trouble once difficulties are encountered. Winter hazards really hold no terrors for those with reasonably level heads who are willing to learn from their adventures. The rules to keep out of trouble are fairly simple, and when they don't suffice, one can still usually get by without too great a sacrifice. One of the great lessons of the wilderness is that you can manage very nicely by yourself when you know you have to. I have had several skiing injuries on commercial slopes, but not one in the thousands of miles of wilderness skiing I have done, despite the more difficult conditions encountered in the backcountry.

The main dangers of wilderness travel in winter are: avalanches, storms, becoming lost, and personal injury or medical emergency. All will be covered in some detail in later chapters, and all have certain unique aspects in connection with cold weather. Avalanches will be the most unfamiliar to the experienced backpacker newly arrived to the cold seasons. They are treacherous even for the expert, and it takes years to become an expert in this field. Anyone going into mountain country in the winter must learn to exercise the utmost care concerning steep snow. Chapter 11 offers an introduction to the problem of avalanches.

EQUIPMENT

The obvious dodge for the author talking about equipment is to tell the beginner to take everything necessary but not one ounce more. Good advice, except that even the expert never really knows what may be needed. Most of us arrive at the solution of taking only what we *know* we'll need, plus a light combination of *essential* emergency equipment. Appendix D may be used as a checklist.

The novice is faced with a greater equipment problem than the expert; the beginner must not only decide what to take but also what to buy. The best rule is to buy only what you need for the next trip. If you're learning your way by taking day trips, don't buy a mountain tent until you plan on using it. This will spread out your costs and enable you to make intelligent choices of equipment based on more experience. Both costs and experience may be spread out even farther by judicious use of the rental services of any backpacking or mountaineering stores in your area.

The reader will find most equipment discussed in the chapter concerned with its use. Advice about technique is often handled easily by discussing the merits of various sorts of equipment, and I have used this plan frequently. There is a risk in this method of placing too much importance on the equipment itself, which is, or ought to be, of secondary importance. This book is about equipment and technique, but what is important is the traveler's experience of the wilderness itself. It's always fun to talk about equipment, but this can become a fetish. I hope I have not obscured the real meaning of the white wilderness in this book, but the problem will be easily solved if the reader gets out and experiences it. No piece of equipment is so essential it cannot be done without or replaced with a substitute.

2 | Cold-Weather Clothing

The art of dressing for cold weather is fairly simple when the principles discussed in the preceding chapter are followed. Your clothing must provide enough insulation to keep you warm in the temperatures you will encounter, with windchill taken into account. It must breathe well enough to pass the water vapor produced by your body into the outside air. It must be readily adjustable for varying temperatures and exercise. It must allow free movement; clothes that bind will cut circulation and compress insulation. You must have shell clothing that is windproof and capable of shedding any precipitation you might encounter.

There are a number of effective clothing combinations, and the one you choose will probably depend as much on your finances and on personal taste as on the exact weight and insulating capacity of each garment. The increasing popularity of ski touring and other outdoor winter activities has encouraged manufacturers to make a variety of excellent and attractive items. However, it is also still possible to obtain many basic pieces of clothing quite cheaply from surplus stores.

The fundamental principles you should keep in mind while choosing clothing are to dress in layers, so that you can regulate your body temperature and avoid sweating too much in widely varying conditions, to choose insulators for basic garments that will retain some warmth even if they get wet, and to pick shell garments that will stop the wind and shed snow as much as possible.

Traditional combinations do not necessarily have to be followed in layering, so long as the final combination works well for you, providing as much versatility as possible. The standard arrangement for pants called for long johns—perhaps even two pairs in extreme conditions—under a pair of pants that provided most of the insulation for the legs. These might be made of wool or a double layer with wool on the inside and poplin on the outside to shed snow and provide abrasion resistance. Windpants would then probably be carried that could be worn over the regular pants in severe conditions, during lunch stops, or while digging a snow cave.

The modern backcountry ski tourer would be likely to choose a different combination, using lightweight long underwear together with a cross-country ski suit of stretchy synthetic and carrying warm-up pants and additional insulation for the upper body. The underwear and ski suit will absorb very little moisture from perspiration and provide enough insulation when the weather is warm or the traveler is exercising vigorously; the bulk of the insulation carried goes on top of this basic outfit. As long as the insulating layers can be easily donned without taking off skis or snowshoes, this approach to clothing is excellent, though it is apt to be fairly expensive.

If cost is no object, you can simply buy your outfit from a good outfitter and be done with it, but for people on a tight budget clothing is the best part of the outfit on which to save money. You probably have a lot of clothing that will do very well in your closet or in a trunk, and if you don't, someone else does. Military surplus is also an excellent source for some items. Other clothing is easy to make, since baggy fit is desirable rather than detrimental unless stretch fabrics are being used.

BASIC CLOTHING

Underwear

Probably the two best materials for long underwear are polyethylene and soft woven wool. Polyethylene is the material used for making tow ropes for water skiers. It absorbs virtually no water at all, so it has the edge in drying out quickly and passing perspiration through. Wool is somewhat warmer but dries a little more slowly. High quality wool underwear is very soft and rarely bothers anyone's skin, but if you are very sensitive, pick a synthetic. Other synthetics, such as bulked Orlon, are also quite good; they absorb about the same amount of moisture as wool and are almost as warm. Cotton is a terrible material for underwear that will be used in cold-weather travel. It is soft when dry, but it becomes very uncomfortable when it gets wet and it dries very slowly. Even double-layer underwear incorporating cotton is a poor substitute for wool or a synthetic material.

Thin, solid long underwear is most common, though fishnet patterns in wool or synthetic have some advantages. They trap large pockets of air next to the skin when worn under another garment, providing warmth and allowing perspiration to evaporate easily. Some snow campers like to wear one layer of thin, solid underwear and one layer of fishnet. Fishnet is also excellent when you overheat, since it allows rapid cooling when you open or strip off the layers outside it. Interesting tan patterns can be developed from wearing fishnet underwear during spring trips.

Briefs, bras, and such items worn under your long johns will be far more comfortable if they are made from lightweight synthetics. Cotton is likely to become abrasive and clammy after a hard day on the trail.

Shirts, Sweaters, Vests, Jackets, and Pullovers

Any combination of garments for the upper body that will keep you warm enough on the trail will do, and each arrangement has its advocates. Long underwear, a heavy wool shirt, and a fuzzy sweater would make up a typical traditional combination, perhaps supplemented by a vest insulated with polyester batting in cold temperatures. Currently, a very popular arrangement is to wear a stretch ski suit over long underwear and to carry a pile jacket for use over the ski suit.

In any case, the garments you plan to wear a lot while working on the trail should be made almost exclusively of wool or synthetics. They will inevitably pick up a fair amount of moisture from perspiration and snow, so insulators that are severely affected by moisture should be avoided for this clothing. Down has important advantages as an insulator in reserve clothing and for extra protection in extremely cold temperatures, but it is a poor choice for basic insulation. Down is useless when it gets wet, and it takes a long time to dry.

It is better to use several layers of insulation for the upper body, providing both for easy adjustment to varied conditions of temperature and work load and for a better reserve. A single heavy garment won't allow for enough ventilation when you are working hard, especially around the back and shoulders under your pack, and when it gets wet from perspiration you have no backup. Several layers also provide extra insulation by trapping layers of air between separate garments.

Light, fuzzy weaves provide more insulation for their weight than heavy solid ones, and a garment that is easily penetrated by moving air also dries more easily. Pile jackets and fuzzy sweaters thus make excellent insulators, provided they are supplemented by a shell to stop the wind and to shed snow when necessary. Garments that will be worn outside when it is snowing or when you expect to fall often in the snow should have a smooth surface. This can be provided either by a shell garment or by a nylon jacket or vest insulated with one of the polyester batting materials: PolarGuard, Thinsulate, and Hollofil are the trademarks of three of the best ones, each having some particular advantages.

A lightweight but very warm down parka, useful in very cold conditions This snow-shoer is wearing wool-lined poplin pants, the smooth outer layer serving to shed snow while the wool lining provides some warmth even if it becomes wet.

Upper garments should be cut long. Short ones ride up, exposing the kidneys, allowing the entrance of snow, and fraying the nerves. Perfectly adequate wool shirts and sweaters can often be found in a trunk in the attic or purchased for low prices in surplus stores if you are trying to save money on your outfit. They are not as fashionable as nylon stretch suits and pile overgarments, but they work almost as well and they are a lot cheaper. It makes more sense to spend your money on good skis, a pack, and boots than on fancy clothing.

Pants

The old standby for pants is a hard-finish wool; it maintains a modicum of warmth if it gets wet, sheds snow reasonably well, and lasts for quite a while. Such pants are available at bargain prices from surplus stores. Air Force flight pants, with knit cuffs and padded seat and pants, are pretty well suited for wilderness use as is. You can convert army pants to knickers if you prefer them. The fuzzier type is warmer but will collect snow unless you wear nylon windpants on top. Pants naturally get into the snow a lot more than upper clothing, so they should be chosen to shed snow.

Stretch synthetic pants are good, but they are much more expensive than surplus woolies. When buying the cheaper pants, though, you need to consider not only the cost of the pants themselves but that of good quality overpants as well, since the basic wool pants will have to be supplemented more quickly in cold weather. The best stretch ski pants (equally good for snowshoeing) have double fabric in the front to help cut the wind. They should be made with a reasonably tight weave to reduce wind penetration.

It is practical to have knit cuffs in the winter, even if you will be wearing gaiters most of the time; they don't pick up ice, they help to seal out snow, and they don't have to be folded as much to fit under gaiters. It is easy to install knit cuffs yourself if you get surplus pants that don't have them, or dig an old pair of wool pants out of a trunk or a Goodwill store. Knickers are very comfortable and practical for winter use. They allow good freedom of movement to the legs and easy ventilation. Remember, however, that knicker socks cost about twice as much as equivalent short socks.

Hats and Face Masks

Hats are not optional in cold conditions. Because the brain is an essential organ, the body does not shut down the blood supply to the head when the cold temperature drops, as it does to the other extremities. The unprotected head can easily pump over half of the body's heat production into the great outdoors. The old-timer who said, "If your feet are cold, put on your hat," knew what he was talking about. This is a good place to indulge your individuality, but any hat you choose should include ear protection. One of the best choices is the balaclava helmet, which rolls up into a stocking cap in moderate weather and rolls down to protect the face and neck in very cold weather. An opening is provided for the eyes. This opening is also large enough for ski goggles, a feature not found on most face masks. The material should be wool or Orlon. Additional ear protection can be provided for any hat with an ear band or ear muffs. The hood of the parka or anorak covers the hat. An extra balaclava is worth its weight and cost on a winter trip.

For very severe conditions some sort of face protection is necessary, and if a balaclava is not worn, a face mask should be carried. Wool and Orlon are the usual materials and work well in combination with the parka hood. Deerskin masks are excellent. Masks made from foil-covered felt won't tolerate quite so much abuse as natural materials, but they are less prone to freeze up and are very windtight. Silk or light synthetic masks are nice luxury items to be worn under other masks or when conditions are not quite so cold, but they won't substitute for heavier materials.

Socks

Wool remains the standard material for heavy socks, because the feet inevitably become somewhat damp, and no other material retains its springiness and warmth as good virgin wool does. Some nylon is usually added to improve durability, particularly in the heel and toe. It is generally best to wear one heavy outer pair of socks and one lighter inner pair, for increased warmth and to reduce the danger of blisters.

Ragg socks, which are woven from coarse, undyed yarn, seem to be best for outer socks. Socks lined with a loop pile are warmer at first but do not breathe as well, so they are slightly less desirable. The heavier the outer sock, the warmer your feet will be, so long as there is enough room in your boots. Heavier socks or extras will make your feet colder if they make your boots too tight and impair circulation to your feet.

Liners may be made from soft wool or from a synthetic. Preferences vary. Some people use Olefin socks on the theory that they transport moisture away from the foot into the outer sock, as a wick would. Others prefer a light, soft wool sock. Bulked Orlon dress socks also work adequately.

Boots are so closely related to your means of getting around that they are discussed in connection with skiing and snowshoeing. Overboots and the like are covered in the same places.

OUTER CLOTHING

Outer clothing has to provide whatever additional insulation you need both on the trail and during stops when you are not in your sleeping bag. It also must be tough enough to withstand abrasion, must be fairly windtight, and must protect you from snow and from rain in areas where wet conditions are possible in the winter months.

These functions may be combined to some extent, but, as has been suggested earlier, it is often more effective to use several layers and gain versatility at the expense of a little extra weight. The amount of insulation you may need will vary a great deal depending on the conditions you expect to encounter, on your experience, and on your own metabolism. Remember, however, that a great deal more insulation is needed when you stop than when you are working hard on the trail. This requirement for extra insulation is made more acute by the likelihood that when you stop late in the day, you will probably be tired, your clothes may be somewhat damp, and weather conditions may be deteriorating. It is best to be conservative, especially during your first attempts at winter camping, and to be sure to carry enough clothing to put on when conditions become difficult. This is where down clothing, discussed below, can be particularly useful, because it weighs so little and takes up such a small space.

Zippers and Other Closures
The closures on your outer clothing are important. Failure can be dangerous, and the design of closures is also one good indication of the overall quality of a garment. Parkas, shell and down, should have two front closing systems if they open like a jacket. The double closure serves to seal out drafts and also is insurance against jammed zippers and ripped buttons or snaps. Zippers should work perfectly; a zipper that sticks in the store is not something you want to struggle with in icy conditions. Larger zippers, especially nylon ones, are less likely to jam. Light snaps are undesirable but acceptable for a wind seal; they are unacceptable as a main closure. Heavy snaps are excellent for an alternate closure and on a down parka with a wide overlap may be used for both closures. They are not very good for main closures on shell parkas or for pants flies, since they aren't windtight. The same considerations apply to buttons as to snaps. Velcro tape that uses two mating surfaces that stick together makes an excellent closure for pockets or wind seals, but it will not substitute for a long zipper.

Well-made zippers are quite reliable; they can jam, but buttons and snaps can rip off. Double closures on important seams and a few safety pins carried on a belt loop will take care of emergencies.

Two types of waterproof wet-weather gear   On the right, a commercially made rain-
suit. On the left, a home-manufactured cagoule.

Shell Clothing

Shell clothing presents difficult problems for the winter traveler because of the contradictory functions required of it. Ideally, shell clothing should be lightweight, abrasion resistant, and windtight. It should easily shed snow and rain, yet it easily should pass any moisture evaporating from the body out into the air, so that insulating layers do not become soaked with moisture. Traditional types of shell clothing have represented different compromises between these desirable characteristics. Tour skiers and snowshoers in areas like the Rockies, where cold temperatures and dry snow prevail in the winter months, usually chose wind shells of uncoated nylon that would breathe well and shed dry snow, but which were of little use in rain or wet snow. Travelers in areas where cold rain or wet snow occur frequently usually chose standard rain gear made from coated nylon, despite the tremendous condensation problem that is typical of this fabric in cold-weather use. The usual solution for those looking for a compromise was a fabric made either of cotton or a cotton-nylon mixture that would breathe reasonably well and shed some water, but which would freeze very badly in winter conditions.

This compromise gear is still often used, especially by the winter camper making use of clothing he already owns and by those who don't have a lot of money to spend on shell clothing. The newly available shell clothing made with Gore-tex laminates, however, has provided a nearly ideal solution to the winter shell problem in all respects other than price. Gore-tex is the trade name for a very thin film of material that is chemically related to Teflon. The film is penetrated with billions of tiny holes per square inch that are large enough to permit passage of molecules of water vapor but too small for liquid water to pass through. This material is laminated between two layers of conventional fabric, providing protection against rain and snow and giving excellent wind protection but allowing water vapor to pass through as well as it does through any of the standard porous wind shells. Gore-tex garments require a fair amount of care (they have to be kept clean or dirt will act as a wetting agent and cause leaks), but they are hard to beat for versatility and effectiveness in the winter, and they function well as rain garments at other times of the year.

Gore-tex shell garments are made with a variety of backing fabrics. For winter use, I prefer standard nylon taffeta on the outside, which is relatively lightweight and compact. A nonwoven backing is normally used on the inside of fabric intended for parkas and pants to protect the Gore-tex film. A heavier brushed nylon fabric called Taslan is preferred by many climbers and by those who are concerned about the looks of shell clothing for use in town.

All shell clothing should be easy to put on and take off, should have well-designed provisions for ventilation, and should be large enough to fit over the insulation that you would normally wear on the trail in stormy conditions. Adding and stripping off clothing has to be done a lot to stay warm but still avoid perspiring too much. If shell clothing is too inconvenient to don and remove, you will tend to wait too long to do either. Pants that can be put on without removing skis or snowshoes are handy, but it is essential that you at least be able to get into them without taking off your boots. Either the legs must be cut large for this purpose or they must have zippers that open at the bottom.

Parkas should have attached hoods to form a complete seal around the head and neck when it is needed. A parka with a full zipper down the front is probably best because of improved ventilation and convenience, though an anorak with only a partial zipper is lighter and cannot become useless as a result of the failure of the closures. Underarm ventilation zippers are excellent for temperature control, though they do add to the cost and weight of the parka. Pockets should be roomy, sturdily sewn, and have positive closures. These are essential for winter use, because you will have a constant supply of small items that have to be stowed. Losing mittens because you don't have enough pockets or because they don't seal shut is not just inconvenient—it's dangerous.

Insulating Outer Garments
The matter of insulation has been mentioned earlier in the chapter. All your insulation should be considered together as a system. You can't afford the extra weight or volume of half a dozen outfits carried for different conditions you will encounter on a trip, so everything has to be chosen to be complementary. In the coldest conditions or in emergencies you will wear everything you have, and in milder circumstances you will use various combinations. The total amount of equipment will depend on the severity of the weather you are likely to encounter and the allowance that seems necessary for a measure of safety.

As indicated in the earlier section, those insulating garments that will be worn most of the time should be made of materials that lose as little of their effectiveness as possible when they get wet. In outer layers, the best compromises will depend on your particular circumstances. The ultimate insulator, in terms of the amount of warmth provided for a given amount of weight and packed bulk, is still down, the undercoating of waterfowl. However, the quality of most down available to manufacturers has steadily deteriorated over the past few years, while the cost of materials and construction has climbed, making down equipment more and more expensive. At the same time, competitive synthetic insulators have steadily improved, narrowing the performance gap in very cold conditions while demonstrating advantages over down in damp weather. As a result, most cold-weather campers now prefer to rely mainly on synthetics for clothing, perhaps carrying a fairly light down jacket for reserve insulation at rest stops, in camp, and for emergency use. Even most expeditionary mountaineers are relying far less extensively on down than they once did.

Quality of construction and materials is extremely important in choosing down garments, and the reader is referred to the next chapter for a discussion of the ins and outs of the market. Sleeping bags are the items of equipment where down still retains its preeminence as an insulator, so the construction and purchase of down equipment is best considered in the section on down bags.

The principles of insulation are discussed in detail in the next chapter, but virtually all warm clothing worn by the winter traveler insulates with dead air spaces. The wool sweater, down parka, or other garment traps a layer of still air around the body that impedes the flow of heat. The thicker the insulating layer is and the more thoroughly the air is trapped, the slower heat will flow through the material. What keeps you warm in cold weather is the effective trapping of your own body heat next to your skin, so that the natural flow of heat out into a cold environment is reduced below the rate at which your body replaces that heat. You need more insulation when you are resting because you produce so much less heat then than when you are active.

Heat transfer through insulation can take place in a number of ways. If air blows through the garment, the entire insulating thickness of warm air is moved away and body heat is lost. This is why a wind shell is crucial, unless the garment has an effective wind block of its own, as with down parkas that have Gore-tex shells. A fuzzy wool sweater or a pile jacket may be very warm in still, cold air, yet it will become virtually useless in even a light breeze. The effect of wind in reducing the insulating capacity of a permeable garment is even greater than the windchill factor would indicate, but a good shell will greatly reduce this problem. Gore-tex is particularly good at eliminating the effect of the wind.

Assuming that you have eliminated the effect of wind (or your own motion through the air), the effectiveness of most insulators is almost directly proportional to thickness, because it is the immobilized air in the layer that actually does the insulating. Thus, an inch of wool, an inch of down, or an inch of polyester batting provides just about the same insulating effect. There is some variation depending on the degree to which the air within the layer is prevented from moving around. An insulator with large air spaces will be somewhat less effective than one with small air spaces. Thinsulate insulation, made by the Minnesota Mining and Manufacturing Company (3M), manages to achieve considerably more effectiveness per unit thickness than down or polyesters by using very thin fibers that create very small air spaces. It is not as effective per unit weight as down, however, nor does it provide any more freedom of movement.

Any judicious combination of insulating layers will keep you warm. Freedom of movement is important as well, and too much bulk around the armpits or layers that compress each other will make you feel like the Michelin tire man without making the best use of the insulation. One good combination for most purposes is a pile jacket over long underwear, with a Gore-tex shell parka and a fairly light down jacket for reserve insulation. Another good possibility is a heavy wool shirt over long underwear, a vest insulated with polyester batting, a shell parka, and a reserve jacket with down or polyester insulation. The possibilities are endless, but remember that versatility is the key. Overall insulation will be essentially proportional to thickness. Thinsulate has about twice the insulating value of normal fabrics for a given thickness, but the jackets that use it are not very thick so don't expect any miracles. Unlike polyester batting or pile, Thinsulate does not have any price advantage over down, either.

Construction techniques for insulated clothing are similar to those used in sleeping bags illustrated in the next chapter. The thicker an individual layer, the more elaborate the construction techniques have to be to avoid binding and to make efficient use of the insulation. Short fiber polyesters like Hollofil have to be quilted or contained in individual compartments, as down is, to prevent the material from shifting. PolarGuard has long fibers and can be sewn directly to the shell without shifting as long as it is protected by fabric, so extra layers can be arranged and cold seams avoided by sewing separate layers of insulation to the inside and the outside of a garment with offset seams. Quilting directly through a garment produces cold seams; it is appropriate for a relatively thin jacket or vest but is inefficient for a thick one that is supposed to provide a lot of insulation.

Construction details are important in both insulating garments and shell clothing. Zippers and closures have already been mentioned. Seams must be well sewn with synthetic thread, which is stronger and more rot-proof than cotton. Sloppy seams usually indicate poor workmanship throughout. Stress points should be reinforced with extra stitching and extra fabric where necessary. Seams should have at least eight stitches per inch or they will tend to pull out far too easily. Look carefully at any edges that are exposed to see how they are fixed. Nylon that has no coating is particularly prone to unraveling at the edges. This is best prevented by hot cutting that fuses the nylon and then zigzag stitching over a wide edge. Only the best manufacturers hot cut the fabric.

Gaiters

A snowproof closure between the pant legs and boots is essential for winter travel. If you are wearing special footwear that comes up to the knee, such as mukluks or overboots (see Chapters 7 and 8), or if you have pants that seal off the top of the boots, gaiters may not be necessary. With most equipment, however, they are very important both to keep snow out of your footgear and to provide extra protection for the lower legs. Short gaiters may be adequate with heavy pants, but gaiters extending to the knees are usually best for extended winter travel.

Gaiters take a lot of wear and should be made from durable material. Fasteners should be doubled, heavy-duty, and should operate smoothly. Even the best-made ones will be hampered when they are clogged with ice and snow. Cloth using cotton-nylon or cotton-polyester mixtures for the outer layer and uncoated nylon for the lining is a reasonable compromise when the snow is fairly dry. Uncoated nylon soaks through too easily. Coated nylon picks up a lot of condensation inside, but it is preferred by many people who live in areas with wet conditions much of the time. An excellent but expensive combination is a lower section with a double layer of coated nylon pack cloth and an upper section of Gore-tex backed cloth with an uncoated nylon lining.

DRESSING FOR THE COLD

Cold temperatures do not usually require nearly so many clothes as people think they will. Most novices do not become cold because they don't have enough clothing, but because it is the wrong type or is not used properly. All clothing should be roomy rather than tight, except for stretchy garments worn next to the body. Even these should not bind so as to restrict circulation. Footgear should never be tight, though it needs to fit well enough to prevent rubbing that will cause blisters.

The most common mistake of all is to wear too many clothes during active exercise. I have traveled quite a few miles in winter during fairly cold weather with only a net undershirt on above the waist, and

Gaiters form a seal that prevents snow from getting into your boots Long ones like these are best, since they also help keep your lower legs dry and warm. Both functions help to keep the feet from getting cold. This pair is closed with zippers at the back; the snaps keep the zipper covered and provide an auxiliary closure.

even when the wind comes up, I rarely need to add more than a shirt and shell anorak. Stopping is a different matter: A lunch stop calls for immediate donning of extra clothes.

A lot of thick clothing is needed by the ice fisherman, the sentry, and the belayer in ice climbing, all of whom have to stand still in the cold for long periods. The active wilderness traveler needs far less, but it is important to be aware of the state of your body, adjusting your insulation as soon as you start to get warm. The novice generally takes off that extra sweater about ten minutes after his shirt becomes damp with perspiration. This is a dangerous mistake, because he won't have the warmth when he needs it.

It *is* necessary to have adequate clothing available on wilderness trips, however. A lot of downhill pleasure skiers injured on the slopes are getting pretty cold when the ski patrol reaches them ten minutes later. The wilderness traveler has to be equipped for the emergency situation—that is the surest way of preventing difficulties from arising. Some extra protection will be carried in the form of sleeping gear, but clothing needs to be sufficient for fatigue and storm conditions. The person most likely to get caught is the snowshoer, ski tourer, or climber out for a day trip. If you are going off patrolled or well-used trails, carry emergency clothing. Carry it, but don't wear it while you are sweating up that hill!

3 | Sleeping Warm

If you intend to enjoy a trip, instead of just enduring it, you should pay particular attention to the equipment necessary for a good night's sleep. Food and sleep can ease the memory of a lot of daytime discomforts, but a bad night or an empty stomach will sour the finest day. Obviously you can't get a good night's sleep if you're cold, and in winter conditions, staying warm at night requires good equipment and technique. Temperatures drop far below those experienced during the day, and so does your body's production of heat.

The days when reasonable wilderness travelers could build all-night bonfires to keep warm are gone forever. The use of fires in emergency situations is discussed later in the book, but in many areas even cooking fires should be avoided as a general practice for environmental reasons. There are just too many people using popular wilderness areas during all seasons of the year for fires to be justified. Fires were never a very satisfactory way of keeping warm during really cold weather, anyway. Even with a good arrangement of reflectors, an enormous amount of wood was required, and the fire-builders generally broiled on one side and froze on the other. Well-designed sleeping bags and shelters are far more satisfactory both in terms of comfort and good conservation practice.

Shelters are an important factor in determining your sleeping comfort; the more effective the shelter, the less protection your sleeping bag has to provide. This chapter will concentrate on bags and associated equipment, however, leaving consideration of shelters to the next chapter.

HOW MUCH SLEEPING BAG DO YOU NEED?

The purpose of a sleeping bag is to keep you warm by preventing your body heat from being lost at a greater rate than you are producing it. If the bag fails to do this for any length of time, your body will first begin to shut down blood circulation to your skin and extremities, the most apparent result of which will be cold feet. You will probably begin to sleep badly, and eventually you will wake up shivering as your body becomes alert to the need for increased heat production.

Clearly, then, an adequate sleeping bag for you is one that will prevent this uncomfortable train of events from occurring where you will be using the bag. In this chapter the factors that make a bag warm will be discussed in a way that will give you a basis for comparing bags. The evaluation of your needs is something you will have to make on the basis of your own experience with your body, your estimation of the conditions you will encounter, and consideration of the other equipment you plan on using.

The biggest variable in this equation is your own body. Different people are in better or worse physical condition, have different metabolic rates, different amounts of body fat to insulate them, and different circulatory characteristics that may help or hinder their staying warm. Some people "sleep cold," while others tend to "sleep warm." For example, my wife and I can sleep in identical sleeping bags, on identical pads, in the same tent; I am likely to be warm as toast sleeping nude inside my bag, while she is just barely keeping warm wearing a big down parka inside her bag. Clearly, she needs a heavier bag than I do under the same conditions.

The conditions you will meet are complicated, but fairly obvious. You need to consider the lowest temperature at which the bag will normally be used. Inside a tent, outside in the cold, or in the shelter of a windproof snow cave? With or without a sleeping-bag cover? Sheltered from the sky? With how much additional allowance needed for fatigue, dampness, and the like?

One other condition that might not be so obvious is the altitude at which you plan to use the bag. Altitude affects both temperature and weather, of course, in ways that are discussed more fully in the section on weather. In addition, however, it affects the body functions directly, especially in an individual who has come recently from lower altitudes. Decreased oxygen pressure and some other more complicated effects have the general result of depressing all the body functions, so that your capacity to produce heat is liable to be decreased the higher you go. For this reason you can expect to need a warmer bag for zero temperatures at high altitudes than for the same temperatures at sea level. To make things even more complicated, the altitude may make you sleep badly to begin with, so that cold feet are more likely to keep you awake than they would be at sea level.

Finally, in evaluating your needs for a sleeping bag, you'll have to consider the other equipment you plan to take. It is hard to overstress the need to make every piece of equipment serve as many purposes as possible on any lightweight trip, and this is much more true in winter than in more temperate seasons. Your dry clothing will serve to extend the range of your sleeping bag, and it should be taken into account when you decide how warm a bag to purchase.

It isn't necessary to wear every stitch of clothing you have with you every night. What you should try to do is to adjust the combination of clothing and bag so that it is adequate to handle the worst conditions you can reasonably expect to meet. Then on warmer nights you won't need it all, but on cold nights you will be adequately protected without carrying unnecessary weight or spending more on your outfit than necessary. Thus, a down jacket may serve the combined purpose of providing welcome warmth during lunch stops and in camp, serving as spare clothing for emergencies or severe conditions, and of extending the range of your sleeping bag on a particularly cold night. Clearly, some allowances have to be made for the possibility of some clothing getting wet, but spare items should be as versatile as possible.

The methods of camping you use in different circumstances have important ramifications for your insulation needs. For example, the use of snow caves in high, windy areas can significantly reduce the need of the experienced winter camper for a heavy sleeping bag, because caves are warmer than tents and virtually eliminate the cooling effects of the wind. Some caution is necessary for the beginner in relying on such techniques, however, since they require practice before they can be safely depended upon.

Finally, a layering system can be used with sleeping equipment just as it can with clothing, and a good choice of elements—discussed later in this chapter—can provide the camper with more flexibility, excellent design, and some relief for a strained budget.

A BUYER'S GUIDE TO SLEEPING BAGS

The first choice with which the prospective buyer is confronted in shopping for a sleeping bag is the insulating material. The standard against which other insulators are measured is high quality goose down. The reasons are simple. For a given weight of insulation, even allowing for the extra fabric that is required for baffling a down bag, down provides more warmth than any other material. It can also be compressed into a smaller space, is comfortable over a wider range of temperatures, and is much more durable than any other insulator. The disadvantages that make down of questionable superiority to synthetic insulators in garments are of far less importance in sleeping bags.

Down's light weight and easy compression are advantageous, because the bag will be carried all the time on the trail; it won't be worn. The tendency of down to be compressed by body movements is of little consequence when you are sleeping; it is easy to take full advantage of down's lofting characteristics in designing a sleeping bag, as it is not in constructing a parka. Down's vulnerability to moisture is far less telling in a sleeping bag than in clothing, because you will not be sweating up a trail in your sleeping bag.

Synthetic insulators have made significant inroads during the last few years, however, and they can be expected to become more and more important. There are several reasons for this. The most important is probably price. Polyester batting is cheaper than down, and the construction methods that are used in working with it are simpler, so labor costs are reduced as well. Sleeping bags are time-consuming constructions, so this is an important factor. This price advantage is reduced over the long run by the less durable quality of the synthetics, but such considerations are not likely to be persuasive to anyone looking at the high initial cost of equipment for winter camping these days. Besides, a well-made sleeping bag of either material lasts a long time and is an excellent investment. The differences are relative.

The other major advantage of the synthetic insulators is that they are much less affected by moisture than down and are easier to dry if they do get wet. The polyesters are certainly colder if they get wet, but they don't collapse completely as down does. Down is almost impossible to dry in the field, whereas synthetics will dry. This gives them advantages for those camping in very wet areas and for mountaineers experiencing severe conditions where it is not always possible to keep a bag dry. It makes them far more foolproof, so that bags with synthetic insulation are particularly attractive for people taking out large groups of novices.

The synthetic insulators have also shown steady improvement, while the quality of down that is generally available has declined just as steadily. Synthetics can therefore be expected to become more and more popular. For the skilled camper who wants to reduce the size and weight of the pack to a minimum, however, down remains the best insulator for the basic sleeping bag. A well-designed bag using high-quality down can provide a tremendous amount of insulation with minimal weight and bulk.

Combinations are also possible either in a single bag or by the use of a layering system that provides versatility and makes the most efficient use of the qualities of each material. One such system is described later in this chapter. First, however, it is necessary to consider the design features important in both down and synthetic bags.

Shape

The shape of a bag for lightweight winter use should be roughly the same as that of the human body—a so-called "mummy" bag. Big rectangular bags tend to be prohibitively heavy even in summer, and in winter weights, they are even heavier. They are also very expensive when they are made of down. The reason is twofold: Not only is the bag itself larger, using more materials, but it is also much less efficient so that a thicker bag is needed.

Within the mummy classification, however, there is a lot of room for choice, because bags are now made which range all the way from a modified rectangular bag tapered at each end to reduce weight and surface area to extremely lightweight bags that fit very closely.

The choice you make in terms of how closely your bag fits and how severely it is tapered will depend both on personal preference and body build. It is pointless to buy a bag that is so closely cut that you tend to squish the insulation just by getting in and moving your body. I would strongly recommend, however, that for winter use you buy the closest fitting bag that is practical. Such bags tend to feel a bit cramped to the beginner, because you can't curl up *inside* the bag. It usually is quite easy to learn to turn about with the bag, though, and the closer the bag fits, the more efficient it will be.

A well-designed bag should taper rapidly at the top, to the hood, should be fairly broad through the midsection, from shoulders to hips, and should then taper down to the foot. There should be a bottom large enough so that when you are lying in the bag with your feet sticking up, they do not press against the bag. Otherwise, there will be a cold spot. The hood should fit smoothly around your head without compressing the insulation, and the devices that tighten the opening should be easy to distinguish and work when you are in the bag.

Differential Cut

An important design feature in cold-weather bags, particularly if they are shaped to fit the camper snugly and if they are insulated with easily compressed down, is the cut of the inner and outer shells. Any bag will actually consist of two bags, one inside the other, with the insulation in between. If the two bags are the same size, then whenever you stretch inside the bag you will push the inner bag against the outer one, and the insulation between will compress. You will then have a cold spot at each pressure point. With a differential cut the inner bag is cut smaller than the outer one, so that when you press against it the outer bag will still be held away from the inner one by the down insulating layer.

It is considerably more difficult to make a bag with a differential

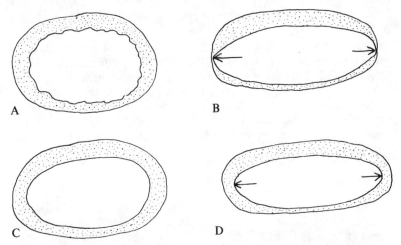

Differential cut in a sleeping bag The upper two figures show a schematic cross-section of a sleeping bag with the inside shell cut the same size as the outside. The same amount of insulation is provided (*A*), but when the occupant pushes out on the bag (*B*), the insulation is pressed between the two shells, resulting in cold spots.

 C is a bag with a differential cut; the inside shell has a smaller circumference, so that when the sleeper presses out (*D*), some insulation space is maintained.

cut than simply to cut the inner and the outer shells to the same pattern, and even some of the best outdoor suppliers manufacture bags without this feature. Such bags are not well suited for cold-weather use; under winter conditions when you scrunch up from the cold, you will soon find that your back is freezing because you have pressed the inner shell against the outer one. Even though a differential cut is less important in a roomier bag, for sleepers who move around less, and in bags insulated with synthetic fibers, a properly sewn bag with a differential cut will be lighter and more efficient than one without it.

Fabric

The standard material for sleeping bags is nylon. The reasons are simple: For a particular fabric weight, nylon is stronger and will take more wear than any other type of cloth; it is not subject to mildew or rot; it can be woven tightly so that it is downproof. The major disadvantage of nylon cloth is that it cannot be treated very effectively with water repellants, but this is of little importance in sleeping bags. The disadvantage of initial expense is offset by the durability of nylon. A cotton cover, even a quite heavy one, will wear out long before the down it is enclosing.

The lightness of high-strength nylon fabric gives greater freedom to the sleeping-bag designer, because a heavyweight fabric will tend to reduce the expansion of the down by its very weight. Even so, a well-designed sleeping bag uses different weights of fabric throughout the bag. The heaviest weight fabric is used on the outer shell, while the inside of the bag is made of a durable lightweight material, woven tightly enough to prevent escape of the down. An even lighter fabric is used between the two layers for down baffles, and it is also the proper material for a removable liner.

Closures

Most lightweight sleeping bags have an opening that is closed by a zipper running at least halfway down one side or the top of the bag, as well as being open at the head of the bag. The zipper should be made from nylon in a large size with opening tabs both inside and outside the bag. It should operate perfectly, and a sticking or jamming zipper is the sign of an inferior bag. Don't buy it. Zippers with heavy standard teeth are strongest and do not jam as easily, while coil zippers are lighter and a little less vulnerable to permanent damage. Inside the bag there should be sewn along the opening a down-filled tube that covers the zipper from the inside when it is closed. This tube prevents a cold breeze from blowing through the zipper at night and dusting your spine with powder snow. Other closures besides zippers are possible, but they are not currently being used by the manufacturers of good down bags. Two zippers are used by a few companies to substitute for the insulated tube in forming a draftproof closure.

Other considerations are of less importance than good zipper operation and insulated tube. A side zipper has some advantage over a top one. When the weather warms up a bit and you want ventilation, or when you open the zipper for freedom of movement, the side zipper allows some air circulation without having the bag fall completely off your chest, as happens with the top zipper. A full-length zipper has some advantages in drying the bag on sunny days, a matter that makes it worth considering the small extra weight and expense. Finally, many manufacturers now make all their bags that have full-length zippers in such a way that they will zip together as long as the zippers are on opposite sides.

Most hood designs are adequate. When you buy a bag, test the operation and make sure the hood can be opened all the way and closed to any desired degree down to an opening large enough for the tip of the nose. The simpler the whole operation, the better. When the call of nature gets strong enough to make you brave the midnight cold, fussing with fifteen different tangled and unidentifiable strings is annoying—to say the least!

The old miniature awnings at the head of the bag, which are often depicted as shedding torrential rains from the head of the peacefully sleeping camper, are rarely found on lightweight bags. They are useless, and their presence on bags you are being shown should send you packing to another store.

Occasionally, you may find ultra-light bags with no side openings; entry is through the top. Most manufacturers don't make these bags because of their major disadvantage: they lack flexibility in temperature range. If you need a really ultra-light bag for one temperature range and can afford it, you can either make a bag of this type or have one custom-made. Usually, they are not worth the weight saved.

Down

The quality of the down itself is an important factor in the warmth of a bag. Down is a natural material and does not have the uniformity of some man-made materials. It is important to distinguish down from feathers. The latter have quills, but down consists of a mass of filaments extending out from a tiny pod. Down always has small feathers mixed with it, but a down-and-feather mixture, labeled as such, is greatly inferior in insulating quality to true down.

The best down is plucked from geese raised to maturity in a cold climate, and it is not surprising that it is expensive. Its quality is measured by the volume of air that a given weight of down will immobilize. Thus, the standard filling capacity of down used by most manufacturers of high-quality sleeping bags is 550 cubic inches per ounce. Some makers use a very high-quality down with a filling capacity of up to 700 cubic inches per ounce.

Unfortunately, the quality of down has deteriorated in the last ten years, even as demand and price have skyrocketed. This has occurred because of a combination of the greatly expanded market with changed practices in the poultry industry abroad, the source of virtually all good down. Geese are rarely raised to maturity anymore, because the best meat production per pound of feed is obtained by slaughtering poultry at a younger age, when the down is less fully developed. The down plumules from immature geese and from ducks are not as large, complex, or durable as those from mature geese, and the resulting down has less loft and a shorter life, despite increasing sophistication in machine separation of the down.

Adding to the problems of the puzzled prospective purchaser is the fact that manufacturers are not at all uniform in their methods of testing, labeling, or quality control. You *cannot* assume that catalog ratings of the loft of bags, temperature ratings, or fill standards are even roughly comparable. This lack of uniformity is true even of the more reputable makers. Discount operations and bags marketed by large garment manufacturers and department stores are even less reliable, because they obtain their products from many factories in the Far East, and quality often varies dramatically. Direct comparison and recent reputation are your best guides. Fluff up bags, measure the loft, weigh them yourself, feel the plumpness, and talk to as many knowledgeable people as possible before buying a bag. Remember that backpacking suppliers are being bought at a rapid rate by large conglomerate corporations and that quality can show a marked deterioration in a short time. The maker's reputation remains one of the best guides in choosing a sleeping bag, but it can change in a short time. At the time this is written, some good makers of down bags to use as standards for comparison are Sierra Designs, Warmlite, Marmot, North Face, Trailwise, Camp 7, and Holubar.

Synthetic Insulators

Some winter campers prefer synthetic insulators as primary filling for sleeping bags because of their low initial cost and reduced vulnerability to moisture. Because the fibers themselves are largely impervious to moisture, bags using synthetic insulation can be dried effectively even in winter, and can retain their loft and much of their warmth even when they are wet. Even the best-designed synthetic insulated bags will usually weigh about half again as much as a comparable down bag, however, and will require at least 50 percent more space in your pack.

The most frequently used synthetic for sleeping bag construction is PolarGuard (a trademark of Celanese), because the batting has continuous fibers in a relatively stable batt. This allows bags to be constructed with fewer attachments between the insulation and the shell and without intervening baffles. Good loft can thus be achieved with less added baffling material and associated labor than with looser fill polyester fibers. Some typical constructions using PolarGuard insulation are shown in the illustration on the next page. Thinsulate (a 3M trademark) has the advantage of providing more insulation per unit thickness because of its very fine fibers, so it could partially solve the bulk problem of the polyesters, but its expense and inferiority to down in efficiency per unit weight have so far limited its use in sleeping bags to experimental models. Hollofil II (a Du Pont trademark) has better lofting and draping characteristics than PolarGuard and is used in sleeping bags by a few manufacturers, but its shorter fibers require nearly as much baffling as down to prevent the insulation from shifting and leaving cold spots.

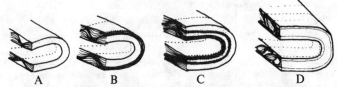

Construction of PolarGuard insulated sleeping bags   *A* shows a bag using a single layer of insulation, which is quilted to one shell of the bag. The stitching can be done to either shell, but should not go through both, since the cold-seam effect is reduced by sewing through only one. This type of construction is good only for very light bags, like the outer shell shown later in the chapter. *B* shows the most common construction for PolarGuard bags, using two layers of insulation, one quilted to each shell with offset seams, so that no cold spots are formed. *C* shows the construction that is most appropriate for winter-weight bags. Two layers are quilted to the shells with offset seams, and a floating layer of PolarGuard is sandwiched in between, held by friction and by anchoring stitching at the sides. *D* shows a final method that has been used successfully in three-season bags, with short, overlapping layers of batting sewn to both shells, rather like the slant-wall baffles in down bags.

Internal Construction of Sleeping Bags

The method of construction of a sleeping bag's interior layers is of crucial importance to the snow camper, though unfortunately most of it cannot be seen directly. Down, because it is a loose material that is highly compressible, will drift into a few corners and pack there unless it is distributed into many isolated compartments in the bag. The most obvious way to do this—quilting the inner and outer shells together— is not suitable for winter bags, because each seam presents a line through which your body heat will leak. Ideally, the bag should be designed so that the whole shell lofts to an equal distance above the sleeper. The more baffles that can be sewn between the two shells, the smaller the compartments enclosing the down will be, and the more efficiently the insulation can be used. Unfortunately, weight is added in baffling material and labor in sewing it, so a sleeping bag designer has to make the best compromise possible. Some of the most common constructions are shown in the illustration on the next page.

The baffling material itself should be made from a very light-weight material, but one that will hold the down where it is wanted. Some manufacturers prefer a very light conventional nylon material, while others use a stretchy netting. There are some good arguments in favor of each. The most important feature in the baffling and other inside edges, however, is that they be finished in such a way that they will not fray and unravel. Light synthetic fabrics are particularly

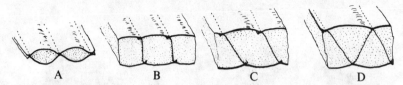

A   B   C   D

Construction of down sleeping bags, showing several methods of compartmentalizing the down A shows a quilted bag, with the down held in sections by sewing the two shells together. Cold seams are left, and the lofting capacity of the down is partly wasted. This method is good only for very light bags, which in winter could only be used for inner bags in a combination. B shows I-beam or box baffling, in which baffles are sewn straight across between the two shells. A light material is used for the baffles. This method is very effective for lightweight, close-cut bags. C shows slant-wall baffling, which most manufacturers feel controls down better and allows better lofting than box construction in thicker sleeping bags. D shows V-baffling, which provides maximum control of the down and prevents compression by an occupant shifting the inside shell against the outer. The weight of baffling is doubled, however, and this construction is normally used only in expedition bags.

prone to pulling out on the edges. Hot cutting to fuse edges and then double or zigzag stitching is needed to produce a bag that will hold up over the years. You can't see most of this work, but you can at least ask salespeople and inspect catalogs. Stitching between the baffling and the shell, which is visible on the outside and inside of the bag, should have at least eight stitches to the inch. Wider spacing in these or other seams is one sign of shoddy construction.

In the case of PolarGuard insulated bags, baffling is not used to hold the insulation in place, since the batting itself has a good deal of stability and strength. The insulation has to be fastened to the shells at intervals to keep it in place, and along the seams the batting will be compressed. For a single bag to be used in winter, these cold seams are clearly not acceptable, and a number of constructions can be used to avoid them, as shown in the illustration below. Since battings are available with different average weights, the designer of the bag has some flexibility in working with these methods. PolarGuard is not subject to the variations of natural insulators like down, but quality control is just as important, since batting can come with thin spots. Check your bag and its construction carefully.

INNOVATIONS AND SPECIAL DESIGNS

There are a number of variations in standard sleeping bag design that may prove particularly useful to the winter camper, both in individual bag construction and in systems using several components. Some are aimed at improving the efficiency of the bag and some at providing better value for the money. One obvious point of attack is the bottom layer of a down-insulated bag. Because of the compressibility of down, the sleeper obviously will squash the bottom portion of an all-down bag to an almost negligible thickness, one reason why foam pads are essential supplements to a standard bag. For this reason, some manufacturers have made bags with a less compressible insulator incorporated into the bottom, eliminating the need for some down and incorporating at least some of the ground bed into the bag. Some examples include the use of shredded foam in the bottom of the bag, as with Frostline kits, and the use of polyester insulation in the bottom with a down top. Probably the most successful such design is Warmlite's bottom compartment, into which a special pad or down-filled air mattress is slipped. The difficulty that most makers have found is in making an efficient, close-fitting bag in which the mixed materials do not either leave cold joints where they come together or reduce one another's effectiveness. Thus, a pad attached to the bottom of a bag can tend to pull the top against the sleeper and reduce the loft of the down. Those who roll around a lot are also likely to find that a close-cut bag of this design will end up the down under them and the foam off to the side. A larger bag eliminates this problem, but it can also eliminate the savings in weight and down filling that were sought.

Vapor-Barrier Liners

VBLs are an invention of Jack Stephenson of Warmlite that has been taken up recently by several other manufacturers. The idea is to introduce a layer of coated material on the *inside* of the sleeping bag (not the outside!) to prevent moisture from the body from migrating out through the insulation. This approach has several advantages for the winter camper. The humidity inside the bag rapidly reaches the saturation point, and then evaporation of water from the skin drops to a very low level. (There is always some moisture escaping through the head of the bag, and so on.) The heat loss that occurs through this evaporation is greatly reduced as well, and so is the loss of moisture from the body. Dehydration, always a problem in winter, also is therefore reduced. Finally, the usual condensation of moisture within the insulation of the bag, as the water vapor moves out into colder and colder layers, is almost wholly eliminated.

There are a few disadvantages to the vapor-barrier liner. Contrary to the fears of many, the bag does not turn into a Turkish bath, as long as you don't get so hot that you begin to sweat. In this case you would want to open a zipper to prevent soaking the bag, anyway. The VBL does make the inside of the bag feel slightly dank, however. A light bag with a VBL cannot be used in combination with a heavy down parka, since the vapor barrier would cause condensation in the parka. This is not a problem in most situations, however. Tentmates of VBL users have been known to protest the opening of the bag next morning, with complaints of concentrated odor filling the living space.

Vapor-barrier liners either can be built into a bag by using coated material for the inside or can be added as an accessory. The latter solution is excellent, since the VBL can be used to increase the warmth of the bag in severe conditions and left at home when it isn't wanted.

Sleeping bags can be designed with adjustable insulation, and again the major credit for innovation in this area goes to Stephenson and Warmlite. Their bags include zip-on tops of different thickness, which can be used separately or in combination, so that you take just the bag you want. Other combinations have been made at various times by other manufacturers.

One other variation that has been used with success is to make the outer shell of the sleeping bag from a Gore-tex laminate material. The advantages are that the bag is far less vulnerable to moisture penetrating from outside and that the sleeper will be cooled less by convection currents because Gore-tex is very windtight. Such bags can be used confidently in tents and snow shelters without bivy sacks, since snow and condensation are easily shed by the outer fabric. (Forget about sleeping out in direct rain, however. There are too many seams on a sleeping bag to be effectively sealed.) The main disadvantage is the added cost of the bag. This innovation was pioneered by Marmot Mountain Works, and their bags incorporating it typically cost about $100 more than comparable bags that use conventional fabric. Some additional weight and difficulty in washing must also be put up with.

The use of Gore-tex for sleeping bag shells, though it has some definite advantages, should therefore be considered as something of a luxury feature. The gains are not as great as for many other items of equipment, and the cost is quite high. Those looking for the ultimate in equipment who are willing to pay a premium price for it may find the feature worthwhile.

A RECOMMENDED SYSTEM

For economy, versatility, and the advantage of allowing a beginner to spread out purchases over a period of time, a sleeping bag system is usually ideal. The one preferred by the author is described below. You may find that another combination suits your needs better, but this one should serve well as an example.

I prefer a lightweight, close-fitting, three-season down bag. These

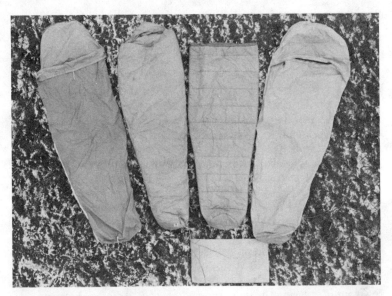

A versatile and very effective sleeping bag system At the bottom is a small ethafoam pad, an essential element of any winter sleeping combination. *From left to right*: a vapor-barrier liner, with ties to attach it inside the bag; a very efficient closely cut down bag made by Trailwise; the Camp 7 Pioneer PolarGuard overbag; and a Goretex bivouac sack made by Early Winters. The pad, down bag, and bivy sack are more than adequate for most winter camping, and the two other elements can be added for severe conditions.

are reasonably economical, they can be used for backpacking trips in the mountains the rest of the year, and they are often adequate for winter camping with the addition of a sleeping bag cover for use in snow caves. Such bags typically weigh about three pounds or a little less, depending on the model and your height. Good examples are the Trailwise Slimline, the Holubar Trimlite, Sierra Designs' Cirrus and Narrowlite, Camp 7's Arete, the Marmot Pocket Gopher, and the North Face Superlight.

The second important component of the system for winter use (ignoring the ground pad, which is discussed below) is a sleeping bag cover, a fabric sack that is slipped over the whole bag. The cover increases the warmth of the bag in any circumstances, serves as a ground cloth when a tent is not used, and helps to protect the bag from wetting by loose snow or condensation within a tent. The bottom of a cover should be made of urethane-coated nylon, while the top should breathe. Any lightweight uncoated nylon can be used on top, but Gore-tex laminates are definitely most satisfactory. They are more windproof, can be made fully watertight if the seams are sealed, and reduce condensation significantly even over standard uncoated nylon fabric. Sleeping bag covers (or bivy sacks) with Gore-tex tops are expensive, though remnants can easily be used to make your own if you can obtain them. (See Appendix A.) I prefer to avoid the heavier and more elaborate bivy sacks in order to save weight. A homemade one can weigh in at less than a pound; a good commercial example is Early Winters' Sleep Inn.

A pad, sleeping bag cover, and light three-season down bag will probably serve you well for most winter camping situations, particularly if you rely mainly on snow shelters, which are warmer than tents. If these do not provide quite enough warmth for you, however, or if you are sleeping in less than ideal circumstances—outside, on climbing expeditions, or the like—adding two more components will result in a very warm, weatherproof, and versatile system at a reasonable weight.

The first is a vapor-barrier liner, discussed above. You can easily sew your own, using the lightest available coated material, or you can purchase a separate one from Camp 7. Finally, the best way to increase the warmth of a closely cut down bag is to add a very light PolarGuard insulated outer bag on the outside. Design here is important if you want to get maximum advantage from the system. Most manufacturers who have come up with combinations have also made major errors that result in a lot of extra weight and bulk without much extra warmth. The advantages and theory of the system should be discussed briefly first.

A light PolarGuard insulated overbag will add an inch of loft around your basic bag, an extra dead air space between the bags, and a little extra insulation underneath you. Just as important, it increases the ability of your equipment to be kept dry and efficient in difficult weather and camping conditions. Condensation occurring in your sleeping insulation will be confined mainly to the outer PolarGuard layer, because that is where water vapor will be cooled the most. This layer is easy to dry, both because of the material and because the bags come apart and can be hung out separately for drying. Your down bag thus stays much drier, lighter, and fluffier, even if a bag cover and vapor-barrier liner are not used. With all these elements it is easy to keep your sleeping system dry and warm in the nastiest wet-cold conditions.

It is important to note that this system can be effective only with a close-out down inner bag. A larger mummy bag, especially without a differential cut, would require a much larger outer PolarGuard bag, which would weigh a lot more and be much more bulky, in order to prevent the outer bag from squashing the down insulation inside. A similar diminishing of returns occurs when the outer synthetic bag is made heavier: The overall loft is not significantly improved, because a heavier outer bag pushes on the down and reduces its loft. On my own system I measured the loft using a two-pound outer bag and a four-pound one; the loft was exactly the same! Typically, the outer bag should use a single layer of PolarGuard sewn to one shell only, reducing the cold-seam effect slightly. The outer bag also does not need to go farther than the shoulders of the inner bag when they are used together, since tightening an additional hood just tends to push the inside one down. A bag that is shoulder length when used over an inside down bag will be just about right for a light summer bag when used alone. It is also excellent for sleeping in cabins, on boating trips, or for emergency bivouac gear. Ideally, such a bag should be made with very light nylon fabric and should have about a three-foot lightweight zipper to allow some mobility. The closest commercially available bag to these specifications is Camp 7's Pioneer; it weighs two pounds, is cut correctly, and is reasonable in price. It has no zipper, however, and is made of fabric a little heavier than necessary.

My own system weighs under six pounds, including a short foam pad, a down bag that is adequate even under most winter conditions without additional elements, a Gore-tex bivy sack, a vapor-barrier liner, and a PolarGuard overbag. This combination provides a comfortable margin of warmth and safety in the most severe expeditionary conditions and compares well with the weight of down expedition-grade bags. The price compares well also, and a system can be bought piece by piece, instead of all at once. Finally, the versatility is useful both throughout the year and in harsh conditions. On a long day trip from camp or on a load carry on an expedition, you can choose to take one or two pieces from a system to provide an extra margin of safety. With a single heavy bag, it is all or nothing.

SHOPPING FOR SLEEPING BAGS

The use of rentals has been mentioned earlier in this book, and sleeping bags are especially profitable to rent. Borrowing from a friend is a cheaper equivalent, of course, if this alternative is available. If you know from previous experience what kind of bag you need and you have the money to buy it, don't go through the expense and inconvenience of renting. By the same token, if you have a medium-weight bag and enough clothing to extend its range for winter use, don't rent a heavier bag you can do without. But if you don't own a bag that can be made adequate for cold-weather use and you either aren't sure what type of bag to buy or don't have the money to put out at one time, rent your sleeping bag the first few trips. If you get a different bag each time, you can build up more experience with different makes of bags than most veteran snow campers ever acquire. Sleeping bags last so long, most active mountaineers only own a few in a lifetime. The rental alternative is only open to you if there is a mountaineering-backpacking shop near your home, of course.

Let us say that you have only very limited knowledge of snow camping and can't try out equipment by renting or borrowing. (Obviously, if you can get such experience you will be ahead of the game; you will rapidly develop your own prejudices and can ignore some of mine.)

The first step in buying a major piece of equipment like a sleeping bag is to get all the catalogs you can. Even if you end up buying your bag at a store, you will have a better idea of what is available after reading the offerings of other manufacturers. A list of mail-order suppliers is found in Appendix C. Many of the catalogs available from these houses contain very valuable advice and information. With a bit of work and consideration of the features discussed in this chapter, you should be able to compare the bags offered and get some idea of the comparative prices of different manufacturers. There are some pretty big differences, though price is a good guide to relative quality in any one maker's line.

One minor caution is to read all the information about each bag. Most reputable manufacturers of lightweight bags readily admit that temperature ranges are only suggestive: they tell you that one bag made by Joe Smith is warmer than another but not that it is warmer than one by Frank Jones. The same thing applies to loft measurements, down ratings, and so forth.

Finally, if you do go to a store, take a good look at the catalog before you get into a discussion with the sales clerk. Almost all good stores selling this type of equipment put a lot of care into their catalog statements. Their customers demand honesty and frankness, but they cannot be expected to screen their clerks quite as carefully. Most are very good indeed; that salesperson you're talking to may very well be one of the best mountain climbers in the world. Unfortunately, some are not as competent. They may have strong opinions but weak experience, or they may simply have developed a cynical attitude toward customers. Do your homework beforehand and then listen to the salespeople; they may be very helpful, but they will be more so if you know what you want.

GROUND INSULATION

Since any reasonable insulation for use in a sleeping bag must be quite compressible, it will be squeezed to a thin layer under the weight of a sleeper. Because the snow camper frequently has to sleep directly on the snow, some separate insulation under the body is essential, whether it is included in the sleeping bag or carried separately. Most sleeping bags do not include special ground insulation, so the snow camper must normally take a separate pad. Bags insulated with synthetics provide a little more insulation under the sleeper than those filled with down, but additional material is still essential if major heat loss to the snow is to be avoided.

The three major types of ground bed used by backpackers are air mattresses; foam pads made from comfortable, spongelike urethane foam; and pads of closed-cell foam in which each air pocket is completely closed off. There are also a few hybrid devices like air mats that are self-inflated by enclosed foam pads.

In general, closed-cell foam pads are most satisfactory for winter use, though the other alternatives can be used if you have them in your summer equipment and want to avoid special purchases. Air mattresses are cold in winter because of air convection inside the tubes, unless they are filled with compressible insulation as a sleeping bag is. Many materials used for mattresses also become brittle at low temperatures. Conventional urethane pads covered with nylon can be used in winter, but they are relatively heavy and bulky for the insulation they provide and can freeze in a compressed state. Since the padding they give is less essential in winter, it is usually better to choose the closed-cell pads for sleeping on snow because they yield maximum insulation for a given amount of weight and space in the pack.

The most widely known and distributed of the closed-cell foam pads is Ensolite (the Uniroyal brand name for polyvinyl-chloride), but the same insulation can be obtained with half the weight by using ethafoam or one of its more exotic relatives, such as ethylene-vinyl-acetate. Ethafoam is most commonly sold in a light blue version, so it is often known as "blue foam."

The size and thickness of pads are largely a matter of personal compromise between weight and bulk versus comfort and convenience. A thickness of ⅜″ will do in most situations, but ½″ foam is warmer for extensive camping on snow in cold temperatures. In a small pad the extra thickness adds very little extra weight and bulk. I prefer to carry a narrow pad just long enough to extend from the top of my shoulders to a little below my hips. The pad I usually carry is ½″ × 16″ × 31″. I use my pack and spare clothing and equipment for a pillow and to pad under my legs and feet. Others prefer to carry a longer pad. One can also compromise by carrying a full-length ¼″ pad with extra thicknesses glued on at those points where the main weight of the body is borne.

SLEEPING WARM

The first technique for sleeping warm is *keeping* warm. During the day you will usually keep warm from sheer physical effort, combined sometimes with the welcome rays of the sun. You will notice at every rest stop, though, that the air is cold, and when you stop you feel it. This is much more true on stopping toward the end of the day, for the sun is usually going down, and your tired body joins dropping temperatures and damp clothes to produce a situation where very sudden chilling often results.

The proper way to meet this situation is simple. Make your camp and then get into your sleeping bag before you start to feel cold. If you're still warm, the sun is in the sky, the woods invite exploring, and camp is made, by all means answer the call. However, watch your body, and always try to bed down before you get cold. If you use a stove, the standard pattern in winter is to cook supper in your sleeping bag. At any rate, your camp should be completely ready before you start exploring. The days are much shorter in winter, and the cold really seeps into your bones in a hurry when the sun goes down and you stop moving. Even if you don't get into your sleeping bag, change to dry socks and mittens, and loosen boot laces. Put on extra clothes if you are sitting around.

Keep your body warmth in mind as you are pitching camp. Follow the techniques for choosing a warm campsite, which are discussed later in the book. Then arrange your bed so that you are well protected underneath. If you are cold in your bag, then it is only common sense to use all the insulation you have available. There shouldn't be any extra dry sweaters in your pack.

Fluff up your sleeping bags well as soon as you have the tent pitched or the snow shelter built. They will gain extra loft and warmth if they are shaken up several times and allowed to expand while you are getting other things ready. Sleeping close together will conserve quite a lot of warmth.

For all-night warmth, you need food; the digestion of food releases energy in the form of heat. There is one slight qualification here: If you are really cold when you first get into your bag, start off with hot drinks and perhaps something sweet. Though you need lots of food to keep you warm, eating a lot of heavy things forces the body to divert blood to the stomach, when you need it temporarily for thawing out.

To warm up when you get in your bag, snug everything tightly, and then try contracting your muscles hard, a few at a time. This serves the same function as shivering: The muscular activity produces warmth. The contractions are good because you avoid moving around and creating air currents to carry away the heat you are producing.

If anyone is *really* cold, don't neglect the possibility that he may be suffering from hypothermia, popularly known as exposure. This subject is discussed in another chapter, and the symptoms should be memorized by cold-weather campers. It is important for each person to take responsibility for his companions, since a person suffering from too much heat loss often becomes irrational and may not realize he is seriously sick. A person suffering from hypothermia cannot always generate enough heat to get warm inside a sleeping bag; someone else must get in with him.

One piece of clothing is often neglected at night, though it can cut more heat loss than almost any other. If you're cold, *wear a hat*. High blood circulation is maintained in the surface skin of the head, even when the body is cold, and this can result in tremendous losses of heat. This is particularly true at night, when cooking and other chores are still being done from the sleeping bag, so that the hood isn't covering the head. *If your feet are cold, put on your hat.*

Drying Out Clothes

If you want to start a good argument in a group of experienced winter campers, just inject this subject into the conversation, and then sit back and watch the fun. The question is whether to wear your damp clothes to bed at night in order to dry them out with your body heat.

Those who favor this technique argue that "During the earlier and warmer part of the night much of the moisture from damp clothes can be evaporated and will pass right through the sleeping bag in the form of water vapor. This way you wake up with dry clothes, rather than a frozen heap at the foot of the tent, and you have a particular advantage if the sun doesn't come out."

"Nuts!" says the opponent, the sleep-in-dry-clothes proponent. "You probably won't succeed in drying your clothes very much, but you will have a bad night's sleep. What is more dangerous, if you do this regularly on a long trip, your sleeping bag will pick up more and more moisture, eventually becoming useless and losing significant insulation even the first night."

Obviously, there is some truth in each of these arguments, and your practice should be governed by personal trial coupled with a few basic principles. The first is fairly obvious: If you use body heat to evaporate water from your clothes, that heat is not available for keeping your body warm. Clearly, you should never try to dry out wet clothes in your bag unless you are quite warm and can afford the heat loss. Also, it is clear that the amount of drying you can expect to do is limited, and it should be confined to damp woolens and synthetics which aren't too uncomfortable. It is absurd to lose a night's sleep trying to dry out clothes. If you can't sleep, you're making a mistake.

The major problem, however, is the problem of wetting the bag. It works like this: The air inside your bag is warm, and some of the water in your clothes evaporates in this air, mixing with insensible perspiration from your body. Since this air doesn't circulate very much, the humidity inside the bag gets quite high. Gradually the water vapor circulates through the air cells trapped in the down insulation of your sleeping bag, and those air cells are colder near the outside of the bag. The colder air cannot hold as much water, and if too much water vapor is being produced, the water may condense into dew in the down. This may not be serious if the weather is not too cold, since the water may evaporate again later. If the weather *is* very cold, the air cells in the outer part of the bag are often well below freezing, so that when the water vapor condenses, it freezes, forming ice crystals in the down. In very cold weather these keep forming, and the bag finally becomes completely useless. On long trips, this can be a problem even if clothing is not dried in the bag, since insensible perspiration can cause the same difficulty. The problem arises much more quickly if clothes are dried in the bag.

The condensation is also serious in damp weather around the freezing point. Under these circumstances the moisture does not freeze in the down, but it condenses into liquid and does not evaporate because the air is already too wet. As with the dry-cold problem, the only real solution is to dry things either in the sun or on the trail, when you are producing a surplus of heat.

The reader has probably guessed that the author tends to side with the sleep-in-dry-clothes advocates. The main reason is that clothing is generally a lot easier to dry than a sleeping bag. A damp sleeping bag on a cold-weather trip is a very serious matter. So are damp clothes, but except for down clothing, nothing you wear is nearly so hard to dry as your bag. Finally, as I suggested at the beginning of the chapter, a little misery in the day is soothed a lot by a good night's sleep. Having dry, warm sleeping gear available at the end of the day provides both a psychological boost and a significant safety margin.

CARING FOR YOUR SLEEPING BAG

Aside from the obvious matter of repairing rips and broken hardware, the two main things you can do for your sleeping gear, at home and in the field, are to keep it dry and clean. Both dirt and moisture rob down of its insulating value. When the opportunity arises on a trip, open the bag and air it out, preferably in the sun. When you get it home, hang it out in the sun or in a warm spot in the house until you are sure it is thoroughly dry. Then store it in a dry place.

Unless you spill the stew on your bag or perspire much in it, you won't need to clean it too often. Most dirt will rub off on the liner, if you have one, and this can be cleaned separately. Too much perspiring in a bag will get salt in the down, and this in turn will absorb moisture when the bag is in use. A bag can be cleaned by a reputable dry cleaner who is experienced in handling down products, though I prefer washing. If you take your down bag to a dry cleaner, be sure to ask questions before leaving the bag; improper handling can ruin it. Ask what kind of fluid the cleaner uses for down bags. Stoddard fluid should be used. If the cleaner indicates that "perk" (perchlorethylene) works fine, take your bag home with you. Never clean any bag in a coin-operated dry cleaner or dry clean bags with Gore-tex shells, synthetic insulation, or foam bottoms.

Bags can be washed in the large, front-loading machines found in laundromats or by hand in bathtubs. Use Ivory Snow powder or one of the special down soaps. It is simplest to immerse the bag while it is compressed, since air is difficult to squeeze out once the surface of the nylon shell is wet. Rinse several times if you are using a machine or until all soap is clearly out if you are washing by hand. Squeeze and press if you are hand washing, but be wary of lifting a wet down bag in such a way that clumps of wet down will be held up by the baffles. The weight can rip baffling out. Move the wet bag carefully to a place where it can drip or to a spin extractor in a laundromat. I hang the bag in a net hammock for dripping. You can then either dry the bag in the wind and sun, turning it and gently pulling clumps of down apart occasionally, or you can dry the bag in a large dryer at low heat. Put a clean tennis shoe in with it to help break up the down clumps and to build up an electrostatic charge that fluffs the down.

Proper washing of your sleeping bag will more than restore its original loft. With proper care a good down bag should last for many years. Bags insulated with synthetics fatigue a little faster but should still give good service if they are kept clean. Store your bag by hanging it or stuffing it in a roomy storage bag. Leaving the bag stuffed in a tight stuff sack between trips will reduce its life. Never leave a damp bag stuffed any longer than necessary.

4 | Camping on Snow

The fascination of winter is hard to grasp fully until you have tried camping on the snow. On day-long tours with skis or snowshoes you can experience the beauty of brilliant white slopes meeting blue sky in a line somehow sharper than any seen in summer. Still, it is only during longer stays that you can feel the full intensity of the background silence, sometimes bright and clear, sometimes muffled and close.

The challenges of winter are also felt more strongly when one lives for a time on the snow, in addition to walking on it. Challenges are often worth meeting for their own sake, but there are other more important reasons for snow camping. Especially when you begin snow camping, before the techniques become second nature and begin to make you feel at home, you may feel very strongly how tenuous your existence is in this world of cold and light. The beginner has one great advantage over the expert in this situation, because this consciousness of not belonging in the cold, stark, and beautiful world around you can lead to a realization of the independent value of that world—a value that can only be experienced in its own terms.

To meet the winter on its own terms you have to get away from the knowledge that a warm cabin is waiting. To me this is what snow camping is all about. It's also a great challenge in its more extreme forms. Finally, it can be a lot of fun.

GETTING STARTED

It's best to get your first couple of experiences camping on snow that's not too far from your base. If you live in a forested area, try walking into the woods behind your house for the first try. Otherwise, get just far enough from the road for peace and quiet. A little experience in easy conditions can prevent your first real trip from turning into a survival ordeal. There's a lot to learn about snow camping, and you might just as well learn it pleasantly.

For your first trip pick a weekend that seems to offer reasonable prospects for decent weather. Winter weather is unsettled enough so that you'll have your chance to experience a blizzard soon enough; try to avoid it the first time out.

If you have bought or rented new equipment, make sure to inspect it and try it out at home or at some other warm location. A cold, snowy evening is no time to find out how to operate a self-priming gasoline stove from the Swedish directions, or to discover that the last guy who rented that tent left the zipper on top of Horrible Ridge. Incidentally, later on you'll find that this applies to the first trip of every season, anyway. By then you will have forgotten that broken fortzwaffler that you were going to fix during the summer—and never did.

This is a good place to mention again a couple of principles in getting equipment. A useful rule of thumb is to never buy anything you don't need for the next trip. This way you don't get a lot of stuff that you don't need and you are likely to make more intelligent selections of the things that you do need. Naturally, you'll have to modify this rule a bit if you're buying equipment by mail order from a place that takes six weeks to reply.

If there is a store near you specializing in mountaineering and backpacking equipment, they probably have a rental service. Renting is obviously a good way to spread the cost of basic equipment over a reasonable period. It is also a good way to try out various types of gear before putting out the large sums needed to purchase them.

SHELTERS TO CARRY WITH YOU

For winter camping you will almost always need a shelter, whether it is one you carry with you or one you construct in the field. It needs to do a good deal more than is required of the type of shelter used in most summer camping, and for this reason many of the types of tents and shelters that are used in summer camping are inadvisable for camping on snow. An example is the plastic tube tent, which is an ideal shelter in many areas during the summer. At best it is emergency equipment in the winter; you should not plan on camping in it.

Shelters that are made on the spot will be discussed later in the chapter, but it might be useful to point out that they will usually come later in your camping experience, too. You won't be able to plan on using improvised shelters until you have had quite a bit of experience, and this means you'll have to carry a tent at least while you're learning.

Except in the mountains, most tents for use in the warmer seasons on the trail function mainly to shed the rain. In crowded campgrounds the matter of privacy becomes important, but for go-light campers, this does not usually need to be considered. Open-front tents have had great and well-deserved popularity, because they cover a lot of area without weighing or costing too much, and because they don't give one the feeling of claustrophobia that many closed, lightweight tents do.

Especially with the widespread use of down sleeping bags, these tents aren't used primarily to keep warm. Many backpackers, myself included, prefer to sleep without a tent when the weather permits. This can sometimes be managed even in winter, but as a rule the tent in winter has to help keep you warm, to protect you from snow and from cold winds. Usually, this means either a closed tent or an all-night fire. The traditional north-woods arrangement of a lean-to (tent or boughs) and all-night fire is obsolete for environmental reasons. A closed tent is warmer and less work, anyway. In the mountains where high winds may be expected, a closed, stable tent is absolutely essential.

The closed tent for winter camping should have a sewn-in, waterproof floor, preferably extending up the sides six inches or so, in "bathtub" fashion.

A-frame and Pyramid Tents

The standard types of tents for use in severe conditions such as winter camping and mountaineering are usually the A-frame type tent—a sort of glorified pup tent—for two to three occupants and the pyramid-type tent for three to four. Most of the better models are made with a canopy of uncoated nylon sewn directly to a coated floor and lower walls with an extra canopy, the flysheet, which is made from coated nylon and pitches a few inches over the first. The fly serves to shed rain and to provide some extra insulation in cold weather, so that condensation on the inside is reduced. Where the weather is cold enough so that no rain will be encountered, however, the tent can be used without the fly to save weight, at the expense of some extra condensation inside. In the simplest A-frame tents, single poles may be used at each end for pitching, but better tents use pairs of poles to increase strength and leave a clear doorway. Such tents may be tilted toward one end to save weight, but there is a definite advantage to the extra room of two high ends in winter, particularly if there are two entrances. This enables the second person to get in without either kicking over the stew or dropping snow in the face of his tentmate.

Traditional tents, both A-frame and pyramid, have some other major advantages. If they are well designed, they can be made so that they achieve a lot of floor area for a reasonable weight, though trends among manufacturers in the last few years have generally favored

A typical two-person tent with A-frame poles at the high end, tapered at the rear As long as they are not made from a single layer of coated nylon, such tents are practical for winter use, but they are not as roomy as hemicylindrical types, nor do they shed snow as well.

heavier traditional models rather than lighter ones. Poles can be replaced with ski poles, ties to trees, and other makeshifts in order to save weight in the pack or in case of pole breakage. It is also relatively easy to make such tents yourself, unlike the hemispherical and hemicylindrical models discussed below. On the other hand, the traditional tents are less resistant to wind than the new types, they require more stakes and ties to pitch in any given situation, they become loaded down with snow more easily, and they are far less roomy inside above the level of the floor.

Dome and Quonset-shaped Tents

Tents with rounded shapes supported by curved poles are becoming increasingly common, both because of fashion and because of the much more comfortable living space that they offer. Such tents rarely offer much advantage over traditional designs in floor area for a given weight, but because the walls rise quickly from the floor, the occupants are not forced to huddle in the center of the tent to sit. This advantage becomes more pronounced in winter, when snow loading and condensation typically make the walls of a traditional tent sag inward. Such tents employ a variety of systems of frames and variations in shape,

A traditional pyramid tent with a central pole This one sleeps four people and is made by Holubar Mountaineering. The steep sides shed snow well, and the center is high enough to allow the occupants to stand occasionally. The layer visible here is the fly-sheet, pitched above the main canopy of the tent.

A dome tent made by Holubar for two or three people This type of tent has some major advantages in comfort and ease of use for winter camping, but damaging or losing a pole creates more problems than with conventional designs.

but poles usually fit into sleeves sewn to the canopy, either crossing one another for strength or working against the tension of the tent and the tie-downs. Besides being comfortable, such tents are usually more stable aerodynamically, responding well in wind and building up less of a snow load. They usually require fewer stakes and tie-downs to pitch, often none at all in calm weather. They must be well tied down in the wind, however, and pitching them in the wind is not always easy.

There are a few major disadvantages to the dome and quonset-shaped tents. They are usually quite expensive and are not easy to make yourself, since the geometry is complex. There is usually no way to improvise poles, so you must be confident of the strength of the ones you buy, treat them with care, and have spares or repair kits in some circumstances. The cheaper versions generally use poles that are not strong enough to be reliable. Aluminum poles have to use sophisticated alloys and engineering, and fiberglass ones require special materials and quality control. In both cases you have to rely on the tent maker to watch these points for you. You won't be able to use your ski pole for a spare. The best such tents, however, are a joy to use and are very reliable if the poles are treated with care. (They are light, and if you step on one you have left lying about, you will almost certainly break it.)

Three styles of canopy construction are generally used in the curved tents. The first is the conventional kind with an uncoated nylon roof and a separate coated flysheet that fits over the outside of the frame. This method permits the choice of using the tent without the flysheet in cold weather, but it usually adds a little time in pitching the tent and results in a heavier combination than the alternatives. This style is used in the dome tents made by North Face and Holubar. A second method also includes two walls, but they are constructed to form a single unit. Typically the poles support the outer canopy and the inner one is suspended from that. This system originated in frost liners for conventional tents and was refined by Jack Stephenson of Warmlite for his very light hemicylindrical tents. It is also used in Sierra Designs' dome and quonset-shaped tents and in Early Winters' Omnipotent. A third method is to use a single canopy of Gore-tex laminate, the construction of most of Early Winters' designs.

There are many excellent versions of the new-style tents. Unquestionably the lightest for any given size are those made by Warmlite, a series of hemicylinders using arches held under tension by the skin. These tents are very well-designed double-skin tents relying on sophisticated venting to reduce condensation. They can be successfully used in winter, and the two-person tent is quite roomy and tips the scales at less than three pounds! However, these tents are made with extremely light materials, and I consider them too light duty for regular winter use or for expeditions. The venting system is also less than satisfactory in wet-cold conditions and when the wind is whipping powder snow around.

The next lightest tents are those made by Early Winters, ranging from a little under four pounds for their lightest two-person tent to a little under ten pounds for their four-person dome. These are very well constructed and rugged, and they serve as a good basis for comparison. Other strong, well-made domes and arch tents are made by Holubar, Sierra Designs, and North Face.

Spend some time looking around before choosing a tent for winter camping, since it is an expensive proposition. Consider carefully the number of people with whom you will normally camp. Larger tents are generally lighter in weight per person and roomier than smaller ones, but of course you have to carry the whole tent whether you need it or not. Strong construction is essential for winter tents, especially for use in the mountains. Bargain-basement tents can be satisfactory for summer use, but they can be dangerous to rely on in winter. After you buy a tent, carefully pitch it in the back yard over a plastic sheet and inspect it carefully before using it to make sure you are satisfied with the workmanship and design. Any reputable shop or mail-order house will let you return it in new condition. This will also allow you to familiarize yourself with the method of pitching and the lines and stakes needed before you get off into the backcountry.

Pitching a Tent on Snow

You will frequently have to pitch a tent directly on snow in winter. This has the advantage of allowing you to construct a level site anywhere, but it requires a lot more work than settling down in a meadow in summer. Other considerations for picking a campsite are mentioned later in the chapter, but the main ones related to the tent are wind direction, hardness of the snow, availability of anchors, and an area clear of possibly hazardous tree branches above. A dead branch can break under snow loading or in the wind and put a hole in your tent.

Soft snow has to be packed down to form a solid platform before you pitch the tent. Otherwise you will find yourself wallowing around in the tent floor. Eventually soft snow underneath will either collapse the tent or freeze into huge bumps and hollows. Pack as much snow as you can with skis or snowshoes first; then finish the job with boots and allow the smooth platform to freeze for a few minutes before laying out the tent. It's worth taking this trouble early for a smooth bed later on.

Conventional stakes are usually worthless in snow. Stakes that are long with a wide cross-section can be used in packed and frozen snow. These can be made from plastic or aluminum with a U-shaped cross-section. Regular stakes work only on very hard snow. In soft snow, the best solution is often to use deadmen, objects buried in the snow and packed in with lines tied around them. Branches, sticks, and rocks can be used, as can stakes buried in trenches. If you are using natural objects, tie the lines so that they can be untied and pulled out in the morning without digging out the frozen-in deadmen. For this purpose, it is often a good idea to leave parachute cord tied to all stake loops of a winter tent. Shock cord can be tied into guy lines to help reduce the shock of gusty winds. Skis, poles, and the like can be used for staking and guying a tent that will be moved next morning, but not if you plan to leave the tent pitched while you go on a day trip.

In general it is best to pitch the tent in the most sheltered spot possible, but not in one that will collect drifting snow. This sometimes means that there is no choice but to pitch the tent in a fairly windy spot. If the wind comes mainly from one direction, the tent usually should be pitched into the wind if there is only one entrance. The tent then tends to billow up and may flap a little less. Tents with two entrances are often best pitched with the secondary entrance into the wind. You should experiment with your own tent to see what method works best.

SNOW SHELTERS

Oddly enough, the best shelter from winter gales is usually to be found in the snow. Snow shelters are warmer and more comfortable to live in than tents. The snow camper relying on caves, igloos, and other snow shelters can reduce the pack's weight both by eliminating the tent and by carrying lighter sleeping gear. Caves and igloos eliminate the wind that causes convection currents in the best of tents, and their snow walls act as insulation. It is no accident that most animals living in the white wilderness use a blanket of snow for warmth, or that Eskimos traveling in Arctic regions in winter built their houses of snow.

Every snow camper should begin learning how to build snow shelters as early as possible. If nothing else, the rudimentary techniques for digging caves and other improvised shelters are basic survival skills that can greatly increase your margin of safety in the backcountry during the winter months. In stretching your limits on day trips, you will be far safer if you know that you can fashion a shelter should the need arise.

Igloos get stronger overnight. After spending the night in their snow houses, these snow campers stand on top of them. Others in this windy camp dug caves instead.

Many of us also choose to rely on snow shelters most of the time in preference to tents, significantly reducing the weight and bulk that have to be carried and improving the comfort and security of camp. There is as well a strong aesthetic appeal to snow shelters: The cave digger and igloo builder feel more at home in the winter, better in tune with the surroundings. In many circumstances, particularly in high winds, snow shelters are far more stable and reliable than tents. In the mountains near my home I have not used a tent for winter camping for years, relying by choice on snow caves from the time the large drifts first form in early winter until the spring melt begins.

There are a few inherent disadvantages to snow shelters, however. The first and most obvious is that it takes some time to learn to use them effectively, so they can't be relied on until you have acquired some practice. This difficulty is exacerbated by the variety of conditions found in different areas and at different times. In some areas and snow conditions, caves work best; in others, igloos; and in still others, trenches, snow tents, or tree pits. It takes some practice in learning to adapt to different situations before you can confidently take off in the middle of January with the knowledge that you will be able to fashion a comfortable shelter ten or fifteen miles up the trail.

Finally, snow shelters typically require a larger expenditure of energy to build than tents do to pitch. This is not universally true. A survival cave can be dug very quickly and tree pits sometimes take little effort, whereas constructing an adequate tent platform in some circumstances may require a major effort. On an average, however, pitching a tent does require less initial work and relying on snow shelters requires better budgeting of your time and energy, another difficult point of judgment for the beginner. Once you have acquired some experience, there are some additional advantages to snow shelters, however. In exposed, windy areas, for example, the snow caver escapes the wind almost immediately, while a person trying to pitch a tent is subjected to the fury of the wind until the tent is completely pitched. This can be a serious matter above timberline in the mountains. Snow shelters also require far less additional effort and attention than tents once they are built. They don't have to be taken down and packed in the morning. You don't have to get up in the middle of a stormy night to shovel out a properly built cave or igloo; instead, they will be so quiet you probably won't even be aware of the arrival of a storm until the next morning.

Only a brief synopsis can be given below of methods for the construction of snow shelters, which can take on a tremendous variety. The two main ingredients are ingenuity and practice. Caves are fairly easy to dig, for example, but it will inevitably take you twice as long to dig a cave when you are a beginner as it will later on when you are experienced. You will also get far wetter on your first attempt than you will when you have learned to watch your body heat and the accumulation of snow on your clothes more carefully. You should therefore either go with experienced people at first or get some practice on day trips or on overnights near the car or cabin.

Snow Caves and Holes

Caves are among the most comfortable and adaptable of snow shelters. They can be built in many situations, but the ideal location is in a wind-deposited drift. Look for the kinds of drifts that form where the wind has been channeled around rocks, lakes, stands of trees, or small rises, rather than the formations on the lee sides of ridge crests. The latter can be used under some circumstances, but they pose hazards both of avalanche terrain and of heavy deposit during storms. The drifts that form in the eddies around boulders will grow bigger as the winter progresses, but the sides stay in essentially the same position, so there is no danger of having the entrance deeply buried during the night.

There are two advantages to digging caves in drifts. Snow consolidates and becomes mechanically stronger when it is disturbed, and a drift will be harder and stronger than the surrounding snow, just as avalanche debris and plowed snow are. Many drifts also have vertical sides that permit more efficient construction of a cave. If the drift is only just big enough to accommodate your cave, or if you have limited time or energy, dig straight in, enlarging the chamber as soon as you get inside the drift, and cover the entrance with your pack and anything else available. The warmest caves have entrances below the level of the floor, permitting cold air to sink out, and if you have the time and the space it is best to dig this type. It takes a bit longer because of the need to move the snow out through the entrance tunnel.

Virtually any wind drift is normally strong enough structurally to support a cave, unless very warm temperatures are causing melting. Try to figure out the shape of the cave you plan before you start digging to make sure the dimensions are right for your plans. The roof does not have to be very thick, but you should check the thickness of new, unconsolidated snow on top of the drift before you start digging and be sure you don't penetrate into this layer. Light coming in through the roof normally will give you plenty of warning that you are getting close to the top of the drift, unless you get stuck after dark. The roof of the cave should be domed to prevent slow sagging during the night. The warmer the snow, the more crucial the dome shape is, since warmer snow will deform more quickly. As long as the final roof is relatively smooth, dripping will not be a problem, because any meltwater will be absorbed by the walls. Large projections will drip, however.

The usual mistake made by beginners is to make a long, upward-sloping tunnel, which requires more effort to move the snow from the final chamber. If you are making an entrance below the planned floor level, dig the entrance in and start excavating the chamber as soon as possible, leaving a minimum distance for removal of snow. Dig a vertical wall in the drift before even starting the tunnel in order to minimize its length. It is also possible to dig a large, keyhole-shaped entrance, allowing a larger space through which to excavate, and to fill the top of the keyhole with blocks later. This works efficiently in some snow conditions but not in others.

Probably the most efficient caves to dig are two-person ones, because one digger is soon working inside while the other shovels the debris out from the entrance tunnel. Larger caves are fun and can be very comfortable if you have room for them, but they are far less efficient to dig, because the cave is almost finished before a second person can work inside. If time is limited or people are getting cold, it is best to dig two-occupant caves, perhaps linking them as they near completion.

When you are digging caves, the most important point to remember is to avoid getting wet. One tends to get enthusiastic about digging, especially inside, and to forget about keeping dry. Usually, the best strategy is to take off most of your insulation and to wear shell clothing while you are digging. It is possible to stay dry even without shell gear, but only by paying attention and carefully brushing off snow accumulation before it has time to melt. The biggest problem is overheating and sweating, however.

The rules discussed below for living in camp are important in caves. A large airhole high in the cave is crucial when you are cooking to prevent carbon monoxide poisoning and insure an adequate supply of air. You should leave a hole at night, too, but I have never had air supply problems even with snowed-over ventilation holes except at high altitude (16,000 feet or so). A stove uses a lot of oxygen, however, and good ventilation is critical. Equally important are the cautions about care for equipment. It is embarrassingly easy to leave equipment lying around when you start digging a cave and to bury it yourself.

Even when wind drifts are not available, snow holes can often be dug with a little imaginative use of the surroundings. In areas with heavy snow accumulation, like the Sierra Nevada and the Cascades, it is often possible to find a place where a sapling has been bent over by the snow load and buried. By digging under the sapling, you can often excavate a comfortable chamber. In other areas a dead tree will often provide the same roof support. A drift that is too small for a complete cave may provide enough space for a dugout that can then be walled in with blocks, and the same possibilities can be presented by fallen trees, boulders, and clumps of brush. Each situation presents its own possibilities, but it is always possible to devise some sort of shelter.

Igloos

An igloo is a very comfortable shelter, and, contrary to many opinions, it is easy to build when the snow has the right consistency. Unconsolidated snow can be packed and allowed to harden, but this is hard work, and under such conditions another type of structure should be chosen, if possible. Hybrids between snow holes and igloos are very practical, especially for one- and two-person shelters. The igloo structure forms only the roof over the hole, so that less work is involved. Most blocks are cut inside the hole, lowering the floor and raising the roof at the same time.

Snow for the blocks should be hard enough so that the foot sinks very little when standing without skis or snowshoes, and the snow must be of the same consistency throughout the block, not just crusted on top. Often, good snow for blocks can be found in a layer below the

Digging a snow cave Wind-formed drifts like this one make the best places to dig snow caves, because of their convenient shapes and their consolidated snow. These skiers have just finished forming a comfortable bi-level cave.

surface where the snow has had more time to consolidate. Packing, first with skis or snowshoes and then with boots, will usually form a good layer, but this is a measure of last resort. Allow the snow to sit for a few minutes after packing. It will harden as a result of both the increased density and the mechanical disturbance. I have built igloos from very shallow snow by shoveling it into a pile, packing it, and then cutting out blocks, but this requires time and effort. The one condition in which it seems impossible to build an igloo is in deep, unconsolidated snow in very cold temperatures. There are many circumstances in which other types of shelters are faster, however. With favorable conditions a four-person igloo can be built in an hour, but in more difficult circumstances it may take two or three.

An inside bottom diameter of eight or nine feet will make an igloo large enough for four, and this is the largest size which should be attempted by any but true experts. Larger sizes require very accurately shaped domes to prevent collapse, and they should be practiced on occasions when their failure will be amusing.

Blocks for the igloo should be about 2½ × 1½ × ½′. They should be cut out on the bottom as well as the sides, otherwise the inside of the igloo will be irregular and will drip. Each block is then beveled on the bottom, so that the wall will tilt inward at the proper angle, and on each side, so that each block is kept from falling by the preceding block, as shown in the illustration.

The diameter of the igloo should be marked out on the snow at the beginning. The first row of blocks is then placed and all joints chinked with snow. This chinking should be continued as construction proceeds, since it will help stabilize the structure, unless the snow is very strong. If the blocks are strong enough, chinking can be left until the structure is finished. The next step is to make a diagonal cut from top to bottom across three blocks, which forms a ramp to begin the next layer. The first block of the next layer is put at the bottom of this ramp, and the rest of the igloo is a continuous spiral. One person working inside puts up the blocks cut by the rest of the party working outside. When the dome is complete, loose snow is used to smooth the surface, especially on the inside. A smooth inside will prevent drips. An entrance tunnel should be dug under the wall; the entrance below floor level makes a much warmer igloo. The entrance tunnel is covered by a small arch. This tunnel should be perpendicular to the direction of the prevailing wind—that is, the wind should blow across the entrance. Finally, a vent hole should be punched in the roof opposite the entrance. The entrance may be partly blocked, but both the vent hole and some ventilation space at the entrance must be left open whenever the igloo is occupied, and ventilation must be increased when a stove or fire is in use.

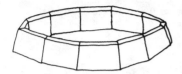

Building an igloo Begin by drawing a circle on the ground using a ski or another device to get the curve right. Some blocks may be cut from the floor area in order to excavate a basement and reduce the size of the dome required. Lay the first row of blocks exactly around the circle, fitting the edges carefully.

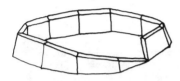

Cut a ramp through three of the blocks, diagonally from the top corner of one to the far lower corner of the third over. When subsequent blocks are laid beginning at the bottom of the ramp, a continuous spiral will be formed for the rest of the igloo.

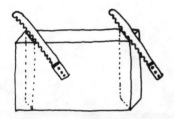

Each block for the upper part of the igloo should be beveled so it can lean on the one before and support the subsequent block. This fitting becomes critical as the roof tilts far in. The larger the blocks the better this keying works. Don't worry about open spaces, which can be filled in later.

The second row half-finished. Cracks must be filled as each block goes in unless the blocks are quite strong. This snow is barely consolidated enough for igloo building.

Each layer tilts in further. This igloo would be comfortable for four.
(*Continued*)

67

Each block must be held in place by the preceding block and the one below. Note the beveled edges.

Once cracks are chinked, the blocks will stay in place. The beveling alone will hold the blocks if the snow is hard enough.

The igloo nearly finished. Entrance is dug under the side to prevent warm air escaping.

Coming in through the tunnel.

Building a two-person snow tent This camper, standing in the trench, is forming an A-frame roof by leaning together the blocks cut by her partner.

Trenches

In deep, unconsolidated snow in forested areas, it can be difficult to construct igloos or caves. Holes under saplings, tree holes (described below), or holes in brushy areas or under trees are often possible, but a trench is often another good possibility. You can dig or stamp a trench in the snow. In calm weather with good sleeping gear, this may be enough in itself, or the trench can be made weathertight by roofing it over with blocks leaned over it to form an A-frame (a snow tent). If you carry a piece of light plastic sheeting or a couple of large plastic bags, it is easy to roof over a trench by forming a frame with skis, snowshoes, packs, and the like, spreading the sheeting over, anchoring the edges well, and then covering the whole roof with snow. In very loose snow, blocks for a snow tent can be obtained by first packing down the trench, waiting for a little until the snow freezes, and then cutting the blocks from the trench itself.

IMPROVISED SHELTERS

Tree Hollows

In forested areas with heavy snow, there are often deep hollows around the bases of large trees, caused partly because of melting and partly by the shelter of the branches above. A judicious choice of one of these hollows will give you a comfortable shelter with a minimum of excavation. The best ones are formed by conifers when the snow level reaches the lower branches. These form a fine roof over the hollow below. Stairs or a ramp are cut down into the chamber, which must usually be enlarged and tramped down a bit. A small fire can often be built on the floor for warmth, cooking, and cheer. Sleeping platforms should be cut or stamped above the lowest level of the chamber, for even a few feet of elevation will make for a warmer bed. Cold air sinks, and this disadvantage will be felt in the tree hollow even with raised sleeping platforms.

Brush Shelters

When there is only a small snow cover, snow holes are impossible and other snow shelters are tedious to build. In brushy areas quick shelter may often be found by burrowing into a thicket. When a reasonable chamber (the smaller, the better) is found, the walls and roof should be tightened as much as possible with broken brush. When the walls are tight enough, snow can be heaped on the top of the shelter for wind protection and insulation. A plastic sheet or tarp can be used to advantage in forming the roof, but is not essential. (Do not break any

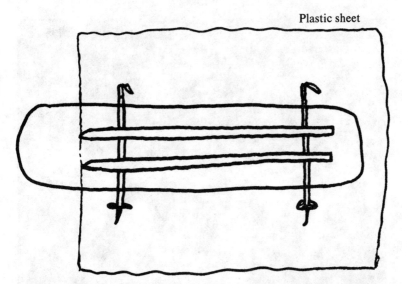

Plastic sheet

Another trench shelter The trench is dug first, then the poles and skis are laid as shown. These are covered with a tarp or plastic sheet. The edges of the sheet are weighted with rocks and snow, and then the whole sheet is covered with snow. The entrance can be covered with the backpack.

brush in the timberline stands of small conifers found in high mountain areas. These plants take many years to grow and should not be disturbed except in a survival situation. Caves in wind drifts make better shelters in such regions, anyway.)

TOOLS

Igloo blocks can be cut with skis, and survival caves dug with snowshoes, but digging or cutting tools are essential for building comfortable snow shelters with reasonable effort. Such tools often make excellent safety equipment in any case. A small aluminum folding shovel serves as a rescue device in avalanche terrain and as a tool for digging snow caves as well. I rarely go on a long trip without one. Larger shovels may be useful on expeditions or in a good-sized party to speed work on caves. The cut-down grain scoop shown in the photograph weighs about three pounds and the folding shovel about one and one-quarter pounds.

Three excellent shovels for cave digging, avalanche rescue, and other winter chores
The one on the left is a very durable light model of the type that would most often be carried. The large one in the center, made by Mountain Safety Research, is made to fit an ice ax and is shown here with a homemade auxiliary handle. On the right is an excellent heavy-duty shovel made from a cut-down aluminum grain scoop, available in some hardware stores.

Many types of saws and knives can be used successfully for cutting blocks. For regular igloo construction on a long trip, I prefer a large snow knife, a pruning saw, or a small carpenter's saw. For occasional and emergency use, though, I have had good success in sharpening an edge of one of the aluminum alloy stays in my pack. It is always with me, and it works quite well when it is needed.

LIVING IN THE SNOW

Whether you are camping in a tent or in a snow shelter, there are a few general points that should be made about choosing campsites and about routine in camp. One important consideration in choosing a site should be the availability of liquid water. It saves fuel and time if you can find a site near a stream with a patch that is open or can be chopped through.

Wherever the campsite is located, the camper must be certain that no dangers are present. This is mainly a problem in the mountains, where the possibility of avalanches exists, a matter which is discussed at some length elsewhere in the book. With tents, some care should be exercised in the woods to be sure that large quantities of snow and dead branches will not fall onto the tent from nearby trees.

With real luck, the winter camper may be able to find a campsite that is not only safe and supplied with water but is warm as well. If there are strong winds, of course, it's well to seek protection from them. With real storms, though, beware of the lee side of a ridge. A large drift often builds up at this point, and moving a tent out from under a snowdrift in the middle of the night is not conducive to restful sleep.

In the absence of prevailing winds, remember that cold air sinks. On a calm night the bottom of a bowl may be twenty degrees colder than a knoll fifty feet higher. Also, if the bowl is a large one, the gullies leading into it are usually the paths for rivers of cold air flowing down at night. Pitch your tent a little out of the gully from which you're getting your water.

Radiational cooling accounts for the fact that clear nights tend to be the coldest. Under a clear sky your tent will get colder than it will if it is sheltered by an overhanging rock or some other shelter, and it will build up much more frost. This fact should be considered if you are having trouble with cold.

Try to stop early. Snow camping should be enjoyable, and it is more likely to be so if camp is made and sunset can be watched with a hot drink in hand, perhaps from the sleeping bag. Sometimes it is worth sacrificing other desirable features for the right scenery. Melting snow may be worth the improved view from the ridge.

Finally, the campsite should be situated with consideration of the route of your trip. It should be far enough along so that not too much distance is left for the next day. More important, consider what might happen if you have to retreat. For example, if there is danger of a storm in the mountains, you must not only pick a campsite free of avalanche danger but also try to avoid having your escape route pass over the avalanche slope.

Once you have chosen a campsite, it is best to get all the standard chores out of the way before lying around in the sun or going for a last ski run without your pack. If conditions are good, hang out your equipment to dry, making sure that nothing can blow away in the wind. It is usually most effective to split up the duties. A couple of people may start to pack a tent platform or dig a cave, for example, while one sorts out the food and another fetches water or starts to melt it.

It is extremely important to avoid leaving gear lying around in a winter camp. A light dusting of snow or a careless kick can make small items disappear, and snowshoes or skis left lying on top of the snow can easily be lost if a storm comes up overnight. Keep things in your pack when they aren't being used and take the pack into your shelter at night, if possible. Anything left out should be placed so that it can be positively located next morning, even in a blizzard. Digging tools should be taken into any snow shelter as a safety precaution.

Keeping things as dry as possible is the major housekeeping chore in a winter camp. The ways of doing so are obvious but largely a matter of habitual attention: kicking the snow off your boots before pulling your feet into the tent, brushing off your back after crawling into your snow cave, and so on. The same goes for staying warm once you have stopped moving vigorously. Put on extra clothing right away if you aren't getting into your sleeping bag.

A path should be stamped out to a suitable latrine location, so that the party can answer calls of nature without having to don skis or snowshoes. In choosing a spot the winter camper should recall that things melt in the spring and are well preserved until then. Pick a place that would not otherwise be an ideal campsite for backpackers next spring or a water supply for other winter campers. Toilet paper should be burned. If the snow cover is light, a hole can be dug to the ground and eight inches into the dirt. In any case, your latrine should be well buried before you leave. The good wilderness traveler in any season takes pride in leaving as few signs of his passage as possible.

CARS

Whether you're car camping or simply driving to a take-off point in snow country, don't forget to take the usual precautions for snowy driving. One recent serious case of frostbite occurred because of difficulty and delay in starting the car after the chilled victim reached it. Besides chains, shovel, sand, and so forth, it is worth leaving a dry, warm change of clothes and some extra food in the car. A key should be left at the car, and each member of the party should know its location. Try to leave the car where it will be neither snowed in nor plowed under. Remember that in case of accident someone may need it to get out for help. It is a good idea to tape a note to the windshield indicating your plans, especially if you will be gone more than a couple of days.

5 | Cooking Out in the Snow

For anyone who has done a lot of cooking outdoors, cooking in winter will not be very hard to learn. A few things are a bit different. Water is easy to find, for instance, but usually has to be melted before it can be used. The principles of cooking on light-weight trips are essentially the same all year round, however. Proper planning and packaging at home are the keys to an easy time at camp.

Still, what is easy after you have learned how is not always so simple for the novice. Get your first experiences cooking over backpacking stoves somewhere that's warm and dry. Then try your techniques out in the snow on a picnic. Save your first experience in a tent on a cold night until you are confident of your technique. One good method is to cook lunch a few times on day trips on skis or snowshoes. Supper on your first overnight trip will then come easily.

Successful cooking in winter camps begins at home. The ingredients for each meal should be measured out, placed in plastic bags along with any instructions necessary (such as the number of cups of water to add), and then packaged together with the rest of the meal. The principle is to leave no more work to do in camp than necessary. The planning of menus and nutritional principles will be discussed later in this chapter, but obviously where weight is a factor, the ingredients will contain as little water as possible.

The standard method of cooking for winter camps is the boiling of a "one-pot meal." This is the backpacking stove-top version of a cross between a casserole, a stew, and a soup. The main reason for the one-pot meal is ease of preparation. If one is cooking on a stove, only one burner is available, and it is a waste of time to go through the struggle of preparing three or four courses. A well-planned one-pot meal can be very good, anyhow, and you may find your favorite camp recipes are good enough to be used in your menus at home. The technique results in meals that taste just right in a winter camp. Dehydration is a common problem in winter, and soupy meals help to provide the liquid and salt everyone needs.

STOVES VERSUS FIRES

Building fires is a standard survival skill that should be cultivated by all winter campers. You should learn to build fires easily without having to rely on the use of a carload of dry newspaper, even in nasty conditions when most of the wood around you is wet. Practice is the only way to acquire this ability, which consists mainly of patience in finding and collecting a large store of dry kindling in all sizes, ranging from small shavings to good-sized sticks. The usual beginner's mistake is to get a nice pile of shavings or twigs, a few large sticks, and then to light the pile without enough intermediate-sized material to get the fire really going. No matter how good a fire builder you are, however, there are a lot of circumstances in which you will not be able to kindle a blaze, and these situations are often the ones most likely to result in an emergency. High altitude is one example, and very wet woods are another. In the latter case it may be impossible to start a fire without tools for cutting and splitting standing wood.

In any case, quite apart from emergencies, small pressurized stoves have become standard equipment for normal cooking on snow-camping trips. There are several reasons: convenience, independence of wood supplies, and environmental considerations. Stoves are more convenient because they can be used in any weather and in much more varied circumstances than fires. In extreme cold or high wind it is possible to cook inside a tent or snow shelter, though it is better to cook outside when feasible. Despite the attractions of a wood fire, it is often warmer to get into your sleeping bag and cook in front of your tent entrance than it is to stand in front of a fire, melting your parka in front and freezing behind. Most important, popular wilderness areas receive too much use these days for fires to be justified much of the time. The best course to follow under the circumstances is to use portable stoves as a matter of course and to build fires only in emergencies or for pleasure when there is adequate wood and when they will cause no environmental or aesthetic damage.

CHOOSING A STOVE

Any good portable backpacking stove can be used for winter camping, but many of the standard types are less than ideal for winter use. If you already have a backpacking stove, it will do for your first few trips, providing you make allowances for any shortcomings it may have. If you are buying a stove specifically for winter use, note the recommendations that follow.

Cartridge-type stoves using butane, iso-butane, and propane or LP gas are extremely popular for summer use because of their convenience. They require a good deal of nursing in winter, however. The volatility of the gases is severely reduced in cold weather, though the effect varies both with the type of gas and the way the cartridge feeds into the stove. It is usually a good idea and is often essential to warm the cartridge before trying to light the stove. You should therefore stuff the cartridge into your shirt while making camp and take it to bed with you at night if you want to be sure the stove works. Other problems of these stoves for winter use are: They are generally badly affected by wind, making complete shelter while cooking essential; the fuels are less efficient per unit weight; and the heat-producing capacity of the stoves themselves is relatively low. The latter two problems are much more significant in circumstances where you have to melt your water from snow and where a good deal of heat is lost to the surroundings.

Somewhat more satisfactory in winter are the self-pressurized stoves using white gas (naphtha) for fuel. These stoves—the Svea, Primus, and Optimus models, for example—are primed with some of their own fuel, and once they are operating, the heat of the stove serves to vaporize the fuel and to maintain pressure in the tank. The Svea 123 is the most widely available stove of this type. Self-pressurized stoves are quite light and reliable once you have learned their idiosyncrasies. Especially when supplemented with the new Optimus mini-pump, available wherever the stoves are sold, they will do reasonably well for winter use.

There is a real advantage in winter camping, however, to having a very high-capacity stove. It enables you to melt all the water you need, so that the party is less likely to become dehydrated. It also makes cooking much easier and uses fuel more efficiently in a cold environment. (The faster you boil water, the less waste heat is dissipated into your surroundings.) The best stoves for the purpose are stoves with pumps to pressurize the fuel tanks, powered either by white gas or kerosene. White gas is more convenient; white gas stoves can be lighted faster and don't require a special priming fuel. Kerosene is safer because it is less volatile; any stove fuel can be dangerous, particularly in a tent, but kerosene will burn where white gas will explode. Kerosene stoves are also necessary in many foreign countries where white gas is unobtainable.

There are a number of good pumped stoves. The old standbys are made by Optimus and Phoebus. I think the two that stand out are those made by Mountain Safety Research (MSR) and Coleman. The MSR is the lightest really high-output stove, a characteristic achieved by using standard fuel bottles to substitute for the fuel tank. By using a long feed tube, the bottle is kept well away from the stove so that it will not be heated and does not have to be beefed up to withstand high pressure. One model of the MSR will also burn kerosene, white gas, or diesel fuel; it is the only stove with this versatility. The MSR stoves have the usual number of idiosyncrasies, and they do not simmer very well. The Coleman Peak 1 is the other particularly notable high-output stove. It runs on white gas; it is heavier than the MSR but lighter than most pumped stoves, runs very well in the entire range from simmer to full blast, and is somewhat less temperamental than most backpacking stoves. Coleman recommends using priming paste in extreme cold, though I have had good success by warming the generator with a butane lighter carried in my pocket.

A Coleman Peak 1 white-gas stove and a metal fuel can This type of fuel container fits into the pockets of packs easily and pours well without spilling. Stoves with pumps like this one are the most efficient for winter use because of their high heat output.

COOKING INSIDE

The standard procedure mentioned earlier for really cold weather is to cook from a sleeping bag. This requires a certain finesse, since the crowded quarters of a mountain tent or snow shelter make spilling the soup an easy thing to do. One night in a soupy sleeping bag generally induces the necessary care. If the tent has two entrances, the cooking can begin as soon as it is set up, but if there is only one, it is usually best either to wait until everyone is settled or to start melting snow outside and move the stove in after all but the cook have arranged themselves.

Cook in front of the shelter if at all possible, since there are extra hazards to cooking inside that should be risked only when necessary. A snow shelter is less dangerous than a tent, since spillage can be absorbed by a snow floor and because the walls are not flammable. Use great care in handling any stove indoors, however. *Never* fill a stove inside, no matter what the weather. Burning a tent down over your head in a bad storm is inadvisable. The hazard should not be great, but a surprising number of competent mountaineers have accomplished it. Think out possible actions in case of an accident, and have the stove near a doorway where it can be tossed outside if necessary.

If you are cooking inside either a tent or a snow shelter, make sure there is good ventilation while the stove is on. Stoves use a lot more oxygen than people breathing and they also produce carbon monoxide. Make sure there is a vent open high in the shelter and another low down near the stove, so that there is a source of fresh air and hot, rising exhaust gases will leave through the top vent without swirling around people's faces on the way. Avoid lying with your face next to the stove while you are cooking. A lot of headaches blamed on other causes are really mild cases of carbon monoxide poisoning. If possible, light the stove outside. The worst production of fumes and the greatest danger from flames occur while the stove is being lighted.

The Water Problem

The difficulty of obtaining water is decreased in the winter when snow is all around, but then one is faced with the new problem of how to use it. If liquid water is available, it should be used, since melting snow consumes time, effort, and fuel. Usually, one is faced with the necessity of melting snow, however, and there are a few tricks to remember. If wet snow is available, it is preferred, and the second choice is ice or crusty snow. Powder snow is worst, since a large volume is required to make a small amount of water.

Another trick to remember is the maintenance of a snow supply as close as possible to the cook. If the tent has a vestibule or cooking hole, that may serve as a snow supply. If you are getting your snow near the front door, make sure to keep it clean. A toilet area should be designated, and if the tent has two entrances, the second one should be used. The sanitary reasons for this are obvious, but friendships are also saved: it's harder to kick over the stew pot if you enter at the foot of the tent.

MEALS

Choosing Food

Food tastes vary, and there is plenty of room for individual preferences. The main requirements that must be satisfied for lightweight winter camping are high caloric content per unit weight and ease of preparation. Spoilage is not generally a problem in cold-weather camping, so that some tastes can be indulged in winter that cannot in warmer weather.

Nutritional requirements are somewhat different in winter camping than they are in daily life in the city. Vitamin requirements can generally be ignored on short trips, though they should be considered if you are heading away for two weeks or more. A working understanding of some facts about the three main food categories is very helpful, however; they are fats, proteins, and carbohydrates.

Carbohydrates are the sugars and starches. They are easily and quickly digested, and they are therefore the best foods for quick energy and for fuel while the body is working and cannot afford any more blood for digestion than necessary. Thus, dried fruit, candy, sweet drinks, biscuits, and such are good trail snacks. Such carbohydrate-rich foods as rice, noodles, bread, spaghetti, dried potatoes, and bulgur wheat provide plenty of easily digested energy and are the main ingredients for most one-pot meals.

Proteins have about the same number of calories per pound as carbohydrates. They are used to rebuild tissue in the body, and some should be included with each meal. The digestion of protein also liberates more heat than that of carbohydrates, making it a good bedtime food to help prevent chilliness at night. Proteins take more time to digest than carbohydrates, so that they tend to stave off hunger for a longer period but produce less quick energy. Only modest quantities of protein are needed by the body, and excessive amounts are often wasted. Including some meat, cheese, fish, or vegetable protein for flavor in meals generally provides an adequate supply.

Fats provide over twice as many calories per pound as either carbohydrates or proteins and are therefore valuable as a lightweight food. They take more time to digest and liberate more heat in digestion than sugars and starches. It has been my experience that people working outside in the cold have a far greater appetite for fats than they would in other circumstances; food that would be excessively greasy is suddenly just what is wanted. Because of their long digestion time, the fats also help to provide energy later in the day when they are eaten at meals, but carbohydrates should be emphasized for quick-energy snacks.

All these considerations should be thought of as merely introductory. Various people adjust best to different foods. This is particularly true on weekend trips, where the body is in a transition state and never gets a chance to acclimatize completely. Before going on, two other details should be mentioned. If you are going to high altitudes, be wary of fats. Many people cannot digest them at high altitudes, and carbohydrates should be emphasized unless all members of the party have had experience with fats at the altitude where you plan to go. Vegetable proteins do not have all the ingredients of animal proteins, and they cannot be used as effectively by the body unless their combination is carefully planned. The easiest way to avoid this problem is to include some animal protein—milk, cheese, jerky, and so forth—in a meal relying on vegetable protein. The quality of the latter is effectively improved by the combination with small amounts of animal protein. Those wishing to rely on vegetable protein can purchase meat substitutes or use combinations like those suggested in *Diet for a Small Planet* by Frances Lappé.

For summer backpacking, dehydrated foods have become the method preferred to achieve the objective of maximum food value coupled with minimum weight and bulk. While this is often true in winter as well, the problems of obtaining water and the need for emergency food that can be eaten without melting snow modify winter menus somewhat. Each camper will probably find his own solutions, but a few suggestions are made here for the beginner.

On short trips I often carry canned meat or fish for economy. Canned tuna (packed in oil—more calories than water), canned salmon, or canned meat makes a good one-pot meal combined with margarine or butter, seasonings, noodles, spaghetti, instant mashed potato, or rice. In an emergency the fish or meat can be eaten without preparation. On longer trips, when weight and bulk become more important, Wilson's meat and bacon bars take the place of the canned meat.

For very cold weather the meat or fish can be removed from the can at home and frozen in heavy plastic bags, eliminating the problem and weight of the cans.

Cheese is one of the best sources of fat and protein. No heavy containers are needed, and the cheese can be used in one-pot meals or eaten alone. Salami and sausages fall in the same category.

So called multipurpose food, a nutritionally well-planned combination of vegetable protein, makes a good addition to one-pot meals. It is now available both in unflavored form and in various synthetic meat flavors.

An easy starch to use in suppers is instant mashed potato. I mix it with dried powdered milk, margarine, and seasonings before a trip. At camp, hot water and meat, fish, or cheese is added and the whole thing is edible after sitting five minutes with occasional stirring. No further cooking is needed, and the remaining hot water can be used for drinks. No burned pan results.

Many dried soups make good bases for stews. Add some extra protein, noodles, margarine, and seasoning and a good meal will result. Another good base for easily cooked meals is provided by the instant Japanese noodle packages—Top Ramen, for example. Other ingredients can be added to the noodles and seasoning to produce a quick one-pot dish.

Preparing Meals

Decisions about meals are again partly a matter of experimentation. The question of whether or not to have a cooked breakfast, for example, is a matter to be decided by compromise among the various members of a group. A lot of friction on trips can be saved if the member planning the food makes sure to find out the prejudices of all the members beforehand. The black-coffee drinker who doesn't bring a cream substitute will not be a popular person.

The one-pot meal for supper has already been recommended. A starch base, such as noodles, macaroni, rice, beans, bulgur wheat, or instant potatoes, is usual. Other ingredients are then added for proteins, fats, and flavor. The only limit to these meals is your imagination. Water content should be low in foods that are to be carried, and heavy, bulky containers should be discarded; the food should be repacked in lightweight plastic bags and containers. Enough dried foods are now available in the supermarket so that the beginner can use this as the source for most food. Backpacking stores carry excellent, well-packaged, expensive foods. These may ease some of the pains of planning and packaging on the first few trips, but beware of menus that are too elaborate. That dried cheesecake is best saved for some other time than your first cramped meal in a mountain tent. If you buy the standard, freeze-dried, one-pot meals to simplify planning, it is usually wise to cut the listed number of servings per package in half. A meal that is supposed to serve four is usually about right for two. Freeze-dried meals are generally easy to prepare and excellent, if one allows for their usually being too small after a hard day. Their defects are high cost and high bulk. The bulk can usually be accommodated on shorter trips. The other problem is between the reader and his wallet.

My own method is to buy all my camp food at once—every six months or so. I keep it in a couple of boxes, and I get it out and make up my meals sometime during the week before a trip (actually, almost always the night before the trip, but this is not recommended). This method avoids the last-minute rushes to the market, and it enables me to save money by getting my dehydrated food in bulk. It is much cheaper that way, and the supermarket stuff almost always has to be repackaged anyway.

After a few trips you will have no problem devising your own meals, as long as a systematic method is followed. One of my own favorite recipes, easily packaged and easily prepared, is as follows.

TUNA WITH NOODLES AND SOUR CREAM
(serves four; for two, reduce amounts of noodles, cheese, margarine)

At home, put two large handfuls of egg noodles in a plastic bag. In another bag empty a package of dried sour cream sauce, a half-cup of dried milk, a teaspoon each of paprika, oregano, sage, and marjoram, a half-teaspoon of pepper, and about four ounces of grated Parmesan cheese. Put these two bags in a larger bag with an eighth of a pound of margarine and a six- or seven-oz. can of tuna.

In camp, melt snow in a pan, or get a panful of water. Pour the mixture bag into a pan or bowl, add about a cup of water, and stir for a minute. The remaining water should be brought to a boil. About six cups of boiling water are needed. Add about a teaspoon of salt to the boiling water. Add the noodles to the boiling water and stir. When the noodles are cooked (about eight minutes), drain them, add the tuna, the margarine, and the mixture. Stir, heat, and salt to taste. Eat.

Many other one-pot meals are made in this fashion using different starches, meats, cheeses, and substituting gravies, soup mixes, and such for sour cream.

Breakfasts are a matter of taste and the amount of effort to which you are willing to go. Some people can't start the day without a hot breakfast. Most will want at least a hot drink, but a lot of us prefer cold food and a quick start. Some combination of biscuits, fruit bars, nuts, meat bars with a cup of hot cocoa, tea, or coffee gets us off and serves as the first installment on our all-day lunch. A possible compromise is a pot of hot water that can be mixed with instant cereal in the cup and used for the drinks. For those who want full-scale breakfasts, cooked cereal with butter, sugar, and dried fruit added or dried eggs mixed with cheese or dried meat are the most common choices.

Lunches are almost always eaten cold, and are usually composed of a long series of snacks on the trail. A lot of small meals keep warmth and energy flowing, and they avoid the competition for blood between the stomach and the legs that follows a large meal. Trail foods are a matter of taste. The variety of possibilities is immense. Even with a cold lunch, a party can indulge in a hot drink if the stove and pot are carried near the top of the pack.

Planning

With a small party camping in a single tent or cave, meals are best planned by one delegated person. The most experienced member should be chosen by a group of beginners. This applies to all supplies for cooked meals. Snacks, lunches, and trail food are usually left to the individual. Larger groups should usually plan and cook their food by tent. That is, a party of nine carrying three tents would usually carry three stoves and cook their meals separately. This arrangement is usually the most practical when using small stoves. Swapping is in order, of course, and for groups planning on using a campfire, menus may be planned for larger numbers. Those who do a lot of camping together may work out other arrangements, each person planning certain meals, for instance, but assigning things to one member per tent eliminates confusion over who was to bring the stove, the butter, or the salt.

Until you have developed another system, the best method is the checklist. Write down all the general supplies that need to go—salt and so forth—then list all the meals that must be planned. When you have decided what is to go into each meal, write it down. Package each of the meals separately; the meat for Tuesday's stew should not be buried under Saturday's oatmeal. Then check off each meal as you pack. Make sure that everything is well labeled, and that any necessary instructions are included.

In considering cooking time, don't forget that the boiling point of water decreases with increasing altitude. A thirty-minute cooking time is a bit long even in New England, but in the Rockies it means that you will eat the food still half-raw after boiling it for an hour or two. Foods for high altitudes should be "instant." Cooking time should be kept as short as possible if you are cooking inside. Boiling creates a lot of condensation in a tent or snow hole.

Emergency Food

In planning the food for any trip, allowance should be made for various unpleasant possibilities; bad storms, injuries, nonfunctioning stoves, and so on. Emergency reserves should be of a type that can be eaten cold if necessary, in case of the useless stove or the necessity of splitting the party. Extra trail food may be the best solution.

Fuel

In planning the amount of fuel to be carried on a trip much more must be allowed for a winter trip, when snow is to be melted for water. It takes almost as much fuel to melt the snow as it does to heat water all the way to boiling. It also takes just as long. The beginner should allow about one to one and a half pints of fuel per stove per day. Always pack both your fuel and your stove as far away from your food as possible, ideally in a separate pack. No experience can quite duplicate that of eating gasoline-contaminated granola for a week, and Murphy's Law for backpackers dictates that given the most remote possibility, the fuel will soak into the largest available food bag.

Dishwashing
Full-scale dishwashing on winter trips tends to waste a lot of fuel to little purpose. Cooking food in a well-planned sequence eliminates a lot of washing, as does avoiding items that tend to stick to pots. Crusty snow will take care of a lot of the cleaning, and there is little danger of spoilage in winter temperatures if a few calories are carried over from one meal to another. When washing is needed, a 3M scouring pad with a little heated water will do the trick. These pads are light in weight, have no soap, and don't rust.

It is usually unwise to use soap in cleaning pans and dishes in winter camping. Unless enough hot water and energy are available to rinse the cooking gear thoroughly, the soap is likely to mix with grease in the pots, forming a bad-tasting contribution to the next meal. This soap residue will cause the digestive upsets that leftover food will not.

6 On the Trail

The main requisite for enjoying the white wilderness is to get out into it—away from your car, house, ski lodge, and highway. You have to escape the sound and stench of gasoline motors to hear and smell the world of snow. It helps to go for at least a couple of days; that allows enough time for the sounds of civilization to die away in your ears and its smells to fade from your nose.

Of course, getting away from that noise can be a problem when snow lies on the ground to a depth of six feet. In that case you'll need skis or snowshoes to hold you up, and these special tools are discussed in the next two chapters. Sometimes, when the snow isn't very deep, or at higher altitudes in spring and summer when it is well consolidated, you can walk into the white wilderness with nothing more on your feet than a sturdy pair of boots. Whatever your means of staying on top of the snow, the general techniques of travel don't vary too much.

PLANNING YOUR TRIP

Whether you are starting off on a weekend snow-camping jaunt in the mountains or a half-day tour in the woods around home, it is important to remember that the winter wilderness is a somewhat harsher place than the summer woods. A certain amount of planning and care is essential if you are to avoid unpleasant experiences. Planning in this case includes means of transportation, clothing, food, cooking gear, shelter, certain essential personal items, the means to find your way and cope with any emergencies, and the capacity to handle the trip you have in mind. By "planning" I don't mean that you have to have all these things written down or that certain set rules of organization have to be followed, but none of these items should be overlooked or left to chance. The winter traveler must have a system to insure that essentials are not forgotten. The beginner obviously has to consciously plan more of them than does the expert, who has learned to take care of some details automatically.

Several of these subjects are discussed at greater length in other chapters, but there is always a danger that the novice will forget that they apply to him, even at the most elementary level. Getting lost is one of the most obvious examples. You don't have to be on a week-long expedition to get lost; it can be done in ten minutes by a perfect amateur with no trouble at all. There are plenty of ways to keep yourself oriented other than by map and compass—you might follow a power line on an afternoon ski tour, for example—but if you trust your "natural sense of direction," you will be making a mistake. You don't have one. The tricks you really use have to be modified to cope with the winter landscape. For instance, your morning tracks won't do you much good in the afternoon when they are filled with drifted snow.

These same sorts of considerations apply to the other items on the list. You don't need a written menu for a day-long snowshoe hike, but good planning does include some extra trail food in case of the unexpected.

The last item, the capacity to handle the trip you are undertaking, is the trickiest. It's best to plan trips conservatively until you develop the experience to judge their difficulty in advance with some accuracy. This doesn't mean you shouldn't hope to get a lot farther than you may be able to travel, just that you shouldn't bet your life that you will. Don't, for example, plan on getting to a wilderness hut your party may not be able to reach and leave yourself unprepared for snow camping. With luck in weather and snow conditions, you might make it, but only by exceeding your capacity and courting disaster. A more experienced group might spend a cold night in a snow cave after running into bad weather but would not have taken unnecessary risks if preparations were made for a night out.

As you gain experience, you will learn the limits of your equipment and ability, enabling you to approach the limits of safety if you wish, but the experience is necessary to find out just where those limits are. The novice must be more cautious and allow a larger margin for error.

Some risks may also be worth taking, if they are outweighed by advantages. The experienced traveler may want to try some solo trips, for instance. A sensible backcountry skier may choose to take a calculated risk walking under an avalanche gully, but the innocent who wanders by without even being aware of the possibility of a slide is not taking a calculated risk or being brave. He's merely being foolish.

Planning in the narrower sense is also necessary, and the longer the trip the more it is needed. Food and equipment are best handled by checklists. Forgetting one item can make a trip impossible. It can also lose you some friends if you've just driven a few hundred miles for the big weekend and you discover at the trailhead that you forgot the tent.

Other slips of memory can have more serious consequences; if you forget the first-aid kit, you probably won't cancel the trip, but later you may wish you had. As you gain experience, you may develop some system to substitute for lists, such as keeping your rucksack packed with the items you need.

Community equipment should be carefully arranged in advance to avoid the "But I thought you were bringing the tent!" scenes. The passage of a good deal of time is often required to enable one to appreciate the humor of such situations. The reverse of this type of planning is also required of groups. The weight of each pack is everyone's concern, and unnecessary duplication of community items has to be avoided. Four complete cooksets are not needed to cook for a party of five.

PACE AND CONDITIONING

The importance of pace in wilderness travel was brought home to me when I was a teenager hiking in the Swiss Alps. Every Sunday many of the villagers go for walks in the mountains. Young and old, still dressed for church, they climb steadily up the trails. The tourists go zipping past them and then sit panting on rocks by the side of the trail, while the little old ladies in their black dresses climb steadily by, always keeping the same slow, ground-covering rhythm. It is an amusing and educational experience, though it may cause some reddening around the ears of those visitors impressed with their own *machismo*. The little old ladies are in fairly good condition, of course, but more important, they know how to pace themselves.

Pace is even more important in winter than summer, because of the need to avoid excessive perspiration and the more strenuous character of winter travel. The trick of pacing oneself or a party is to try to set a rhythm that can be maintained for long periods with few stops or none at all. The start should be slow, and during the first half or three-quarters of an hour there are always numerous brief stops for adjusting equipment and removing clothing. After this, you should try to keep your pace adjusted so that one ten-minute break each hour is adequate. It is better yet not to stop at all except for food and adjusting clothing or equipment. Long stops should be avoided; muscles stiffen and rhythm is broken. The necessity for frequent short stops is a sign that the party is going too fast.

There is nothing wrong with a leisurely trip, if that is what is wanted, or with photography and gawking at the scenery. The point here is simply that you should try to set a pace you can maintain, rather than spurting up a hill for a few hundred yards and then collapsing by the side of the trail for fifteen minutes. There are several important reasons for pacing yourself or your party.

The first reason is a consequence of the physiology of muscular action. If you force your muscles to work beyond the capacity they can maintain steadily, waste products accumulate in the muscles, and pretty soon you have to stop to allow the waste products to be carried away by the blood, and to allow the oxygen deficit of the muscles to be made up. The muscles are inherently less efficient when they are operated this way than when they operate within their normal capacity. Fatigue occurs quickly with this start-and-stop traveling. The sign that you are going too fast is that you begin to pant; when you do or someone in your party does, *slow down.* Your circulatory system also will adjust itself to your physical activity much better if your pace is fairly steady. This adjustment is the familiar experience of the "second wind." If you go too fast, you will be exhausted before ever catching your second wind.

The second reason for pacing a party properly is primarily a winter problem, that of perspiration. The need to avoid sweating whenever possible has already been stressed. To do this, it is necessary to regulate your body's heat loss by removing clothing as you get warmer from exercise. This is fairly easy to do when a steady pace is maintained. If you go by spurts and stops, it is almost impossible. You will have soaked your shirt before you realize that you are warmed up, and yet you will already be stopped for a rest and beginning to shiver with cold.

Another reason for steady pacing is psychological, and it is especially important for groups of uneven strength. A common mistake you should avoid is the familiar pattern of the strong members of the group rushing ahead for twenty minutes and then sitting down to wait for the stragglers. The slower members are usually pushed too hard, because they feel they are holding back the group, and they go faster than they should. When they catch up they are tired and panting. By this time the speed demons have already rested and are impatient to be off again, so that the stragglers feel compelled to go before they are ready, and the cycle repeats itself. The result of this sort of syndrome is that the group gets only about half as far as it would have if a proper pace had been set in the first place.

As a final word on pace, I would simply remind you of the tortoise, the hare, and the little old Swiss ladies.

Conditioning is something you can't affect during a trip, but it is important to recognize that the conditioning of the weakest member of the party inescapably sets the limits to the capacity of the group.

Winter travel is definitely more strenuous than wilderness wandering in summer, so it is important to maintain reserve strength in each member and in the party as a whole. The variations in the effort that may be required to cover a particular distance are also far greater in winter. A group may easily cover ten miles to get to a remote lake on Saturday and find that the return journey through two feet of new snow and against a headwind turns into a survival epic. For safe and enjoyable travel in the winter it is essential that all members have good reserves of strength. In addition to the rigors of cold and of breaking trail, virtually everything you do in the winter takes a little more energy than in the milder seasons. Packs are usually heavier, you have to pack a platform down before you can pitch the tent, and so on.

People with widely varying levels of conditioning can enjoy snow camping, but it is important to pick goals that are commensurate with the strength of the party. It is harder to get by if you aren't in good shape. Driving one member of the group too hard will not only insure an unenjoyable trip for everyone, it may be dangerous as well. If you want to undertake ambitious wilderness jaunts in winter, you'll need to put in the necessary training beforehand.

CARRYING YOUR GEAR

Even on short snowshoe hikes, it is usually necessary to carry more equipment in the winter than one would on a hike of similar duration in the summer. Extra clothing and food are normally required in winter even for half-day trips. During fast cross-country skiing you may travel a long way keeping warm just with exercise, but if you plan on stopping you are likely to need extra clothing. If the trail is not well traveled, you should also picture the consequences of a broken ski tip before leaving the extra sweater, candy bar, and repair kit in the pack at home.

On trips that last overnight, you must carry your food, shelter, and emergency equipment on your back. Since travel in snow is generally more demanding than travel on bare ground, you must also try to keep this weight to a minimum. Extra ounces must be pared off ruthlessly. This is another function of planning. Without it you will find yourself with an eighty-pound pack and still discover you have forgotten something important.

The problem of weight actually boils down to a question of what to take. The winter traveler must get as much use as possible out of each item. Multiple uses can often help cut down on weight. Items that are not either necessary for emergency gear or definitely needed for the level of comfort you consider essential are left behind. If the best reason you can think of for bringing an item is that it "might come in handy," leave it at home or in the car.

Weight is also a function of equipment design, and here it is sometimes necessary to make a few compromises in the interests of economy or durability. Most of the best equipment made these days is also very lightweight. Long-range economy dictates the purchase of the best equipment possible, but most of us cannot always afford this, so we have to make do with the best compromise possible. Fairly good compromises *are* possible, though. In fact, the budget-minded traveler has some advantages over his wealthy counterpart, since he will be inclined to stick to essentials, which is the main secret to keeping weight at a minimum. It's hard to leave an expensive gadget at home once you've bought it.

A party as a whole must be just as concerned with keeping its weight down as the individual. Duplication should be avoided where it is not necessary, and even the strongest member of the party should be tactfully told to leave frivolous junk at the car. Reserve strength may be needed for more important duties.

MAKING UP THE PARTY

Generally, recreational winter travelers have better criteria for making up parties than organizers of expeditions; considerations of friendship and convenience are usually foremost, as they should be. There are a few special points to be kept in mind, however, especially for large parties. If no one in the group has had much experience, everyone will be learning together. This an enjoyable way to do things, but in this case the group size should be kept fairly small; the occupants of two tents make a good party. Large groups of relatively inexperienced people can turn emergency situations into disasters. A party of four inexperienced people is stronger than a party of two, but a group of twelve neophytes is much weaker than either. At least a few experienced winter travelers should be included in any large group of novices.

All parties should be made up with consideration of both the prospective trip and the relative strengths of the members. It is common sense that no one should be asked on a trip that is too much for him; he will feel like a drag on the party rather than enjoy himself. A more subtle mistake is made by the relatively experienced person who takes a group of beginners on a trip they would have the good sense never to undertake alone. Don't forget: *You* may be the one who breaks a leg. If no one else has the ability to find his way back out or the stamina to break trail, how are you going to get out? Under these circumstances, the leader is undertaking a solo trip with other people.

Assuming roughly equal ability, a group of three or more is safer than a party of two. In case of injury, this leaves at least one person to go for help and one to stay with the injured person. Most other problems of making up and handling a group are matters of common sense and goodwill. Weight should be divided equitably, though in parties where there are great disparities in skill and strength, it often helps to give more weight to the strongest members of the party. One essential party item that should be carried by everyone is a sense of humor. There's nothing like a good laugh in a cramped mountain tent when the stew gets tipped over.

SOLO TRIPS

Traveling alone in the winter wilderness has been frequently condemned, for no particularly good reason. The fine companionship that is the virtue of group travel is lost, but there are many unique attractions to occasional solo trips. Obviously, traveling alone is riskier than traveling with others, so it is only prudent not to undertake solo trips until you know what you are doing. Once you understand the risks, the choice of whether or not they are worth taking is a personal matter.

Since the safety margin is quite a bit thinner on a solo trip, other safety matters should be given more attention. One of the advantages to group travel is that one does not have to be so conservative as when traveling alone. An injury is always serious in winter. If you are alone, it is much more so. The difficulties of survival with a badly sprained ankle under winter conditions should not be underestimated. The importance of leaving word of your plans with a responsible person is much greater for a lone traveler. With proper foresight you can survive most injuries for quite a while, but there is a good chance you will not be able to travel. If no one knows where you are or when you expect to be back, a broken leg may well be fatal.

ROUTE FINDING

The subject of finding your way is discussed in detail in another chapter, but in addition to the larger problems of route finding, the winter traveler is faced with hundreds of smaller decisions during the day, and the cumulative results can make the difference of many miles of progress. Intelligent route finding requires an observant eye and a consideration of your equipment and that of your party. The best route for the skier is not always the same as the best one for the snowshoer. If the lead skier is wearing skins, he should remember to choose an angle of ascent which can be followed by his companion using climbing waxes, or the effort of trail breaking will have to be duplicated. Many small details like these are the stuff of making a winter trail, and the observant beginner will not be long in picking up the most important tricks.

One of the most important considerations of small-scale route finding is the condition of the snow. Some snow conditions are very tiring, but it may be possible to avoid them by small changes in route, and the careful observer will not only reap the pleasures of seeing a few more of nature's patterns but may also save himself a good deal of unnecessary travail. For example, one side of a ridge may be deep in heavy powder snow, requiring hard plowing to make headway, while the other side is hard windboard, a highway for the skier or snowshoer. In late afternoon, the breakable crust on the south-facing side of a valley may not exist on the north-facing side, which received less sun during the day. At one time of the day the wooded portion of a slope may make much easier traveling than the open part, while a few hours later the reverse may be true. It would be impossible to catalog this sort of thing here, but novices can rapidly build up their own fund of knowledge about the way the snow conditions change in the areas they frequent.

Obstacles and dangers along the route should be anticipated when possible from your examination of the map or previous experience in an area. Avalanche slopes are discussed in some detail in Chapter 11, but it can't be overemphasized that these present an important and unfamiliar danger to the novice wilderness traveler. Streams and rivers also present special winter problems. Large rivers that are not frozen over should generally be crossed by bridge, since they otherwise present expeditionary problems, requiring rafts and wide detours.

In the North, rivers freeze over to a safe depth, but if your trip involves a crossing you should check to see that the river is safe before leaving, if possible. Except in the far North, it is usually best to plan to use a bridge for large rivers. Great care should be exercised in crossing, if a bridge is not used, since rivers have very uneven layers of ice. Skis or snowshoes should be worn to distribute weight over a larger area, unless the ice is very thick, but bindings should be adjusted so that they can be kicked off in the event of breaking through. A long pole will help in case of accidents, and so will a safety rope between members of the party. Wide spacing should be observed on any lake or river.

Rivers that freeze over to great depth have a peculiar hazard in the spring when break-up is approaching. The ice, while still thick, becomes very unstable, forming long vertical crystals called candle ice, which will support very little weight. At this time of year it is best to stay off the ice, but a pole should be used for probing when a crossing is unavoidable. Another common phenomenon on rivers with thick ice is the overflow of water on top of the ice. The feet can become quickly wet by this condition, which sometimes occurs in very cold weather, when waterproof footwear is not usually worn.

Lakes generally form safer crossings than rivers, because their quieter water freezes to a safe depth more quickly, and there are less likely to be thin spots and places where the water has sunk below the level of the ice, making an unstable bridge. The same general precautions should be observed on lakes as rivers, though crossings can usually be undertaken with more confidence. When the weather is cold for long periods, lakes are often preferred routes, offering flat highways free of obstacles. Thin spots are more likely to occur near shore, especially where streams and rivers enter or leave the lake. In guessing the thickness of the ice when planning a trip, the history of the winter should be considered. When heavy snows come early in the winter, the ice sometimes remains thin despite very cold weather because of a thick insulating blanket of snow. A long period of freezing weather before the first deep snow produces thick ice much earlier in the year. Chopping a hole is the most reliable way of assuring the safety of the ice layer when you reach a crossing.

Streams are more likely to be encountered by the weekend traveler than rivers, and stream crossings are often quite difficult. Unless the stream is completely and deeply covered over, a man-made or natural bridge must be found. A good deal of care should be exercised in approaching a stream because the water tends to undercut the snow on the sides, so that an unsupported bench of snow overhangs the stream. In the event of its collapse the unwary traveler will be precipitated into water that is at freezing temperatures with overhanging snowbanks in all directions. If he is unroped, his chances of survival in a deep stream will be quite slim. When streams are well bridged, this problem does not occur, but crossings should not be attempted unless you are sure of the safety of your snow bridge. Mountaineers may use rope techniques to extend their safety margin. Bridges are more likely to be safe early in the morning than on a sunny afternoon. When in doubt, follow the stream course to a safe crossing.

Snow bridge, late winter in the California Sierra Snow often overhangs streams and requires finding a snow bridge to cross.

The crests of ridges present a problem similar to the overhanging sides of stream beds. The wind blowing snow across the ridge often forms an overhanging structure of snow called a cornice. These are often impossible to detect from above, until the traveler is already standing out over space. The cornice appears from above as a convex slope, and the observer may not realize that, instead of sloping off continuously, the cornice drops off into thin air. Cornices form a particular hazard in stormy weather, when the traveler is likely to be so anxious to get across a pass and out of the wind that he does not even think of the possibility of a cornice. The rule to follow is simply not to go out onto anything that might be a cornice. On a curving ridge, a look can often be gotten farther down the ridge. Cornices also present a great avalanche hazard, a subject which is taken up in Chapter 11.

More mundane route-finding problems simply involve the best angles at which to climb slopes that present no hazards. A long angling climb is usually best, especially on skis. Sometimes such a traverse on a steep slope is uncomfortable on snowshoes, and a direct climb is preferred if it can be handled. A traversing ascent helps the party to maintain pace, and a traversing descent is often nearly effortless on skis. The snowshoer again sometimes prefers a short direct descent, followed by a distance on the flat.

Summer snow No snowshoes or skis are needed on this summer snow, which easily supports hikers. The depressions in the snow are called suncups.

WALKING IN WINTER

When the snow is not very deep, snowshoes and skis are neither necessary nor practical, and winter travel consists merely of walking. This same method can sometimes be used when the snow is very well consolidated, so that one walks on top of what may be a very deep layer of snow. In either case, there is no particular problem of technique, except when the snow becomes steep, a subject introduced in Chapter 10. The main differences between winter walking and backpacking in other seasons are that progress is slowed considerably and that special attention must be paid to footwear. One must also remain aware of the possibility of being caught by a heavy snowfall or softening snow. An easy walk in can become a nightmare going out. For this reason, it is often necessary to carry snowshoes or skis on longer trips. Unless they will definitely be used, at higher altitudes, for example, skis are inferior to snowshoes for this purpose, since they are much more difficult to pack.

BOOTS

Footwear is a problem at any time of the year, but winter exacerbates every difficulty in choosing boots. More waterproofing is needed at the same time that better breathing qualities are important—two contradictory requirements. Much more insulation is needed, because even when the upper body is baking in the sun, the feet may be surrounded by snow at subzero temperatures. Thus, these essential parts of the body with their poor circulation are subject to the most severe cold. They are also more likely to get wet than the rest of the body. It is more of a problem to provide insulation for the feet, because the body's weight rests on them, so that compressible insulation cannot be used. Finally, in winter travel, the special demands of footwear for skiing, snowshoeing, climbing steep snow and ice, or all of these must often be met.

The first thing to remember in choosing winter boots is that the winter foot traveler is a generalist, whether he is a skier, a snowshoer, or a climber. His boots or other footwear must serve many functions. Any boot that he wears will be a compromise among the many conflicting demands that will be made on it. There are many excellent types of winter footwear on the market that are completely useless to him. The modern downhill ski boot is excellent for its purpose, but it is hard to walk in it from the door of the lodge to the bar, much less through twenty miles of rough country. The same thing applies to many types of footwear designed for snowmobiling, ice fishing, duck hunting, and sentry duty.

There are particular types of boots that are preferred for skiing on various types of terrain, and these are discussed in the chapter on skiing. Snowshoeing is a bit more versatile in the types of footwear that can be used, and some types are also discussed in that chapter. Very wet weather, when there is as much water as snow, coupled with easy terrain may call for the rubber-footed boots mentioned in the snowshoe chapter. The most versatile footwear for the rough terrain that most of the readers of this book will encounter is the heavy-duty mountain boot.

A good general-purpose mountaineering boot can be used for hiking, climbing steep slopes, slogging through powder snow or mud, snowshoeing, and skiing. It is generally the best compromise available. Softer footwear is more comfortable if conditions are just right for it, but a heavy pack and a little rough terrain will make you curse it. It is impossible for skiing or for steep slopes.

A good winter mountaineering boot must be fairly heavy with a rubber-lug sole. The uppers should have as few seams as possible, and these should be designed to minimize leakage. The tongue should open widely without too much difficulty, or the boots will be impossible to put on when they are frozen. It should also be gusseted, so that snow and water can't get into the boot around the sides.

Double boots are good for extreme conditions, especially for mountaineering, but they are more expensive and not at all essential for most conditions. True double boots have one or more pairs of remov-

Boots for winter use in moderate conditions Left to right: heavy-weight and medium-weight mountaineering boots, both with the smooth side out for water repellency, and rubber-bottom boots. In very cold weather any of these boots must be supplemented by overboots or replaced with double or vapor-barrier boots. Excellent rubber-bottom boots are made by Sorel with lug soles and replaceable felt liners.

A double boot for technical climbing in cold conditions An expensive but effective alternative for winter travelers who also need rigid footwear for difficult climbing or alpine-style skiing.

able inner boots, which are worn inside heavy outer ones and which can be worn separately in the tent. They are very warm. Wool or foam inner boots also can be purchased to convert normal oversized boots into doubles. Boots for winter use should be bought somewhat larger than those that are used exclusively in milder seasons. Room should be allowed for the inner boot, if any, and at least one pair of heavy socks and one pair of lighter socks without cramping the feet. The heels should be snug but not tight, and it should be easy to wiggle the toes. Cold feet have poor circulation without any extra constriction from the boots. Tight footwear is the cause of many cases of frostbite.

Your summer mountain boots will be perfectly good for winter use, provided they are not too light or too tight. Light and medium-weight mountain boots do not generally provide enough insulation or water repellency for winter use. For snowshoeing they may be adequate if worn with a pair of overboots. These fabric covers will extend the temperature range of any boot, especially if they have pockets for closed-cell foam insulation pads. Plans for making them are included in one of the books mentioned in the do-it-yourself section. They can also be purchased from a number of suppliers listed in Appendix C.

CARE OF THE BOOTS AND THE FEET

A good pair of mountain boots will last through several pairs of soles, but only if they are properly cared for. Water will ruin leather if it is not treated regularly with good preservatives. The silicon-based waxes are usually the best, since they preserve the leather with less tendency to soften it. The best thickness for the wax layer depends on the conditions prevailing at the time. For wet conditions—in fall and spring and all winter in some areas—a thick layer of wax worked into the boot will make it completely waterproof, but it will also prevent the leather from breathing. In colder weather, a thinner layer of wax will give enough water repellency without completely closing the pores of the leather.

The boots should be taken care of after you return from each trip. They should be cleaned, using saddle soap if necessary, and then allowed to dry at room temperature (excessive heat will ruin leather as fast as it will your skin). The boots should be warmed slightly to open the pores, and then the wax should be applied. Work the preservative into the leather, paying particular attention to seams. Several coats may be necessary at twenty-four-hour intervals if the leather is dried out. When enough wax has been applied and dried, polish the boots with a cloth and put them away. On long trips it may be necessary to apply wax on the trail, but this is much less effective on cold, wet boots. If preservatives have to be applied on trips, try to do it on a sunny day during a lunch stop, when the boots can be warmed and partially dried.

Care of the feet is a particular problem on any backpacking trip, but it is much greater under winter conditions, when cold and circulation problems are added to dampness and friction. The first couple of rules of foot care have already been mentioned: proper socks and adequate room in the boots. The latter point is difficult to overemphasize. Tight boots can cause difficulty and discomfort on any winter trip, and they are likely to cause frostbite in a survival situation. Nails should be trimmed before the trip, and special problems like bunions or corns should be taken care of well in advance.

On the trail the traveler will always have adequate warning of foot troubles, and the main trick is simply to heed these warnings when they occur, rather than waiting until it is convenient and too late. Gaiters, anklets, or overboots should be put on when they are needed to keep snow and wet out of the boots. Otherwise you will have to change your socks a little later, which will be more time-consuming. The upper body has to be kept reasonably warm for the feet to be warm; circulation to the feet will be cut down if the trunk is chilled, and once the blood supply to cold feet is reduced, insulation will not warm the feet.

Blisters are often a particular problem in winter. Socks become damp and friction increases, while skis and snowshoes often cause more rubbing at the heel than would occur with summer walking. If you feel uncomfortable friction at some point on the foot, stop and take care of it; otherwise, you will soon have a blister. Moleskin, a felt backed with adhesive, is excellent for covering trouble spots. It should be carried somewhere that is readily accessible. If a blister has already appeared, moleskin should still be applied, preferably without breaking the blister. The technique involves cutting a hole in the center of the moleskin pad for the blister. The pad transfers further friction to the surrounding area. If you catch the irritation before a blister forms, there is no need for the hole. If the blister has already broken, or if its size makes draining necessary, clean it as well as possible, leaving the skin layer over the affected area, apply an antiseptic to the whole area, and apply moleskin. Draining should be done from one side with a sterilized point and as little disturbance of the skin layer as possible. In the case of a large blister with the skin already pulled off, you will probably have to apply a dressing of either plastic or gauze covered with a slippery antiseptic cream and then cover the whole thing with moleskin. Adhesive tape can be used for any of these purposes instead of moleskin, but will not work quite so well. Remember that the best time to apply the cover is *before* the blister forms.

When you stop for a snack or a rest, try to get your feet up out of the snow. It is sometimes amazing how great a difference in temperature can exist between the top of the snow and the layer a few inches down, which is often much colder because it is insulated by the top layer. Your feet will be warmer if you prop them out of the snow. This is also the time to change your socks if they need it. If the stop is to last more than a few minutes it is a good idea to loosen the laces of your boots to improve circulation.

During travel, frequent wiggling of the toes will help improve circulation in cold feet. If your feet are painfully cold and the discomfort stops, you should stop immediately and warm the feet. This numbness is a prelude to frostbite. A more detailed discussion of frostbite and related problems is included in Chapter 12.

EQUIPMENT

When you are carrying your gear on your back, you'll first have to put it all in a pack, so we might as well start off with that. If you've done much mild-season backpacking, you probably already have one or more packs, and they will generally be adequate for winter use as well, at least for a start. Various types of packs will be discussed in this section with some recommendations for the best uses of each, but don't immediately go out and buy a new one unless the pack you have is completely inadequate for the first trip you have in mind. You may find that you like your old pack just as well even if it's not the "ideal" one for this or that type of trip.

Contoured Frames

The contoured aluminum and magnesium frame packs, invented by A. I. Kelty, have rapidly become almost universally accepted as the standard pack for the backpacker. Most snowshoe travelers will find that these packs suit them well, too. Some ski tourers use them also, but most skiers and climbers prefer the new internal-frame rucksacks, because they interfere less with balance and fluid movement.

Frames of various sorts have been around for quite a while, and they have always had the advantages of keeping the load away from the back, of providing ventilation while preventing gouges in the anatomy, of allowing all sorts of odd parcels to be packed comfortably, of getting the load fairly high and close to the body so that less forward lean is required, and of controlling the shape of the load. The contoured frames do all these things, generally better than the old frames like the Trapper Nelson, but the main innovation that they provided was a design that enabled the packer to carry most of the load on his hips. Most weekend wilderness travelers have a hard time with older-type packs, not only because the center of gravity is often far behind the wearer, forcing him to lean forward against the load, but also because his back and shoulder muscles just aren't in good enough shape to carry the load comfortably even if the center of gravity is right over his shoulders. The contoured frame gets the center of gravity very close to the back, so that it is over the hips with a very slight lean, and then the load is transferred to the hips by means of a broad waist belt attached to the bottom of the frame. The weight of the pack then rests on the strong muscles of the legs directly, instead of being transmitted through the back. The newer internal-frame packs accomplish the same weight transfer, a little less effectively, while leaving the wearer a little more freedom of motion.

This waist belt is often not well understood by novices (or by some pack manufacturers). Lots of packs have waist belts, but many of them are designed just to keep the pack from flopping. With a properly designed contour frame the belt can be used to carry most of the load. Sometimes a wide front belt in combination with the bands on the frame itself serves to transmit the weight to the hips. On many newer models a full belt going all the way around the waist is used, and the lower part of the pack is then hung on a couple of side tabs, which are attached to the belt. Either arrangement is all right if it is well designed, but the second is better for really heavy loads (the kind you shouldn't carry unless you're going in for at least a week). When you try a pack frame on, you'll never be able to tell if the waist strap will do its job if you wear only the empty pack. Load it up with thirty or forty pounds of stuff and then adjust the pack so that all the weight rides on the hips, the shoulders merely balancing the pack. Walk around and imagine carrying the thing over ten miles of rough country. Bounce up and down. You'll be able to feel the difference between well-designed waistbands and poor imitations pretty quickly.

There are several big disadvantages to the contoured frames, and they are felt more in winter than at other times. The main problem is that by getting the center of gravity high the wearer is made more unstable, which is a disadvantage in snow, especially to skiers. For this reason rucksacks are preferred by most ski tourers and mountaineers, except perhaps on long expeditions, when heavy and awkward loads will be carried.

The rigidity of frames tends to cramp body movement, which again troubles the skier more than other wilderness travelers. This disadvantage is also strongly felt by the mountaineer, who also dislikes the extension of the frame behind his head, making it difficult to look up.

Rucksacks

Rucksacks have always been preferred by many climbers and skiers because of their low center of gravity and minimal interference with the movement of the body. It was difficult to carry heavy loads in older-style rucksacks, however, because they were made with short sacks, and larger loads projected so far back that they required an exaggerated forward lean. The rucksack designs developed in the last decade have changed all that, and present the winter traveler with a very wide variety of possibilities. The best of these packs are relatively expensive because of the materials and the amount of sewing they require, but if you can afford them, they are usually the best choice for winter camping.

There are many fine small rucksacks, often using light internal frames or removable foam pads to protect the back and to help shape the pack. Such packs are perfectly suited for day trips and for tours of a few days by those who can travel very light. However, if you can afford only one pack, it makes sense to get a larger one that can be used for everything, rather than a small sack that is ill suited for trips requiring larger loads.

The best of the larger rucksacks represent one of the most important advances in equipment design of the last few years. They can be divided roughly into three categories. First, there are rucksacks that use fairly traditional design, except that the sack is longer and equipped with a good waistband so that if the pack is filled it forms a long, relatively stiff cylinder and the wearer can transfer quite a bit of the load to the waistband. A padded back is usually used, but if there are any stays at all, they don't form a frame connecting the shoulder straps and waistband. Such packs have advantages for climbers, but using them for heavy loads usually requires that the wearer have well-developed shoulders. The other two types of rucksacks are easier for most snow campers to use. Some good examples of this first type are made by Millet, Karrimor, and Forrest Mountaineering.

A second type of pack uses a compartmentalized and shaped bag that is shaped by the placement of the load in the different chambers. The original pack of this type is the Jensen Pack, now made in several versions by Rivendell Mountain Works. The sleeping bag is stuffed into the large lower compartment, which then forms the back of the waistband and a shelf to support the rest of the pack. These packs work very well when properly packed, though they tend to cause more than the usual perspiration buildup on your back. They ride close to the back and are great for skiing and climbing. Personally, however, I find them less adaptable to different loads and no more comfortable to wear than the internal-frame packs.

Large packs using flexible aluminum stays to connect a large integral waistband to padded straps that go well over the shoulders form the last category of large rucksacks, the one that I think is the best group for most winter campers. There are a number of variations: Some of the packs open through large zippered panels in the back and others load more conventionally at the top. The zippered panels give ready access to any part of the load, but have less flexibility in the loads they will carry and are vulnerable to zipper failure. Many of these packs have compression straps to improve the profile when small loads are carried, accessory pockets that fasten on the outside, and so on. Excellent versions of this type of pack are made by Hine Snowbridge, Synergy Works, and Early Winters.

In trying out these packs it is necessary to experiment a good deal with the suspension to achieve the proper fit. As with pack frames, you should test them for comfort with a load comparable to the ones you intend to carry. If the pack doesn't feel comfortable in the store, it will feel miserable on the trail. Most of the internal-frame packs have suspensions that adjust to people of widely varying size. Jensen-style packs and many frame packs have to be chosen in the correct size for the length of your torso. Make a close inspection of the materials used in the pack, the stitching, and the design of the suspension. Packs take more abuse than any other item of equipment except for your boots. A pack with sloppy stitching or a frame with the waistband hanging on a tab attached with only a few threads will not hold up very long under rugged use.

Lights

For most purposes in winter, battery-operated flashlights or headlamps are standard lightweight gear. A headlamp has great advantages when the hands are needed for other things, such as cooking, gathering wood, or making midnight repairs on a guy line. The separate battery pack of the headlamp also enables one to get the batteries close to the body, where they will stay warm and hence operate efficiently. As any car owner in a cold area knows, batteries become progressively less powerful as the temperature drops. Because of their greater temperature range, longer life, and superiority in heavy use, alkaline batteries or one of the more exotic types of long-life cells should be used in preference to standard flashlight cells. Lithium cells, available from a few of the suppliers listed in Appendix C, give the best performance for the weight and are least affected by cold weather. They are expensive, but they last much longer than even alkaline cells.

Batteries last longer if they are used intermittently, so if you have two flashlights available, it is a good idea to alternate them every ten minutes or so during extended use. Spare batteries and bulbs should normally be carried for each flashlight or headlamp. Bulbs can often be taped somewhere inside the lamp to make sure they are always available. Be sure to disable your flashlight in some way whenever it is carried in the pack, so that it can't be switched on accidentally. Keep your batteries warm whenever they may be needed so that they will operate with maximum efficiency.

Sun Protection

It seems rather contradictory that in winter when the sun is lowest, the danger of sunburn can be particularly great. Snow is an almost perfect reflector of light in the ranges that burn the skin and eyes. In a large snow bowl, you may consider yourself to be the focal point of a giant reflector oven. Cloudy days can be most deceptive, since visible light is shut out to a large degree, but this is not always the case for the burning ultraviolet portion of the spectrum. Skin and eye protection should always be carried, unless you know you won't need them. In high mountains, everyone must carry sun protection, since the danger there is much greater. Much of the ultraviolet that is filtered out before reaching sea level is still present in the light of the mountains. At lower altitudes, most people will find conventional suntan preparations satisfactory. At higher altitudes, a special cream should be carried, and it may be wanted by people with sensitive skin at all times. Several good preparations are available in mountaineering shops. The budget-minded can use mineral oil for the milder sort of protection, and the zinc oxide ointment usually marketed for baby's diaper rash gives complete protection against high-altitude burning rays. Sun preparations are now frequently labeled with a number indicating the degree of protection offered, on a scale of one to ten. Choose one with a high number.

Sunglasses or goggles do not have to be expensive, but they must be of good quality. Some types of cheap plastic glasses can do more harm than good, since they cut out visible rays, thus making the pupils dilate, while allowing the ultraviolet rays that do the damage to pass through. Snow blindness is disabling and very painful, and it must be avoided by foresight and care, since the victim rarely feels pain until the damage has been done. Lenses of glasses for use in snow should be darker than conventional sunglasses, and they should be good enough optically so that they do not produce eyestrain after a few hours. Climbing shops and some ski stores have excellent models. Glare from the side should be cut out by some means, but as much ventilation as possible is desirable to prevent fogging.

For some reason, most of the manufacturers of goggles and sunglasses seem to believe that all mountaineers and winter travelers possess perfect vision because they generally pay little attention to the needs of eyeglass wearers. Some goggles will fit over eyeglasses, but if they aren't well ventilated you will have a lot of trouble with fogging. Even with those that are well ventilated, you will probably need some antifogging compound to smear on the lenses of your goggles and glasses. The double set of lenses causes far more trouble than a single set. Probably the best alternative for the wearer of eyeglasses who can afford them is a set of prescription sunglasses with large dark lenses and colored or opaque side visors to cut glare.

Two other special needs of the eyeglass wearer are a spare set of glasses and some sort of holder to prevent him from losing his specs in a tumble. A piece of cord and a pair of rubber bands will do if nothing else is available. Contact lens wearers should carry an extra set.

Toilet Articles
A small piece of hand soap or, better, a tiny tube of liquid hand soap will take care of washing needs. Washing the face and hands more often than necessary should be avoided, since the removal of the skin's

protective oils will aid chapping and sunburn. Those who don't possess weather-toughened skin are well advised to carry a small container of oil-based skin lotion for chapping. A tiny tube of petroleum jelly takes care of chafed spots and can be carried in a pocket of the clothing or pack. Everyone should have a special stick or cream for the lips, which are particularly prone to cracking and chapping. For high altitudes a special opaque cream to protect the lips from sunburn may be desirable, since the protection used for the rest of the face often comes off the lips too easily. Desitin baby ointment works well.

Toothbrushes are a necessity for some, while others never bother with them on a trip. Suit yourself, but remember that a little plastic bag of tooth powder attached to the toothbrush with a rubber band is a lot lighter than a tube of toothpaste and is less messy if it gets broken. Dental floss is light in weight, and it makes a good heavy thread besides keeping your mouth clean.

Don't forget to take the toilet paper! Rerolled into small bundles, it will fit into convenient spots in your pocket and pack.

Tools and Repair Kit

A knife is needed for many purposes, and one should be carried by each member of a party. A sharp pocket knife is usually adequate. A small whetstone may be worthwhile on longer trips. If you are building fires to keep you warm, you will need a saw or an ax. A saw is much lighter than any adequate ax. A Hudson Bay ax with a one-and-a-half-pound head is about the smallest practical size. There are several folding saws that are fairly light and compact. Some of these can also be used for cutting snow blocks. For a lightweight emergency saw, a hacksaw blade can be carried or a lightweight wire saw can be purchased.

A repair kit will vary with your own experience. Wilderness tourers, like armies, tend always to be prepared for the last war rather than the next one. Aside from this personal aspect, your repair kit will depend on your equipment. Skiers, who might have to repair the hardware of bindings, may want to carry a plier-screwdriver-crescent wrench combination tool and any spare parts that seem appropriate. An emergency ski tip should be carried by skiers with wooden skis. I prefer to carry most emergency equipment together in one small package, including spare matches in a waterproof container, fire starter, and medical supplies, which are covered in Chapter 12. Some items like adhesive tape serve for repairs of both equipment and people. Other items like parachute cord serve many ordinary camping uses as well as being useful for emergency repairs, and they will usually be carried in the pack or a pocket. Any repair kit should include a needle and some nylon thread for mending clothing; ripstop nylon tape is also handy for fabric repairs. About a yard of wire is very useful for some kinds of repairs on skis and snowshoes. For quick repairs a few safety pins should be carried somewhere; I leave mine on one of the belt loops of my trousers, where they are handy. Some quick-curing epoxy glue can be useful for extensive repairs on skis or snowshoes, though everything has to be warmed to make it cure. Over-sized screws and epoxy are good insurance against bindings pulled out of skis.

If an emergency kit is to do any good, it must be available when it is needed, and this means that it should be light and compact. If it is too complete it is likely to be left in the tent when you go off on a day trip. One kit will do for a small party, if there are no plans of splitting the group for day trips or on the trail.

If you plan to split into smaller groups at some point, one emergency kit must be carried for each group. Some experienced travelers carry their emergency items in two packages. Medicine, extra bandages, and other items are left with the tent, while a lighter kit is carried at all times. The items left at the tent can serve a large party, and the smaller kit is duplicated for each small group that is going off by itself. Detailed lists for suggested emergency kits are included in Appendix D.

Containers and Utensils

It is important to have a container in which you can carry liquid water after finding or melting it. Such a container has innumerable other uses in the jugglery of camp cooking. The most serviceable type I know is a strong polyethylene flask with a wide mouth. Marks can be made on the side with a hot knife for measuring water in cooking. The wide mouth is essential so that snow can be added to already melted water. Pick a bottle that doesn't leak. An excessively large thread area on the cap will make the bottle more difficult to open when the water starts to freeze.

Whatever type of water bottle you have, remember to fill it whenever there is an opportunity. If you have extra hot water at breakfast, you can make a hot drink for lunch and wrap the bottle in the middle of your sleeping bag to keep it warm. If you like a fast start in the morning, make some sort of nourishing drink at night and keep the bottle in your sleeping bag to prevent it from freezing overnight. This can be combined with normal trail food for a fast breakfast.

For eating, I usually carry one plastic cup and one light plastic bowl for each person. These are easier to use in a crowded tent than metal dishes, since they don't get so hot that people burn their hands and spill things on the floor and sleeping bags. Plastic dishes are light, and the flexible ones are quite strong. Make sure that the ones you get are shaped so that you can pack them easily. One tablespoon per person is usually adequate for a utensil, together with personal penknives. One or two clamp potholders are very useful for handling hot pans. When held, they grip the pot like a saucepan handle. If you plan to fry anything in the thin cooking kit covers that double as frying pans, it helps to bring a light spatula, since it is nearly impossible to keep things from sticking to these pans.

If you are using a gasoline stove for cooking, you will need a gasoline container. The best type is the rectangular metal kind with a narrow pouring spout on one side and a vent spout on the other. Test the container at home to make sure it doesn't leak. Pack it in a plastic bag for extra safety, and then put it somewhere in the pack as far away from food as possible, to prevent any accidental leaks from doing too much damage. Gasoline, even used in small quantities, gives food a very distinctive flavor. In testing the can at home, make sure you can pour easily into the stove from a full can without much spilling. If you can't, carry a small plastic funnel for filling the stove. A pricker for the jet should also be carried by the gasoline-stove user. Don't forget that you must use white (unleaded) gasoline or the special fuel sold in camping stores.

If you carry any canned food, don't forget to bring a miniature can opener, unless you have one on your knife.

Miscellaneous Items

Maps and compasses are discussed in Chapter 9. They are essential, and so is the knowledge of how to use them. Other instruments for navigation are fascinating but are rarely needed on short trips. On trips to the mountains, an altimeter is an interesting luxury item that is useful in navigation and weather forecasting.

Other gadgets will be considered essential by different people, but remember to be stingy both in the store and at the trailhead. Will you really use it? Is it really worth the price and the weight? Photographic equipment is the most commonly carried gadgetry. If you take it, make sure it is accessible enough so that you use it. A camera buried in the pack will be left there with the thought of getting that picture tomorrow. Only tomorrow it usually snows! A light and inexpensive camera often gets the pictures missed with a heavy *SLR*, which can't be carried in a convenient position.

ALONG THE WINTER TRAIL

The main reason for being on the trail in winter is to have a good time, and the need for too much attention to details and worry about problems will spoil your trip. Leave yourself enough time and energy to enjoy the company of your companions and the beauty around you. You are more likely to have a good time if you limit your objectives at first. It's fine to end the day tired, but the slower members of the party shouldn't be shoved along on a forced march, except under unusual circumstances.

Normal procedure is to alternate regularly in the trail-breaking position, which is very tiring in some kinds of snow, especially on snowshoes. Weaker members of the party may be spared this job, but you should be wary of letting the strongest member of the party do all the work. The extra stamina of the toughest individual may be needed later, and the necessity for reliance on one person should indicate to you that the party's strength is being stretched out a little too much. What happens if the bull breaks his leg? If there is a heavy fall of new snow? Parties of uneven strength should keep their goals on the conservative side.

With larger parties, it is common to go into camp and then split up for day trips. This sort of arrangement is fine, but groups should always be aware of the dangers of dividing the party. Each separate party must have the capacity for handling any emergencies and problems it may encounter.

A dangerous and common mistake is for all the strong members of the party to go on a hard trip, while the beginners take a trip of their own through country in which they are not competent to travel. The only emergency kit is taken by one group, and is not available to the other. The same will be true of the map, if only one is carried. This sort of situation has all the makings of disaster, and that fact is obvious when it is presented in this way, but otherwise sensible people still make this type of mistake rather frequently.

Parties should never be split up in dangerous situations except in the specific circumstances discussed in the chapter on emergencies. The most common mistake of this kind is to allow the party to separate in whiteout conditions when blowing snow reduces visibility to a few yards: A few members of the party may stop to rest, while their companions proceed out of calling range in the howling winds, or two groups may split to investigate different routes, losing each other before they realize what they are doing. In any case, the result is that they are soon looking for each other as well as the trail. When a group is in any difficulty, special efforts must be made to keep it together, and even during normal trail travel, morale will be higher if the group does not spread out too far because of uneven pace. Experienced parties made up of members of equal strength who want a little of the silence afforded by a ten-minute spacing can indulge themselves as long as there is no danger of skiing down different valleys. In good conditions this does not pose any danger, but as soon as tracks start drifting in rapidly, the party should get together and stay that way.

CHILDREN ON THE TRAIL

Taking children on winter trips can be quite enjoyable, but some special attention is needed in planning, and ambitions will have to be scaled down somewhat. With children of about ten years and over, there aren't many differences from planning a tour for adults, except for appropriate evaluations of strength and the length of the trip.

One thing you should remember is that children generally do not have the reserve strength of adults, either physically or emotionally. A very strong and energetic child will still usually be nearly spent once he is tired. The transition from incredible energy to exhaustion and collapse is quick. This is especially true in cold weather. Special care is necessary in guarding against the effects of cold. Children also cannot usually be expected to pace themselves, and it is important that some care be exercised, especially with large groups of young people. Those who are used to the outdoors and have developed some habits of foresight and self-reliance may have better judgment than their

Children and winter camping With proper clothing, children can be taken on winter trips with easy itineraries.

adult companions, but most boys and girls have not had a chance to develop that kind of maturity.

Children between the ages of five and ten can also undertake trips on their own power, with objectives appropriate to their size and stamina. Older members of the party will have to carry some or all of the supplies for this age group.

Below the age of five, children usually have to be carried, along with their clothing and regular equipment. Older children are rather heavy, and with younger ones the problem of bulk is considerable due to diapers and changes of clothing. The frame carriers in which the child faces forward are effective, though not as durable as they should be. These carriers can also be lashed high on a packframe equipped with an extension bar, and a packbag will fit below.

A child who is riding should be dressed very warmly; he is not climbing a hill to generate heat. The problem of insulation is not too great, however, since the child is sitting in one place and is easily padded.

The biggest problem in snow camping with small children is that they can't play around the tent or lunch spot in deep snow, since the packed platform doesn't extend very far. This means they don't get any real break from the monotony of sitting, and they become understandably bored and cranky. Another real difficulty of winter weekends with small children is the changing of diapers and clothes.

With small children the most enjoyable alternative is usually to take day trips from a car camp or cabin. Most of the difficulties are manageable on day jaunts. On longer trips they can be handled, but in winter they are likely to turn your trip into more of an ordeal than a pleasure. Overnight backpacking with small children is best saved for milder seasons.

STAYING ON TOP OF THE SNOW

Skis and snowshoes are dealt with in the next two chapters. Besides the choice between these two methods of staying atop the snow, there are many types of skis and many snowshoe patterns. If you already have a pair of webs or skis, you can use them, at least for a while, without worrying about whether they are perfect for the conditions you expect. You may also be able to try out different types of equipment by renting them.

However, if you have to put down the money to purchase skis or snowshoes you will want to study the different types with care, and these are discussed in some detail in the following chapter. The basics are easy. In mountainous country skis are trickier to use and some skill at managing them must be acquired in advance. Thus, the non-skier who wants to head for the high country right away will probably choose snowshoes. Technique with touring skis for easier terrain is not hard to learn, and the beginner needn't worry about starting right off with skis.

Mountains that don't usually get a heavy cover of snow often require snowshoes for winter climbing, since a deep snow cover is necessary for skiing in really rough terrain. In the Northeast, for example, ski tourers are often confined to gentler trails. In the high Western mountains, the skier can manage terrain as difficult as any that can be traversed by snowshoe, since the snow cover is usually deep. In fact, skis are generally easier to use on open difficult terrain when snow depth is adequate.

On steep terrain snowshoes are far easier to learn to use effectively than skis, but skiers admit few other advantages to the plodding webs. Snowshoes are much simpler to carry for intermittent use, but they are usually slower for strong parties.

Whatever sort of equipment you already have or decide to buy, you'll be able to handle a wide variety of terrain from snowy beaches to mountain peaks. Though each ski and snowshoe design is best in one type of terrain, it can be used in a much wider range of situations. Picking equipment simply amounts to choosing the best compromise for your purposes.

7 | Snowshoeing: Walking on the Drifts

When winter really settles in and the drifts begin to pile up, slogging through the snow can become impossible unless you spread your weight over a larger area than the soles of your boots. The way to do this that is the easiest, cheapest, and requires the least practice is with snowshoes. It is the traditional American way because snowshoes were invented by indigenous Americans, the Indians, and there have been few significant improvements in design since.

The greatest advantage of snowshoes over skis is that you can learn to walk on them in about five minutes. Using skis requires that you learn to ski. This advantage is not nearly so great if the country where you plan to tour is flat or rolling, since Nordic-style ski touring is fairly easy to learn. Mountain-touring technique with skis takes some time to master, however. The snowshoer needs to learn only the fine points of technique, not the basics, because he already knows how to walk. This means that he can learn on trips rather than practice slopes, a great boon.

There have always been myriad patterns of snowshoes, for each Indian tribe that used them had its own distinctive design. The features of a particular type were dictated by tradition and available materials, but most of all by the snow conditions prevailing in the area where they were used and the activities for which they were designed. The same conditions govern the design and choice of snowshoes today.

There are a few additional advantages to snowshoes that should be mentioned. Snowshoes are superior to skis for many jobs in the woods; that is, for work rather than travel. Felling trees and hauling loads is easier on snowshoes than skis. Almost any footwear suitable for winter wear can be worn with snowshoes. This can save money and be of considerable advantage on a trip where some particular type of shoe or boot is needed for other reasons. Finally, on trips with terrain alternating between soft snow and walking or climbing conditions when only boots are needed, snowshoes are much easier than skis to carry between drifts.

Snowshoes are simply webs of thin, strong material stretched over a rigid frame that are attached to the feet and spread the wearer's weight over a wide area of snow. The snowshoes are held to the foot in such a way that the foot pivots forward freely but is held fairly strongly from sideways motion. The standard snowshoe is made of varnished strips of cowhide on a curved wooden frame. Good snowshoes are also made from a number of high-technology materials, the most popular being aluminum frames with neoprene-coated nylon webbing and binding.

Walking technique on webs varies somewhat with design and terrain, but basically a long, gliding gait is used when possible. The feet are a bit farther apart than in normal walking, but not so far apart as one would think from looking at a pair of snowshoes sitting side-by-side on the floor. The widest part of a large snowshoe is beside the foot, with the frame tapering in both forward and backward directions. In walking, the wide parts are not placed beside one another; instead, the forward curve of the rear shoe fits beside the back curve of the leading shoe, as shown on page 119. In walking, the rear shoe is lifted just enough to clear the front one as it comes forward. The legs are just far enough apart so that the shoe doesn't strike the opposite leg as it comes forward. Mountaineering-style snowshoes are uniformly narrow through their entire length.

The design of snowshoes is supremely functional, and choosing the right type is fairly simple if you know the conditions that prevail where

Some types of snowshoes Left to right: modified bearpaw with H binding, a Maine shoe with ties for a squaw hitch, a modified bearpaw with a Howe binding, and a standard bearpaw with an army sandal binding.

they will be used. How much do you weigh, and how big a pack do you normally carry? Does deep, dry, light powder cover the woods in the part of the country where you live, or is heavy, wet snow or breakable crust the rule? Will you be traveling mostly in brushy, dense country or in the wide, open spaces? Are you thinking of steep mountains, flat plains, or rolling country? Or do you have some special use in mind, such as utility shoes for use around a cabin where the main transportation will be on skis?

The main features of design are: length, width, general shape, tail, and upturn of the toe. Many other differences, such as rounded or pointed toes, are relatively unimportant. Models are more standardized than they once were. The features mentioned above will be discussed, and then the general types of shoe will be listed with the conditions in which they are preferred. The main types each have a number of practically synonymous names. Niceties such as the differences between Michigan and Maine shoes will be left for the interested reader to find for himself.

The larger the area of the snowshoe, the more weight it will support without sinking too much into the snow. The smallest shoe that will do the job for you is the best. Every extra ounce on the feet is tiring, and larger sizes are more awkward as well. Where hard snow conditions prevail, smaller shoes than normal may suffice. The designs that are suitable for regions with deep, soft snow are usually made with fairly large areas. The recommended sizes below are for general use.

Width tends to increase the general awkwardness of snowshoes and makes them slower because the legs must be kept wide. Fourteen inches should be a maximum shoe width. Where long shoes are not a disadvantage, area is increased with length rather than width, but where maneuverability is more important than speed, width is increased. The general shape of a shoe will be dictated both by the area needed for adequate support and by handling characteristics.

A tail is always desirable for hiking, but it makes the shoe slightly less maneuverable. The tail makes the snowshoe somewhat heavier to the rear of the pivot axis. When the foot is lifted, the tail remains on the snow, supporting some of the weight of the shoe, and the toe turns up out of the snow. A tail-less snowshoe can be made either with the weight to the rear of the pivot, like the tailed variety, or with the weight approximately balanced. If the weight is balanced, more weight has to be lifted by the leg, because no weight is supported by the tail, and it must be lifted higher, because the toe is not pulled up by the heavier tail. A tail-less snowshoe with a heavy pack also slows the wearer, because the rear of the shoe drags badly on the snow. Instead of a narrow width of smooth wood, one drags a small snowplow. The great advantage of the tail-less shoes is their maneuverability. They are also very convenient to carry on a pack due to their reduced length.

An upturned toe is another essential feature of snowshoes made for the trail. A straight toe tends to dive into the snow or at least to act like a snow shovel, especially in downhill travel. Shoveling a ten-mile path with your legs is rather tiring. One compensates for this defect by stepping very high, and this is almost as tiring as shoveling. With an upturned toe and a heavier tail, deep snow can be handled without excessively high steps. The amount of upturn depends on the conditions for which the snowshoe is designed. Too high and long a toe merely adds weight to the shoe without increasing its carrying capacity. Extra weight must also be added to the heel for balance. The additional length makes the shoe more awkward to handle. Ideally, the toe should be long enough and with just enough upturn to handle the depth of snow expected.

TYPES OF SNOWSHOES

The Maine or Michigan Snowshoe

The Maine or Michigan is the standard all-purpose snowshoe and the one against which the performance of other types should be measured. The toe is tapered and turned up slightly, and the tail insures good tracking. Standard sizes are available that will provide enough flotation to handle just about any snow conditions and load. The pattern of the shoes is such that the legs do not have to be spread too far for a stride to be maintained. The shoes are reasonably maneuverable, and they are not impossible in bushy country. The standard lengths of forty-eight inches or less are short enough to carry on a pack without being terribly awkward. This is the snowshoe that most beginners should buy. The following are recommended sizes:

Weight with pack up to	*Standard snowshoe*
125 lbs.	12 × 42″
170 lbs.	13 × 48″
225 lbs.	14 × 48″

Some Canadian varieties with pointed toes will be a bit longer in each size.

The Pickerel Snowshoe

Also known as the Alaskan trail shoe and the Yukon trail shoe, the pickerel snowshoe is long and narrow, designed for fast going on open ground. The standard size is about 10 inches wide and 48 to 60 inches long. The tips of these shoes are turned high to clear deep snow, and the narrow track enables the experienced user to attain good speed. Shoes of this design were originally used for running down game. Their large area gives good flotation in deep, soft snow. For the beginner who plans to do a lot of hiking in open country with deep, powdery snow, a pickerel design is a good choice. It is even more inconvenient to carry on a pack than the Michigan shoe and is a horror in heavy brush. Like the Michigan, it is poor for steep, soft slopes.

The pickerel- and Yukon trail-type shoes are best made with a fairly pointed front and the toe hole placed well forward of the center of gravity. Some badly designed models with a wide front and centrally spaced toe hole pick up a great deal of snow on the front. The extra weight of the snow is very tiresome. The sizes of pickerel-type shoes are generally 10 × 48 inches for light people with packs, 10 × 56 inches for most men, and 12 × 60 inches for heavy men with packs.

Cross-Country Snowshoes

Similar to the pickerel type, cross-country snowshoes taper less and are a bit shorter. The toe hole is closer to the front of the shoe, which turns up more sharply. These features make the cross-country shoe somewhat more maneuverable than the pickerel and reduce the possibility of snow piling up on the front of the shoe. Overlapping is not quite so good, however. Generally speaking, the cross-country model is good and bad in the same conditions as the pickerel. The standard size is 10 × 46 inches, and it is adequate for most people. The shorter length makes it easier to pack than the longer pickerel.

Bearpaws

There are several types of bearpaw snowshoe, the standard bearpaw and variations that modify both its defects and advantages. The standard bearpaw is flat; it has no upturn at the toe. It is roughly oval shaped, usually with a slight taper toward the heel, and the foot hole is far forward. There is no tail. Bearpaws are very maneuverable in areas where uncovered brush and obstacles cause the wearer of long, tailed shoes to tear his hair. On short, steep slopes that are soft enough to require snowshoes, bearpaws are excellent. The straight toe can be kicked into the slope, giving the climber a flat surface to stand on, a feat that is almost impossible with long curved toes. The foot rests in the step even when it is not kicked deeply, because the foot is well forward on the shoe. Bearpaws are excellent for doing chores, because of their maneuverability and because the toes do not stick far in front of you, keeping you from your work. They are easy to pack.

The list of vices for the bearpaw is not long, but it is convincing for

Tracks of Maine shoes The feet need not be kept very far apart, because the shoes are shaped so that the curves fit together. In walking, the edge of the moving shoe just clears the stationary one. Note the tail tracks. The tail drags behind, carrying some of the weight of the shoe.

anyone who does not absolutely require its virtues. The straight toe, excessive width, and wide, dragging heel make it a tiresome curse on the trail, especially in soft snow. If you need a bearpaw, check to see if one of its modifications will suit you as well, while ameliorating a few of its vices.

The modified bearpaw tapers more to the front and rear, adding some length to maintain area. The toe is raised somewhat to reduce diving, and the foot is placed farther back. There is still no tail, but the rear of the shoe is narrower than that of the true bearpaw, reducing the drag. The modified bearpaw retains the maneuverability of the original, while being a bit more feasible for trail use. Feet do not have to be quite so far apart, since the tapering allows the shoes to fit together when one is placed ahead. The modified design is still a poor trail snowshoe, but it is much better than the original. It is just as good in brush and generally rough terrain, and it is almost as good for utility uses around a cabin or camp. It is inferior to the standard bearpaw in steep snow, however, for the upturned front, which sticks out farther in front of the toe hole, is harder to kick into the slope. The modified bearpaw is generally preferable to the standard for all-

Mountain snowshoes A modified type of bearpaw, mountain snowshoes are narrow and have bindings that provide a lot of control; one can set them well on sidehills where the snow is not too hard. They have aluminum frames and neoprene-coated nylon webbing.

around use in brushy areas, except where the straight toes are definitely needed for kicking steps. Even on steep slopes, the straight toes become an annoyance on the descent, when they dive under the snow with every step.

Modern mountain snowshoes were designed as a compromise shape that could be used effectively on the trail, in dense woods, and on steep slopes. The original design, constructed with conventional materials, was called the Green Mountain bearpaw, but excellent models with improved bindings are now made with aluminum frames and membranes and webbing of neoprene-coated nylon. This material is durable, is unaffected by moisture, and is less prone to snow buildup than traditional lacing.

The mountain snowshoes, made by Sherpa and various other manufacturers, are narrow so that one can climb diagonally up soft snow, with the shoes biting in like skis. They have upturned toes and toe holes well forward so that they give reasonable performance on the trail. Like the old army bearpaws, they have fairly rigid bindings that pivot on a metal rod and incorporate a crampon for hard snow. The part that actually holds the foot, however, is much improved over older bindings; it uses a combination of a neoprene-nylon sandal with a nylon tightening band that is held by hooks and is much easier to use and more effective than traditional bindings. These snowshoes work very nicely in the conditions that would call for maneuverable, tailless shoes. They are significantly more expensive and somewhat lighter than a comparable snowshoe with a wood frame and neoprene-nylon lacing.

Recommended sizes of the different types of bearpaws are listed below for the maximum weights of the wearer and pack.

Weight with pack up to	Standard bearpaw	Modified bearpaw	Mountain bearpaw
100 lbs.	12 × 26″		8 × 25″
125 lbs.	12 × 30″		
150 lbs.	13 × 28″		9 × 30″
200 lbs.	13 × 33″, 14 × 30″	13 × 33″	10 × 36″
250 lbs.	15 × 30″	14 × 36″	10 × 42″

CHOOSING SNOWSHOES

If all the endless advantages and disadvantages just listed sound a bit confusing, don't worry about it. Just about any snowshoe will do what it's supposed to do—hold you up in the snow. Obviously, it's a good idea to get a type that will be most likely to suit the terrain where you'll be traveling if you're going to plunk down a lot of money for a pair. If you already have access to snowshoes, though, don't worry if they're the right type. As long as they are of reasonable size and are sturdy, they will serve well enough to get you started.

The recommended sizes listed in the earlier sections are not gospel, either. They are intended merely to give you a rough idea of what to expect from a particular size. Snow conditions that prevail where you plan to use the snowshoes may influence you to pick larger or smaller models. Mountaineers using the shoes mainly in spring conditions, for example, typically use smaller models. Shoes that are a little smaller than those recommended can still be used even in average winter conditions; you'll just sink a little deeper at each step.

Neoprene-nylon is rapidly becoming the standard filler for snowshoes, replacing the traditional varnished rawhide because it is more durable, is less vulnerable to moisture, is almost maintenance-free, and freezes up a little less easily. There is nothing wrong with rawhide, however, and it does have a nice aesthetic appeal. The best wood frames are made of ash. Good tubular aluminum alloy frames are lighter and a little stronger. They are maintenance-free but harder to repair if they do get broken.

HITCHES AND BINDINGS

The traditional method of attaching snowshoes to the feet was the lampwicking snowshoe hitch. Aside from the difficulty of finding

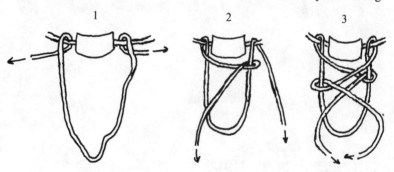

1   2   3

How to tie a squaw hitch. Some sort of soft webbing makes the best squaw hitch. The one shown is tied on a snowshoe with a permanent toe strap, which is always preferable, and which is essential with hard-toed boots. The same squaw hitch can be tied without a toe strap, or a separate toe strap can be tied. Finish the hitch off with a square knot behind the heel.

lampwicking these days, the main difficulty with this hitch is its floppiness and absence of control. Some people still like it, some for its virtues and some for its snob appeal. It is worth trying for fun and learning for emergency use, anyway, and a drawing is included. Soft nylon webbing will work well as a substitute for lampwicking, but rope is not satisfactory and should be reserved for emergencies.

The bindings that have gradually replaced hitches give good control when they are well designed. The normal material is leather, and this is satisfactory, but the new neoprene-nylon types are much better. They don't freeze, and snow and ice don't stick to them. They will also wear longer than leather bindings. Best of all, the neoprene-nylon material doesn't stretch, so that the curse of tightening your bindings a dozen times a day is gone. Somehow, the adjustment was always needed just when you were halfway across a barbed wire fence.

Aside from the material, there are several types of bindings. Conventional strap-type bindings start with a simple design using a broad toe strap and a heel strap. Additional control and stability are gained by adding extra straps over the instep, around the front of the toe, and so on. The one providing the most control is called the Howe binding. The sandal bindings mounted on a metal plate that is hinged to a metal piece attached to the shoe, like those made by Sherpa, are the easiest to use, the most comfortable, and give the best control. They usually include a crampon as part of the binding. They are also the most expensive.

FOOTWEAR

What you wear between your foot and your snowshoe will depend on the terrain you will frequent, the temperatures that are likely, and what you may already have. If you are going into the mountains and you plan to climb up steep slopes, you will have to have some kind of mountaineering boot. For gentle terrain, lighter and more flexible footwear is cheaper and more comfortable. In any case, lightweight hiking or work boots are inadequate for winter conditions, unless you get overboots to supplement them.

Moderate Terrain, Moderate Temperatures

The biggest problem in moderate conditions is the wetting of the boots and socks, which then lose all their insulating qualities. Wet or melted snow can rapidly soak through lightweight boots, and the snow then chills the feet thoroughly, with subsequent frostbite becoming a distinct possibility.

Cheap, light footwear Here are an overshoe with buckles cut off and left open for ventilation, a wool felt liner, and a long gaiter to keep snow out. Spare liners must be carried in case these get wet.

Probably the best footwear in these conditions is the rubber-bottom boots with leather tops. These are completely waterproof on the bottom, and proper care keeps the tops very water-repellent. They are much more comfortable to wear than all-rubber pacs; they are lighter and do not present nearly so much of a condensation problem. Insoles should be worn with them for insulation and to absorb moisture, and several pairs of spare insoles should be carried. The bottoms may be insulated, and the insulated models can be worn in quite cold temperatures. The best insulation for this purpose is closed-cell foam, such as Ensolite, the cells of which cannot absorb water. Some rubber-bottom boots are now available with lug soles, which wear longer and give better footing and insulation to the bottom of the foot. Probably the best snowshoeing boots available for those who do not need the rigidity of mountaineering boots are the Sorel rubber-bottom boots with leather tops, removable wool liners, and lug soles. Get an extra pair of liners to change to when the first set gets damp from condensation.

Korean-type double-vapor-barrier rubber boots are sometimes used for moderate conditions. Insulation is sealed between the inside and outside layers of rubber so that they can't get wet. These boots retain their insulation unless they are punctured, but if this happens they can become useless. They are rather heavy as well.

One inexpensive type of alternative footwear for these conditions is a normal rubberized fabric overshoe. I have used these fairly successfully with wool felt liners and heavy wool socks by cutting off all but the bottom buckle and wearing long nylon gaiters overlapping the top to keep the snow out. No shoes are worn, so the combination is light and comfortable. The overshoes open widely enough to allow quite a bit of air circulation while walking, so that the condensation problem is reduced. Even so, an extra pair of felt liners should be carried, and they can also be used to keep the feet warm in the sleeping bag. For trips longer than three or four days, you should make a pair of closed-cell foam liners to the same pattern as the felt liners. These cannot accidentally be wet through as the open-cell foam-type can.

With any rubberized footwear, no matter how well it is designed, the condensation problem will plague you, and you should plan for it by carrying more socks and inner soles than you would with other footwear.

Moderate Terrain, Cold Temperatures

The classical footwear of the North—high-topped moccasin shoe pacs—is the most practical and comfortable footgear when the weather is cold but the terrain is moderate. The pacs are high-topped moccasins with flexible leather soles. They are very light. They should be large enough for several pairs of heavy socks to be worn inside. Sokkets, low felt socks that are worn over a regular pair of heavy socks, can also be used. This combination is light and warm—a joy to wear.

The temperature range of moccasin pacs can be greatly extended with the use of a pair of fabric overboots, not the normal heavy over-shoe, but a pair like the type described in the previous chapter. These are light, adding hardly any weight to the foot, even when an insulation layer is included. They extend the lower temperature range of moccasins down to anything you are likely to encounter, and if they are made of coated fabric, they will also enable you to use this type of footwear in wet conditions where running water is not present. You can make overboots fairly easily, or you can obtain them from one of the suppliers listed in Appendix C.

Steep or Rough Terrain

In mountainous areas where a lot of steep terrain will be encountered, mountaineering boots are necessary, as discussed in the preceding chapter. Occasional steep slopes can be handled with the footwear described above, if snowshoe crampons are used, and if all climbing is on moderate slopes that are well covered with snow, boots may not be necessary in the mountains. Really rough terrain often requires carrying snowshoes, however, and footwear with rigid soles is necessary. Mountaineering boots are also adaptable to wet or cold conditions, using the methods described earlier.

GETTING AROUND ON SNOWSHOES

Snowshoeing is, as stated in the beginning of the chapter, fairly easy to learn, and the techniques can be practiced on real trips. Most snowshoers carry one or two ski poles as an aid to balance and a particular help in righting themselves after spills. Poles are particularly useful in rough country, when they serve as props during awkward maneuvers over and around obstacles and as aids for climbing slopes.

Ski-pole length does not much matter, but the basket width should be six inches or so, rather than the narrow sort now preferred by skiers. This is to your budgetary advantage, since many of the older types can now be gotten cheaply secondhand. Mountaineers carrying ice axes can obtain removable baskets to attach to ice-ax shafts for use in soft snow.

Snowshoe crampons of some sort are necessary in steep terrain and are often very useful on slippery crusted snow at any angle. The built-in models included on mountaineering snowshoes are very helpful, but they will not always substitute for longer removable types, because they don't penetrate deeply enough. Longer crampons or claws are a nuisance when they aren't needed, but they can be crucial on steep slopes with a hard crust too fragile to walk on without snowshoes but too hard to obtain good purchase on with them. Several models are available commercially, and many types have been improvised. What is needed is simply a few points about an inch and a half long attached to the snowshoe just under the ball of the foot. They should be easily removable, and almost any device that satisfies these requirements will do the trick. My own preference is for a pair of aluminum-alloy instep crampons that can be attached to either snowshoes or boots. It is hard to find instep crampons that can be attached rigidly to snowshoes without removing the side tabs, but there are some available, and the versatility of the dual purpose makes them worthwhile. Almost any instep crampons will work after the tabs are broken or sawed off. A cross-strapping arrangement that will hold the crampons securely should be devised and tested ahead of time. Sections of T-shaped aluminum rod can also be used to make effective snowshoe crampons.

Climbing slopes with snowshoes is fairly easy to learn after a little practice. It is not always easy, but the beginner will do as well as the expert before too long. On moderate slopes and on steep, hard slopes when crampons are being used, the shoe is simply stamped flat on the slope, while the toe of the boot protrudes through the toe hole. The toe gains some purchase on the snow itself, and the ball of the foot rests on the snowshoe thongs. With straight-toed bearpaws on steep, soft slopes, the shoe is kicked straight into the snow. With mountaineering

A set of modern mountaineering snowshoes showing the built-in claw on the bottom of the binding The simple but effective sandal binding using nylon webbing, hooks, and a spring buckle for holding the boot is also shown. These snowshoes, made by Sherpa, have aluminum-alloy frames and neoprene-coated nylon membranes.

designs the snowshoer traverses diagonally as long as the shoes can be made to bite in enough, and switches to reliance on the crampon and the toe of the boot when the snow gets too hard. Other models will require experimentation, but the toes of even Maine and Michigan models can often be kicked into the slope when you are going uphill.

Descent is somewhat trickier, and in soft snow or breakable crust it can be just as tiring, since the toe of the shoe tends to drive under the snow. The only real trick is to stand up fairly straight. Sometimes a slide or a sliding step can be achieved, similar to skiing. In this case the poles are usually held together, and they can then be used for braking. Be careful not to slide where there is a dangerous drop-off below or where it is so slippery that you may not be able to control the slide. A shuffling step keeps the toes from diving under.

Climbing in steep, soft snow with bearpaws The snowshoer kicks directly into the slope to form a platform for each step.

8 | Skiing the White Wilderness

Skis are unquestionably the most elegant way to stay atop the snow, and under the right circumstances they are much more than that, for they give the skier the feeling of soaring flight. Even on flat terrain, the skier has the great advantage of being able to glide with each step. When the depth of snow is adequate, the skier can do just about everything that the snowshoer can, and a good deal more besides.

The skier's only problem is the depth of the snow cover. Skis tend to require somewhat deeper snow than snowshoes, especially on rough terrain. Once the snow lies deep enough to cover most of the small brush and rocks, this disadvantage is unimportant. In the western mountains, where the snow lies heavy all winter long, it is rarely a disadvantage at all. In some other regions, such as New England, where the brush is heavy and snow is sometimes light, snowshoes often have an edge over skis except on prepared tracks. Skis can be used on a golf course with only a few inches of snow, but fighting through brushy country with only a few feet of snow is easier with just boots or with bearpaw snowshoes; long skis or long snowshoes are a nuisance.

Once the snow is deep enough, skiers have most of the advantages. On little bumps or big hills, they can slide down the downhill sides, while snowshoers must keep on walking. Skis are easier to use on steep slopes, because the edges can be dug into the slope. On the flat, a gliding step can be developed that eats up the miles more quickly and pleasantly than can ever be managed with snowshoes.

The primary objection to skis as a means of wilderness travel is that at any given level of difficulty in terrain, skis require somewhat more skill to use than snowshoes do. On relatively flat ground, skis are not very hard to manage, but snowshoes are still easier. Steep slopes can be challenging using either type of equipment, but certainly skis do require better technique. Your choice may thus depend a lot on your temperament. If learning the technique for skiing the most difficult slopes appeals to you, the objection may present rather an attraction. Similarly, if you are willing to be patient and stick to easier terrain until your skiing improves, skis may be ideal for you. If, on the other hand, you are more interested in getting out into the mountains on long trips now than you are in developing your skiing technique for trips next year, you might prefer snowshoes.

More technical arguments over the relative virtues of skis and snowshoes on special types of trips—expeditions to big mountains, for example—are too involved and esoteric to go into here. In general, the same rule applies: Skis work well provided the skiers are skilled enough to handle them in the particular situation and equipment is properly chosen, but snowshoes are a better choice for those who have not perfected their technique to the proper level.

THE EQUIPMENT REVOLUTION

The most important changes in winter backcountry travel in the last few decades have resulted from improvements in ski-touring equipment and improvements in skiing technique made possible by this new equipment. These developments have accompanied the explosion in nordic-style skiing in the U.S. Nordic-style skiing, using lightweight, flexible equipment, is ideally suited for covering long distance over varied terrain. Alpine-style skiing, as it developed in Europe during the last half century, emphasized increased control for steep and difficult downhill runs at the expense of light weight, flexibility, and mobility. Even though the use of nordic technique in North America has a long history, dating back to the nineteenth century, most of the active wilderness skiers in the country came from a background of alpine skiing instead. Really light nordic equipment also presented problems for wilderness use, because of the danger of breakage of light wooden skis.

In the late fifties and early sixties, many backcountry enthusiasts began to discover what a few aficionados scattered around the country had known all along—that lightweight nordic skis with flexible boots were far better suited for many favorite tours than heavy modified alpine skiing gear. The popularity of cross-country skiing soared, and large numbers of nordic skis started to become available in the U.S. and Canada. The increased market, coupled with offshoots from the downhill skiing industry, stimulated a lot of experimentation into strengthening lightweight skis with metal or with fiberglass and epoxy

Skiing in wooded areas The heavy snow in places like Yosemite National Park covers underbrush and small trees, making skiing easy even in wooded areas.

resins. The result has been that in the last few years it has become possible to obtain skis for backcountry use that are very responsive, lighter than most wooden skis designed for trail use a few years ago, and stronger than the old wooden downhill skis.

The wilderness skier can now have his cake and eat it too. You can buy equipment that is light and flexible for easy skiing on the trail, reliable enough for serious wilderness trips, and sufficiently responsive to allow the adventurous skier to handle very exciting skiing. Finally, with nordic equipment, everything is sufficiently flexible so that an excellent safety margin can be maintained. It is possible to break an ankle while skiing with light equipment, of course, just as it is while hiking or snowshoeing. With a reasonable amount of prudence, however, the likelihood is rather small.

Since the first edition of this book, equipment developments have greatly reduced the number of choices that the wilderness skier has to make in deciding on equipment. There is no need to suffer with heavy alpine equipment on the trail in order to have skis with metal edges that will enable you to cross steep hard slopes or to have a good time parallel skiing on the windboard high above timberline. There are light touring skis with this capability. Nor is it necessary to take relatively fragile skis in order to be able to kick and glide up a long gentle valley at the beginning of your trip. The same skis will do well there, too.

As a result, there will be little discussion in this chapter of equipment extremes, though there are still some reasons for choosing much heavier or lighter gear than that emphasized here. Climbers skiing in to do technical climbs, for example, may want bindings and skis that can be used with heavy, stiff double boots. Alpine skiers who want to ski very steep couloirs in the backcountry may want high-performance equipment that also permits reasonable touring. Excellent developments have been made in equipment for this kind of skiing, too. For most wilderness skiers, however, the newer nordic gear is ideal. By developing your technique, you can learn to ski quite difficult terrain with it, achieving both the satisfaction of wilderness travel and the excitement of downhill skiing.

EQUIPMENT RECOMMENDATIONS

A wide variety of skis, boots, and bindings can be used successfully for wilderness skiing, and the recommendations given here should be considered to be no more than that—recommendations. There are many specialized circumstances that might dictate completely differ-

Nordic equipment Modern nordic equipment, light and flexible, can be used on a wide variety of terrain.

Equipment suited for both difficult alpine skiing and technical climbing, while retaining reasonable touring capacity A double boot is used with a Ramer binding, which holds the boot rigidly to the ski and has a full safety release like any downhill binding, but can be released at the heel to pivot 90° at the toe.

Steel edges Modern light touring skis can be made with full steel edges like these, so that the accomplished skier can handle very difficult downhill skiing without sacrificing mobility. The edges on these skis are offset so that they can be sharpened.

ent choices. The possibilities suggested here represent compromises that have proven to be adaptable to most wilderness travel, however, and the backcountry skier should consider them carefully.

For most wilderness skiing you should pick a ski in the range between what used to be called light touring and extra-light touring skis. Modern construction makes such skis strong enough for wilderness use, and their light weight is a delight on the trail. Such relatively narrow skis still give reasonable flotation in soft snow, but they are much better for breaking trail than wider models. The tips of this type of ski will generally range from 55 to 65 millimeters in width and the centers from about 50 to 60 millimeters. Skis much narrower than this, though they can sometimes be used for wilderness skiing, have less flotation and are generally designed for skiing on tracks and broken trails. Wider skis give better stability, but a penalty must be paid in weight and in difficulty of breaking trail.

Touring skis are long compared with modern downhill fashions, so downhill skiing with them takes more skill than does skiing with short, wide alpine skis, particularly since their narrowness requires better balance and more positive control of the edges. However, the improved flotation and glide of the longer skis are significant. The discussion of design considerations below refers to this type of ski. The design of an alpine ski or a ski intended for cross-country racing on a prepared track will be quite different.

Construction

Construction of modern touring skis can take a number of forms. The most common basic designs use either a wood core with epoxy-resin-bonded fiberglass layers on the top and bottom or a lightweight foam core with epoxy-resin-bonded fiberglass wrapped around it. There are advantages to either construction and to the almost infinite variations. The details change every year, and they will not be considered here, partly because the subject becomes too esoteric, and partly because the manufacturers' quality control is even more important than the exact construction of the ski. Fiberglass and epoxies can be nasty materials to work with, and an excellent ski one year may be a poor one the next. A reliable shop will both keep abreast of the latest constructions and advise you of the way particular skis have been holding up.

On top of the basic construction, most modern skis are covered with plastic tops and plastic or paint sidewalls, both for protection of the inside layers and for cosmetic purposes. Ski bottoms are made from a plastic, usually polyethylene, that is intended to provide a good compromise between durability, easy gliding, and a reasonable ability to hold wax for traction. Waxless skis will have a section, usually just in the center, with whatever gripping device is used. These are discussed in more detail below. Both of the basic construction techniques have been used to make very satisfactory and durable skis. In discussing skis with salespeople or perusing catalogs, remember that reliability and durability are of prime importance. One question worth asking is about the construction under the binding. Foam and soft woods do not provide a very good anchor for mounting screws, and an insert often improves the reliability of the ski.

Camber and Flex Pattern

The upward curve of the bottom of the ski is called camber. At the most basic level, it is important to insure that the ski is more or less flat on the snow when you are skiing. Skis are flexible, and if the ski were perfectly flat to begin with, your weight and that of your pack would make it sink in the center on soft snow. Skis that are bowed down this way are slow and give poor performance in all conditions. Thus, the ski should have enough camber to make it lie relatively flat when you are actually skiing. The exact camber and flex pattern of a ski are much more complex than this, however, particularly with modern ski design, which can be used to control these factors far more exactly than was possible with traditional wooden skis.

A cross-country racer, for example, usually prefers what is called a double-camber flex pattern. A ski is chosen so that during the gliding phase of the stride, the forward and rear sections of the ski lie flat on the track. These are waxed with a very smooth, fast wax. The center section of the ski, which is waxed with a *kicker* of traction wax, or which has the gripping section of the ski bottom, is built with a much stiffer camber, so that it does not come in contact with the snow at all, except when the racer kicks the ski down into the snow during the propulsive phase of the stride. The ideal flex patterns of racing skis will depend on the racer's weight, skiing style, and the power of the kick.

The double-camber flex pattern will be obvious if you compare a pair of high-performance racing skis with a pair of recreational touring skis. If you put the bottoms of the touring skis together and squeeze the two skis toward one another, they will approach each other smoothly and touch without your having to squeeze too hard. Racing skis will start the same way, but you will have to squeeze very hard to make the centers touch. Backcountry skiers sometimes like more than average stiffness at the centers of their skis, too, particu-

Mountain touring far from the roads This kind of skiing puts a premium on reliability, but much lighter equipment than this alpine touring gear now can be used without compromising safety.

larly if they have strong kicks. Most skiers are better off with a fairly smooth and easy flex pattern for wilderness skiing.

There are many other variations in stiffness and flex patterns as well, and the suitability of one or another will depend on your build, experience, the type of skiing you plan to do, and on personal preference. Heavier people need slightly stiffer skis, as do those who plan on carrying heavy packs. Longer skis of a particular brand are generally a little stiffer; they are made with heavier individuals in mind. In general, a softer ski with a smoother flex pattern is easier for the beginning and intermediate skier. Stiffer skis require stronger kicks and more skill to turn, though they will be more responsive to an expert skier.

Regardless of the overall stiffness of the ski, the tip may be relatively stiff and rigid, especially in its resistance to twisting motions (torsional rigidity). Thus, two skis may require just the same amount of force to push them all the way to the snow, but one may have a rather stiff tip while the other has a rather loose and flexible one. It is easier to learn to telemark and to ski in soft snow on a ski with a flexible tip, but an expert skier will have more control in breakable crust and on hard snow with a more rigid tip.

Edges
The edges of modern skis are of less concern than they were with wood skis. The now standard polyethylene bases form edges that are fairly effective and durable. Plastic edges chip only locally when they hit rocks, unlike the wood ones they replaced. Metal edges have some advantages, but they have probably become more popular than they deserve to be, since they add weight and expense to the ski while reducing its traction when the skier is climbing. Unless you plan to ski hardpack and windboard fairly frequently, encounter steep traverses on very hard snow, or ski in similar conditions, you will probably be better off without metal edges. Compromise experimental skis have been made with edges of harder plastic, roughly comparable to aluminum in effectiveness, but it remains to be seen whether they will be widely marketed.

If metal edges are required for touring skis, as they are for those who plan to do a lot of traveling on very hard snow, they should be quite narrow, because wax won't adhere to the metal, and no-wax climbing surfaces don't extend into them. A narrow edge is achieved by using an angled piece anchored in the ski, with only a small edge protruding. Aluminum edges are lightest, but they will not hold a really sharp edge. Higher performance, for those who feel they need it, is achieved with a steel edge, preferably one that protrudes slightly from the side of the ski so that it can be filed sharp, like a downhill ski.

Steel edges can be left in a single piece, or they can have cracks every few inches. Cracked edges usually result in a softer, more forgiving ski, and they are therefore preferable for most skiers.

Sidecut

Sidecut, or side camber, is a curvature in the side of the ski. It is much less exaggerated and less easily seen than the vertical camber. Holding a pair of skis together side by side shows the side camber. A typical backcountry touring ski might have a 65-millimeter tip, a 55-millimeter center, and a 60-millimeter tail, but there may be either more or less sidecut. The function of the sidecut is to help the skier to turn when the ski is edged into the snow. In general, wilderness touring skis should have some sidecut, but it is important to note that, unlike some other factors, the effect on performance is a subtle one. The way the skis respond and their turning characteristics will be as dependent on the flex pattern and your skiing style as they are on the sidecut. In a carved turn on hardpack, for example, the actual curvature of the edge of the ski will be dependent not only on the sidecut but on your weighting and the amount that the ski flexes under that weight.

Waxless Skis

Waxless skis have been around for a decade and have been gradually refined to present a real alternative to waxing, a subject discussed at length later in the chapter. A number of new waxless surfaces have made their appearance during the last two years, and they can be expected to be improved in the next few years, so that ski waxing may eventually disappear except in top-level racing. For the time being, however, waxless skis still have major disadvantages that persuade many wilderness skiers to stick with wax, at least through most of the year.

One important distinction in considering waxless skis is between racing and touring models. Racing skis with waxless surfaces, like their touring counterparts, have advantages in particular kinds of snow. However, racing models have a strong double camber, so that the kicker does not touch the track during the glide phase, unlike a touring ski. Touring skis also are likely to be abused more, dragged over rough surfaces, and subjected to more skidding turns. The ideal waxless gripping surfaces for racing and touring skis are therefore not always the same.

So far, three main types of waxless surfaces have been developed: mohair strips attached to the bottom of the ski, step- or fish-scale-like edges machined into the plastic bottom, and flaky crystals of mica or a similar material imbedded in the plastic bottom at a slant. Mohair strips have worked well on racing skis, but have not generally been so successful for touring and backcountry use. Steps and fish scales are the standard waxless devices; they were the first introduced, and they have been refined over the years. As the sharp edges wear down and become rounded, however, the kick becomes less effective. These surfaces also create some drag. The two hopes for the mica and similar crystal bottoms is that they will be as smooth in gliding forward as standard bottoms and that they will not wear out so quickly, since new crystals will be exposed as the bottoms are abraded down. There have been some problems with early models, and it remains to be seen whether these hopes will be realized.

So far, the waxless skis have proved to be best where waxes are weakest, in wet conditions and transition situations where the skier moves back and forth between wet and dry snow. Waxing is trickiest when the snow is wet and when it changes constantly. Waxless surfaces grip well on wet snow. For these reasons, waxless skis have been most popular among experienced skiers in those parts of the country where transition snow is common throughout the year: in the Sierra Nevada and in the Northeast, for example. They perform less well in dry, cold snow, so they have not been nearly so popular in areas like the Rockies where transition snow is common only in spring. For experienced skiers, waxless gripping areas should be comfined to the center portion of the ski.

Bindings

Standard three-pin, 75-millimeter cross-country bindings are excellent for backcountry use. They provide a positive attachment to the skis, allow easy forward touring movement, give adequate downhill control, yet are flexible enough to be quite safe for backcountry use. There are many good models, but you should choose one that is rugged and adaptable for emergency repairs. Side holes for straps are helpful, for example. The farther back the bail presses down on the front of the boot, the less likely the boot sole will be to wear out at the edges so that it can slip free. Older, wider pin bindings, such as the 79-millimeter (nordic norms refer to the width of the binding where the pins are placed) and the old four pins, have their advocates, but the 75-millimeter models have the great virtue of interchangeability, and this outweighs other minor advantages.

Some of the new narrow bindings that have been developed for racing can be used for wilderness travel as well, but the advantages and shortcomings apply mainly to the boots they are made to fit, and these will be discussed below.

Standard three-pin touring bindings These bindings are satisfactory even for demanding wilderness use if they are made sturdily. The pins in the toepiece fit into matching holes in the toe of the boot, preferably reinforced with a metal plate like the one shown. A spring holds the toe on the pins, giving torsional control of the ski but allowing the boot to flex completely for freedom of movement and for safety. A tether should be attached to the binding and the boot for use on steep slopes, in order to prevent loss of a ski in case the binding releases. A spare spring should be carried in the repair kit also.

Boots

Conventional, well-made leather touring boots serve reasonably well for wilderness skiing in most respects, so alternative possibilities will be discussed in comparison with them. Generally, an ankle-height boot made to provide good support is best, giving a little more control in downhill skiing and maneuvering with a heavy pack. If most of your skiing will be on moderate terrain, however, a lighter boot may be satisfactory. Most touring boots are made with an injection-molded sole. These are molded directly onto the edge of the leather, and they often give good service, but they cannot be repaired if they pull loose or if the sole is damaged. I prefer a conventional sewn welt, which can be resoled.

The main defect of conventional touring boots for multiday wilderness travel is that they are not very warm, particularly when you are tramping around in camp, putting up a tent or digging a cave. Many people also have trouble with cold feet when touring, particularly in cold powder snow. Several good solutions are possible. Booties are available that fit over touring boots, work with three-pin bindings, and provide insulation over the boot. The best ones extend up over the calf and substitute for gaiters as well. Good ones are made by Rivendell and Early Winters. Double boots provide an excellent but expensive solution. The inner boot can be worn in the tent or cave and makes donning of cold boots in the morning far more pleasant. A combination of double boots and overbooties is warm enough for expedition use. A third possible solution is a pair of fabric overboots to put over your boots in camp. They can also be worn in camp over down or PolarGuard booties, but they cannot be used on the trail.

Double touring boots used with light skis and pin bindings The felt liner insures warm feet and is very convenient for snow camping. The lug soles also make it possible for the camper to do moderate climbing when not on skis.

Another possible problem with conventional touring boots is encountered by climbers. Most touring boots have smooth soles, and they are not well suited for much walking, especially on slippery terrain. They are impossible for climbing. Climbing boots can be worn with specialized bindings if they are absolutely necessary, or they can be carried in the pack. For moderate climbing, a touring boot with a lug sole provides a better solution. They are available in a few single touring boots. Both models of double boots available in the U.S.—Galibier and Kastinger—are also equipped with lug soles and can be used on moderate rock and ice climbs.

In the last few years, boots for cross-country racing have increasingly been made from nylon fabric or from very light leathers and leather substitutes attached to a molded nylon sole that attaches directly to a special narrow binding. Some of the bindings are quite strong, and the two bindings are identical—there is no left or right distinction. There are some good arguments for using this same approach for wilderness boots and bindings. Leather has the virtue of durability, but it is not very warm, and packing insulation inside a boot has always presented problems of condensation, compression, and cramping of the foot. There is a good argument for using a very light boot that breathes well and won't freeze, designing this boot to provide the skiing control that is wanted, and adding insulation on the outside with booties. Some high-top boots have been introduced for this purpose by Adidas and Suverin to fit the 50- and 38-millimeter bindings.

So far, however, I don't believe that these boots really fit the needs of the wilderness traveler, though they can certainly be made to work, particularly on moderate terrain. None of these boots provides as much lateral control as good touring boots, so downhill control in heavy snow suffers. One can make up for this problem with good technique, but the skiing is less enjoyable. It is also questionable whether the soles of the present boots will hold up well enough for safe wilderness use. Because of the design, breakage presents a serious problem. It is much harder to improvise a repair than with conventional equipment. The soles of these boots are also very slippery, and the protruding toes can be a nuisance in walking. With some development specifically for wilderness use, this type of equipment may prove excellent for snow camping, but major improvements are needed first.

Poles

Touring poles for backcountry use should be durable and should have a basket large enough to give reasonable flotation and a tip that will grip hard snow well when pushing well behind the body. The curved tips on most touring poles serve both to catch the snow when the pole is extended back at an angle and to keep the pole from sticking in medium hard snow as it tilts forward. The straps and handles of conventional touring poles are also designed to allow a long pole thrust and follow-through. There are some good reasons to carry adjustable poles that convert to avalanche probes, but unfortunately none of those available are very well designed for touring.

Good poles have been made both of aluminum and epoxy-bonded

fiberglass. In either case, it is a good idea to carry a short tube of aluminum alloy tubing of the correct diameter in order to repair a broken pole.

Some poles have handles that will pull off in case the wearer is caught in an avalanche or catches the pole on a tree. If your poles are not so equipped, don't wear the straps in possible avalanche terrain or when skiing downhill in thick woods.

Straps on touring poles are not always long enough to fit easily over heavy mittens. Backcountry poles should have straps that adjust easily and that are sufficiently long.

TOURING ON SKIS

The technique of touring cross-country on skis doesn't vary much, whether one is using light touring skis or heavy, modified downhill equipment. The main difference is that the light equipment enables the skier on easy trails to make much faster progress with much lesss effort. A skier with good touring technique strides along with as much glide as possible, and this requires that the heel of his boot be free to lift off the ski. The more free play allowed the heel by the binding and the flexibility of the boot, the longer strides the skier will be able to take. For this reason, the tourer should pick the most flexible combination of boots and bindings that will also satisfy the other requirements of the terrain on which he will ski.

The technique of getting a glide at the end of each step is much easier to learn than to explain. The skier plants one ski and the opposite pole, leans forward slightly, and pushes with both the foot and the pole. The other leg comes forward rapidly to throw extra power into the stride and the skier's weight is shifted to this ski as the push is finished. There is a glide, and then the procedure is repeated with the other ski and pole. The amount of glide that can be achieved is quite variable. With light touring skis and a day pack, some glide can often be gotten even on uphill stretches, and the speed that can be reached on packed trails is phenomenal. On the other hand, with heavy skis, a heavy pack, and unbroken snow, the skier usually gets little glide even on the flat. Under such circumstances he settles for a walk or, better, a swinging stride.

You have to have some traction when you plant your ski, otherwise it will simply slip backward when you push forward, especially when climbing a hill. This traction is normally achieved by applying an appropriate wax to the bottom of the ski. Cross-country waxes are chosen to be soft enough at the temperature of the snow so that snow crystals will make tiny impressions in the surface of the wax, producing a high static friction. At the same time the wax must be hard enough to run forward in the snow. No one wax will satisfy these conditions for all types and temperatures of snow, so the tourer must carry a number of waxes. The technique of waxing will be discussed in more detail later in the chapter.

Basic touring technique can be improved a good deal by skiing hard occasionally without a pack on a packed trail or, better yet, on a prepared track. Practicing your kick-and-glide at full speed is the best way to develop a fluid motion and effective kicking and follow-through with both the arms and legs.

WAXING YOUR SKIS

In touring, the purpose of wax is to provide enough traction so that you can push along, even up moderate slopes, while still allowing your skis to slide on the snow without sticking. These seemingly contradictory properties can be achieved if the wax layer is soft enough to allow the crystals of snow to form tiny indentations in the wax when the ski is planted, yet hard enough to melt a thin layer of snow into a water film with the friction of sliding. This water film forms the actual sliding surface. If the wax layer is too hard or too thin, the indentations will not be numerous enough or deep enough to hold your pushing ski. If, on the other hand, the wax layer is too soft or too thick, your skis will not slide forward, and clumps of snow will begin to stick to them.

These principles form the basis for waxing. Waxing is an art, since there are many varieties of snow and some mixed snow conditions are very tricky, but the essentials of waxing are not really too difficult to learn. You should remember that the colder the snow for which you are waxing, the harder the wax should be to produce the necessary friction. Warmer snow will require a softer wax to enable your ski to obtain purchase. Snow will never be warmer than thirty-two degrees Fahrenheit, of course, since this is the freezing point of water. Under melting conditions, however, the snow layer will become wetter and better lubricated, and this requires a softer wax to develop adequate static friction between snow and ski.

The form of the snow, as well as its temperature, should influence your choice of a wax. Dry, starlike crystals with many fine points will make many more indentations in the wax than old, rounded pellets at the same temperature. Thus, fine crystals will require a harder wax or thinner wax layer than the pellets in order to allow the ski to slide properly, or, alternatively, a thicker wax layer or softer wax will be used to allow the rounded pellets to bite deeply enough. In general, a thicker layer of wax tends to have the effect of a slightly softer wax.

Types of Wax

There are three main types of wax: base waxes, binders, and running waxes. The running waxes are the ones that we have just been discussing, waxes you apply to meet particular conditions. Base waxes and pine tar are preparations that protect the bottoms of wooden-soled skis and form a surface to which the running waxes can bond. They are not used for modern plastic-bottomed skis. Binder waxes are special waxes used to provide a better bonding surface between base and running waxes so that the running waxes will wear longer. They are useful in preparing polyethylene bottoms for waxing, particularly with new skis.

Terminology

The beginner is likely to have more trouble coping with the various systems of labeling waxes and of describing the snow conditions for which they are used than he will have with the actual problem of waxing. Most modern development in touring has taken place in the Scandinavian countries, and most touring equipment is made there, as are most touring waxes. Thus, many waxing terms have been borrowed from one or another of the Scandinavian languages, but the meaning of a borrowed term is often different for each user. I think the novice is best advised to stay away from all these complications until he has a basic familiarity with waxing.

In this book the only distinctions made are between *running waxes,* which provide the actual surface contacting the snow, *base waxes,* meaning any preparation intended to be applied on the bare surface of a wooden-soled ski, and *binder waxes,* which are intended for use between a base and the running wax. Running waxes are divided into two categories that can be easily separated by the beginner: *cake waxes,* which are packed in little cylinders and rubbed on, and *tube waxes,* which come packed in containers like toothpaste tubes, and are spread on the ski surface like peanut butter. Binder wax and some running waxes are also available in aerosol cans.

Glider Waxes

Glider waxes are cake and liquid waxes used by racers on the tips and tails of skis in conjunction with a kicker of normal wax in the center, in order to improve the glide. They are not needed for touring, but a harder wax is often used for the same purpose.

Base Preparation

New skis with polyethylene bases often do not hold wax very well at first. Adherence improves as the pores are filled with wax. Some skis come from the factory with the bottom already roughed. If yours are perfectly smooth, rough the surface first by sanding lightly with 180-grit sandpaper. Then melt in either a binder wax or a hard cake wax like Swix Polar with an iron or a torch the whole length of the ski. You can use glider wax on the tip and tail if you like. If you use binder wax, follow it with a hard cake wax. Make sure the surface is heated well, so that the wax penetrates the pores. This treatment should insure that your regular waxing bonds well to the ski bottom.

Binder Waxes

Binder waxes are not essential, but they make a normal waxing hold longer. Regular waxes must be used to cover binder wax. You can either put binder on the whole length of the ski, following this up with a hard wax, or put binder only in the center where you apply your kicker. Binder wax should be applied in a very thin layer and corked down well or smoothed with an iron or torch.

Running Waxes

Because regular tarring or base waxing is no longer needed since the advent of plastic bottoms, the art of waxing now consists almost completely of choosing the proper running waxes. This has to be done at the beginning of each tour and sometimes several more times during the day. There is no point in trying to guess the waxing conditions before you leave home, though some skiers like to iron or torch in a hard wax (one intended for very cold weather) before leaving home. On a cold day, they start skiing with it and see how it works. If the snow calls for a softer wax, they put it on over the first.

It's not really too difficult to acquire a good basic waxing technique. Start off by buying a beginning kit of waxes from one manufacturer and stick with these same waxes until you know their characteristics well. Then you can start adding a few more waxes from the same manufacturer or trying a couple from another company. Don't do too much switching around at first, though. No two lines are quite the same, and if you change early in the game, you won't know whether differences in performance are due to your method of application, your skiing technique, the snow conditions, or the wax. Several manufacturers make up beginners' kits, and these are the easiest way to start. Typically, they include basic sets of waxes, a scraper-spreader, and a cork or foam rubbing block. The waxes can be replenished as you use them. Alternatively, if you can't find a made-up kit, choose one brand of wax, and get a basic selection like one of the ones discussed below.

Basic Wax Kits

The selections of waxes below are intended to give you an idea of what you need to buy in order to make a beginning at touring. Other brands will do as well, but those listed are the most commonly available in the United States. A kit from a manufacturer is also a good way of getting a starting selection. Before buying waxes, look at the instructions on the packages and compare them with the conditions in your own area. Someone beginning touring in the Rockies in midwinter, for example, might wish to buy a couple of extra cold snow waxes and drop the wet snow ones. You should stay with one brand, though, and learn the characteristics of the basic waxes before gradually adding others.

The selections listed below are not quite equivalent, but any of them should enable the beginner to wax adequately, if not ideally, for most conditions. The cake waxes are listed first, then the tube waxes, each roughly in order from colder to warmer snow conditions.

SWIX	cake waxes: Green, Extra Blue, Purple, Red tube waxes: Blue, Red
REX	cake waxes: Green, Blue, Purple, Red tube waxes: Blue, Violet
ØSTBYE	cake waxes: Mix (also in aerosol), Mixolinvox, Klistervox tube waxes: Skare, Klister
BRATLIE	cake waxes: Silke, Blandingsføre, Klistervox tube waxes: Skareklister, Våtsnø Klister

Judging Snow Conditions

Since a particular wax is designed to handle a particular range of snow conditions, the first and most important thing you must learn about waxing is how to judge snow conditions. Directions on wax packages most often refer to "new" or "old" snow, to the air temperature, and sometimes to special characteristics—crust, powder, and so on. All these are necessarily subjective and imprecise ways of describing conditions. How old is "old"? Well, it depends on other circumstances. Even the temperature, which seems straightforward enough, is only an indication of what snow conditions are likely to be, since wind and previous temperatures affect both falling snow and the cover already on the ground.

In general, the newer the snow, the more sharp points the crystals are likely to have, and the harder your wax will have to be to prevent sticking. Colder snow also calls for harder wax. As snow grows older, the points disappear and the snow crystals grow rounded, and a softer wax must be used. Wetter snow, which is better lubricated, also makes softer wax necessary. Warm temperatures tend both to make the sharp points on snow crystals disappear more quickly and (if they are above freezing) to provide more of a lubricating film; cold temperatures have the opposite effect. Also, as I mentioned earlier in the chapter, thicker layers of wax tend to have the effect of a softer wax, thinner layers the effect of a harder wax.

Speaking of the hardness of a wax is an oversimplification, but it gives a good rough idea of the characteristics of different waxes. The novice should remember that "hardness" refers to the state of the wax in touring conditions, after it is applied to the ski and is at the temperature of the snow layer. Tube waxes designed for crusty snow, for example, are sticky fluids when squeezed from the tube, but they form very tough layers on the bottoms of the skis.

For practical purposes, there are a few simple tests that will tell you quite a bit about snow conditions. The first and most obvious question is: "Is it snowing?" If it is snowing, you are obviously faced with "new" snow. If snow is not falling, look at the snow, kick it, walk in it. If the snow has begun to consolidate and the layer holds together, either holding you up or leaving distinct footprints, which don't tend to collapse at the sides, it is becoming metamorphized "old" snow, and a softer wax will be called for than for new snow at the same temperatures. In very cold weather, the snow may remain powdery and fluffy for weeks, while in warmer weather metamorphosis takes place very quickly.

Next, scoop up some snow with mittens on. Look at it. Is it crusty, granular, powdery? Blow on it. Dry powder snow fluffs away like flour. Squeeze it into a snowball. Very cold, dry snow, whether it is powdery or granular, just won't stick together at all. Older dry snow that is not quite so cold but is not icy or granular will form snowballs with difficulty, but they fall apart if you squeeze the wrong way. Damp snow will form snowballs easily, and if the snow is really wet it will pack tightly and leave your mittens wet.

By this time you should know enough to wax for the snow condition that you have observed. You pull your wax kit out of the pack and set the skis up against the car and begin to puzzle through the descriptions on the labels. You will probably find that the store clerk placed the price sticker on the English directions, leaving you a choice of Norwegian, French, and Swahili.

Which Wax?

New snow generally calls for one of the cake waxes—the colder the snow, the harder the wax. A manufacturer will have one, two, or three waxes intended for dry, new snow, with the differences usually broken down by air temperature. As the snow gets older, the same wax change is required as for new snow of a higher temperature—a thicker coat or a softer wax. If, for example, you go out touring during a storm with temperatures of around twenty-five degrees, you may find that things go very well with Swix or Rex Green, which are fairly hard waxes. The next day, with temperatures about the same, you might find that the snow had settled enough to prevent your getting good grip with Green, and you would then go to Blue, which is somewhat softer.

Along with the wax or group of waxes intended for new dry snow, the manufacturer will have a group of softer cake waxes intended for damp or wet, new snow and for settled snow, ranging from dry snow near the freezing point to sopping wet. Each brand often includes quite a number of waxes in this category because these conditions are the most difficult for which to wax. The beginner should probably start by experimenting with only a couple of waxes in this group.

The tube waxes, or klisters, are intended almost exclusively for older snow. The method of application naturally produces a fairly thick layer of wax, so tube waxes cannot be used for dry powder snow, in which they would stick badly. Tube waxes follow the same range as the cake waxes; however there are some that form a hard layer for cold snow, and progressively softer ones are used as the snow gets wetter. The hard tube waxes are very tough once they are applied. They are used for crusty, icy, and dry, hard, granular conditions, when the thin layer of a cake wax does not grip well and wears off rapidly. Softer tube waxes are used for old snow as it becomes progressively wetter. Occasionally, these soft tube waxes are useful for very wet, new-fallen snow.

After you have inspected the snow conditions and looked over the labels on your waxes you should have some idea which wax to use; you should at least have narrowed the possibilities down to two or three waxes. If the wind is whipping along at temperatures not much above zero and the new powder is lying on the ground to a depth of a couple of feet, you won't be considering any of your tube waxes or the cake waxes intended for thawing conditions. This will leave you no more than two or three waxes to choose from. There are a few general rules for choosing and applying these that save a lot of trouble.

The first rule in picking a wax is to start with a thin coat of the hardest wax you think will work. The reason for this method is simple: One can always apply a second coat of this wax or a coat of a softer wax over the first layer to give more grip, but if a harder wax is needed because of sticking, it is usually necessary to completely scrape the ski, a tedious business. The rule may not always be followed: If the weather is getting warmer, for instance, you may choose a wax that will maintain its grip in slightly warmer snow; but it is often best even in these circumstances to add a little soft wax for grip later in the morning than to risk sticking by using too soft a wax to start off.

The second rule is to test adequately before adding more wax. Don't expect the wax to grip properly until you have skied a quarter mile or so. The elasticity of the wax does not develop until you have skied some distance. You should get some grip right away, but you may find that a slight slip at the push in your stride disappears after you have gone a few hundred yards. If your skis are sticking badly, though, you may as well start over, since things will get worse rather than better.

After you have checked your first wax, you may want to add more to get a better grip. Unless you greatly misjudged the snow condition and found that your skis were not gripping at all, you should add more wax of the same or the next softer grade in the center of the ski only. This will give extra grip with less danger of causing sticking. If you find that you still need more grip, you may want to continue this second layer to cover the middle three feet of each ski.

A third important rule is to learn to anticipate conditions. This is a matter of experience, attention to maps and weather forecasts, and luck. Some changes should be obvious. If you are starting before sunrise on a beautiful spring day, you may expect the air to get warmer and the snow softer. On the other hand, if you are starting up a climb of several thousand feet you should anticipate snow conditions generally reflecting the colder conditions and stronger winds that occur at high altitudes. In either case, it would be worthwhile to try to pick a wax that might work in both types of snow. You should look around the area before waxing, checking for variable snow conditions. In windy areas during cold snaps, you may find that conditions alternate between hard crust or windslab and drifted powder. In this situation, if you looked only at the crust and used a tube wax, you would probably find yourself sticking in the powder. Waxing for changing conditions and anticipating those conditions is part of the art of waxing— it is a very tricky business—but the first step to mastery is to be alert to possible changes and watch for their signs.

Applying Waxes

Waxes are usually most easily applied in warm rooms, preferably with accessories like solvents and blowtorches. All this is unfortunately not of much use to the wilderness tourer, who usually has no warm room available even at the beginning of the tour, when he is likely to be standing out in the early-morning cold beside some highway, anxious to get off before he freezes from standing around. In actual touring conditions, body warmth is usually the best available; any extra heat beyond that must be supplied by friction. Some tourers do carry a light blowtorch, a waxing iron that uses tablets for heating, or use their cooking stove to the same end, but usually the only fuel used is elbow grease. Cake waxes are rubbed on in a thin layer and then smoothed out by rubbing with a foam or cork block or with the heel of your hand. Care is necessary with the latter method, since a blister will be raised pretty quickly on a city-softened hand. Hand rubbing of skis with steel edges should be done with extreme care. Tube waxes should be spread on with the stick provided, with a spreader-scraper, or with a putty knife.

With modern skis, the skier usually puts on only a kicker of wax in the center of the ski, leaving the rest of the ski unwaxed or covered with a smooth coat of hard wax. Experienced skiers generally use kickers ranging in length from six inches to two feet. Beginners will probably want to use about three feet of wax. If you are adding a softer wax to get just a little more traction, however, you may want to start with only a foot or so of the second wax. In wet snow, for example, if you are getting some traction from Swix Purple and want just a little more climb, try a few dabs of Red right under your foot.

Application of the softer cake waxes and the tube waxes is easier if they are kept near the body for warmth. This is especially true of the tougher tube waxes, which are almost impossible to squeeze out when they are cold. If you forget to keep them warm you may have to get out the stove and heat the front of the tube. The harder cake waxes are usually easier to use when they are cold. Incidentally, if you are carrying the tube waxes in a pocket—or anywhere else, for that matter—keep them wrapped in a good plastic bag, since there is no stickier substance known to man, and the tubes always leak. The tube waxes are usually smoothed with the spreader or the heel of the hand, since bits of cork tend to stick in the wax if a rubbing block is used. A putty knife makes a good spreader. The skis should be dry and free of any snow before they are waxed, and they should be allowed to stand a few minutes after waxing. Sticking problems are likely if snow gets mixed into the wax. If you do have a chance to wax the skis where it's warm, make sure they cool before use without getting snow on them; otherwise the bottoms will freeze up.

When you are going from a softer to a harder wax, it is almost always necessary to scrape the ski clean before applying the new wax. A combination scraper-spreader works, as do any number of individualistic instruments from putty knives to implements that look more like the tools of an assassin than a ski tourer. The job is easier if you use some solvent. Several are available where waxes are sold, though almost any solvent like gasoline will work. Trichlorethane, which can be purchased in hardware stores, is the best inexpensive solvent.

Whatever the wax, remember to spread it or rub it on in thin layers and to smooth it well. If you need a thicker layer for grip, use two or three thin layers instead of one thick one. Thick layers tend to be lumpy, and lumpy wax invites freezing and sticking. Hard waxes should be rubbed well until they are smooth. Squeeze soft waxes on in thin lines before spreading them into the smoothest and thinnest layer you can manage.

Waxing Problems

There are some snow conditions that are particularly tricky and a few that are just plain nightmares. I think the worst is a thin layer of very wet snow that has fallen over cold, dry powder. The skis get wet as you slide them over the top layer of snow, and when weight is put on them they sink into the cold powder and freeze up. After a few steps in this (you never do get a glide), each of your skis has about ten or fifteen pounds of snow stuck to the bottom. This is a difficult condition, and I know of no really satisfactory solution. If you have made the mistake of using a soft wax for the wet snow, this must first be removed. A downhill wax or plain paraffin should be applied for most of the length of the ski, with perhaps a thin layer of fairly hard climbing wax in the middle for grip. Try to use a stride that keeps the skis moving; they will have less chance of sticking if they don't stay in one spot on the snow very long. When the icing gets bad, stop and rub the iced spots with the downhill wax. You may be able to do this quickly without removing the ski.

Another difficult condition occurs when wet snow is falling because of a high layer of warm air, while the air temperature around you is below freezing. Skis tend to ice up in these conditions when they become wet and are chilled by the air. Try not to lift the skis off the snow at all in these conditions and keep them moving as much as possible.

The problem of anticipating changing conditions has already been mentioned. There are far too many possibilities to discuss here, but one of the most common occurs in mountain touring, when one normally encounters colder snow with increasing altitude. A couple of thin layers of wax that is too hard for the condition at the lower altitude can be applied, with one thin kicker of a softer wax to finish off the job. Much of the softer wax will probably have worn off when you reach colder snow and you have a good chance of not having to stop and rewax.

Another of the most common changing conditions is the softening of the snow during the day. This is an easy condition to wax for, since you simply have to add a bit of softer wax if your skis stop gripping.

Some of the uses of standard downhill wax or paraffin have been mentioned already, and the tourer should always carry a small lump. This can also be used to help prevent snow from sticking in various places under the heel, for example. It is most useful to help solve icing problems on the ski bottoms. Just rub the icing spots with the hard downhill wax. Finally, it can be used on top of many of the tougher touring waxes for a fast downhill run. It will tend to wear off by the end of a long downhill stretch. Don't try this over the softer touring waxes; the downhill wax is too hard to rub over them.

CLIMBERS

Where a tour involves a great deal of steep climbing, especially with heavy packs, it is useful to be able to climb steeper slopes than climbing waxes permit. Under these conditions, which occur mainly in mountain touring, it is useful to have a pair of climbers, also known as "skins," because they were originally made of sealskin. The sealskin variety no longer exists, and climbers are now made of a synthetic fur. In either case, the climber is a long strip of material covered on one side with fur-like hairs. It is attached to the bottom of the ski with the bristles running toward the tail of the ski. The ski will slide forward fairly easily with the grain of the fur but will not slide backward even on hills that are quite steep.

There are several ways to attach the climbers to the skis. One of the best is to use adhesive, so that no hardware is required to hold the climber to the ski except at the tip. Climbers of this type come with the adhesive already on, and it is renewed from a tube every three or four uses. It will stick to any reasonably dry ski. Since these climbers use no hardware, only a loop needs to be sewn at the front end, and I make the climbers for touring skis by buying a set in alpine width and cutting them in half lengthwise to reduce the cost. The only defect of the adhesive-backed climbers is that applying them can be a problem if they are being used repeatedly in bad weather, as on some expeditions. In these situations it may be better to carry climbers that attach with hardware.

Avoid skins that attach with canvas straps. They freeze easily, interfere with edging, are soon cut through, and the climbers tend to roll off to one side. Much better are skins that attach to the ski with rigid metal fittings, which hold the skins on the skis quite effectively. Two types are now widely available. Trima climbers use matching

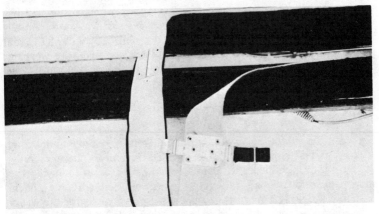

Two types of skins, actually made of synthetic fur On top is the Trima rail type; below is the Vinersa rigid strap.

rails and grooves on the skis and climbers. This type has several great advantages: The skins are held on very well and will not tend to slip off; they are fairly simple to put on and can be taken off without removing the pack or skis; they will not slip from side to side; and the steel edges of the skis are completely free when they are needed for edging. The Trimas have the disadvantage of requiring that you install all the fittings on both climbers and skis and that holes be drilled in the skis.

The second currently available climber with metal fittings is the Vinersa. It is fixed to the ski with straps like older climbers, but instead of being made of canvas the straps are metal. The metal straps are not cut by steel edges, of course, and their rigidity eliminates the tendency of the skins to roll off the skis. The Vinersas have an advantage over the Trimas in not requiring that your skis be drilled and in having fittings that are already attached. They are not held to the skis quite so rigidly, however, and you may find that the rear bracket tends to slip off your skis unless you make some modification. Finally, one of the straps on the Vinersa skin is placed in a spot that coincides with the position of some bindings, so it may not work on your skis. Make sure to check this before you bend the rear brackets to fit your skis, in case you want to return the skins. In either case, you must be sure that the hardware and its placement are compatible with your skis. Most climbers are made for alpine skis, and even if you cut down the skin, the hardware may be too wide to fit your skis.

Any type of climber will enable you to climb much steeper slopes than climbing waxes, but you cannot glide or sideslip with skins. For this reason, they never really replace climbing waxes. Even in mountain touring, a party equipped with skins may want to use touring waxes on long rolling sections of the trip or on long, gentle climbs. Waxing enables you to glide down short downhill sections and to slide your skis forward with much less effort than when you are wearing climbers.

BEGINNING SKIING TECHNIQUE

Skiing in the wilderness is quite different from either downhill skiing on commercial slopes or touring on well-used cross-country trails, though it is much closer to cross-country than it is to following the snow packer down a carefully manicured slope. You will have a pack, probably weighing around thirty pounds if you are out for the weekend. Even the accomplished downhill skier will find challenges he didn't know existed when he tries to make a downhill run with all that extra inertia strapped to his back. The snow will be unbroken and may change condition every few yards. To top it off, the ski patrol isn't waiting at the top of the hill to whisk you off if you take a flying somersault. You will quickly develop a conservative technique if you give a little thought to the consequences of a broken leg.

Let's start at the beginning, though. If the terrain is easy, moderate ski tours can be attempted even by a group of beginning skiers if they have already mastered the art of winter camping. It's better to do a few day tours first, if possible. If not, plan to camp fairly close to the roadhead.

The first thing to do after getting out of your car or cabin is to wax your skis. Chances are that the beginning of the tour is either flat or uphill, so you won't have to worry about warming up. Beginners should spend an hour or so getting used to the feel of walking on skis before putting the pack on. Push off with one ski and the opposite pole, and try to get as much glide as you can with each stride. Get your rear leg moving forward during the push; then as it comes forward it will put extra power behind your glide. When you put your weight down on the foot that is about to push, plant it on the snow and leave it there, pushing off with a smooth thrust. A jerky push will break the ski loose, especially going uphill. The position for touring is more like jogging than walking since your weight is a bit forward, but the tread is light, not heavy, and the glide is smooth, not choppy.

If you really aren't getting any traction when you plant your skis you may have to put on a softer wax. A soft wax can usually be put on right over the harder one. Start off by just putting some on in the middle, under your foot; this may be enough, and if it starts to stick, you won't have as much to scrape off. If your skis are sticking badly, you need a harder wax, and this cannot usually be put on over the soft one. Before you stop for scraping and rewaxing, make sure you can't prevent the sticking with just a steady pace. Snow will stick to the bottom of a ski much faster when you are standing still, and an even, slow rhythm will often solve the sticking problem. You should also check to see that the wax layer is smooth and thin; sticking will occur sooner on a thick, lumpy wax job.

As soon as you feel comfortable on level terrain, try climbing some bumps, and experiment a little to find out how steep a slope you can climb. Vigorous use of the poles will increase the angle. Even a beginner can often manage a respectable slope with waxes, and improved climbing and waxing technique will help quite a bit. You cannot expect to climb the slopes that a cross-country racer would, however, Your pack will keep you back and so will a sensible conservation of energy and dry clothing; sweat and exhaustion are best saved for short training jaunts.

Turns

The most common turn used by the ski tourer is the step turn. The skier simply picks up the tip of the ski on the side toward which he wants to turn, points it over a comfortable distance, and follows with the other ski, repeating the operation as many times as necessary to achieve the turn. When the skier becomes more practiced, this operation is combined with a skating stride to achieve smooth turns without losing stride, especially in skiing downhill with touring bindings. This turn in its simplest form is easy to learn, being almost instinctive. It is a bit harder to perform while the skier is sliding downhill, the trick being to bring the second ski over quickly, before the two have traveled far in different directions.

Step turn In a step turn, the skier simply lifts the toe of his ski and moves it in the direction of the turn. The other ski follows.

A more difficult turn for one who has never learned it is the kick turn. This is a skill that should be mastered immediately by the beginner, since it is used to extract oneself from all kinds of difficulties from steep slopes to fence crossings. The turn is more easily illustrated than described, so the reader is referred to the pictures of the execution of the turn. It will take a few tries to get the knack of this turn, but the advantage is that once mastered it can be executed easily even on very steep slopes, allowing the skier to proceed down or up in a series of traverses linked by kick turns. Incidentally, you really don't have to wait until you're on the snow to learn a kick turn. It can be learned and practiced in your back yard on any surface that won't damage your skis; a good lawn or an old rug will do. A kick turn can be used to get over any obstacle up to crotch height.

Kick turn to right The skier faces right. Left pole is near the front of skis, right pole is behind and very close to skis.

Right foot is kicked up and the heel of the ski is planted well forward, close to the left ski.

Right ski is swung down parallel to the left and facing in the opposite direction.

Weight is transferred to the right ski.

Left pole is replanted and the left ski brought around to complete the turn.

The skier ends facing in the opposite direction. On slopes the turn should be executed *away* from the slope.

Skating

Skating is a useful technique that may already be known by experienced downhill skiers. Practice it after you are fairly confident and stable on your skis. It is easiest to learn with a slight downhill slope that is not quite steep enough to allow you to slide down without an extra push. The pushing ski is angled out from the other at an angle of perhaps 30° and is edged into the snow, while both the poles are planted as far ahead as the skier can reach and still get a good push. The skier pushes off with his poles and his foot at the same time, carrying the push as far as possible. At the end of the push the arms and the pushing leg will be well behind the skier and the body will be leaning well forward over the running ski to counterbalance the leg. The skier takes as much glide as possible and then brings his back ski, still in the air, forward next to his running ski. His weight then shifts as he pushes off with the second ski and both poles. At first, your skating stride will be rather anemic, but as you learn to lean out farther with a longer push, you will find that the skating stride can be very powerful.

The skating stride is generally only used for short stretches. The standard touring stride is just as effective over long stretches and is much less tiring, but the skating stride is quite useful for some special circumstances such as picking up speed on a gradual downhill section and maintaining speed over short hills.

Double Poling

Double poling is similar to the skating stride in that both poles are used for a vigorous push, except that a normal kick is used rather than an angled one. The kick is vigorous, throwing the body forward for a push with the arms. Double poling is a standard racing technique, but it takes too much energy for extended use on tours, so only one or two strokes are commonly used to get over the top of a hill or to pick up speed.

Climbing

As previously mentioned, the best way to climb a slope is to just ski up it, using the traction provided by your wax. The steepness of the slope you can go up in this way will increase as you gain experience, but the upper limit is somewhere around fifteen or twenty degrees. As long as the slope is open enough to permit traversing, the normal method of climbing is simply to cut across the slope going upward at the maximum angle that your wax and digging the edges of your skis into the slope will permit. Occasionally, the direction of the traverse is reversed by a kick turn.

On short, steep sections of narrow trails either a herringbone or a sidestep may be used, the sidestep being much less tiring. In the herringbone the skier faces straight up the slope, his skis in a V with the tails together, one slightly above the other, the inside edges of the skis dug into the slope and the poles dug in behind the skis for support. The herringboner then walks up the slope, maintaining the V. The steeper and more slippery the slope, the wider the V must be and the more the edges and the poles must be dug into the snow. An accidental slip while climbing with the herringbone is most undignified, unless you have mastered the art of skiing backward.

The sidestep is less tiring, and it is generally preferred by the tourer. The skier simply stands across the slope, his ski edges dug into the slope on the uphill side as much as necessary to prevent slipping. He steps up with the uphill ski and then brings the downhill ski up to meet it. This step is best used in combination with an uphill traverse if the width of the slope permits: The skier works up diagonally with both a sidestep and a forward slide. Occasional kick turns will change the direction of edging and provide relief for the feet as well as keeping the skier on course. When edging becomes tiring, the climber can rest his feet by planting his downhill pole and allowing the skis to slide down onto it, allowing a halt without edging.

For long, steep slopes, climbers and steel edges on the skis may be helpful. The procedures are similar to those described above, except that a much steeper angle may be pursued. When some members of the party are using climbers and others are climbing on waxed skis, the member breaking trail should keep his angle of climb low enough for all to follow; otherwise the work of trail breaking will have to be duplicated.

Downhill Technique

The novice skier must pick up downhill technique from experience. As your balance and confidence improve, you will be able to handle more and more difficult runs with confidence. On moderate downhills, particularly on trails, step turns are perhaps the most frequently used maneuvers. A pack makes things considerably more difficult, so it is helpful to learn some of the basics on a few day tours before you try to descend steep trails with a heavy pack.

The convert from downhill skiing will be a little thrown off at first by the extra complication of the pack and the fact that the heels are not tied down. All of the familiar downhill turns can be accomplished on touring skis, however, once you have learned to make allowances.

The beginner can get down open slopes that are too steep for his technique by either sideslipping—using the edges of the skis for a brake and then allowing a controlled slip to occur—or by traversing back and forth with kick turns in between. A bigger problem occurs on steep, forested trails. To handle these, the basic maneuvers that need to be learned are the snowplow and the pole drag. Downhill skiers will already know how to snowplow. To snowplow, spread the tails of your skis apart and keep the tips close together. This V will slow your descent. To brake more, push your knees together so that your ski edges are forced into the snow and spread the tails farther apart. Once you have mastered slowing down this way, get out on an open slope and practice snowplow turns. By edging one ski more than the other you can steer in whatever direction you like.

A pole brake can be used separately or in conjunction with a snow-plow on any slope, but both are particularly useful in descending steep, narrow chutes. Grab both handles in one hand, hold the poles on the other side of your body and grasp them with the other hand two-thirds of the way down, and lean on the baskets to make a brake.

Snowplow In a snowplow the tails of the skis are pushed apart. The skier's knees are pushed in slightly, forcing the inside edges of the skis into the snow. Steered turns are easy to make.

IMPROVING YOUR SKIING

The techniques of advanced skiing on light skis with pin bindings deserve a whole book themselves and can only be touched on here. All of the standard techniques of downhill skiing can be mastered on skinny skis, including linked parallel turns, wedeln, and so on. In general, parallel techniques cannot be used in snow that is very heavy or in breakable crust, because edge control is more sensitive with touring skis. Parallel techniques are easiest on hardpack, packed powder, and powder skiing. The easiest way to learn quickly is to practice skiing at a regular downhill area, so that a lot of practice can be packed into a single day. A good skier on touring skis can easily handle expert runs at a downhill area, but don't try them your first time out.

Similarly, the most efficient way to improve your touring technique is to spend a weekend concentrating on technique at a cross-country center with prepared tracks. Occasional participation in cross-country citizens' races is fun and does a lot for your basic stride.

The most important turn for the backcountry skier is one that goes back to an earlier era of skiing—the telemark turn. The telemark is both the most satisfying turn to do on light skis and the most versatile. It is ideal in steep, deep powder, for swinging around the trees, but it can also be used in crud and on hardpack or steep spring corn. With light skis it can be used in a wider range of conditions than parallel turns.

The telemark is a steered turn accomplished by pushing one ski ahead, knee only slightly bent, dropping down somewhat on the rear knee, and canting the front leg inward slightly to steer the turn. The skis are very close together, the arms raised and out for balance. The two skis effectively act like one long curved ski. Balance is the main problem. The exact weighting depends somewhat on individual style and on conditions. In deep powder the front ski is farther forward and carries most of the weight at the beginning of the turn. On hard snow the weight is more evenly distributed and the angle of the front ski more exaggerated, while the legs are closer together.

Telemark The telemark is the most versatile turn for skiing downhill on light skis. The rear heel must lift easily, one reason this turn faded from the alpine repertory as more rigid bindings came into vogue. The turn is easiest to learn in powder snow.

Telemark on hard spring snow The telemark position is easier to see in this photo of a tour skier on hard spring snow. Here he has just completed one turn and is starting to advance his left ski for a turn to his right across the fall line. Tight form is necessary on hard bumpy snow like this.

Around across the fall line The same turn as the skier comes around across the fall line. Note how his right knee has dropped; his right tip is bouncing up slightly on a bump. In linked turns, the torso should remain facing down the fall line, as it does in parallel skiing downhill.

Telemarks are somewhat more difficult for ex-downhill skiers to learn, because they tend to go into a half-snowplow, rather than bringing the front ski well forward and bending the back knee. The easiest way to learn the turn is to stand at the top of a short, steep slope of powder, push off straight down, and push the front ski well forward. Tilt your front knee in a little and hold the position. You will turn. Keep practicing until you can turn across the fall line both ways, and then start linking turns. Work into more difficult snow, and you will be on your way to advanced skiing.

9 | Finding Your Way

A snowy landscape presents many route-finding problems that are not encountered by the summer traveler. Obviously, if you are going into wilderness areas in winter you need to be skillful enough to find your way. This is true whether you are going on a two-week trip or an afternoon ramble; many fatal incidents involving lost people have occurred near roads and dwellings. It is quite possible to wander for days within a mile of the nearest road. Short trips may require less elaborate preparation than long ones, but the winter traveler must still have some method of route finding, particularly since a night in the open is a much more serious matter in winter than in summer.

Many experienced mild-weather backpackers are used to finding their way by simply following trails, using signposts or guidebooks as direction finders at intersections. In many areas this technique is so effective that there is no real need for walkers to develop the skill of finding their way without blazes, cairns, and tracks. This method is rarely adequate in winter, since snow often covers the familiar trail signs. Even when a summer trail can be followed for a time, it may be obscured a few miles farther on, or a fresh snow in the night may obliterate it. For example, you may successfully follow the line of a trail through thick woods but lose it completely above timberline.

The most common mistake made by novices in the winter is reliance on their own tracks as a means of finding the way back to their point of departure. The tracks make such an obvious and comforting line that one relies on them without even thinking about it. Unfortunately, fresh or windblown snow can completely cover them in minutes or even seconds, leaving you at a complete loss concerning your whereabouts.

The way to avoid this problem is to develop the habit of always knowing where you are. This injunction may have different meanings in different situations. Sometimes it is essential to know your exact location at all times, keeping a record of compass bearings and distances. In another situation it suffices to know that you are in a certain valley or just to know the general direction and distance in traveling

165

time you've gone from some sort of boundary. The important thing is the habit of constant awareness of your position and understanding of what you need to know in order to find your way in a particular area.

LEARNING TO LOOK

In order to find your way around the wilderness in winter, you must first develop some skill in observing your surroundings. We all have this skill in some environments—we have learned, for example, where to look for street signs in the city—but navigation in snowy woods or mountains requires that we look for quite different things than most of us are used to noticing. In fact, different kinds of wilderness often require looking for different signposts.

Many routine tricks are part of keeping yourself oriented. One of them is looking backward as you go along. Remembering landmarks as they look when you are going into the woods may do you no good in finding your way back out; the trail tends to look very different when you are looking at it from the opposite direction. Hence, you should develop the habit of looking back frequently, memorizing landmarks that might help you retrace your steps. This is worthwhile even if you are not planning on returning by the same route. You might have to go back the same way in the event of trouble.

The habit of looking backward is particularly important at various kinds of junctions. If, for instance, you are going up one of a number of gullies to a long ridge and then turning right, the intersection with the ridge is obvious when you are coming out of the gully, and you are likely to go on without giving further thought to the matter except for a feeling of gratitude that the hard climbing is over. Coming back, however, there are likely to be half a dozen gullies heading off to the left, and unless you have foreseen the problem you will have difficulty in deciding which one to follow. The time to meet the problem is on the way in, when you should carefully note the distinguishing features of the gully you came up.

Another similar trick of observation is to make your landmarks as weatherproof as possible. While this is only feasible to a limited degree, it is a method that should be kept constantly in mind. It is certainly a good idea to remember that you traveled a whole day in the direction of a certain peak and that you will want to keep it at your back on the return journey, but you will need alternative landmarks as well, since the mountain may be obscured by a cloud bank. The possibility of a blanket of snow or poor visibility should also be considered in choosing landmarks. The only method that can be used to find your way in really bad weather is with a compass, which will be discussed later in the chapter, but some care in picking different kinds of landmarks will save you a great deal of trouble.

No matter how well they are chosen, landmarks are of little use if your memory of them is fragmentary and confused. This is a good reason for writing down key landmarks as an aid to memory. There are many ways of doing this, though a rough map is usually the best. Everyone uses different systems in remembering things, and for this reason, there is no "best" way to remember, list, or map landmarks. You will develop your own methods, which will improve in accuracy and will require less effort as time goes on and you acquire experience. The important thing to remember in the beginning is that we all tend to flatter ourselves on the accuracy of our memories. You may think that you could not possible mistake that distinctive-looking rock when you first see it, but you may find a dozen that look the same when you return a couple of days later, cold, tired, and confused. And was the rock before or after the pass? Develop your own system of mapping, observing, and memory jogging, but be realistic in your expectations of it. Your memory isn't as good as you think it is.

On short trips you may be able to guide yourself by landmarks alone, particularly if you are following some prominent line, whether it is a river, road, or power line. For longer trips and many shorter ones, you will have to use a map to orient yourself to the landscape, even if you draw the map yourself.

MAPS

A map is of little use unless you can read it. The map is a symbolic depiction of an area of land, and in order to use it effectively you will have to learn to read the symbols. This is less a matter of instruction than experience, since most of the symbols themselves are fairly simple. With a bit of practice you can learn to visualize the landscape that is represented by a particular map. Once this knack has been acquired, the map becomes a really helpful tool. With it you can plan trips in wilderness areas you have never seen, estimating with fair accuracy the time it will take to reach your destination. Once you are in the woods you can often find your own position quickly by relating the visible landmarks to those shown on a map.

Many types of maps are available. They are designed for many different purposes, and since any one map is limited in the number of things it can show, it may be more or less useful to you. It may, of course, be well or badly designed even for the purpose for which it was intended. You might be interested in a ski tour in coastal marshes, for example. Many nautical charts are probably available for the area in which you are interested, some good and some bad, but they would be of little use to you, since they are designed to aid someone traveling by water and not by land. The charts may show the location of sand bars but not jeep roads, when you want the opposite emphasis. Road maps are usually just as useless to the wilderness traveler, since they are generally drawn to the wrong scale and ignore the features in which the tourer is most interested.

Even the maps that are of help to the wilderness user are of many different types, and you may often need more than one to serve the several purposes you have in mind. One map may show trails, while it gives only a small number of reference points on the local landscape, for reasons of scale or economy. You may need to use a map like this, which will show you where trails have been cleared in the forest, in combination with a detailed map of the topography, which may not show the existing trails.

By far the most useful maps of most wilderness areas in the United States are those published by the U.S. Geological Survey (USGS). They are quite accurate and very cheap. Several series and types of maps are published by the Survey, including special sheets on the national parks. The series of most interest to the wilderness traveler are the seven-and-a-half-minute series and the fifteen-minute series. There are maps of the fifteen-minute series available for most of the United States, except for Alaska, where a different scale is used. These maps are detailed enough to be very useful. The scale is 1:62,500, which is very nearly one inch to the mile. The seven-and-a-half-minute series is even more useful; the maps are drawn to a 1:24,000 scale. The mapping of the country in the seven-and-a-half-minute series will be completed in a few more years.

The Geological Survey maps are accurate even in areas that are rarely traveled, since they are compiled primarily from a complicated process of aerial photography. They are generally completely reliable for topographic features, but they should be used with more caution with reference to man-made features and vegetation. The survey date is printed in the lower right-hand corner, and changes subsequent to that date will not appear on the map. The magnetic declination, which will be discussed below, is usually updated more frequently. Another complication in using the survey maps for trails, jeep roads, and the like, is that the policy on which ones should be included seems to vary with area and time. These maps cannot be revised very often, and those who make them up must decide whether a trail should be included, recognizing that it may be allowed to disappear the next year. For this reason, some quadrangles show only very heavily used and well-maintained trails and roads. Others include every track. For trail information it is usually best to consult another map in conjunction with the USGS map. If you are traveling without trails, this will not be a problem.

The USGS maps are available in several overlays; that is, additional information is printed over the basic map, sometimes in different colors. The most useful overlay for wilderness use is that in the contour edition with a green vegetation overlay. The height of land is shown by the use of contour lines, and green coloring shows forested and clear areas. Contour lines are the most accurate way of showing differences in elevation, though a bit of practice is required to read them. Contour mapping is discussed more fully below.

USGS maps are available at local offices, from the central offices listed in Appendix C, and from many backpacking shops. Index maps of individual states are available free; they show the names and locations of all the quadrangle maps. Sheets that explain all the symbols used on the maps are also available free of charge.

There are many other sources of maps, some of which are excellent and most of which are not. Commercially available maps made for sportsmen are sometimes good for trails, but they are often just badly reproduced and expensive copies of maps made by some government agency that will supply them free of charge. Since your taxes paid for the survey to begin with, you might as well reap the benefits, if any. The quality of the maps of conservation agencies, counties, fish and game departments, and so on, is variable. The Forest Service will provide maps of national forest areas. Those that are of recent date are often very good for trails and access roads, but many are out of date and should be used with caution. They are usually not terribly good representations of the topography of the area, and they should usually be used in conjunction with USGS maps.

Private lands such as those owned by lumber companies have often been mapped by the owner. It is usually wise to get permission before using such areas, anyhow, and you can ask about maps at the same time.

The best sources of information on trails and routes are usually the guidebooks and maps published by outing clubs or by companies aiming specifically at wilderness travelers. Such information is usually much more up to date than that included on maps designed mainly for other purposes, and it often includes descriptions of routes that are very helpful, even though they may be designed for the summer walker. In some cases, such maps may be adequate by themselves, like the excellent series published by the Appalachian Mountain Club.

Other maps are more sketchy and should be used to supplement USGS maps. Even a guide with no map at all that includes a recent description of a trail will often be enough to tell you that a trail shown on a ten-year-old map still exists, and you may then hope that the brush won't be too thick. In areas like the Sierra Nevada where the small brush is covered over by the first few snows, the winter traveler can steer by the topographic map and compass without concerning himself about trails. In other areas, where cover is thick and snows not so deep, a trail will often greatly increase your speed.

READING THE MAP

Those who have become experienced in the use of topographic maps learn to read them as easily as they do the printed page or road map. All these skills are learned, however, not inbred, and to the novice looking at his first topo map everything except for lakes and roads is likely to be completely unfamiliar. The main difficulty is presented by the *contour lines*. A contour line represents a particular height of land. That is, it follows the same route on the map that you would follow if you were to walk along being careful never to move up or down, but staying at the same altitude. If you were on a hillside and you followed a contour line, you would eventually walk all the way around the hill, ending at the same place you started. Put another way, the contour describes the shoreline that would be formed by an ocean at its altitude. Contour lines are drawn to represent steps in altitude, so that the altitude change between any two contour lines is always the same on a particular map. If the contour interval is twenty feet, for example, you could reach the next contour line on your hill by walking up the hill until you were twenty feet above your earlier track. If the hill is very gentle, this might be a long way; if it is very steep, it will be a short distance. If you now follow your new contour line around the hill, you will be staying inside the contour you traced before. Where the hill is gentle you will be farther away from the lower contour, and where it is steep, the lower contour will be just below you.

The illustrations show a few common patterns on contour maps. One of the best ways to learn to read them is to buy a few contour maps of different kinds of terrain and study them for a while, picturing the features they represent. It may be worthwhile to get a couple of USGS maps of the same area, one a contour edition with a vegetation overlay and the other a shaded relief edition. The latter gives a more pictorial version of the landforms and may help you relate them to the contours. Pick up the map of an area near your home; then take it out and compare the map with the actual landforms.

A simplified contour map, and photograph of the same place The cross on the map shows the spot where the picture was taken, and the arrow shows the direction. The contours are at 200-foot intervals from 7,600 to 9,000 feet. Note that the rock gendarme on the left does not show as a separate summit on the map, because the contours are too widely spaced. The large cliffs on the peak show as closely spaced contours. and the ridges and gullies are easily discerned.

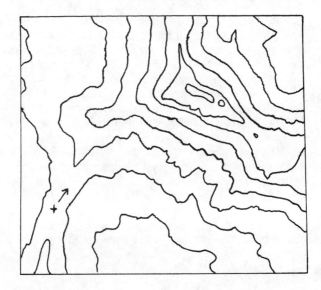

You will notice that contour lines do not cross, since they represent different heights of land. In the case of a vertical cliff, a number of contour lines may come together for the length of the cliff. (Technically, the lines cross to show an overhanging cliff, but this situation is naturally rare.) The altitude gain represented by each contour line is listed in the legend of the map and will vary a great deal depending on the scale of the map and the terrain that is being depicted.

Within the limits of the scale of the map, the contours will give you a very good picture of the pattern of the landscape. Even if visibility is limited, by keeping track of where you are located on the map, you can tell a great deal about the terrain around you. If the visibility is fairly good, you will probably be able to establish your position on the map by simply comparing the landforms around you with those shown by the contours. As you go up a valley, for example, you need only keep track of the landmarks you pass. In climbing a mountain in clear weather, you can estimate your altitude fairly accurately by checking the altitude of some high point of land that is at the same level you are. Such a check might save you from the mistake of a late afternoon dash for a peak or pass that is still several thousand feet above you.

As you become more skilled at reading maps, you will be able to tell more and more about the landscape by just looking at the map, but there are limitations imposed by both vertical and horizontal scale. If the map has 200-foot contours, for example, which is quite common in mountainous regions, a ridge full of jagged 100-foot cliffs and hills might look quite smooth on the map. Details of terrain other than general forestation, swamps, and so on, will not appear on the map. This provides the adventure of discovery, of course, but it is important to remember when you are planning a trip from a map or steering a course in a snowstorm. A map with 100-foot contours will not show the 50-foot cliff you are about to step over.

The easiest way to steer a course with a map is by matching the details of terrain of the map and the country around you, but this is not always possible. In flat country it may be a long way between recognizable features like rivers. You may be in an area that is so heavily forested you cannot see more than a few yards. Some mountainous areas and some lake country include so many features of almost the same kind that it is impossible to tell one hill or lake from another by comparison with the map. Finally, a really bad storm in any country can reduce visibility almost to zero, so that you may be lucky to be able to see your footing, never mind any landmarks. In any of these circumstances, it is necessary to keep track of the direction you are traveling if you are not to become lost.

DIRECTION FINDING

The first maxim in determining or maintaining a direction is a negative one: Convince yourself that you don't have any sense of direction. You may be an astute observer and have learned all sorts of tricks for finding your way in various kinds of surroundings, but whatever methods you have, they are based on outside clues, not some internal compass. It has been proven a number of times that no one can walk a straight line without some external guide.

Most people who have spent much time in the wilderness have had this fact demonstrated to them at some time or other. One very common experience in storms, dense woods, and similar situations is the feeling that the compass is wrong, that it is broken or being deflected by a metallic deposit. This feeling is almost always incorrect, but it sometimes takes a good deal of self-control to keep oneself from dashing off in circles, following instinct. People who become seriously lost often do just this. Remember, if your compass is really acting erratically, the last direction finder you should substitute for it is your instinct, which is guaranteed erratic, one hundred percent of the time.

One method of determining direction, by reference to landmarks, has already been discussed. There are two other means of use to the wilderness sojourner: reference to celestial objects and the use of a magnetic compass. Other reference systems, from moss on trees to prevailing winds, are generally unreliable and are, in any case, too local to be of much use in navigating a strange area.

Celestial bodies allow precise position finding, but only through the use of instruments that the snowshoer or ski tourer is unlikely to carry. Some types of expeditions may need such devices and the knowledge of their use, and interested readers are referred to Appendix B. The tourer may want to check his compass by use of the North Star, but referring to the declination shown on the map is easier. It is unwise to depend on navigation by the stars in preference to a compass. You may get hungry waiting for the clouds to break. Using the stars for direction is greatly facilitated by a good knowledge of the constellations. The pointers and the North Star are the only accurate way to check declination on a compass, but if you are using the sky as a rough directional beacon—perhaps for an early-morning start—it is pleasant to recognize other constellations and to know where to expect them to be at the time you are looking.

Many methods have been suggested for establishing bearings using the sun. At best they are time-consuming and dependent on a touching faith that the sun will be shining when you want to find your way home. At worst they are often grossly inaccurate. Those who are interested can look into some of the books suggested in Appendix B, but these methods are of little use to the traveler on trips of a few days or weeks in the wilderness. Get a good compass and a good map of the area to which you are going, learn to use them, and take them. If you can't remember to take your compass, you are unlikely to remember the exact direction of the sunrise on a particular day. The wilderness traveler should never travel without a compass, unless he is in an area where terrain alone will guide him out, even in blizzard conditions.

COMPASSES

A pocket compass is the standard direction-finding device for general use in the wilderness. It will not enable you to find your position, unless you have some additional information. It will, however, give you an essentially constant directional reference, which can be used to keep you going in a straight line, to keep track of changes you make in direction, and to establish the relation between directions on the ground and those shown on a map.

A compass is simply a magnet mounted on a pivot so that it is free to turn. The case is supposed to protect the moving parts and to help you to relate the position of the magnet to the land around you and to your map. The magnet itself may be in the form of a needle or it may be glued to a round dial, so that the whole dial turns. In either case, the magnet will turn until it is oriented along the lines of the earth's magnetic field (providing there is nothing else around to deflect it).

WHERE THE COMPASS POINTS

The directions marked on a compass tend to lead to misconceptions, and it is important for anyone who travels much in the wilderness to understand that the compass needle or face rarely points toward the North Pole. It lines up with the earth's magnetic field, which is rather irregular, and which wanders around enough to confuse anyone. The earth's magnetic North Pole is in northern Canada over a thousand miles from the geographic North Pole. If you think of your compass needle as pointing at the magnetic North Pole you will begin to understand that in many parts of the country the error between magnetic North and true North is quite large. The situation is even more confusing, however, since the actual field is deflected by many factors.

The difference between the direction the compass shows and true

North is called the *magnetic declination*. The average declination in a particular area will be shown on the border of the USGS map of the area. This declination figure is updated frequently, since the earth's magnetic field fluctuates. In the eastern United States and Canada the compass will point west of true North; in the western parts of those countries it will point to the east of true North.

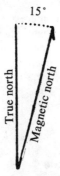

Approximate mean declination, 1959

How declination is shown on maps The arrow showing magnetic north shows the direction a compass needle would point, and the true north arrow shows the direction of the geographic North Pole. A third arrow may show UTM (Universal Transverse Mercator Grid) direction.

If you are using your compass to take bearings as you travel, effectively making your own map, you can simply use magnetic bearings. Except on very long trips, you would be able to ignore declination altogether, since you are not likely to travel far enough for the declination to change singnificantly. In this case you are simply using the compass for a constant direction finder, and you are not concerned about the relation between your directions and true North. If you are referring to a map of the area, however, you must convert your bearings to true bearings by adding or subtracting the declination. Except in a few areas, the declination is great enough to throw you completely off course if you assume that magnetic and true North are essentially the same. Around Mount Washington in New Hampshire, for example, you would be a mile and a half off course in five miles if you followed a magnetic instead of a true bearing. Methods of correcting for declination will be discussed more fully, but you are unlikely to get into trouble if you remember where your compass is actually pointing whenever you use it.

WHAT GOOD IS DIRECTION?

The compass gives you a directional reference that has some relation (declination) to the direction of the North Pole, but so what? You will rarely be interested in going to the North Pole. If you find that you are lost in the woods in a blinding snowstorm and you pull out your trusty pocket compass, it will tell you the direction of the earth's magnetic field at the spot on which you are standing, but you may have difficulty working up an interest in this piece of information. The direction of the earth's magnetic field will not tell you where your car is parked unless you know some other things as well.

Even in the situation just described, when you have neglected to keep track of the other information you need to steer back to your car, the compass will do you some good. It will enable you to steer in a relatively straight line, rather than walking in aimless circles, which is what you will do if you follow your nose. In this case you should sit down and think about what you know of the area you are in, and decide which direction you should go to get out. Then you steer a straight line in that direction.

You will not be able to steer a very straight line by simply holding the compass in front of you and trying to head southeast; you have to walk around obstacles, push on your ski poles, blow your nose, and try to keep the compass needle steady. Probably you will end up by tripping over a log while looking at your compass and then losing it in the snow. The normal way to cope with all this is to take bearings. Taking a bearing is simply sighting an object in the direction you want to go, preferably one at some distance. You can sight over your compass, determining that a prominent dead tree is southwest of you. You put the compass in your pocket and walk to the dead tree by the easiest route. Then you take another bearing.

Bearings can be used to solve quite a few other problems. Let's suppose you have been more prudent. You have brought a map and kept track of your position on it during a mountain trip. The terrain may have been sufficiently distinctive so that there was no need for the compass. You simply followed your topo map and camped in a large round valley, but during the night a storm came up. If the visibility is poor it may be impossible to steer up out of the valley and hit the right pass just by looking at your surroundings; you might end up climbing a mountain, instead. In this case you can look at your map and determine which direction you should go to hit the pass. You can then correct for declination and take a bearing in the direction of the pass. In this way, you can steer yourself to the pass.

The compass can, of course, be used to orient your map with

respect to the land around you, and this will often enable you to identify landmarks, since you will be able to relate their general direction to the map, as well as their shapes. If you can identify two or more landmarks in this way, you can use bearings to find your exact position by reversing the procedure mentioned above. Bearings are taken on the two landmarks and the directions transferred to the map. Where the directional lines cross is your position.

Finally, bearings may be used to keep track of your position, either in conjunction with a map or without one. You may draw your own map as you go along, keeping track of the distances traveled and determining precise directions by taking bearings. All these uses of the compass will be described in more detail below, but since the exact procedure varies with different kinds of compasses, it will be necessary to discuss them first.

TYPES OF COMPASSES

Any compass intended for wilderness use should have a large enough face and sufficiently detailed markings to enable you to take bearings that are accurate within a couple of degrees. The more accurate it is, of course, the better. The tiny compasses divided into eight or sixteen directions are not really adequate for most purposes. Obviously, the compass should be sturdy. At a minimum, it must have a line or marks on opposite sides of the compass, which will enable you to sight landmarks for bearings. Sights attached to the compass are better, and they allow more precision with less effort.

The compass dial should be marked with azimuth readings, as well as the points of the compass. Azimuth marks are simply degree marks, the compass face being divided into 360° running clockwise from North, which is 0° and 360°. East is thus 90°, South is 180°, Southwest is 225°, and so on. This may sound a bit complicated, but if you think about adjusting for a 17° East declination from North Northeast by East, you'll see that it's easier to add or subtract from a numerical direction. For precise bearings the 360° system is much simpler to use than points of the compass. The actual markings may run either clockwise or counterclockwise for reasons explained below. The markings may either be on the case or on a face that turns with the magnet, called the compass card.

The most common type of compass has a rotating needle with directional and azimuth markings running clockwise on a face that is fixed solidly to the case. The case will include some sort of sighting device or line that corresponds to the marking for North (0°, 360°).

We'll refer to this type as the standard compass in the discussions that follow. A detailed description of the method of taking a bearing with the standard compass will clarify the design of the other types to be described. These designs have arisen because of certain problems with the standard pocket compass.

The illustration shows the process of taking a bearing with four different types of compass. (The bearings shown here are magnetic bearings and still need to be corrected for declination if they are to be used with reference to a standard map.) With the standard compass the sighting line is aimed at the landmark that is 45° from magnetic North, or simply 45°, magnetic. There is no way to read this bearing directly, however. We must obtain it by noting that the north end of the needle points to 315° and that this is the same number of degrees counterclockwise from magnetic North (360°) as our landmark is clockwise. Thus, the bearing is 360° − 315° = 45°.

This correction becomes natural to make after some practice, but there are other types of compass that are designed to remove this complication from the start. The simplest, but also the strangest when one first looks at it, is the cruiser compass, which is the same as the standard except that the markings on the case are reversed; instead of running clockwise, they run counterclockwise. Thus, at right angles to North (0°, 360°) and to the right, we find not East (90°) but West 270°). The advantage to this system is obvious from the illustration. To find a magnetic bearing you simply orient the sighting line and read the bearing where the north end of the needle points.

A second method of solving this problem is to use a compass card attached to the top of the needle on which the directions and azimuth markings are printed. This whole card rotates, so that each directional marking is oriented toward that magnetic direction. The markings are made in the usual clockwise fashion. With this type of compass, taking a magnetic bearing is again simplified. The sighting line is pointed toward the landmark and the bearing is read where this line intersects the compass card.

A fourth method of correcting this problem is used on the orienteering compasses, which also include several other useful innovations to be discussed below. The orienteering arrangement uses a three-part system instead of a two-part one. The sighting line is on a case or a plastic base on which is mounted a compass housing that is free to rotate on the base. The directional markings are on this housing. Inside the housing is the compass needle. The sighting line is aimed at the landmark, and the housing is then turned until North corresponds with the needle. The bearing is read at the intersection of the sighting line and the housing dial.

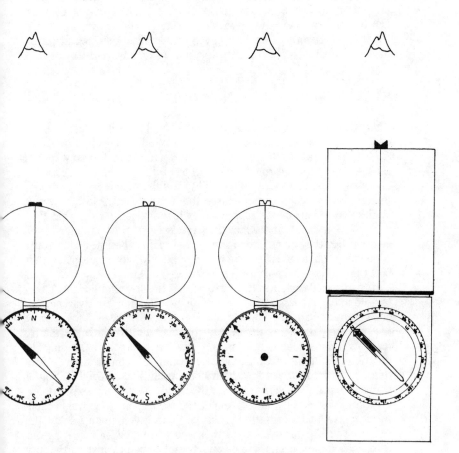

Taking a bearing with four types of compasses On the left is a standard compass; next is a cruiser type, with reversed directions; in the third, a card type, the entire face rotates; and on the right is an orienteering compass, generally the most satisfactory type for wilderness use. It features both a rotating needle and a movable dial mounted on a transparent plastic base.

This basic method of taking a bearing is used whether one is recording the bearing for future reference, finding a landmark guide for a line of progress that has been determined from a map, or using landmarks to locate his position. Any reasonably accurate compass can be used, but the advantages of the three modified systems should be obvious. Before going into any more detail about special procedures, we'll discuss the standard methods of finding your way.

SYSTEMS FOR KNOWING YOUR LOCATION

There are many ways to guide yourself around the wilderness, and the one you choose will depend very much on individual circumstances. An afternoon jaunt along a narrow valley will not require any special thought about the return trip; you will just follow the valley back without even thinking about it. This ability to follow some routes without thought is the most common reason that people become lost, however. While they are following such a valley it is obvious to them that they can follow it back, and when they cross a path into another much larger valley they do not stop to think and realize that the return route is no longer obvious. By the time they suddenly become aware of that fact they no longer know where they are.

It was stated earlier in this chapter that the art of finding one's way in wilderness areas consists largely of maintaining an awareness of one's position in a way appropriate to the terrain and the objective of the trip. In many areas that are fairly open and that have distinctive features, this is done simply by an occasional glance at the map. In the high mountains of California, for example, a compass may sometimes be carried for years without being used, since a combination of map and terrain will serve to guide the wanderer. As long as you maintain an awareness of your location on the map, no bearings are needed. In case of a bad storm, you need only check your map to find the bearing you should follow, and then you can follow this bearing out with the compass, even though you have taken no bearings on the way in.

Since this method of route finding is a pleasant one to use, it is unfortunate that there are many kinds of terrain where it will not work. Some areas have a few prominent landmarks, yet include no distinctive features in the surrounding terrain. It would hardly be prudent to wander around in the tundra south of the Alaska range without taking bearings occasionally, since there is enough country "generally south of McKinley" for a man to wander for the rest of his life, and one square mile often looks just like hundreds of others around it.

Base Lines

One very convenient system for many situations is to use any long base line that may be available. The most common would be a road on which your car is parked, but a river, the shore of a large lake, a railroad line, a power-line cut, or many other such lines may be used. In using the base-line system, one simply keeps track of the direction and distance of the base line and the approximate distance and direction along it of the car, camp, or supply dump. With the base-line system, much less precision is needed in this information than with most other methods. The idea is that you need only find your way back to the reference line and follow it to your objective.

An example of this method is shown on the next page. The degree of accuracy that is needed depends on the length of the available base line and the distance you are traveling. It is important to be sure that your error is not so great as to cause you to miss the line. Make sure that you know the character of a base line from a map or from examination. The twists and turns of roads and rivers can be very confusing, and unless you are sure of your location when you hit the base line, you are likely to search back and forth along a section of the line instead of traveling far enough along it to reach your objective. Unless the scenery along the line is familiar to you, it is important to aim to one side or the other of your objective. Otherwise, you will not know which way to turn when you reach the line. By deliberately missing the point to which you want to go, by aiming to one side, you will know which way to turn when you reach the base line.

Base-line methods can be used in many sorts of terrain and on many scales. In forested areas with little visibility and no landmarks, it is possible to set up your own base line by marking out a path in either direction from your camp by the methods discussed below for marking trails. In flat country that has good visibility and at least one landmark, a serviceable base line can be simply a bearing on a landmark that can be seen from a long distance. Where considerable distances are involved, a subsidiary marked line can be set up perpendicular to this bearing line, running far enough on each side of it to compensate for compass error.

Steering by Compass Bearings

In many areas it is simply not feasible to use the map alone or to navigate roughly from a line of position. Under storm conditions, this becomes the case in almost any sort of terrian, unless one is following a very well-defined geographical feature. In such a situation it is necessary to find one's way by using compass bearings. There are several ways of relating the map and the compass, depending on what you

Base-line road

Wrong way

Right way

Using a road as a base line Here the party has proceeded generally south from the base line. When they wish to return, they should not attempt to head directly north to the car, since if they miss it, they will not know which way to turn. Rather, they should bear either east or west of North, and when they reach the road they will know which way the car is. Many other types of base lines are used the same way.

know and what you need to know. These are discussed below, but first we may as well cover the actual method of taking and following a bearing.

Walking on a bearing is the method used when it is necessary to actually guide yourself with the compass. This is done in a number of situations. If you know where you are on a map, but there is no way for you to guide yourself by landmarks alone, you can mark your desired line of progress on the map. Then the angle between your lines of progress and North is measured, either with a protractor or with the compass used as a protractor. This angle, measured clockwise from North, is the azimuth bearing for the direction you want to travel.

Another situation in which it is necessary to travel on a bearing occurs when you are guiding yourself by a large landmark, though you are not actually traveling to it. You might be heading for a lake ten miles northeast of a particular mountain, and the easiest way to find the lake might be by maintaining a bearing on the mountain behind you. Even if you were going to the mountain, in some kinds of country it might be impossible to see it for miles at a time. In this case you would maintain your direction in between views of the mountain by taking intermediate bearings.

Finally, in many kinds of flat country, in mountains that all look the same, and in bad storms, it is often necessary to base your whole knowledge of your position on bearings you follow. This is often true whether a map is available or whether you are drawing your own along the way. In such cases your knowledge of your position is only as good as the bearings themselves.

Let's suppose you are traveling to a mile-long lake five miles distant through fairly thick and featureless woods. Five miles farther on the other side of the lake is a large mountain that can be seen most of the time. Taking a bearing on the mountain, you check your map and determine that the lake is on a line between you and the mountain. You reason that by heading for the mountain you will hit the lake. If you just travel toward the mountain, though, there is a good chance that by nightfall you will find yourself within a couple of miles of the mountain but with no lake in sight. The reason is that your course through the dense woods will wander here and there, with a good chance of missing the lake altogether in the middle. If you want to follow a fairly straight line to be sure of hitting your lake, you need two points along your bearing that you can keep lined up as you go along.

To do this, when you take your original bearing on the mountain you should pick a prominent tree as far along the line as possible. By keeping the tree and the mountain lined up you will stay on a straight line. You will make detours, but always having two points to line up will enable you to keep correcting for errors as you go. When you are about halfway to your tree, pick another in the same line. It is not necessary to take a new bearing each time, but you should recheck the bearing occasionally. The farther away the trees are, the more accurate your line will be, and the less often you will have to check your bearing.

In very dense forest or very bad weather, you may have to take bearings very frequently to keep from getting off course. On the other hand, if you can line up two distant hills you may be able to travel all day on a very accurate bearing without ever rechecking the compass. In poor conditions, when bearings are taken on trees just a short distance ahead, a large accumulation of error will be inevitable unless bearings are rechecked constantly. In any case, however, it is always best to try to line up two objects if at all possible, rather than using only one.

Where no landmarks are available, the members of the party itself should be used to keep your bearing. If you are alone, of course, you will simply have to keep your compass out and follow it as best you can. If there are several in the party, however, the last person should carry the compass, with the party stretched out as far as safety and audibility permit. The rear member lines up on the others and shouts directions. With two people ahead of you, you can keep the party on

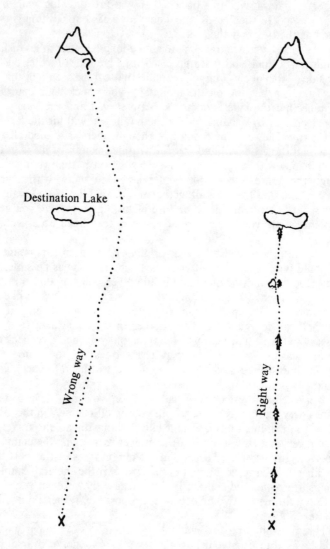

Destination Lake

Wrong way

Right way

Choose intermediate points with distant bearing When using a distant point for a bearing, be sure to choose intermediate points. In the left-hand diagram, a snowshoer intended to go to a lake on the same bearing as a distant peak. He simply headed for the peak, but natural deviations made him miss the lake altogether. On the right, he kept picking intermediate landmarks along the same line, and this tactic enabled him to follow a relatively straight course.

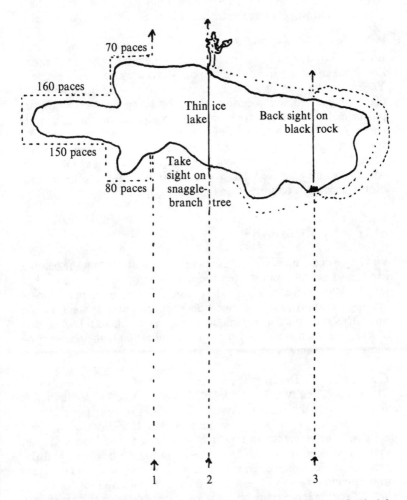

Three ways of going around obstacles while following a compass bearing On the left is the only method that can be used when visibility is bad and the most practical one at some other times. The party paces off their deviation from their course, and deviates at known angles, right angles being the easiest. Then, when the obstacle is cleared, they pace back to their original course. The party in the center sighted a prominent landmark on the other side of the obstacle, walked around to it, and then resumed their course. The right-hand group could see no landmark on the other side, but found one where they were (or could have left a mark). They proceeded around the obstacle and took a back sighting with their compass to get back on their bearing.

a fairly accurate bearing, even when the landscape is completely blotted out. This method is clearly more time-consuming than others, however, and will only be used when it is essential, as it is in whiteout conditions.

In following a bearing or a series of bearings over a long distance it will almost always be necessary to make detours. When the bearing line is taken on a pair of distant points this may cause no problem. You might be able to work up a river to a good crossing and then diagonal back to your bearing simply by lining up the two distant points again. When you are steering by compass alone or using trees and rocks only a short distance away, this is not possible. In this case you must keep track of your deviations, reversing them as soon as possible. This is generally best done by pacing off each leg of the detour. Any angles may be used, but a series of right angles is often easiest, simply because it requires little thought to execute.

MAP AND COMPASS

Walking a compass bearing is used in many situations, but the bearing itself must be determined from the map or marked on some kind of map for later reference if it is to be of use. The simplest use of compass bearings is simply to steer a course between recognizable points on the map. This is an obvious technique, almost as simple to follow as that of using the map alone, and the only complication is the necessity of allowing for compass declination.

Correcting for Declination
The main difficulty to be surmounted in correcting for declination is simply that of developing a system that eliminates the possibility of time-consuming confusion or serious mistakes. If the compass is being used without reference to any map except your own rough sketch, there is no need to convert from magnetic to true bearings, and the problem can be ignored. If, however, you are using map and compass in conjunction there will be a need to convert back and forth.

The particular system you develop for converting will depend on the type of compass you use. In taking notes it is best to distinguish between magnetic and true bearings. I use "m" or "t" following the azimuth in my notes to indicate this distinction, so that I won't have to ask myself later whether or not I made a particular conversion. For example, after crossing a broad, flat saddle before starting down a ravine, I might take a bearing back across the route just used in case of a storm on the return trip. The note might read, "top of ravine, rtn.

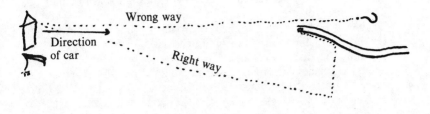

Direction
of car

Wrong way

Right way

Deliberate deviation Hitting trails, roads, or streams endwise requires deliberate deviation, like that used in hitting a base line. If you try to head straight for the line and miss it, you won't know which way to go. Deviate deliberately, turn to cut the line, and then backtrack if necessary.

To hit a point like a camp without a base line, continue until you know you are past the point. Then turn at right angles, again continue past the camp, repeat this, crossing your original trail, and continuing until you are sure you have passed the possible location in that direction. Now cross back into your rough square, which has become a search perimeter. Keep going around inside the square, closing it as much as possible each time, until you hit the camp.

X

from big birch 136° m," meaning that the return route lies along magnetic azimuth 136°, sighted from the prominent birch tree at the top of the ravine.

More commonly, the compass is used in direct conjunction with the map, and the correction must be made at the time. The most convenient compasses have a declination-offsetting device that is set to make the correction automatically. If you have one of the more common types of compass, you must simply make the correction each time you use the compass. For example, you might be laying out a line on the map and then following the bearing.

The illustration shows that you are on the shore of a large lake. Your car is parked at the end of a road five miles away. You decide on a line of progress that will take you somewhat south of the road. Then, when you are sure you have gone more than five miles, you will be able to head due north and cut the road. If you were to aim straight for the end of the road, you would not know which way to turn after traveling this distance.

Having decided the line you wish to follow, you draw it on the map, extending it to the border, which runs north and south. Using a protractor or the markings on your compass, you measure the angle from North, and this is the true azimuth that you wish to follow. Marked on the map, usually in the graphic way shown, is the average magnetic declination in the area. It might be "declination 16° East." This would mean that your compass will indicate a "North" that is 16° east of true North, which is the same as to say that 0° on your compass is at true azimuth 16°. If the bearing you measured for your line of progress was 96°, the compass or magnetic bearing you want to follow would be 96° − 16° = 80°m. If you were in the eastern part of the country the declination would be West instead of East, and you would then have to add the declination instead of subtracting it.

Orienting the Map and Determining Positions

In the example just given and in many other possible situations, the exact location on the map of both the party and its objective were known. In this case it is possible to calculate a compass bearing directly and then to follow it. In many other circumstances, however, it may be necessary to determine one's position on the map before this procedure can be followed. This may not always be possible, and in cases where such a difficulty is anticipated the party maintains its own map of compass bearings, landmarks, and distances, a method discussed below. As long as landmarks are visible occasionally, however, positions can usually be found using the map and compass.

As a first step, the map should be placed on something flat and stable and oriented to the ground. This may be possible without use of the compass; for example, if you are going up a long, narrow valley, you may not know where you are in the valley, but directions may still be clear. If this is not the case, the map is oriented by simply lining up magnetic North as shown by your compass and that shown in the declination diagram of the map.

Once the map is oriented, it may be possible to relate the terrain shown on the map to the land surrounding it. If at least two landmarks are reconizable, it is possible to establish one's position exactly, though at least three landmarks are preferred. Even one landmark will serve to establish a line of position, which may then serve to help identify a second point of reference.

The easiest way to find your position on the map once your landmarks have been identified is by sighting directly. (You may also sight with the compass and then transfer the bearings, but this is usually both more complicated and less accurate.) Make sure your map is accurately oriented, and be careful not to rotate it while you make your sightings. Now take two small, straight objects to serve as sights; pine needles, matches, or pins would do. Stand one of them on the map point that represents your landmark. Then sight across the tip to the actual landmark. Place the second sighting point on the map somewhere along your sighting line. Now draw a line between the two sights, an operation that can be performed by your companion or by you once you have figured the proper sequence to let you get by with only two hands. The line you have just drawn is a line of position, and your location lies somewhere along it. Another line to a different landmark will give a second line of position, and your location will be determined by the intersection of the lines. The method's accuracy is increased if at least one more landmark is used. It is also best to use landmarks that are approximately 90° from one another, since the error is increased by using points more nearly in line with one another.

There are obviously many applications of this method of determining your position. For example, it can be used with the base-line method; one line from a landmark intersecting a base line will determine your position on it. The procedure can be reversed to help identify an unknown landmark. Once some practice in the basic techniques of using the map and compass has been acquired, common sense will suggest other uses when the need arises.

KEEPING TRACK OF WHERE YOU'VE BEEN

The most important route-finding problem in the wilderness is finding your way out. It's not usually a very serious matter if you miss your objective on the way in, since you can always try again another day—providing you know how to get back to your starting point! Of course, the situation is different if you are traveling between food caches, since you then have a more compelling reason to get to your destination than the reputed view. When you are carrying your food and shelter, though, it's knowing the way back that keeps your trip from turning into a survival test instead of a pleasure tour.

The most common and useful ways of finding the way back to your car or cabin have already been discussed: keeping an eye on your back trail, knowing your location on a good topo map, following some continuous landmark like a river, using a base-line system of route finding, or some combination of these.

There are two other important methods that are frequently used to keep track of the return route. The first has already been mentioned incidentally; it entails maintaining a continuous record of landmarks and bearings that can be followed back out. This method is useful if you don't have an adequate topo map, and it may sometimes be called for in featureless terrain or bad weather. A record of bearings and landmarks must be kept, often right on the topo map if one is carried. If no standard map has been taken, the best way to keep a record is usually to draw a rough map as you go along. A sample map is shown in the illustration, but the methods are for the most part self-evident.

One useful point to remember is to use bearings over short distances when possible. A long route is thus broken into a number of

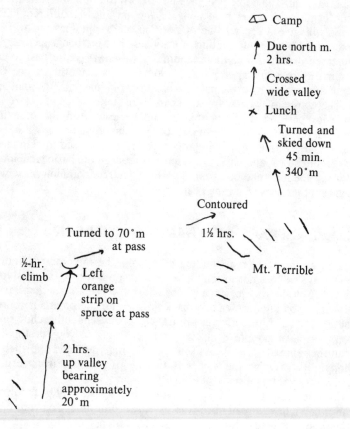

An example of a hand-drawn map kept during a trip Enough information is included for a return trip even in a storm.

shorter legs. Small base-line systems can be used to cover sections of
the route. The track followed can be planned so that landmarks that
are easily relocated are encountered frequently. Each time such a
landmark is encountered, it should be marked on the map, distances
(in units of length or time) ought to be recorded, and new bearings
should be taken. For example, instead of passing near the end of a
lake while walking a bearing, you should use the shore of the lake as
a new base line and take a new bearing from some easily recognizable
point on the shore. In this way the errors that are inherent in walking
a bearing frequently can be reduced to zero before they accumulate
into large distances.

Blazing a Trail

The time-honored method for finding a way back to camp is to blaze
a trail, either one that you can follow all the way back or one that you
can intersect. In some situations this principle is still useful, though
the method of gouging trees is now justified only for trails that will be
maintained with some permanence. If the weekend traveler can't find
his way without hacking live trees, he has no business in the woods.

If you anticipate a possible need to blaze a trail, the easiest way is
to carry a packet of brightly colored strips of plastic. (Rolls of bright
plastic in a convenient width can be purchased in any store that supplies surveyors.) These are light and compact, and they are practically
indestructible except by fire. They can be quickly tied to branches
along your route. Reach as high as you comfortably can, so that subsequent snowfall will not bury your trail. Look back occasionally to
make sure that the markers are visible from the direction from which
you will be returning. Anticipate bad weather in judging the distance
you will be able to see.

If you should have occasion to use plastic strips as markers, take
them *all* down on your return. They will probably look beautiful to
you if you are coming back in a bad storm, but to anyone else they are
just unsightly trash, falling into roughly the same category as aluminum beer cans. They stay bright and conspicuous for years. If some
emergency makes it really impossible for you to clean your route when
you leave, then have the grace to come back the next time you can to
clean your trail. We go to the wilderness for a bit of adventure, but
finding it is no excuse to litter the woods with junk.

Above timberline and in other treeless areas, there may be nothing
to tie your plastic strips to. If no natural projections are available, the
best method of blazing a trail is with wands—sticks three or four feet
long. The light bamboo sticks sold for gardens make good wands,
especially if a bit of bright plastic is tied to the top for visibility. The

longer the wand, the better chance it will have of staying above the level of newly fallen snow. Try to pick windblown spots for the wands, where they will be less likely to be covered by drifts. This is an easy matter, since such spots are also often the most visible places available. Wands should be picked up on the return trip and carried home.

Either streamers or wands can be used in conjunction with another system. Bearings can be taken to and from them, and a line of markers can be used to form a base line in the woods. A marker can be left on one side of an obstacle to give a quick back bearing from the other side. For example, suppose you walk on a bearing to a river, but cannot cross at the point you reach. A marker can be tied at that point, and you can then find a crossing without pacing off distances or worrying about direction. When the other side is reached, you can walk along the shore until you are back on your original line as shown by the marker. On the return trip it serves as a blaze. The reader will have no difficulty thinking of other uses.

ERRATIC COMPASS?

The vagaries of the earth's magnetic field have been mentioned, as has the fact that the compass cannot be trusted to point toward any particular spot. The compass declination in both the Northwest and the Northeast is greater than it would be if the needle pointed directly to the magnetic pole. Within a particular area, however, the declination is fairly constant from one mile to the next, and the foot traveler rarely needs to concern himself about the small variations that do exist. Surveyors and mechanized travelers are not so lucky, but their problems will be left for others to explore.

It is common knowledge that a compass will be deflected by the proximity of any magnetic material such as iron or steel. Obviously, one should not take compass readings near knives, on top of cooksets, or next to steel belt buckles.

There remains the problem of local magnetic disturbance, which occasionally occurs when large ore deposits and the like are nearby. Such spots are rare, and the likelihood of your actually coming upon one while using your compass is small. Areas of magnetic disturbance stir the imagination like the hungry wolf packs of the North. People who have gotten themselves turned around commonly panic and immediately blame the attack of a wandering magnetic field for the fact that their compass does not point where they instinctively feel it should. Chances are overwhelming that the compass is pointing in just the direction shown by the declination diagram on the map. If you are really in doubt, take a series of careful bearings as you move along a straight line. If the bearings don't vary within a mile or so, there is no problem with the compass.

Incidentally, with a compass having a needle, make sure you know which end is which. If the ends are colored or marked in some other way that might be ambiguous, mark the compass "white = N," or something similar. Confusion in an emergency might raise doubts in your mind that wouldn't occur on a warm afternoon.

MORE ON COMPASS FEATURES

Some of the basic types of compass have already been discussed, along with the essentials for wilderness use. Though any compass with provisions for sighting and reading bearings with fair accuracy is adequate, there are a number of other features that are convenient. Three ways of facilitating the reading of azimuths have already been mentioned: reversing the direction of the numbers on the dial, using a compass card, and using a dial enclosing the needle, which also rotates on the base plate.

The convenience of the sighting device is worth studying if you are buying a compass. The best models will usually allow you to sight in a number of different ways to meet different circumstances. Mirrors are included on many compasses, but they are of two types. One merely enables you to read the dial while you are sighting, without moving your eye from the sight. This is a convenience, but is not to be compared to the true sighting mirror. The latter can also be used to read a bearing, but it is intended primarily to allow you to sight through the mirror, using the compass in many positions that would be inconvenient or impossible without the mirror. The sights are even usable with the compass on the ground. A sighting mirror combined with a fairly large and clear dial makes for a very accurate compass.

The best sighting method for wilderness use is one with an optical system which allows sighting and reading a bearing with minimal eye movement and refocusing. The Wilkie Bearing compass and the Suunto KB14 and KB20 are more accurate sighting compasses for wilderness use than any other lightweight ones. Unfortunately, they do not have the transparent bases that make modern orienteering compasses so easy to use.

Declination-offsetting devices have been mentioned as a convenience. They usually operate by having the scale rotate with respect to the sight, though the exact method varies with the type of compass. The declination is set at the beginning of a short trip and left alone, though occasional changes may be necessary on a longer trip. In any case, the declination offset is not changed constantly and doesn't have to be as convenient to change as other settings. It may even be an advantage if a screw is used which doesn't permit accidental changing.

A field compass is much more convenient to use if the needle is damped so that it comes quickly to rest. This is especially true when a compass bearing is being walked in poor weather, so that constant reference to the compass is necessary. The best damping is achieved in liquid-filled compasses. An alternative method is induction damping, which uses an electromagnetic force generated by the needle's motion to damp that motion. The induction method is satisfactory, but does not work as well as a good liquid-filled compass with no bubbles.

Several features make the use of a compass in conjunction with the map much easier. A straightedge attached to the compass case or frame in line with the sights makes it much simpler to orient the map and to transfer bearings back and forth between map and compass. An arrangement on the compass that can be used as a protractor is very helpful. Finally, the use of transparent base plates on compasses, so that the map can be seen through the compass, is extremely helpful. Many operations such as orienting the map are more convenient with this type of compass.

A few accessories are helpful in map work. If the compass cannot be used as a protractor, a light, flexible one should be carried for measuring bearings. A straightedge is often needed, though some item like a saw blade usually will serve. A small pencil should be available to draw lines and make notes. (Ink will run if it gets wet.) A couple of folded sheets of tracing paper serve for notes, and in a pinch they can be used for triangulation if you're doubtful about landmarks. Sighting can be made on as many landmarks as possible across a center point on the paper and lines drawn along the sighting. Then the tracing paper is tried out in various positions over the map, in hopes of finding the combination of landmarks that line up.

Paper, map, and pencil are usually carried in a transparent plastic map case, which may be tied to the pack or clothing. Frequent reference can then be made to the map without getting it wet and worn. The professional method is to cut the map in sections and mount it on cloth. Spaces are left between the cuts to allow folding without damaging the map. I have used this method, and and it is the best way to preserve the map, but I confess that I generally just put the map in plastic folded so that the section in which I am immediately interested faces out. As I move along I refold the map or switch maps. Enough trips to the same area require the purchase of a new map because of wear, but with this technique, sloppy as it is, my location is usually in the middle of a visible section of the map instead of right along a fold somewhere. If the route lies along the intersection of two quadrangles, I fold the map in the case so that the edges come together.

If you mark your proposed route on the map beforehand it will be easy to find, and keeping track of your actual progress can be done with the pencil. Don't forget to note information you may need to know later. For laying out a route at home an inexpensive map measurer is convenient. This has a little wheel on the bottom that you roll along your proposed route. The scale above shows the length of all the twists and turns. Don't forget to watch the contours. Two miles won't go so quickly if you have to climb 3,000 feet.

There is an extra challenge to finding your way around the hills and the woods in winter. The use of the compass and map take a little time to master if you are not used to them, but they are not very complicated once the knack is acquired. Once the art of finding your way is achieved in winter you are unlikely to have trouble in any other season, and your freedom to travel where you are inclined to will be greatly enhanced.

10 | Steep Snow: An Introduction

For many of us, the very essence of the wilderness is conveyed by the sight of a steep snow slope sweeping up the side of a mountain. The way this white ramp contrasts with darker rock and blue sky awakens a special exhilaration. It seems almost free from the law of gravity. This chapter attempts to survey some of the skills often needed by the skier, snowshoer, and backpacker who likes to travel in steep-snow country and who would like to extend the limits of the terrain that can be traveled safely.

The regions where steep snow abounds are a special province for the tourist of the white wilderness, since the snows linger in the mountains long after they have disappeared from the lowlands. In the high ranges, snow can be found at any time of year, though it takes on a somewhat different character during the summer months. As spring marches in, devotees of snow country can simply travel higher, provided they live in areas convenient to the high mountains. Spring often provides some of the finest touring and camping weather, with long days and sometimes with fewer storms.

Steep snow may provide highways to areas that are hard to reach at other times of the year. An easy snow slope can cover a ramp that in summer is nothing but a tortuous and shifting pile of small stones. Where the snow does not cover scree, it may cover thick brush or treacherous dirt slopes. In addition to an easy climb up, the same slope may provide a thrilling run down on skis. Even the mountain traveler who has no interest in climbing the mountains themselves is likely to encounter occasional spots where it is necessary either to cross or climb a short, steep section or turn back.

Despite all its attractions, steep snow is dangerous to the ill-equipped, the inexperienced, and the overbold. The same slope that provides a safe and easy staircase in one condition may within a few hours turn into a thousand-foot sliding board or an avalanche waiting for the unwary traveler to trigger its collapse. If such a change occurs while you are above the slope, you may find yourself in a very uncomfortable situation when you get back down to it. The hazards of avalanches to those passing below steep-snow slopes are discussed in the next chapter, and they demand the constant attention of anyone traveling in steep-snow country.

On Mount McKinley in Alaska During the spring and summer months, the dedicated snow camper can follow the snows to higher altitude.

HOW STEEP IS STEEP?

The art of dealing with steep snow is the proper province of mountaineering, and it requires the most difficult and the longest apprenticeship of a notoriously demanding craft. Snow that would be considered steep by the experienced mountaineer is a subject that will not be touched on here. A really steep snow slope is a fine subject for contemplation by the general traveler in snow country, as well as a source to be studied for possible avalanche hazards. Negotiating such angles requires equipment and techniques that deserve a book of their own, and trying to cover them here would be impossible. (The subject is discussed thoroughly in the author's *Climbing: A Guide to Mountaineering,* Scribners, 1977.)

"Steep snow," as used in this chapter, means simply snow that is difficult, impossible, or dangerous to negotiate with normal walking, snowshoeing, and skiing techniques and equipment. This definition, like the mountaineer's, has as much to do with equipment and snow conditions as it does with the actual angle of the slope. The snowshoer will often have trouble with slopes that don't really trouble the experienced mountain skier. Hard snow at a rather low angle will give the hiker trouble, while snow that is twice as steep might not be bothersome if it is soft enough to allow step-kicking.

Steep snow slopes Although steep snow slopes like these in the Palisades may provide easy avenues to the peaks, they can be dangerous also.

CLIMBING AIDS AND SAFETY MEASURES

The equipment and techniques that are used to deal with steep snow fall into two categories: those designed to help you climb up the slope in the first place, and those intended to prevent a slip or a fall from having serious consequences. The technical climber is likely to have a rather large arsenal of tools and techniques in each of those categories, but the backpacker's inventory is very small. Crampons, which are rigid frames with spikes protruding at the bottoms, can be attached to boots or snowshoes to keep the feet from slipping, and a similar device is sometimes used on skis. An ice ax provides a means of arresting a fall on snow slopes and makes many passages quite safe that would be exceedingly dangerous without the ax. The ax may also be used as a climbing aid, though for the backpacker it is more important as a safety device.

The safety devices are clearly the more important of the two sorts of equipment, but they are quite useless without practice in their use. Acquiring this experience is the prerequisite to any attempts to cross or climb slopes where a fall would be dangerous. Before delving into the lore of such slopes, however, we should consider the techniques that can be used to handle the many steep sections one sometimes encounters that present obstacles but not hazards.

SNOWSHOE TOOLS AND TECHNIQUES

Snowshoes tend to be particularly awkward when the going is steep, because it is usually impossible to dig the edges into the snow, as can be done with skis or boots alone. Still, snowshoes may be absolutely necessary for the nonskier in soft snow or in snow that has a crust that will hold up a snowshoer but not a walker without skis or snowshoes. In steep-snow country some kind of short, tail-less snowshoe is nearly always the choice, and there is a great advantage in having the foot well forward on the snowshoe, at least going uphill. Modern aluminum-framed shoes modeled after the Green Mountain bearpaw—Sherpa and Northern Lights, for example—are the best choice, for reasons mentioned in Chapter 7.

With any snowshoe design, steep snow calls for the addition of some sort of snowshoe crampon or traction device. In general, any cleat- or spike-like projection will do the job. The more spikes, and the longer they are, the better job they will do in difficult situations like slick crust, but the most effective arrangements with more than a couple of spikes over an inch long will have to be removable or they will cause trouble in normal woods walking. Whatever arrangement you use, remember that it will do the most good under the ball of the foot, where your weight will rest. Sherpa-type shoes and old army bearpaws come with attached crampons that work when there is only a little tendency to slip. Clamp-on snowshoe crampons are now available for steep, hard slopes, so it is no longer necessary to improvise your own, though it is easy to do so.

In soft, steep snow, the usual method of ascent with snowshoes is to kick the toe of the snowshoe directly into the snow. Then you put your weight on it as gingerly as possible, in hopes that the step won't break, causing you to slide back twenty feet. When you do break loose, it's usually better to try a new track the second time, since the first one gets harder and harder with successive attempts, gradually developing a vertical headwall at the top. Alternatively, depending on the width of the slope and the snow characteristics, you may be able to zigzag back and forth in diagonal traverses. This is easier with narrow snowshoes like the Sherpa model.

Where rocks underlie the soft snow by a few feet, you can sometimes get purchase with the toe of your boot sticking through the snowshoe toe hole and get up a steep step on the rocks. This is a rather delicate maneuver, and is advisable only when there is a soft landing below.

When the snow becomes a little harder, the step-kicking usually becomes quite effective, and no difficulties are experienced. As it gets too hard for step-kicking, the snowshoe is stamped flat, with traction coming from the crampons and from the toe of the boot protruding through the toe hole. With either of these methods, the climber should be careful not to move the foot around once it is placed, since this is likely to break the support loose. Step gingerly.

Naturally, when the snow becomes hard enough to support your weight without snowshoes, they are taken off and tied to the pack, and climbing, crossing, or descent proceeds on foot. The most difficult conditions occur on breakable crust that is too weak to climb without snowshoes but too slippery with them; snowshoe crampons usually solve this problem. An equivalent situation occurs when steep snow changes from hard crust to powder every few feet.

On any kind of steep snow a fairly long ski pole is a tremendous help as a prop, and many climbers prefer a pair of them. If an ice ax is carried it may be of some help on difficult steps if the shaft is plunged into the snow and the head used as a handhold. Special baskets are available for ice ax shafts in order to make them more useful in soft snow.

SKIS ON STEEP SNOW

The merits and limitations of various types of skis in steep snow have already been discussed at some length, and there seems no reason to repeat them. Skis that are designed to handle steep snow are generally much easier to use in difficult situations than snowshoes, provided the snow is deep enough and the skier is competent. It is usually easier for the skier to climb a steep slope using climbers than to remove his skis and resort to step-kicking. By the time the slope becomes hard enough to make skiing dangerous, crampons are often required to progress easily without the skis.

The limits of the skis can be extended somewhat for high-mountain skiing with the use of ski crampons called Harscheisen. These are serrated edges that attach to each side of each ski and protrude about an inch below the bottoms. They can be used on hard windpack and icy crust to make short, steep sections safe that would otherwise require normal crampons.

STEP-KICKING

As snow becomes hard and steep enough to prevent the hiker from gaining purchase by just stepping in it, it becomes necessary to kick steps into the slopes. There is nothing very difficult about this in principle, though someone doing it for the first time will probably find it rather tiring. One simply stands on one foot, raises the other to a comfortable height, and kicks the upper foot into the slope. Harder snow may require more than one kick. The procedure is continued until the top of the hill is reached. In coming downhill, the leg is usually straightened and the heel plunged down into the snow. This works on snow that is quite steep as long as it is soft enough, and the necessity of facing into the slope and kicking steps down is not likely to be encountered by the conservative backpacker. If it is, the procedure is to bend the upper knee as much as possible and then to kick a step with the lower foot.

The practice of carrying an ice ax and its use for self-arrest are discussed below, but it should certainly be carried on any slope requiring more than the simplest step-kicking. If an ax is not available, the slope should not be attempted. When it is carried, the shaft is usually plunged into the snow as an anchor whenever extra stability is needed during step-kicking.

When climbing soft snow it is usually easiest to proceed up with traverses and switchbacks. On harder snow, because of the extra effort needed to make the steps, it may require less total effort to climb straight up. It is almost always simplest to follow a straight line going downhill. There is normally no danger in going straight up or down in the sort of climbing being discussed here, since the possibility of a slip should not present great hazard. If such a danger does exist, because a slip might not be controlled, a straight line should not be followed, since it puts the whole party in a line, and if one person slips, everyone below him will also be knocked off. However, no one should be on hazardous terrain without a climbing rope and the skills to use it. Crampons have not yet been discussed, but if they are being worn the climbers should not be in line, since the danger is always present that the crampons of a slipping climber will mutilate the person below even in an otherwise harmless fall.

THE SAFETY FACTOR

Avalanches aside, the greatest danger presented by steep snow is that of an uncontrolled slip. Once a slide is started on a snow slope, it may be very difficult to stop without some special methods. Unless there is a positive means of stopping available, it is foolish to try to cross or climb any slope other than a very short one. As a general rule, you should never attempt any maneuvers on a snow slope unless you are absolutely sure that a slip would not be dangerous, either because the slope is short with no danger at the bottom or because you have the means of stopping.

The means of stopping a fall on steep snow is provided by the ice ax, and this is its main function for the general snow traveler. Stopping a slip with an ice ax is accomplished through the technique of self-arrest. Learning self-arrest will enable the backpacker and winter tourist to extend his horizons considerably and with safety. Learning in this case requires practice, however. It is not enough to know how the arrest is performed intellectually; it must be practiced until it has become instinctive and until the traveler has become a competent judge of its limitations.

The best way to learn the technique of self-arrest is to have an experienced climber teach you, perhaps at one of the beginning snow-climbing seminars sponsored by many climbing clubs in this country. Barring this, you can teach yourself. You'll have to find a fairly steep snow slope with a good smooth runout and no rocks around that you might hit if you lose control. Take some friends along who are interested in learning; spending the day sliding in the snow is a lot more fun with company. It's also a good idea to carry spare clothes, since you'll get wet in the course of a day's falling in the snow. If your slope is a bowl that gets progressively steeper the higher you go, you will be able to practice your technique on more and more difficult terrain, and you will be able to learn enough about self-arrest to handle easy slopes with confidence. The ability to handle and judge more difficult situations only comes after a lot more practice. Pick a day when the snow is fairly well consolidated. Loose snow requires wading to climb or stop, and when it gets steep enough to require arrests it presents an avalanche danger.

The Ice Ax

The ice ax is the indispensable tool of anyone who wants to venture on slopes where an unchecked slip would be dangerous. Without it even the experienced mountaineer will slide helplessly down easy snow slopes. For self-arrest and other such uses, the length of the ax should be about the same as the distance from your palm to the ground. Lengths a few inches longer or shorter than this are perfectly all right, but don't buy one of the very short axes that are now becoming common. Such axes are very practical for the technical climber on severe ice walls, but for the beginner on easy snow they are useless and dan-

Easy summer snow Climbing on summer snow, as here in the Minarets, is quite safe with only an ice ax—and perhaps crampons early in the morning. No rope is needed, but plenty of previous practice in self-arrest is essential.

gerous. Metal and fiberglass shafts are stronger and more reliable than wooden ones.

Other features are not important in occasional use by the wilderness traveler. The ax should have a wrist strap attached to a glide ring, but it will make no difference to you whether there is a carabiner hole or where the teeth are placed on the pick. You will probably be happiest with a fairly light ax, since it will travel most of the time on the pack, and the extra weight of a heavier ax is of use only in step-cutting or belaying by climbers on high-angle slopes.

Self-Arrest

Practicing self-arrest should be begun with the novice simply falling into the basic arrest position on a gentle slope. Dress warmly, with all your clothing zipped up and tucked in, and be sure to wear gloves. To arrest a fall the ax is held diagonally across the front of the body. One hand holds the head of the ax as shown in the illustration, the fingers curling around the top of the head and the thumb underneath the adze. The grip can be reinforced by wearing the wrist loop and wrapping it over the top of the ax head. The pick is held just under the shoulder, and the other hand grips the opposite end of the shaft, next to the spike, holding it firmly down by the hip. The whole weight of the body can then be forced down on the ax, pressing the pick into the snow. With the pick forced into the snow, the back is arched slightly, putting the body's weight on the pick and the toes, which are also dug into the snow.

After you have the feel of the arrest position, climb up the hill to a spot that is steep enough so that you will slide a bit if you slip, and practice going into the arrest position. If the snow is relatively soft, dig everything in immediately. If the snow is harder, dig the pick and your toes in a bit more smoothly and gradually, so that the pick will not be wrenched from your hands as you dig it into hard windboard or crust. As you begin to get the knack, work onto slightly steeper slopes, and simulate real slips. Try to get into the positions you would be in if a slip occurred when you were not expecting it. It should be clear by now that where a slip is possible you should always hold the head of the ax in your hand in the position you would use for self-arrest, with your hand around the head, the pick sticking out from the little finger side of the hand.

After you are completely confident about self-arrests that involve falling forward into the position, you are ready to start practicing with more awkward falls—backward. The problem in falling backward is that you end up sliding downhill head first on your back. As with all slips on steep snow, it is necessary to gain control very quickly, before a lot of speed is picked up. A very short delay will have you bouncing

Holding an ice ax This is the basic arrest position, with the climber grasping the head, pick facing out. The wrist loop is wrapped over the head and around the wrist to reinforce the grip. The other hand holds the shaft near the spike.

Arresting a fall To arrest a fall, the climber rolls over onto the shaft, forcing the pick into the snow or ice with the weight of the body. The right hand (if climber is right-handed) holds the shaft near the spike to keep it from catching and ripping the ax out of position. Arrest can be relied on only after extensive practice, since the position is not instinctive.

every which way, sometimes in the air, with no idea which way is up or down. The most important thing to remember in all slips is to apply the arrest immediately; in hard snow it must be applied smoothly, not by jamming the pick or toes into the snow, which would cause you to somersault or lose the ax, but by beginning a steady application immediately. With the backward fall, the ax is grasped in the arrest position while you are on your back. Then you roll over onto the pick side of your body—not the side where the spike is protruding and might be ripped from your hand. As the pick begins to drag, your feet will rotate around it, and by the time you have turned over onto your stomach, your feet should be headed downhill, and you are back in the normal arrest position. It goes without saying that this maneuver should be practiced on easy ground first; things happen very quickly on steep terrain.

As you acquire experience with the techniques of self-arrest, your confidence will develop, but you should take great care that all practice is carried out on slopes with a runout and with no protruding rocks or other objects. Loss of control above hard objects can lead to very serious injuries. Snow is always unpredictable, and a wide margin must be allowed for error, even by experienced snow mountaineers. An unexpected patch of ice may lie below you that will greatly affect your stopping distance, even if you don't lose your ax to it.

The cardinal rule in all situations where an arrest is being performed or may be called for is to *hang on to your ice ax.* You can't perform an arrest without it, except on very easy snow. On hard snow, the pick must not be jammed into the ice too quickly, or you will not be able to hold onto it; it is pressed in rapidly with a steady pressure, but not jammed. If you start to lose your hold, reduce pressure on the pick. *Maintain control of the ax.* Losing hold of the spike end makes the ax almost as useless as losing it altogether. In addition to this, the ax is sharp, and if your wrist strap is being worn, the flailing ax can injure you or one of your companions as you speed by.

The beginner practicing arrest will presumably be on a slope that does not require crampons, and so will not be wearing them. If you should buy or carry crampons later on, you should practice arrests while wearing them. Great care is needed if the toes are dug in not to catch the points of the crampons in hard snow and cause a backward somersault. While wearing crampons, it is safer to rely on the pick and the knees for arrest, if possible.

The Limits of Self-Arrest
Having learned the techniques of self-arrest, you will be able to undertake a lot of easy climbs and traverses on steep snow with confidence.

More than in any other area discussed in this book, however, a very conservative approach is called for in making safety judgments. Going up a snow slope is often easier than coming down (in a controlled manner, at least), even when the consistency of the snow remains the same. In addition to this fact, it is a rare day in the mountains when snow conditions on a steep slope do not change. If the snow that is just right for step-kicking at noon goes into shadow soon after, you may find it board hard in the afternoon, and it may be quite impossible for you to descend with your skills and equipment. In this case you may have to bivouac until the next day.

Any serious climbing requires the use of rope techniques for safety, at least as a reserve in case of difficulty. The discussion of these techniques is well beyond the scope of this book and requires carrying many extra pounds of equipment as well. For this reason, before you venture onto steep snow, ask yourself the following questions, and answer them carefully:

1. Is there any avalanche danger, or is any likely to develop, that might present a problem on the way back? (Avalanches are discussed in the next chapter.)

2. Can each person in the party easily stop a slip on this terrain with the equipment he has? Is the safety margin wide enough to take into account possible ice patches and changing conditions on the return trip?

3. Are there any dangers below on the slope that negate the value of an arrest as a safety factor—rocks, trees, cliffs, steeper sections, ice—or that might negate it on the return trip? You might be able to arrest before sliding over the cliff below now, but what about this afternoon? What if someone slips and arrests—he has to climb back up—has he also room for a second arrest?

4. Have you thought about the problem of handling this section with an injured person? When you are tired? In a storm? If you misjudge, can you go around another way or will this be the only way out?

CRAMPONS

Crusty or windpacked snow is often so hard that kicking steps in it is difficult or impossible. Such conditions require either cutting steps with the ice ax, the use of crampons to give the feet purchase on the snow, or both. Step-cutting will not be discussed here, since a slope that is steep and slippery enough to require it is also one where a climber, at least an inexperienced one, should be protected with a rope. Crampons may be useful to the general mountain traveler, however, if they are used carefully.

The most common crampons for occasional use on easy terrain are instep crampons, which are small frames with from four to six spikes each. They strap on the insteps of the boots. This type of crampon is relatively light and useful for negotiating occasional stretches of hard snow that may be encountered. It is perfect for the skier, snowshoer, or early spring backpacker to carry in case of a few short steep stretches.

More serious climbing requires a crampon that runs the full length of the boot. This type comes in several designs, but the novice should choose a set that is hinged in the middle to permit some flexing. Rigid crampons require rigid technical climbing boots to prevent breakage. The points should be about one and a half to one and three-quarter inches long; crampons with shorter points are designed for ice and are not as useful for the beginner. Crampons must be fitted to your boots. They have to fit tightly, and the strapping arrangement should be absolutely secure. The boots should not be able to shift on the crampons when they are pulled in different directions. There should be ten points on each crampon and all should be vertical; horizontal or angled front points are intended for technical climbing on steep ice. They are of no use to the backpacker on moderate terrain and make the crampons a little more dangerous for the inexperienced. The front set of points should be flush with the toe of the boot, neither forward nor back of it.

Use of crampons requires practice on progressively steeper slopes. All the cautions that have already been mentioned apply all the more if crampons are being used, since they make it possible for the climber to get into more difficult situations and present additional hazards as well. In principle, the technique is simple; the crampon is stamped or planted flat against the slope and left there until it is lifted for the next step. The ankles must be flexed to the angle of the slope, so that the crampon will be flush with it. If the crampon is planted straight down so that it forms an angle with the slope, it will tend to break out. In practice, the use of crampons on all but the gentlest slopes requires strength and flexibility of the ankles, which can only be developed with time. A few attempts on practice slopes will show the beginner the limits of his craft.

Several special dangers inhere in the use of crampons. They must be kept sharp. Dull crampons tend to break out unexpectedly and require much more force to set. In any case, they make the wearer less secure. Since crampons are sharp, they are also dangerous. The hazards of falling on one's companions have been mentioned. When learning to walk with crampons, take care to avoid snagging your pants legs, which can cause falls or leg injuries. When the crampons are not strapped on your boots they should be in the pack or made safe with some kind of secure shield. They should not be tied loose on the outside of the pack; if you fall they may gouge you, and if you turn around suddenly when one of your companions is nearby, you might make him a customer for the plastic surgeon.

Wet snow tends to pack in between the points of crampons. This is an extremely dangerous situation, since the effect is that the crampon does not bite at all. This is likely to happen at an unexpected moment. If snow conditions make sticking and packing snow a problem, a piece of plastic bag or plastic sheeting can be used to cover the bottom of the boot and crampon. The points of the crampons are poked through, but the plastic is tied on so that the rest of the soles are covered. The snow will adhere much less to the plastic, and packing will be less of a problem.

A FEW NOTES ON SNOW CLIMBING

This chapter has not been written as an introduction to mountaineering or technical climbing. Ascent of steep snow with more advanced techniques than those mentioned here requires the availability of a rope or at least the application of experience that must be acquired with the protection of a rope. The reader interested in pursuing the art of mountaineering is best advised to find an experienced person to teach him. Many climbing clubs have instruction programs for beginners. Several books on the subject are listed in the bibliography.

Use of the climbing tools discussed in this chapter is perfectly safe for general travel in snow country, provided you are conservative in keeping your aims within the limits of your experience. The ice ax is used by the climber to cut steps, to help belay the rope when it is used for protection, and to provide holds, but for the unroped novice it is carried for self-arrest. In soft snow, whether climbing or descending, you may wish to plunge the shaft into the snow so that the head can be used as a hold, or you may use either head or spike as a balance point. You must remember, however, that the primary use of the ax in this sort of climbing is as a safety factor, and whenever this safety factor is needed, the ax must be in a position that will enable you to go into arrest in case of a slip. Use the ax as a hold if you like, but only providing you don't have to sacrifice the arrest position to do it.

The safety strap should be used where you might drop the ax. Don't carry the ax carelessly at the top of a steep section after you no longer need to hold it in preparation for an arrest; if you drop it, you are likely to be stuck with no safe way to get down. The strap is intended to prevent accidents like this.

Glissading

Glissading is simply sliding down a snow slope on your feet or the seat of your pants, using the ice ax as a rudder and brake. The ax is held in the arrest position, except that the slider reaches around enough to drag the spike in the snow behind, so that the hand on the shaft can press it into the snow. Glissading upright is rather like skiing. Sitting down is easier and wetter. Glissading is good fun on the rare occasions when the conditions are right: the snow fast enough, but not so fast that you might lose control; no rocks, cliffs, or other hazards below that might be dangerous in case you do lose control; visibility good enough to be *sure* that glissading is safe. Don't glissade if there is danger of getting cold. Even standing glissades often end in facedown arrests, and if you're getting chilled the last thing you need is a good wallow in the snow. Glissading is great fun, but it has caused far too many accidents. You must be absolutely sure that the slope is safe before you deliberately start a slide, and you should go into arrest at the slightest hint that you are losing control. Glissading down an unknown slope when the entire length is not clearly visible is asking for trouble.

This chapter has deliberately emphasized caution, since there are a number of hazards in steep snow that are not immediately apparent to the beginner. If you are careful to watch for these dangers, however, there is little to fear in crossing and climbing moderate snow slopes. Snow slopes nearly always look steeper than they actually are, and once you are on them they usually instill even more caution than necessary, with no additional advice needed. By remaining aware of less obvious dangers like avalanches and the possibility of later freezing or snowfall, the snow traveler will be able to climb and cross reasonably steep snow with safety and confidence.

11 | Storms and Avalanches

Daily life in our usual surroundings tends to dull our sensitivity to the operation of the world in which people are only a small part. We move from heated or air-conditioned cars to buildings of the same temperature, almost unaware of the progress of the seasons or the day-to-day weather. One of the salutary effects of winter camping is that one becomes rapidly and keenly aware of our size and power in larger schemes of things. It is difficult to spend very much time outdoors in the winter and to still remain oblivious to the cycles of weather and snow and their effects on life.

The winter traveler or camper must learn to adapt to certain forces that are acting all around and to avoid the operations of others. Some weather is bad enough to require the hardiest of outdoor wanderers to hole up and wait until the storms abate; to become wise in the ways of avalanches it is necessary to make one's observations from a safe distance. Storms and avalanches can be viewed as sublime visitations, enthralling spectacles, or powerful and wily adversaries. But whatever the mood of the moment, the prudent winter traveler will always treat these phenomena with respect.

WEATHER IN WINTER

Watching the weather is a fascinating occupation at any time of the year, and the winter months hold a special interest in regions where snow is present. Rain may vary only in intensity, temperature, and the size of the drops, but snow falls in an infinite variety of forms. Besides this, it stays on all sorts of ground, and it continues to change from the time it falls until it melts. It can form a light insulating blanket over the body of a hibernating chipmunk, or it can stick to a tree in huge loads, until the tons of weight bow and break the trunk. It can form a sound and stable slope or a huge and unstable sheet, ready to slide off with the slightest unbalancing influence. It may slide in harmless sluffs or in huge masses possessed of enough energy to flatten a town without slowing down. Finally, after it has fallen, the snow layer itself has profound effects on the weather that originally produced it.

Nor is weather in winter just a colder version of the patterns of summer. The large-scale air movements that are ultimately the source of much of our weather are quite different in summer and winter, so that most areas have quite different weather configurations from one season to the next. The Sierra Nevada mountains of California, for example, have almost continuous good weather in the summer months, but in winter a stormless week is rare. Other regions have more stable weather in winter than in milder seasons. The afternoon thunderstorms that occur in many mountains in the summer, quite independent of large storm systems, are not present in winter, when a blanket of snow prevents the local heating of the air that causes these thunderheads to form.

In the great variety of winter weather it is the storms that most attract our attention. Aesthetically and intellectually we may delight in the differences between balmy afternoons and crisp, cold ones, but inevitably, thoughts of storms sweep milder contrasts aside. Our plans hinge on the presence or absence of signs of storm. We may revise routes or clothing depending on whether it is overcast and snowing, icy cold and clear, or lazily sunny. When signs of a real storm loom, however, choices are reduced to the alternatives of digging in or running. If we are forced onto the trail in a violent storm, the prospect is automatically seen as gloomy. With all this emphasis on bad weather, it is not surprising that most of our observations of the weather are concerned with detection of coming storms.

WATCHING THE WEATHER

The more you learn of the science of meteorology, the more easily you will be able to fit those signs into a coherent pattern. Still, many weather signs are dependent on local conditions, and the best meteorologist will be hard put to go into a strange area and compete with the weather eye of an observant native whose knowledge of local patterns is completely unscientific. Stripped of instruments and bulletins from a network of far-flung observers, the professional is on much the same footing as the amateur. If you want to learn to predict storms in your own skiing and snowshoeing country, you'll have to get out and watch. A weather-wise old-timer will often be able to get you off to a strong start.

On the opposite end of the technological scale from the local sage, the first trick in weather watching for the weekend traveler is to watch or listen to the weather forecasts before leaving. The TV charts of weather systems will tell you a great deal that you could never find out by observation, since they are based on information gathered at observation posts thousands of miles away. The pattern of weather in a particular region also becomes apparent on these charts if you watch them often. Books on weather rarely have a regional point of view. A combination of the knowledge of a few of the general principles of weather, a familiarity with normal regional storm tracks, and a check on the major systems on the map the night before the trip will equip the weekend sojourner with some excellent material on which to base a two-day prediction.

At best, of course, television forecasts give the skier or snowshoer a rough idea of what to expect and a foundation for later speculations. Perhaps this is just as well, since the fascination of weather watching comes in large measure from the uncertainty of the best forecasts. Whether you consider it a challenge or a nuisance, the weather bureau is rarely interested in the same areas that winter travelers concern themselves with, and you may have to extrapolate whatever data you obtain over hundreds of miles horizontally and thousands of feet vertically. Finally, on longer trips you will be on your own after a few days. Once you have obtained some knowledge of the general weather patterns of the areas you frequent, you may prefer to ignore the professional prognosticators altogether, finding your own guesses more interesting, if slightly less accurate.

A rough idea of local and regional patterns is probably the most essential weather-forecasting information wilderness travelers can have, whether for weekends or longer trips. Wind direction will mean different things in different regions. A storm coming through an area near the sea may bring cold rain or snow, depending on whether the low-pressure area at the center of the storm is nearer the sea than the camper, or farther away: thus, whether it is sucking cold, dry, inland air or warm, moist, sea air over him. Patterns in one area are often relatively consistent, but they will differ widely from the norms of another region, even one a few miles away.

In the Northeast, for example, the exact path taken by the storm center very often determines whether a particular mountain will be subjected to cold, dry snow or to rain and sleet. The snow camper may know from watching a Friday weather forecast that a storm is on the way, but he will have to depend on his own observations to guide him in his decisions on the trail. Observations of cloud formations and wind direction can tell a good deal about where the storm center lies, and this is useful not only in predicting the duration of the storm, but in predicting short-term trends in temperatures and precipitation. In the mountains of New Hampshire approaching storm clouds combined with winds from the east and tending southeast imply that the storm track is inland and that the relatively warm, wet air sucked in from the Atlantic will drop rain or wet snow, unless temperatures are quite cold. Storm clouds with winds from the northwest are more likely to bring in drier and colder air with a tendency to snow and colder temperatures. Each area has many patterns of this sort, and the first step in forecasting is to spend some time learning them.

In observing the weather of a particular area, the sequence of events is even more important than most individual signs. This is one reason why many who travel some distance to their wilderness rely on the weather bureau; on a short trip you cannot begin to piece a pattern together until it's about time to go home. If you live near your camping spot or go on longer trips, understanding the sequence of events from your own observations is easier.

The most obvious example of such a sequence is a set of barometric readings. Large-scale storms center around moving air masses in the atmosphere where the pressure is relatively low. Air from the surrounding region is under *relatively* higher pressure and is pushed by this pressure into the low-pressure area. Because of the earth's rotation, the air rushing toward the low-pressure area is deflected toward the right (left in the Southern Hemisphere) and the net effect is a whirlpool of air around the low. This whirlpool may be fairly small or hundreds and hundreds of miles wide, and it tends to move generally from west to east. As it moves over a particular spot, a barometer will measure a generally falling pressure as the low center comes closer, and after the low has passed, the barometer will show a rising pressure. Thus, the rise or fall of the barometer is significant, but one individual reading is not likely to mean much; it is the progression of readings that tells the observer something of what is to come.

Clouds and winds also tell the observer much more if he knows what came before. Many fluffy, white clouds at the same level with gray, flat bottoms (stratocumulus) may herald bad weather if they follow a few days of clear, cold weather and are preceded first by high, wispy clouds gradually thickening into a veil. On the other hand, if these same flocks of gray-bottomed piles of cotton follow a storm, they are more likely to indicate a couple of days of good weather.

Types of snow, likelihood of rain or sleet, and special oddities like warm, dry winds are also very much characteristic of particular areas. Most regions have their prevailing winds, characteristic types of snow, and special deceptive conditions. In some regions it is safe to plan on never having precipitation in winter except in the form of snow, so that waterproof gear does not have to be carried. In other areas, like New England, the most dangerous storms are those whipping cold rain along on high winds and following with very cold temperatures, freezing rain, sleet, ice, and finally snow.

Some patterns are generally dependable: Cold, clear weather following a storm is more likely to persist than relatively warmer pleasant weather. With an observant eye and a bit of reading on the subject, the outdoor wanderer can become sage about the succession of sun, clouds, wind, and snow. The more weather-wise you become, however, the more inclined you are likely to be to explain the weather after its arrival instead of before. Even professional meteorologists, with reams of data before them and banks of computers to analyze it, do well to predict the course of a storm a couple of days in advance. The more important questions to the winter foot tourist—how bad a storm, snow or rain, wet or dry snow, duration, and so on—are usually either obvious or very hard to predict. The amateur may be reduced to pronouncing wisely, "There is a 60 percent chance that there will be weather tomorrow."

Because of all these uncertainties, anyone who spends much time in the winter wilderness is going to be caught by quite a few storms, whether by accident or choice, and it is best to be prepared for them. If adequate preparations have been made, you can sit cozily in a shelter with your friends, while the winds howl about, telling them of the many signs that you observed of the coming storm, and carefully dodging questions that attempt to pin you down on the expected duration.

WEATHERING A STORM

Storm is a relative term, and it will mean different things to different people, depending on their location, equipment, and experience. The mere presence of falling snow, for example, need not stop anyone who is equipped with snowshoes or skis; the skiing is often better and the weather warmer when it is snowing. As the amount of precipitation and especially the wind velocity increase, however, it eventually becomes necessary to seek shelter. You should do your best to anticipate the need and to allow plenty of time for setting up camp or an emergency bivouac. Many factors should influence the decision on when to stop, and these must be balanced against each other in the best judgment of the members of the party, but there are several points that must be given particular weight.

The condition of the individual or party is one of the trickiest matters, but one that must be watched constantly. People who are cold and tired do not exercise their best judgment. An individual who is beginning to suffer from hypothermia (exposure) is likely to make irrational decisions, and this is the origin of many tragedies in the backcountry. The subject of hypothermia is discussed more extensively in the chapter on emergencies, and it will suffice to say here that the more severe the conditions, the more careful winter travelers must be to watch themselves and each other. Waiting too long to stop is likely to make setting up camp a difficult or impossible task. Even if the camp or bivouac is made successfully, a party that has stretched its endurance to the limit may not have the energy left to keep warm.

One of the most common errors in storm conditions is for a party to keep going too long in hopes of reaching a car, camp, or cabin. The decision of when to stop and dig in is always a difficult one. Perhaps the best way to avoid real difficulties is to stop briefly at the first sign of storm or the first suspicion that darkness may come before the party reaches its destination. The party can discuss the problems at this point, while everyone is still reasonably calm and clearheaded, and make a decision on a stopping time based on a reasonable assessment of the situation. For example, if no tent is available and a snow cave must be dug, they might decide that at least two hours before dark would have to be allowed, unless the whole party is proficient at digging caves. In storm conditions, there would be almost complete darkness around sunset, so they would have to stop two hours before sunset at the latest. Later on, unless they found themselves unquestionably less than two hours from their destination at the agreed stopping time, without possibility of being lost, they would definitely stop then. A person traveling alone should adhere to this same plan of deciding on a stopping time early, rather than continuing to the last minute in hopes of reaching camp.

Many complications arise in such situations. A party high in the mountains may decide to take certain risks in order to reach timberline, where shelter is easier to make and firewood is available. They should balance the difficulties and energies required to reach timberline against the possibilities of making a snow shelter where they are. A party that is lost in severe conditions would rarely be wise to continue, since they are likely to be in the same position a few hours later, but with their energies and hopes depleted by fighting against the storm to no advantage. On the other hand, a group with one person suffering from hypothermia but only an hour above timberline might well decide that continuing to a spot where a fire could be built would be more sensible than leaving the hypothermic individual out in the full blast of the weather while a shelter is constructed in the open.

CAMPS AND BIVOUACS IN STORMS

When all the party's equipment is being carried, setting up camp in a storm is not much different from the same task at any other time, except that more care is required in anchoring tents and building walls for windbreaks. Parties in wooded areas should not have too much difficulty, since the forest breaks up the wind quite a bit, reduces drifting, and provides ready-made anchors for guy lines. If you are using a floorless tent in the woods, build up low walls of snow around the sides to keep the wind out. You will also have to build walls to shelter a fire if you intend to build one, and these can be arranged in such a way as to reflect the heat into the tent or shelter. (Remember, fires for warming should be avoided except in emergencies.) Look around for dead trees and branches that might be broken by high winds, and make sure your tent is not pitched in their path.

Tents pitched in the open are likely to encounter much stronger winds. Mountain tents are designed with low profiles (or aerodynamic shapes) so that they will be stable in high winds. When possible, the entrance should be pitched into the wind. Pitching a tent with the entry across or away from the wind causes much more flapping. Openfront tents and other high tents designed for use in the forest are not stable in high winds, and if you are caught out in the open with this kind of tent, you may have to build a snow shelter instead. The tent may serve if it is pitched very well and protected by low snow walls. It may also be possible to lower the tent by weighting the lower parts of the tent walls down with snow and pitching the whole tent a foot or two lower than normal. This will only be possible if heavy snow is available. Another way to accomplish the same end can sometimes be improvised. Rocks or other objects are placed along the tent wall at the height that is to serve as the lowered bottom. These can be tied off with cord, which can then be anchored to the ground in the usual fashion.

Drifting snow tends to bury tents in stormy weather, and to prevent their collapse it may be necessary for someone to go outside periodically to clear the snow from the tent. This is especially true when the falling snow is wet and heavy, since large snow loads can build up much more quickly than with light powder. The problem of drifting should also be considered in choosing a tent site during a storm. Large drifts tend to build up on the lee sides of objects during a storm. When you choose a spot that is sheltered from the wind, be sure that it will not also be the site of a large drift, unless you think you might enjoy moving your tent in the middle of the night. A drifted-in tent can ice up and become airtight, posing the possibility of suffocation if it is not cleared. Modern dome and tunnel tents do not tend to drift in as badly as traditional designs.

Much more difficult situations are encountered when a party is caught by a storm away from camp or base. If possible, of course, one gets back to camp, but once it becomes clear that this may not be possible, the time and energy that remain should be spent on establishing a bivouac that is as comfortable as possible. Whenever you travel very far from your camp or car you should give some thought beforehand to the equipment that will be needed in case you have to bivouac, equipment that will vary somewhat with the terrain and weather conditions.

The basic types of shelters which are used in bivouacs have been discussed in an earlier chapter. Anyone caught in a storm is likely to be short on insulation, since the body needs much more protection against the cold when it is at rest than when it is active. Since a person caught away from camp probably has a deficit in insulation, it is important to use the excellent insulating properties of snow in any survival situation. A snow hole or igloo will provide nearly perfect shelter from the wind and will also usually warm up to around the freezing point or higher in a fairly short time. Even in forested areas where firewood is readily available a snow shelter is often easier to build and warmer than a lean-to shelter with an all-night fire in front. In either case, advance preparation in the form of a few tools and some specialized clothing is important. Building a snow hole or igloo is a relatively simple affair if the proper tools are avilable, but it can be a rather desperate matter if they are not. Proper clothing will not make a winter bivouac comfortable, but it will make the difference between emerging a bit cold and stiff in the morning and being in really serious condition. Even the simple expedient of carrying a couple of large plastic garbage sacks in your pack to help protect you from wind and moisture can be enormously helpful in a survival situation.

Anyone traveling in circumstances that might require a bivouac should carry emergency food. Obviously, it should contain lots of calories and should be edible without cooking or the addition of water; heat and liquid water may be in short supply in a bivouac. Any emergency fuel available should be used for preparing drinks rather than cooking food, unless large quantities of fuel are obtainable. Dehydration is dangerous in itself and contributes to many other physical problems. Amounts of food that need to be carried depend greatly on the circumstances of your trip. They may range from a few candy bars to a couple of weeks' emergency rations. On most trips of several days to a week I carry a little more than an extra day's food; this can be stretched out for several days in a really bad storm.

Clothing and special gear that are intended to serve for a possible bivouac also vary widely with locale and time of year. In very cold regions where wet conditions are not encountered in winter, warmth and protection from the wind will be paramount. On the other hand, where cold, freezing rain *might* occur, it is essential to have some kind of completely waterproof cover, even at the expense of condensation, to keep insulating layers from becoming completely soaked. Gore-tex outer layers are ideal. If you are bivouacking in some kind of bag or parka, waterproofing is much more critical than in trail clothing or tents, because the fabric will tend to form water-catching pockets so that moisture will soak through that would flow off a standing figure or a tightly stretched tent. Seams should therefore be sealed carefully.

Basic clothing for possible bivouacs should begin with a couple of layers of wool, pile, or other synthetics because of their quality of retaining some warmth when wet. Over these go sweaters or down clothing, depending on your budget and the temperatures you may encounter, and these are followed by all the shell clothing you may be carrying. Finally, there is special bivouac covering, which may be a very large anorak into which you can tuck your legs or may be a large sack into which you can crawl. Unless you are sure that natural ground insulation will be available (and that you will be justified in cutting it), you should carry some sort of ground insulation.

Particular attention should be paid to protection of the head and the feet. The head must be well protected because it can radiate so much of the body's heat production to your surroundings. The feet need special attention because they become cold easily and are hard to protect. Hats and hoods with drawstrings pulled tight take care of the head. If no special protection is carried for the feet, you should at least change into dry socks and loosen the laces of your boots. Overboots should be put on if they are carried, and any extra insulation available can be wrapped around. If boots are removed, try to keep them near the body where they won't get frozen: Frozen boots and swollen feet in the morning are no joke. Special footwear for a bivouac may include down booties or foam inserts for overboots.

Large plastic bags are lightweight, compact to carry, and are invaluable both in planned and emergency bivouacs. They can be used as waterproof sacks for the legs, and they should be used in snow shelters to store any down equipment when it is not in use, to keep it from picking up moisture in the humid atmosphere of the igloo or snow hole. Many large bivouac parkas and sacks are available for outer protection, or you can make your own. Plans for two types are included in Appendix A.

For planned bivouacs a good but expensive alternative for insulation is a combination of a half sleeping bag and an expedition down parka. Some down pants have a zipper combination that makes it possible to convert them to half bags. Such alternatives are satisfactory for planned bivouacs in relatively mild winter conditions. Severe weather, however, is not to be toyed with, and these methods should be used mainly for emergencies. If you *plan* to bivouac or camp in winter, you should normally have a good winter sleeping bag with you or a combination of down parka, down pants, and a light overbag.

Special tools for tentless shelters also depend on conditions and plans. Igloos are only practical when snow conditions are good, so a snow knife is not of much use in powdery midwinter snow. Igloos also generally take too long to build to be useful for a one-night shelter, except when snow conditions are ideal. Generally, snow holes are the most practical emergency shelters, and if they are anticipated, a snow shovel should be carried. With one, a snow hole can be dug out quite quickly, but without, the process is likely to be an ordeal.

When snow depth is not sufficient for a snow hole, an igloo may still be built. At worst, walls of snow may be heaped around, and some sort of a roof may be possible to improvise. The walls will at least serve as a windbreak. Snow pits near trees often make excellent shelters with only a little additional excavation. Shelters are discussed more completely in Chapter 4. The important thing to remember in bivouac conditions, when inadequate insulation is available, is that snow shelters can be raised to tolerable temperatures with body heat, and they usually require less effort with a more readily available material (snow) than lean-tos with all-night fires. The last thing the average outdoorsman caught in a winter storm thinks of is digging himself into the snow, but this is usually just what he should do.

My own preference for bivouac equipment in most circumstances, assuming that my basic clothing consists of polypropylene underwear, stretch or wool pants and top, a pile jacket, and a Gore-tex parka and pants, is:

- light, but warm, down jacket with hood
- light pair of down pants, which will zip into a half bag
- a bivouac sack with a coated nylon bottom and Gore-tex top
- small pile sack I have made for my feet, which then go inside my pack
- lightweight folding aluminum shovel
- spare pair of dry socks
- foam pad (part of my pack)

All these items add only five pounds to my pack, and many of them serve double duty. The shovel would usually be carried anyway for avalanche rescue, and the down jacket and pants serve for spare clothing. They are enough to guarantee that I can spend a reasonably comfortable night out in most circumstances, yet they are light enough not to slow me down significantly on the trail.

AVALANCHES

Campers on the great plains or in the north woods have the same difficulties with howling winds and deep new snow that their counterparts in the mountains do. After the end of the storm, however, they have only to dig out and plow their way along the trail. Mountaineers have another problem after and during the storm: Many of those falling tons of snow are going to come sliding down off the sides of the mountains, and it is important to be somewhere else when they do. The next section of this chapter will deal with this problem of the high country. It may be ignored by those who never travel to high altitude, but is important to those who do.

Steep open slopes After a heavy storm, steep open slopes like these at Castle Peak can be a deathtrap for a careless tourer.

Like many other powerful natural phenomena, a big avalanche is spectacular, and it is an event best observed from a safe distance. Most of the major western ski areas have crews of specialists who spend a great deal of time, skill, and money controlling the avalanche paths in the relatively small amount of territory covered by the ski areas themselves. The reason is simple: The danger to recreational skiers would be intolerably high without adequate methods of prediction and control of avalanche slopes.

In the high mountains of the western United States and Canada and on some eastern mountains the dangers presented by avalanches to those who ignore their threat are very real. The hazards are expecially high for the cross-country traveler, who will have no avalanche teams to protect him with signs or artillery, and who is likely to pick avalanche slopes as choice routes of travel, particularly for the skier. Anyone spending much time in backcountry avalanche terrain should learn as much as possible about avalanche conditions. A clear understanding is particularly important for skiers who delight in steep downhill runs.

Avalanches are a complex subject—one that is not completely understood even by experts who have spent their lives studying it—involving the mechanics of the always-changing internal structure of the snow, detailed long-term weather observations, and a great deal of knowledge of particular slopes that cannot be obtained by casual inspection. Despite these complications, however, the basic reasons for the occurrence of avalanches are fairly simple, as are many of the safety rules that follow from them.

What Causes Avalanches?

When snow falls on the ground, the force of gravity continues to act on it. On flat terrain, this force will cause settlement, but since it is not possible for the snow to slide downhill, there are no other important effects. If, on the other hand, the snow comes to rest on a slope, the force of gravity is always trying to pull the snow down the slope. Our concern here is the situation that occurs when a large mass of snow accedes to the constant downward pull suddenly and at a rapid rate. Experience has taught mountaineers that it is unhealthy to be perched on a large quantity of snow at the time that it decides to make its downward trip.

Of course, there are very few truly flat areas of any size, and it is clear that snow will not avalanche on slight inclines. Avalanches will only occur as slopes become steeper and the pull of gravity along the slope increases. On the other hand, snow will not cling to vertical faces in large quantities; the snow falls off these precipices almost as fast as it comes down. It is on the intermediate slopes that avalanches form, where the incline is gentle enough to permit large quantities of snow to build up, but where the pressure on the snow to flow down the slope is still compelling.

Many things besides the angle of the slope are important in determining avalanche formation, however, the next most obvious one being the nature of the slope itself. Snow will not slide down in large masses where it is well anchored to the slope at many closely spaced points. Heavily forested slopes rarely avalanche. Irregular, rough, boulder-strewn slopes will not avalanche until enough snow has fallen to fill in the irregularities of the potential avalanche path and form a

Avalanche danger Even generally safe mountains like this one can present avalanche hazard under the right conditions. Unless you are *sure* those prominent gullies are stable, stay out of them and keep to the trees. The chutes are kept clear of trees by recurring avalanches.

smooth sliding surface. Smooth rock slabs or grass slopes form a fine sliding surface, however, and may avalanche with much smaller amounts of snow than would be required on a rough surface.

We begin to reach more complicated ground in considering the conditions of the snow cover itself. Snow falls in an almost infinite variety of forms and mixtures. It begins to change the instant it is formed in the atmosphere, is continuously modified by temperature, wind, and humidity as it falls to earth, and goes on changing after it becomes a part of the snow cover, under the influence of a bewildering variety of conditions. Still, despite all the factors that influence its course, the basic cause of an avalanche is this: When the forces holding the snow—be it one snowflake or a huge slab—are exceeded by the force of gravity pulling it down along the slope, the snow will slide. In sliding, it will exert pressure on other masses of snow, and if this pressure added to the pull of gravity exceeds the strength of their anchoring forces, they, too, will begin to slide down the mountain.

This unbalancing action that starts the avalanche may occur because of an increase in the forces pulling downward, as when more weight is added to a layer of snow during a storm, it may result from a decrease in the strength of the anchors holding the snow, or it may be the product of the combination of both. In practice, the consideration of this balance is complicated by the variable nature of the snow cover. When the snow is loose with little cohesion between individual snow crystals, the problem is difficult enough, but as the snow layer becomes more coherent, forces are transmitted through it. Thus, an unstable part of a snow slab may be supported by being anchored at its edges to the rest of the cover. Alternatively, a stable portion of the cover may be pulled from its anchors by the weight of neighboring areas of unstable snow. Many different types of avalanches are recognized, and since some of them are very different in character it is convenient to break down the discussion of avalanche danger according to some broad classifications.

Types of Avalanches

The first and most important division of avalanches is between *loose-snow avalanches* and *slab avalanches*. A loose-snow avalanche starts at a point when a small amount of snow is set in motion, perhaps by a clump falling off a tree or by a snowshoer disturbing the slope. This moving mass disturbs and carries off more and more snow as it slides, until the avalanche has run its course, leaving a V-shaped path with the point at the top. Slab avalanches begin with a large mass of snow that begins to move at the same time, forming a long, wall-like break at the top where the slab separated from the rest of the snow cover.

Slab avalanches are subdivided into *hard slabs* and *soft slabs*. Before avalanching, a hard slab tends to hold a skier or walker with little, if any, sinking. The debris of a hard-slab avalanche contains chunks and blocks of various sizes. Soft slabs are formed of softer snow that allows the traveler to sink in his tracks, sometimes half an inch, and sometimes to his hips. When it avalanches the soft slab tends to break up and proceed like a loose-snow avalanche.

Avalanches may be *dry, damp,* or *wet.* Dry avalanches contain no free water and are usually at temperatures below thirty-two degrees Fahrenheit. Damp and wet snow avalanches are at thirty-two degrees; the former will pack easily and contains some moisture, while the latter has considerable free water. Dry-snow avalanches contain a good bit of air in the snow, damp ones much less, and wet avalanches have little air mixed in the snow. Wet avalanches tend to form large snowballs that make a channeled track. They move more slowly than dry avalanches and weigh much more.

Avalanches usually begin by traveling on the ground. They may be temporarily airborne in falling over cliffs, and even while they are sliding down slopes a great deal of snow may roil into the air. A large, fast-moving avalanche will also produce a shock wave in the air. Distinctions among these phenomena need not concern us much, but there is one type of avalanche that departs in character from these in a major way. Apparently, when a dry-powder avalanche reaches a certain speed, the shock wave in the air and the associated turbulence become the main propagating vehicle of the avalanche. The cloud of powder and shock wave from this type of avalanche move at tremendous speeds, on the order of two hundred miles per hour, and they proceed with much less friction than a normal avalanche, so that they can travel much farther beyond the steep slopes where they begin.

Large avalanches are quite likely to be mixtures of the types mentioned above. A loose-snow avalanche may trigger the release of a slab. Dry snow from high slopes will carry along the wet snow it encounters lower down. The main purpose of classification here is to help the winter traveler to recognize dangerous conditions. Any kind of avalanche danger carries with it the possibility that large masses of snow may be released once sliding starts.

The Stability of the Snow Cover

The fact of the continuous metamorphism of the snow cover has already been mentioned. This characteristic and several others are very important in the formation of avalanches. Snow is a plastic material: It will deform under stress and will gradually change its shape in order to eliminate the stresses caused by the deformation.

Avalanche in progress A great avalanche roars down over a cliff, producing a large powder cloud as it becomes airborne.

This plasticity will cause snow that is lying on a slope to creep gradually down the slope. Many of the stresses within the snow layer are caused by different rates of creep from one spot to another.

Metamorphism usually results in the snow layer becoming stronger and more coherent. Settling takes place and bonding occurs between the grains of snow. This process is hastened whenever the snow is moved around and disturbed so that the crystals tend to interlock and fall together. Metamorphism is speeded up by higher temperatures, and mechanical disturbance may be accomplished by avalanching or by wind. The hardening produced by these processes generally contributes to the stability of a slope and decreases the possibility of avalanches. However, when they increase the coherence within one layer of the snow cover that is poorly bonded to the layers below, a slab is created, and it is such slabs that avalanche when the anchors around their edges are no longer strong enough to hold their weight. Stresses generated by creep may serve to snap a bond at one edge of a slab. The release of this anchor often puts undue strain on another, which then snaps in turn. The propagation of the fracture lines around a slab proceeds with incredible rapidity. At this point the slab may either avalanche, perhaps releasing other slabs as well, or it may slump to a new and more stable position.

Unstable slabs are most often created by windblown snow. The crystals of the snow are broken up and stirred together by the turbulence of the wind and are thus given great cohesion. The layer formed by such wind-driven snow is called windslab. Great quantities of snow can be deposited in such a formation, often with poor bonding to the surface of the base below. These slabs formed by windblown snow are the most common source of persistent avalanche danger, especially in the Rockies, Sierra Nevada, and Cascade ranges. Most such slabs are formed on leeward slopes (those facing away from the wind), but in heavy snowstorms they may be deposited on slopes facing in any direction. Slopes facing into the wind are more likely to accumulate windpacked snow that is well bonded to the layers below.

Metamorphism generally tends to produce more rounded, compact, and larger grains of snow and to improve the bonding between layers. This process, erasing the original character of the snow crystals, is known as equitemperature metamorphism, because it occurs within snow layers of more or less even temperature. Sometimes, however, a change known as temperature-gradient (or TG) metamorphism occurs, which produces more complex crystals. These crystals are cup- or scroll-shaped and are known as TG crystals, sugar snow, or depth hoar. They have very little cohesion and form a very weak layer that often forms a sliding base for very dangerous slab avalanches. Depth hoar is particularly hazardous because it undercuts what may previously have been a very stable snow cover. Depth hoar is most common in the Rocky Mountains, but under the right conditions it may occur elsewhere. Once formed, the depth-hoar layer may gradually disappear under the influence of temperature-gradient metamorphism, or it may remain like a cocked trap well into late winter and spring.

Depth hoar is formed when there is a relatively large difference in temperature operating through a fairly thin layer of snow—a high temperature gradient. Several sets of circumstances can cause TG crystals to form, but the most common is extended cold weather while the snow depth on the ground is only a few feet. The interface between the snow and the ground will normally be at exactly the freezing point—thirty-two degrees Fahrenheit or zero degrees Celsius—so if the air is very cold, there will be a large temperature change between the top and bottom of the snow. The resulting transfer of energy over a period of time drives the formation of the characteristic faceted, stepped, cup-shaped crystals of depth hoar. If the snow remains cold through the winter, this layer will persist, and it can act like a layer of ball bearings for any windslabs or heavy snows that cover it. Depth hoar has so little cohesion that it will flow off your mittened hand like sugar. It cannot be packed into snowballs unless it melts somewhat first.

The Rockies are notorious for the formation of depth hoar for the reasons just described: Deep snow often does not come until well into the winter, following a few light snows and weeks of very cold weather. In such conditions a deep layer of depth hoar will usually form, providing a dangerous sliding surface for the windslabs that are also common. Such unstable conditions often persist for months, waiting to trap an unwary skier traversing the slope and cutting the slab loose with the edges of the skis. Similar conditions in any other range can produce the same danger.

Avalanche Slopes

Avalanches can occur on a very wide range of slope gradients. Wet snow avalanches in spring with enough water to lubricate themselves will sometimes occur on slopes of less than 15°. Such avalanches may endanger property, but they are not usually much problem to the winter traveler, because they move so slowly. As the gradient of the slope becomes steeper, dangerous avalanches are more likely to occur; then, as it becomes steeper still, they become less likely again, because the snow slides off before significant amounts accumulate. The most likely angle of a slope on which dangerous avalanches may start is around 25° to 45°, but danger may begin on gentler slopes if a particularly good sliding surface is present or on much steeper ones if snow can accumulate. Such angles are difficult to judge accurately, anyhow, without actual measurement, and they are given as a rough indication of danger. With enough experience, the snow mountaineer will learn to judge the angle at which appreciable danger begins. For the enthusiastic downhill skier, the angle is unfortunately rather easy to judge: The highest probability of avalanches will be found on the best ski slopes. The angles coincide almost perfectly!

These considerations apply to the slope where the avalanche begins. An avalanche already in motion will continue onto much gentler slopes, so that the traveler must remain aware of the slopes above. This information is important, nonetheless. Most avalanche victims trigger the avalanches themselves, so the conditions where avalanches may start are a subject of considerable interest. It is dangerous to pass under an avalanche slope, but the chances of being caught are not nearly so great as those encountered by someone who crosses through the breakaway zone and thus risks triggering the avalanche himself. Avalanches rarely start on heavily forested slopes, but scattered trees yield no protection and should not be taken as an indication of safety. Small clumps of trees are present on many slopes that avalanche with every major storm. Brush and rockfields also keep slopes from avalanching, but only until the drifting snow has filled in the anchoring irregularities; once a smooth snowfield is present they provide no protection against avalanching of the upper layers of snow. Grass and rock slabs form good sliding surfaces for avalanches extending right to the ground.

Gullies and couloirs are natural avalanche paths; that is why they are there in the first place. They are the drainspouts of a mountain and are exceedingly dangerous if any of the slopes above are likely to avalanche. Ridges, high knolls, and similar barriers are the natural safe spots on a mountain.

Because of their tendency to place extra tension on the surface of the snow, convex slopes of a given angle are more likely to avalanche than concave ones. This should not be taken to imply that concave slopes are safe from avalanches, but examining the contour of the slope may enable you to guess the most likely point of fracture of a slope, so that you can keep well above it. Avalanche swaths are often recognizable where they have been cut through timber in a fan-shaped path, usually with the wide end at the bottom.

The orientation of the slope is likely to have a good deal of influence on the likelihood of its avalanching. In the discussion below of particular categories of avalanches, it is pointed out that some types are far more likely to occur on slopes facing in a particular direction. Slabs caused by wind drifting are much more likely on leeward slopes, for example; these same slopes are also the ones most likely to be overhung by cornices whose fall may provide a trigger.

Loose-Snow Avalanches

In general, loose-snow avalanches are less likely to be dangerous than slabs. This is true because the conditions that precede them are much easier to detect, because the danger of their occurrence is less likely to persist, because they are likely to be smaller, and because one is more likely to be able to get out of their way or escape alive if caught.

When temperatures are low, loose-snow avalanches often come down during or shortly after a storm. They tend to develop when dry snow falls in calm conditions. When much wind is present, the snow is more likely to be windpacked or to be deposited in slab formations. Dry, unstable snow is very shifty, providing little flotation for skis or snowshoes, and tending to flow back into your tracks behind you. True powder snow, which is something like bread flour in its lack of cohesion, may often form loose-snow avalanches. Powder results from the metamorphism of dry snow that has not been subjected to much winddrifting. Metamorphism removes the feathery arms that have caused the interlocking of the snow crystals so that they can flow more easily. Such powder-snow avalanches may occur days after a storm if conditions remain well below freezing.

The danger of dry loose-snow avalanches can persist only when temperatures are very cold. Most of them come down during heavy snowfalls and in the few hours afterwards. Some come down after metamorphism has produced true powder conditions. If temperatures warm up to around freezing, the danger is likely to disappear in a few hours, though it will be very high when temperatures first rise. Instability of such powder is easily tested on small slopes with the same exposure and gradient as larger and more dangerous mountainsides. If the snow is unstable on the small slopes, it is likely to be unstable on the large ones. (Remember that different conditions will prevail at the top of a slope with a vertical drop of a few thousand feet.) Fresh tracks and avalanche debris at the bottom of the slopes give an indication of danger. If you are traveling along a valley and note that several possible avalanche paths have been active recently, you should be very wary of one that has not yet slid.

Completely different kinds of loose-snow avalanches occur in warm, thawing conditions, especially in spring. A snow pack that may have been quite stable loses its coherence in thawing and is lubricated by percolating meltwater. Very large and heavy avalanches may occur in these conditions, which, like those preceding dry loose-snow avalanches, are usually fairly easy to detect. The snow may become wet as a result of being warmed by radiation, by generally warm temperatures, by warm wind, or by percolating rain water. The surface layers may become unstable, or the whole slope may become rotten because of the soaking of a layer of depth hoar deep in the snow pack.

Probably the most common avalanches of this type are those that come down in spring in the later morning and early afternoon after the top layers of snow have been softened by the sun. Such avalanches usually occur on sunny days, but the snow may also melt by absorbing radiation from high, warm clouds, even when no sun appears and when air temperatures at ground level are below freezing. Signs of instability can usually be seen from some distance: Sunballs roll down the slopes, small slides may be observed or a large one heard, and small slopes of similar exposure to large ones show signs of surface instability. Damp snow in the top strata will slide off in layers, giving poor footing and even sliding out from under skis. This instability is in marked contrast to the afternoon mushiness that may occur on top of stable spring snow. In the latter case only the top few inches are soft, and there is a firm base underneath.

With really wet snow that has been completely soaked and undercut by rain and meltwater, instability is usually marked by soft snow that will not bear much weight. Even the skier is likely to go in up to his knees or hips. Wet snow is very heavy, and if it is also this soft, it is quite dangerous. Such conditions often indicate that a lower layer of depth hoar has become soaked and has collapsed, and subsequent avalanches are quite likely. If these conditions predominate in the main snow layer, a frozen layer on the top should not be regarded as indicating much stability.

Any of these types of wet-snow avalanche may be produced even in midwinter if a very warm wind should begin blowing. Such winds occur occasionally in many mountain ranges, but they are most common in North America on the eastern side of the Rocky Mountains, where they are known as chinooks. A chinook can raise temperatures eighty degrees in a couple of hours. A chinook is formed when a wet air mass loses its moisture in condensed snow or rain as it goes over the top of the mountain range. The precipitation of the moisture causes the air to be warmed, since the water gives up its heat of vaporization. As the air descends to lower elevations on the far side of the mountain range, it is warmed further by higher pressures. The warm, dry wind that is produced can melt a great deal of snow in a short time, far more than either sun or rain, and the beginning of a chinook will often presage a torrent of avalanches within a few hours.

Slab Avalanches

The greatest danger from slab avalanches derives from the difficulty in predicting them. The slab may lie dormant on a slope for months before a heavy snowfall adds too much weight too rapidly and brings half the mountainside down. Still more difficult for the transient tourer to predict is the slab avalanche resulting from the undercutting effects of depth hoar. Even an expert working in one area for the whole winter cannot predict when or whether a slab will come down. He gets an answer by taking a 75- millimeter recoilless rifle and lobbing a few shells at it or setting charges in the fracture zone by hand. The best for which the backcountry traveler can hope is to be able to recognize a situation of potential danger and to stay clear of it. Pressing the limits of avalanche hazard is risky even where a rescue party is standing by; in wilderness situations it is foolhardy.

Slab formation is generally associated with windblown snow, and while slabs are usually produced during storms, wind-drifted snow may form them with no new precipitation at all. Virtually any type of snow can form slabs, though the characteristics of the slabs themselves will depend on the type of snow. The softer slabs that usually result from snow falling at moderate temperatures will usually slide during or shortly after a storm, and will stabilize fairly quickly, either by avalanching or settling in place. The harder slabs that are most frequently formed by high winds at subzero temperatures may persist in a dangerous state for weeks or months.

Slabs usually form on lee slopes, though during a snowstorm with moderate winds they may form on any slope. With moderate temperatures, stability usually follows not too long after the storm, unless some particularly poor base, such as an ice layer or depth hoar, underlies the structure. Under very cold conditions, any slope prone to slides that has not actually avalanched is suspect. A hard slab can persist for weeks after the last storm and be triggered by a crossing skier.

Conditions of extreme danger from slabs will show in the instability of small slopes as well as large ones. Such instability may reveal itself when cracks shoot out from a traveler's feet, skis, or snowshoes. Small cracks that extend only a few feet may indicate a harmless crust, but if the cracks begin to extend ten feet or more and cut deep into the snow layer, severe avalanche danger is certain to be present. The absence of such signs should not be interpreted as a sign of safety; they may not appear except when it is too late. A hard slab, especially, may be buried under quite a bit of new snow, so that the observation of surface conditions will tell nothing.

JUDGING HAZARDOUS CONDITIONS

Despite the difficulties of avalanche forecasting, the careful mountaineer can usually avoid too much risk to life and limb by watching for danger signs, finding out as much as possible about the condition of the snow pack, and practicing a general conservatism of judgment where avalanches may slide. For the weekend traveler, the first step should be to check with a local expert when that is possible. If you visit an area only a few times a year, you may be reluctant to spend your time digging pits in the snow to find out whether a layer of depth hoar has formed or whether a thick glaze of ice was produced early in a particular year. Such an ice layer may bring down avalanches with every storm in places that never slide in normal years, so that even if you take a particular tour every season it is worthwhile to check with a local snow ranger or ski-area avalanche-control expert. If you find a few such people in the areas you frequent, you can always call them up the night before you leave. They can tell you if there is some particular hazard you ought to know about and what kind of slopes you might need to avoid.

Watch for avalanche slopes. Any slope more than about 25° should be considered suspect unless it is heavily forested. As a rough guide, if you are wearing snowshoes and cannot climb straight up the fall line in normal snow without kicking steps or wearing crampons, the slope is probably steep enough to avalanche. If you are a skier using well-applied touring waxes and you have to angle your skis more than 45° from the fall line to climb, the slope is probably steep enough to avalanche. A skier using climbers and going straight up the fall line is on a potential avalanche slope when the slope starts feeling steep, but well before most climbers stop biting.

Remember that once the steepest part of the slope begins to avalanche, the slide will carry onto gentler slopes and may run over flat land and even up the opposite side of a narrow valley. You must pay nearly as much attention to slopes above and below you as to the angle of the slope on which you are traveling. Be particularly wary of slopes overhung by cornices. These are lee slopes—those most subject to slab formation—and they are topped by potential avalanche triggers. Gullies and slopes that have avalanche tracks cut through trees are particularly dangerous and should be avoided.

In avoiding an avalanche slope, it is safest to go above the area of potential danger. Next safest is traveling below the slope, preferably beyond the potential runout. Most people caught by avalanches have triggered the slides themselves, either by adding extra weight or by cutting away some of the supporting snow of the slab. Even the slight weight of a person can overstrain a small section that is helping to hold up a large slab. By releasing one section, a person can start a redistribution of forces that will cause half the mountainside to start sliding. For this reason, unless slides are coming down every few minutes, it is usually safer to pass under a potential avalanche zone than through it: You take a chance of an avalanche coming down but not the much greater chance of releasing one yourself. If at all possible, however, one should stay completely out of both the potential slide area and the runout zone. It is worth going the long way around to avoid a serious avalanche hazard. After a big storm, a party may have to take a different return route, for example, if the original approach came up a narrow ravine below two steep, open slopes. A slope that has already avalanched is generally safe, providing that there are not more possible slide areas above that might have been undercut by the first avalanche. Remember, though, that the next slope along the trail, if it has similar exposure to the first, is certainly hazardous if it has not been released. If numerous small slides have come down on a loose slope, or if cracks are visible where slabs have released but not avalanched, the underlying slopes are probably stabilized.

Danger Signs

Most avalanches come down during or shortly after storms. The snow falling in the storm may avalanche itself, or the added weight of the new snow may release old unstable layers below. The more rapidly the snow falls and the denser the flakes, the more likely it is that a storm will cause avalanches. Two feet of snow falling in a single night are far more likely to cause major instability than two feet in two days. If temperatures are near freezing at the beginning of a storm and get colder as it goes on, the new snow is much more likely to bond well to the old layer than if temperatures start cold and warm as the storm continues. A great deal of wind-drifting snow will cause slabs to form on lee slopes even if snowfall is not heavy.

After a major storm has passed, if temperatures are near freezing, the main avalanche danger may be avoided by delaying travel a few hours. If temperatures are very cold, danger will persist for much longer. Testing small slopes may give some indication of the condition of larger and more dangerous ones. If the main danger seems to be from windslab, the wind-beaten slopes may be quite safe. Such wind-packed slopes tend to be crusted with a wavy surface, and they are often very stable while their neighbors across the valley are shedding tons of snow.

On sunny days in spring the dangerous period for thawing avalanches is in late morning and in afternoon. If you need to cross avalanche slopes in this weather, get an early start and be across before the sun gets to the snow. Slopes with a northern exposure get less sun and are safe for a longer part of the day. In winter any sudden rise in temperature may release avalanches. Rain, warm winds, or thawing temperatures that remain above freezing for more than a day may produce deep thawing and great danger of thawing avalanches.

CROSSING AVALANCHE TERRAIN

When at all possible, dangerous slopes should be avoided altogether, even if this requires long waits or detours. Occasionally, however, it may be necessary for a party to cross a hazardous zone, and some precautions may save lives if anyone is caught. If there is any possibility of crossing such terrain, each member of the party should carry an *avalanche cord* or an *avalanche beacon* and use them. An avalanche cord is a bright-colored length of nylon parachute cord 50 to 100 feet long. One end is tied to its owner and the other end is allowed to trail. Chances are good that if the wearer is caught in an avalanche, at least some of the cord will be on the surface, and it can then be followed to the victim. The best cords have metal markers every two meters. Each one gives the distance from the end and has an arrow pointing toward the end tied to the victim. If there are a couple of short sections of line showing, the markers can save rescuers time in deciding where to dig first. Minutes are crucial in avalanche rescue and avalanche debris is often very hard, so this is important.

If you regularly accept a certain amount of risk from avalanches, even a rather modest level, you should seriously consider carrying avalanche beacons and small shovels as a matter of routine. Skiers who like to ski reasonably steep terrain in the backcountry, for example, should make the use of beacons normal practice. No matter how conservative you are, such skiing involves some chance of burial, and the combination of shovels and beacons will greatly improve the chance of survival. Beacons are discussed below. Shovels are equally important, and sectional avalanche probes are helpful, particularly if you rely on cords rather than beacons.

Aside from special equipment, a person about to cross an avalanche slope should dress warmly, donning mittens, hat, and so on, zipping up his jacket, and pulling up his hood. All equipment should be adjusted so that it can be jettisoned quickly in case of trouble. Packs, ice axes, ski poles, and the like may help to show the victim's path if they come off in an avalanche. If they remain attached to his body, they will tend to drag him under and to twist his limbs in most uncomfortable ways. The pack may be carried on one shoulder, and the waist strap should be removed. Straps of ski poles and ice axes should be removed from the wrists. Snowshoe bindings should be loosened so that they can be kicked off in case of trouble. Skis are the only possible exception to this rule. The skier may leave his bindings as they are, maintaining some chance of skiing out of the way of an avalanche, or he may loosen them so that the bindngs will release easily, taking the chance that this may trip him if he tries to ski out a slide. In any case, Arlberg straps should be released so that the ski will be freed if the safety bindings do come off.

The most important safety precaution of all is to cross any dangerous area one by one. The rest of the party must stay in a protected spot—perhaps a rock outcropping or heavily forested zone—until the first person is all the way across the danger zone. This procedure should be followed for each member. The first crossing does *not* prove that the slope is safe. Avalanche literature is replete with instances of later members of a group being caught after several have crossed safely. Only one person at a time should be in a danger zone. All the others should watch that person carefully and be ready to make note of his location if he should be caught by a slide.

If you are caught in an avalanche you may be able to get out by quick action if you are on the edge of the slide. This happens quite often because the cutting action of the victim's feet or skis is what precipitates the avalanche in the first place. If this first desperate attempt is unsuccessful, you should jettison your equipment and then try to making swimming motions to stay on top of the avalanche—a gesture unlikely to have very much effect except in a very small slide. Keep your mout shut, and don't get it full of snow. As you come to rest you should try to get your hands in front of your face to make a breathing space. Once the sliding snow stops it becomes quite hard, and you are not likely to be able to move much at all. Experts generally recommend one hard push after you come to rest to try to push out. If that doesn't work, relax and don't panic (easy to say). Some avalanche victims apparently quite literally die of fright. With your companions nearby you have a pretty good chance if you stay calm and don't use up your limited oxygen supply on the luxury of fear. Don't waste much energy shouting. You may hear your companions, but they will not be able to hear you.

For survivors of an accident the first step is to keep calm. Speed is vital, but it is useless if it is also misdirected. The first step when you see the avalanche is to watch the victim and make a careful note of where you last see him. Try to note the relation of this spot to visible landmarks. When the avalanche is over, *mark* the spot where the victim was last seen before you rush off and lose it. Mark it with something that will stay put and stay visible. Don't just drop something on the ground if it's snowing.

The victim will be somewhere down the fall line from where he was last seen. Make a quick search for objects like packs, gloves, and so on, that may show his path. Kick up the snow around the place where he was seen to uncover clues. Is there a section of avalanche cord or a hand or foot showing? There are quite a few cases of survivors of accidents taking off for help twenty miles away when the victim's boot was sticking up like a signpost. A cursory examination may very well save the victim, especially if an avalanche cord was worn. Mark all spots where any objects belonging to the victim were found. Probe around these spots with an avalanche probe if you have one, or with an inverted ski pole, the tail of a ski, or a tent pole. Also probe around any trees or other obstacles in the path the victim would have taken. These are the most likely spots for him to be, together with the bottom and side debris. (Different procedures for when beacons are being worn are discussed in the next section.)

Once a quick cursory examination has been made, several decisions have to be taken regarding the next steps, decisions that will depend on the size of the party and its location. Victims of avalanches who are not killed right away by traumatic injuries ususally die by suffocation. An ice mask forms around the face and prevents the victim from getting air. For this reason and other more complicated ones, the length of time a victim may survive varies a good deal. If he is fortunate enough to have an air space, he may survive for some time, or various factors may limit this time to minutes, depending on the air available, fear, consciousness, cold, and so on. Statistics indicate that half of all victims are dead after thirty minutes, so unless outside help can be brought in very quickly, it is better for the party to conduct the best search posssible. In a backcountry situation there is rarely any point in sending or going for outside help until you have given up hope of finding the victim alive. There is a reasonable chance of this until more than two hours have passed, so the entire energies of the party should normally be devoted to the search.

After the rapid initial search, the area of the fall line below the last seen point should be searched thoroughly. The most likely spots for the victim to have lodged should then be probed as carefully as possible. Have the searchers stand in line and probe every foot of the suspected areas systematically. Keep them in a line, so that effort is not wasted or sections missed. Keep careful track of those areas that have been searched.

Throughout the search, the rescuers should make some attempt to sound calm as well as act that way. The victim can very often hear what they are saying, since sound carries well into the snow but not out of it, and his morale is not likely to be improved by tactless comments or apparent panic.

Whoever takes charge of the search must also take responsibility for the safety of the searchers. Providing no further danger threatens, the search should not be abandoned for twenty-four hours, but if the storm that brought down the first avalanche is continuing, there can be no purpose served in risking the lives of the survivors of the first slide, especially after the first two hours are over. Neither is there any justification in having accidents sustained by exhausted members after the first few hours. Searching an avalanche is very tiring, and once exhaustion sets in, the would-be rescuers are not likely to do any good and are quite likely to get hurt, a prospect that would greatly complicate the situation and could only harm the chances of the avalanche victim, since energies then have to be diverted to care for the new casualty.

Avalanche Beacons

Carrying avalanche beacons will enormously improve the chances that a member of your party caught in an avalanche will survive. The prospects for a small party performing a successful avalanche rescue are really rather poor if the victim is actually buried without clothing, extremities, or sections of avalanche cord showing. (It is because some physical clue often does exist that chances of recovery can be good.) Probing by a small party is a last desperate attempt, and detailed probes by large groups of rescuers in a wilderness context are basically body-recovery operations.

With the advent of lightweight, reliable beacons, all this has changed. It is now possible for backcountry travelers to have a reasonably good rescue capability if they carry beacons and know how to use them. Though the cost of the devices is unfortunately rather high, those who spend much time in avalanche terrain should still own them. The beacons will not substitute for good judgment, but they are a welcome backup. (The electronics involved are not inherently costly, but interest is regarded by manufacturers as specialized, so no one has mass-produced the beacons at a reasonable price.)

An avalanche beacon is a low-frequency radio transceiver, designed to utilize a frequency and signal component that penetrates snow well. Whenever a party is traveling in terrain that could conceivably avalanche, the members turn on their beacons, in the transmit mode, and wear them on their bodies. (The object of a search is to find the victim, not his pack.) The usual practice of spreading out the party is followed, and if someone is buried, the other members switch their sets to the receiving mode and use the signal to locate the victim. With advance practice it is possible to get a buried person out in five or ten minutes, greatly increasing chances of survival.

There is not space here to adequately discuss search procedures with beacons, but it is important to note that they must be practiced in advance to be used effectively. The transceivers are quite simple, but rapid location of the victim requires that you do a few advance drills to learn the most efficient procedure. There are several errors in search technique that can waste a lot of time if they are not learned in advance, time that a buried person cannot afford. Careful observance of all the obvious rules for use of the beacons is also essential if they are to do more than provide a false sense of security. They must be worn whenever the party is in avalanche terrain, turned on, placed in the transmit mode, and kept in a safe place on the body where they cannot be lost in an avalanche.

A FINAL CAUTION

The best way to handle trouble in the wilderness is to avoid it in the first place, and this stricture holds particularly strongly in avalanche terrain. Even a small avalanche can bury a skier or snowshoer, and no one who has had the experience of being buried emerges with any desire to repeat it. If you spend time in steep terrain in the winter and spring, you should learn all you can about avalanche forecasting. It is even more important, however, to avoid overconfidence in your own powers of observation and analysis. A freak avalanche can catch the most experienced mountaineer or skier, but the chances of this are unlikely. Most victims start the slides that bury them on obviously dangerous terrain, either through complete ignorance or as a result of their own poor judgment. Avalanches are very difficult to predict, and the real experts are always extremely cautious about trusting their own predictions as to whether a slope will slide.

The best advice is to stay off steep open slopes unless you are absolutely sure that they are stable, following protected routes instead. Even if you are completely confident of the stability of the snow, follow standard precautions. Cross hazardous slopes one at a time. Pay attention to the possible consequences of a slide. Even a very small avalanche that could carry you into a funneling gully would result in deep burial. A small sluff can be fatal if you are climbing on a slope above a cliff. Be particularly conservative when you go on a trip in a different region from the ones with which you are familiar. A traveler going from the Rockies to the Sierra would be likely to be surprised by the ferocity of the storms and the number of avalanches running during and after them. On the other hand, a regular skier from the Sierra might be unpleasantly surprised by the persistence of dangerous slab conditions in the Rockies.

A healthy respect for the power of storms and of moving snow will insure that you have a chance to enjoy the white wilderness over the years. The wilderness in winter is not a hostile environment, but it can be unforgiving to those who insist on taking uncalculated risks.

12 | Emergencies and Accidents

Storms and avalanches are natural phenomena that occur whether there are people around or not. In a wilderness situation there is nothing you can do to prevent them; you have either to arrange to be somewhere else when they happen or to be prepared for them. Emergencies and accidents are something else: They happen to people. An avalanche or tree becomes part of an accident only if someone manages to be buried or knock his head on a branch. Most accidents and emergencies can be prevented, and the unpleasant consequences of those that occur can be minimized by adequate preparation.

There is nothing inherently dangerous about wilderness travel in the winter, providing the traveler is able and equipped to deal with the various problems that he may encounter. It is true, however, that there are a number of characteristics of the snow country beyond the road-head that can turn a difficult situation into a dangerous one rather quickly. There is much less room for error. In summer an ill-clad fool can wander off into the woods in many areas of North America, and if he doesn't manage to do himself in by falling off a cliff, he has a good chance of still being in fairly good shape when the search party finds him a few days later. Mistakes like this are not so likely to end well when snow is on the ground.

The conditions of winter are likely to exacerbate all sorts of problems, especially since many difficulties are most likely to occur when the special characteristics of the cold months are most in evidence. You are more apt to break your leg or to become lost in a storm at the end of the short winter day than at the beginning, and when snow conditions make travel most arduous rather than when they make it easy. All sorts of complications reinforce one another: A person who is suffering from the cold or fatigue is both more liable to injury and less able to cope with one that occurs; the mind is duller and more apt to lapses of judgment in route finding and in decisions about stopping, splitting the party, and so on.

STAYING OUT OF TROUBLE

Part of the satisfaction of winter travel inheres in meeting the challenge of a difficult environment, and anyone who spends very much time in the wilderness, especially in winter, will encounter some trying situations. There is a difference, however, between losing one's bearings and being totally lost, between being stormbound and being in a desperate survival situation, between being injured and being in danger of death. The difference usually depends on the foresight a party has shown in preparing for difficulties. Winter storms, especially in the mountains, are sometimes of such severity that a person cannot expect to survive in the open. With a few extra rations and bivouac gear one can take shelter and sit out the storm—uncomfortably, perhaps, but without having ever been in an emergency. In this same situation an individual or party that tries to bull through for a few extra hours before stopping may become badly chilled and be in very real danger.

Most of the common sorts of trouble can be completely avoided. Proper route finding will keep you from losing your bearings, and if you do lose them you should still have a good enough idea of your location to find your way out. Adequate clothing, food, and calmly applied common sense will keep a difficulty from turning into a disaster.

The main rules for staying out of trouble are fairly simple. The first is to keep your goals well within the capacity of the party. One experienced person cannot safely make the same trip with six beginners as with only one. A group that is lightly supplied with extra clothing and food will not be able to safely undertake as long a trip as the same party could with more supplies. A large, experienced, and well-supplied group can plan on being capable of evacuating an injured member of the party, while a group lacking any one of these attributes cannot. Judgment of the party's capacity must be made on many levels, but the obvious method is to look for weaknesses and to ask yourself how far they can be safely tested or how they can be eliminated. A three-member ski party may be perfectly safe where help is available, but the same size party would undertake much higher risk in a really remote region. The risk may be well worth taking, but it should be recognized for what it is, and appropriate allowances should be made.

The second rule is one of adequate preparation, and this is again a matter of judgment. Many examples have been mentioned elsewhere, such as the fact that if a party is planning to split up, extra items like maps and emergency kits must be carried for each group. Adequate food and clothing in case of difficulty are obviously needed, though quantities vary; you need not carry so much on a weekend ski tour as on one planned to last several weeks. Less obvious matters for preparation involve the supplies and knowledge necessary to deal with emergency medical problems, which again vary with the type, length, and remoteness of the trip. Each member of the party should have adequate knowledge of first aid and medical care, since if an injury occurs, it may be sustained by the person on which everyone relied for aid. Again, preparations required where aid can easily be summoned are different from those needed deep in wild areas.

Despite the best-laid plans of mice and skiers, difficulties will sometimes occur. Emergencies frequently arise from such situations, not because of the nature of the circumstances themselves, but due to the badly thought-out actions of the party in trouble. Care and thought are most needed just when people are most inclined to act hastily on impulse or panic. Parties do not normally split up in a storm because of a misguided but carefully thought-out plan; they just thrash madly off in different directions and realize too late that they have lost both the trail and the other half of the group. The need for calm and deliberate action is obvious from an armchair view, but it is important to keep reminding oneself and one's party of this need in real situations of stress.

Though every difficulty is somewhat different and some are impossible to anticipate, there are many problems that can be simulated at home so that one can learn to deal with them there. For example, it is obviously advantageous to learn how to build fires in the wet and to lay out a compass bearing before these skills are actually needed. Instruction programs on first aid and emergency medicine can and should include practice with mock-up injuries in difficult situations, enabling the students to make their errors and get over their squeamishness without serious consequences. Even emergencies that cannot be physically simulated will be easier to deal with if they have been mentally pictured and thought out, not just skimmed over in a book. The more you can prepare yourself in advance for problems you may encounter, the wider your safety margin will be.

GETTING LOST

There is a particular instinctive panic that takes over when people realize that they have lost their bearings. The common reaction is to *do* something about it, to rush off in one direction or another in the desperate hope of becoming oriented again by a familiar landmark. The usual result is, of course, that the lost person becomes more and more disoriented, with the pitch of fear and expenditure of wasted energy increasing until exhaustion sets in. Obviously, this is not the best way to go about things, and providing there is no immediate danger threatening, like that posed by an avalanche slope above, it is time to stop and think things over as soon as it is discovered that one is off course or confused about direction.

Until the border of hysteria is crossed, no one is ever *completely* lost, since he is bound to know something about his location. If you should lose your bearings, sit down and make yourself comfortable. Get out your map and compass if you have them, and consult with your companions, if any, about what you *do* know. You must certainly know what continent you are on and a good deal more, besides. You probably know your location within a few miles. If you have a compass, you know which direction is which, and if you also have a map, you can orient it with the compass. Even if you have neither map nor compass, you probably know something about the area you are in. The essence of dealing with your situation is applying what you do know to the problem of finding your way, and this demands a careful and realistic evaluation. Even if your camp is only a mile away, it may be more sensible to head for a road five miles away that is impossible to miss, if there is no systematic way of finding the camp.

If you are lost in a storm, the best course of action is usually to build a shelter and wait for the weather to clear, rather than courting exhaustion by continuing farther along a course that may be in the wrong direction. It should go without saying that a person who is really lost and who expects a search party ought to stay in one place and concentrate his energy on making himself comfortable and visible.

Even without a compass, it is possible to follow a straight line in terrain with some landmarks like trees. Simply line up two distant objects and keep them in line, choosing a third object in the same line before either of the first two is reached. Traveling in an arbitrary straight line is better than circling but still leaves a good deal to be desired. Try to remember everything you know about an area before heading off in a random direction. If it is bordered within reasonable traveling distance by roads or other unmistakable landmarks, moving in a straight line is a good idea, but if you are on the edge of a large wilderness area, it would be better to stay put until you have a directional reference. All this is simply meant to suggest by example that it is necessary to apply common sense and good judgment in emergencies, rather than blindly following half-remembered and often fallacious rules of thumb. There is, for instance, the rule that following a watershed down will lead eventually to civilization. This may apply in the area where you are lost. On the other hand, the watershed might lead through a couple of thousand miles of wilderness before emptying into the Arctic Ocean, or just a few miles to a lake that drains by underground streams. Furthermore, blindly following a watershed is not always the *easiest* way out, even if it does eventually lead where you want to go.

If you make sure to have a compass and map with you whenever you travel in any extensive roadless area, you will not have to worry about this sort of problem. Even if you are lost, there will usually be an obvious route to some kind of landmark, which can then be used to locate your position. The most featureless terrain is luckily also the most likely to have long, straight roads, which can be intersected by simply traveling in the right general direction.

STORMS

Storms are generally a real problem only when they combine with other difficulties. If shelter and adequate food and clothing are available, one can simply wait until the weather lets up. Unfortunately, injuries often occur while a party is traveling in bad weather. Chilling and exhaustion are also more likely to beset a party under these circumstances. It is precisely such pyramiding of difficulties that must be prevented to avoid disastrous consequences.

Preparations are obvious and have been mentioned in the form of adequate clothing and extra food. Parties traveling some distance from camp over difficult terrain should carry bivouac equipment. An injury can slow such a party to a crawl, and a night out without bivouac gear can be fatal.

When a party is caught in a storm, it is important to pitch camp early, especially if the weather is beginning to take its toll on some members. Continuing on until dark in a desperate attempt to reach a road or car is foolish. Setting up camp will take much more time and effort in the dark, fuel will be hard to gather, mittens and other equipment are likely to be lost in the scramble. In a really bad storm—rare except in high mountains—one has no choice but to take shelter for the duration. When the weather is bad enough, there is simply no longer a question of what to do.

Even a party that is short of food will be better off stopping when a storm becomes difficult. Going hungry for a few days is a bad idea, especially in cold weather, but it is not really serious if one does not allow severe chill or exhaustion to occur. If one does, the hungry body's reduced blood sugar will hamper its ability to cope with fatigue and cold.

The great majority of injuries in the wilderness occur when a person is tired. A cold party, stumbling along through a storm at twilight, is asking for trouble. Stop before you find it. Watch for signs of fatigue and chilling in your party, both because they are important in themselves and because these signs may well precede a broken leg. Continuing in a storm calls for greater care than in fine weather.

Never split the party in a storm. It is amazing how easily a person can become separated from the rest of the group in bad weather. People may travel in different directions without even noticing. Someone may stop to clean his glasses or answer a call of nature, without his absence being noticed. He may then be prevented from rejoining the party because its tracks are already filled in, or simply because he is too tired to catch up. A positive effort is required to keep the party together in bad storm conditions, but it is essential that this effort be made. The extra problems of finding a lost member of the party are hardly needed to add to the other difficulties presented by a storm. Even if the party gets together quickly, it will have lost time and may have gotten off course as well.

INJURIES AND MEDICAL EMERGENCIES

If reasonable care is exercised, the wilderness traveler may never have to deal with a serious injury, but it is obvious that if you go very far from the beaten track you must be prepared in case you are not so lucky. Any party traveling in wilderness areas should be capable of taking care of the common types of injuries and medical emergencies. This often involves a good deal more than conventional first aid, which concerns itself with handling a patient for a short time, until a doctor or ambulance can reach him. If you break a leg ten miles from the nearest road, you will have to depend on your companions to take care of the injury for a few days, and perhaps they will have to haul you out as well.

Anyone who spends very much time in the wilderness should get as much training in first aid and emergency medicine as possible. The Red Cross beginning and advanced first-aid courses should be standard preparation, but additional instruction is desirable. A mountaineering club in your area may have a special course in emergency medicine. If not, you might be able to organize one with some friends, finding a doctor who is interested, perhaps one who spends time in the

246 THE NEW COMPLETE SNOW CAMPER'S GUIDE

woods and mountains himself. Such a course should include as much practice as possible, preferably in circumstances that simulate genuine accident situations. Practicing examination for injuries outdoors on a snowy night with a flashlight will give you a better background and a longer memory than the same practice conducted in an overheated room. Appendix B: Selected Reading lists some useful books.

In addition to proper first-aid training, you should have a regular physical checkup, and so should the friends you travel with. Anyone who has special medical problems should talk with his doctor about consequences that might be important in emergency situations in the wilderness and should carry any special medicine he might need. It is important that his companions know about these special problems, so that if he should be injured they will know what to do. A diabetic coma would be recognized quickly by a companion who was aware of the possibility, but anyone who is not a doctor could hardly be expected to make a correct diagnosis if he was not aware that his companion had diabetes.

Finally, a first-aid kit must be carried at all times in wilderness travel. The possibility of carrying one large kit and a number of smaller ones has already been mentioned as a useful approach for larger groups. It may also be worth considering the desirability of carrying supplies that go well beyond the range of "first aid" if you plan many extensive trips in remote regions. The importance of certain prescription drugs in proper care for the injured over a period of days or weeks makes the discussion of this problem with a doctor worthwhile. The use of such drugs falls into the province of medicine rather than first aid, but so does any care that aims at preserving or recovering the health of a patient far from doctors and hospitals. In extensive wilderness travel such tools can mean the difference between life and death for an injured person. Prescriptions and instructions for proper use of pain killers, antibiotics, and the like must be obtained from a doctor, so no attempt will be made to discuss them here. Anyone interested in the subject would be well advised to read *Medicine for Mountaineering,* as a basis for discussion with a physician. It is *the* book on emergency medicine for wilderness use, and is worth many careful readings by anyone who wants to prepare for emergencies in the backcountry.

Provided all members of the party are healthy to begin with and have not greatly exceeded their capacities, the most likely medical emergencies to be encountered are those resulting from accidents or cold. By far the most common sort of accident is a sprain or fracture of an extremity due to a short fall, and this is fortunately not a dangerous injury under normal circumstances. Most accidents in the woods, even when they occur, can be handled without great danger to anyone's life providing they are dealt with in a calm and sensible manner.

INJURIES WHERE SECONDS COUNT

Fortunately, there are not many types of medical problems that require extremely quick action on the part of the person who is rendering aid. Undue delay is bad, of course, but there are only a very few cases where the first aider or rescuer does not have time to think things out and to act carefully and deliberately. In most cases, much more damage is done by hurrying than by working slowly and thoroughly.

There are two main exceptions to this rule that are likely to be encountered in accidents occurring in the winter woods—injuries involving a victim who has stopped breathing or who is bleeding severely. In such cases seconds count, and action must be prompt if it is to do any good at all. For this reason, the first things a would-be rescuer should check when arriving at the scene of a serious accident are the victim's breathing and the possibility of serious external bleeding.

Breath Stoppage
Common reasons for the victim to have stopped breathing, other than his already being dead, are drowning, electrical shock, and poisoning. None of these is nearly as likely in snow-covered wilderness areas as in other locations, but they are all possible. Avalanche victims are also sometimes recovered alive but not breathing. Artificial respiration should begin immediately on any victim who is not breathing but not obviously dead. If a second rescuer is available, he should examine the victim for bleeding, check the victim's pulse, check for other injuries, and insulate the victim from the snow, while the first person continues artificial respiration. If only one rescuer is present, he will have to perform these tasks as best he can without interrupting resuscitation. If a pulse is not present, external heart compression must also be started immediately. Either artificial respiration or cardiac compression alone is useless without the other, if both breathing and the heart have stopped.

Mouth-to-mouth resuscitation is much more effective than any other method of artificial respiration available outside a hospital, and it is less tiring and more foolproof than other types of artificial respiration. The victim's mouth and upper throat should be cleared of any foreign matter—snow, water, vomitus, and so on—a task that may be more easily accomplished if he is lying on his side with his head downhill, but which must be gotten out of the way quickly. The victim is then moved onto his back—carefully—and the head is tilted back as far as possible. The jaw is pulled or pushed forward, either with your thumb hooking under the teeth or by pushing from both sides of the back of the jawbone. The combination of the backward-tilting head and the jutting jaw will keep the victim's tongue clear of the back of his throat, so that the airway to the lungs is open.

With all this accomplished, pinch the victim's nostrils closed with the hand that is not holding his jaw, take a deep breath, cover his mouth with yours, and blow into his lungs until you see his chest rise. Release your mouth from the victim's, and listen for the air escaping his lungs while you are exhaling and taking another breath. Then blow into his lungs again. The cycle should be repeated every four or five seconds. When you blow into the victim's lungs, the air should go in easily. If there is resistance, then the airway is not clear, either because you have not got the tongue away from the back of the throat or because there is foreign matter lodged in the airway. Check the jaw first. If it is well forward, turn the victim on his side, head downward if possible, and give him a few good whacks between the shoulder blades. Situations like this may cause conflicts in cases of a possible spine injury, but the airway must be cleared quickly, regardless of other troubles. Once a person has stopped breathing for five minutes, his chances of recovery dwindle rapidly. Usually, one does not know how long respiration has been stopped when the victim is found, so artificial respiration should be tried, but if you have not started resuscitation within ten or fifteen minutes of the time the victim stopped breathing, you are wasting your efforts.

Resuscitation should be continued as long as the victim's heart is beating, and the rhythm should be coordinated with any attempts to breathe that he makes. The victim's stomach may become bloated with air and expand to prevent the lungs from filling competely. This should be checked every few minutes. Pressure with your hand during exhalation will usually empty the stomach of air, but be alert for vomiting when this is done. If the victim vomits, turn him quickly on his side and clear the vomit before resuming artificial respiration.

There is no point attempting artificial respiration if the victim's heart is not beating, unless some measures are taken to pump the oxygenated blood through his system. Check for a pulse at the carotid artery, rather than at the extremities, since a weak pulse may not be easy to find at spots like the wrist. To find the carotid artery, simply press a forefinger gently into the soft area of the neck immediately adjoining the larynx. This is easy to find on yourself; the pulse can be found on either side, but don't press on both sides at once, lest you knock yourself or your subject out. (The pulse can be quite difficult to find in a person suffering from cold exposure and shock, so advance practice is important before you can have reasonable confidence in your judgment. Fortunately, classes in cardiopulmonary resuscitation, or CPR—the combination of artificial respiration with external cardiac compression—are now easy to obtain in most communities, along with first-aid courses. Call the Red Cross or the Heart Association. There is no substitute for training and practice. This book simply summarizes some aspects of first aid as they apply to a wilderness setting in cold weather.)

If no pulse is felt, CPR must be started immediately. Two rescuers will almost certainly be necessary, since it is far less effective for one person to perform cardiac compression and artificial respiration at the same time.

The idea of external cardiac compression is to pump blood by squeezing the heart between the breastbone and the spine. The back must be resting on a fairly firm surface for this to be accomplished, but there should be no sharp projections that might gouge the victim when pressure is applied. The airway should be cleared first, and four quick inflations of the lungs made while the pulse is checked. It does no good to circulate the blood until it is oxygenated. Kneel beside the victim, and with elbows locked put both your hands on his chest, one on top of the other. The heel of your lower hand should rest in the center of the subject's breastbone, an inch above the lowest point. To pump the victim's heart, lean forward, elbows locked, putting pressure on the breastbone and pushing it down a couple of inches. Pressure is then released, and the cycle is repeated once every second. Your assistant can check for a pulse at the carotid artery while delivering artificial respiration.

One rescuer administering CPR alone has to alternate between external cardiac compression and artificial respiration. There is some disagreement over the optimum ratio, but fifteen compressions followed by two quick breaths is a commonly recommended sequence. As with two rescuers, the heart should be compressed once each second.

Chilling of the victim is a serious problem in a winter setting, particularly if the person is an already cold victim of avalanche or hypothermia (chilling of the body core). It may be worth continuing CPR for some time in such circumstances, since the onset of brain damage can be delayed, but the other members of the party should get to work immediately in erecting a shelter and warming both the victim and the rescuers. When performing CPR on the snow take particular care that the surface is hard enough to support the victim's back. A soft surface can prevent any effective circulation of the blood.

The combination of artificial respiration and cardiac compression is a last desperate effort in a wilderness setting and will probably fail to revive the victim. Since there is a chance that they will work, they should, of course, be tried, but the poor prognosis should be considered if there are conflicting interests. An obviously living accident victim should not be allowed to bleed to death while efforts are being made to revive someone who is probably dead. If the pupils of the victim are dilated and fail to respond to bright light during CPR, the situation is probably hopeless, and the would-be rescuers should not continue efforts if avalanche danger or some other threat to their lives is present.

Major Bleeding

The second possible rush emergency that might occur on a winter tour is the occurrence of massive hemorrhaging. Arterial blood is under quite a bit of pressure, and the total amount of blood in the body is only around ten quarts. Major bleeding has to be stopped right away or it will be fatal. *The proper treatment for bleeding is pressure directly on the wound.* If you have some sterile dressings handy, press those onto the wound. Probably you will have to start with a hand-kerchief or just the palm of your hand. Stop the bleeding first, while someone else looks for the first-aid kit. Sterile dressings are nice but they won't do your patient much good if he is dead. As soon as possible get some large sterile pads on the wound and apply the pressure on those.

Fortunately, most bleeding looks worse than it really is. The sign of arterial bleeding is its vigor—it spurts out hard and rhythmically—and it is harder to stop than venous bleeding. The diagnosis is simple in practical terms, since the treatment of arterial and venous differs only in the amount of pressure and time required to stop the bleeding. Once you get the bleeding stopped, keep the pressure on the wound until you are sure it has clotted. *Don't* look underneath your dressing after a couple of minutes, especially if the bleeding is major, Wait fifteen or twenty minutes. Your patient can't afford the extra blood it will cost him to satisfy your curiosity, and you will lose time because you will have to control the bleeding all over again. If you have anyone to help you, have him maintain the pressure on the dressing while you go on to other things.

Tourniquets should not be used. They are needed so seldom that even doctors in emergency wards, who deal with bleeding every day, often spend years without applying a tourniquet, and the likelihood of needing one on a wilderness trip is very small indeed. Pressure points are also a poor alternative for actually controlling bleeding, though they may be useful for changing dressings without causing additional bleeding, if you really know them well enough to apply pressure in the right place on the first try. Direct pressure on the wound is, however, the way to control the bleeding most effectively, and it has the additional advantage of simplicity.

Fortunately, injuries of the nature just described are less common in the snowy wilderness than on the highways leading to its edge, and the wilderness traveler is more likely to get an opportunity to put his first aid to the test on the drive to the mountains than on the ski slope. My own mountaineering medical kit has had far more use in aiding the victims of auto accidents than anything else. In the backcountry it is usually pulled out to deal with blisters or chapped skin rather than serious traumatic injury.

EXAMINING AN ACCIDENT VICTIM

If someone becomes injured or sick it is important to make a complete examination as soon as possible. You may have to interrupt the examination to stop bleeding, protect the patient from the cold, and treat him for shock, but the examination should be carried out thoroughly as soon as possible. In an accident situation it is very easy to overlook injuries that may be much more serious than superficial but obvious ones. While you are taking great pains with a prominent but relatively inconsequential face wound, your patient may be bleeding to death from a deep laceration in the leg.

The most important thing about the examination is that it be thorough, and for this it is necessary to follow a pattern. The order is not particularly important, but it should be practiced so that nothing will be missed. A routine like this can also be very useful in putting everyone in a better state of mind. Talk to your patient. He is your friend, not a bag of potatoes. If he happens to be a stranger, there is even more reason for you to show him that you know what you are doing and that he can trust you. Ask the victim what happened. Ask him how he feels and what hurts. Watch his face during your examination. If it shows pain, find out why. Be careful not to cause any further injury while you are making the examination. By far the most common serious injuries that are likely to occur on a wilderness trip are fractures, and you will cause additional damage by careless handling of the patient before the broken bones are splinted. Remember that a good "bedside manner" is more than a nicety in an accident situation in the cold. Shock is the most likely cause of death, and fear and pain contribute to shock. It is up to you to calm the person you are trying to help and to alleviate his pain.

If a person is unconscious, these considerations are even more important. It is much easier to injure a person who can't scream at you. He may still indicate pain, which is both a warning and a clue to injuries. You do not know how unconscious he is. Hearing is one of the last senses to be dulled, and your patient may be able to hear you even if he seems quite senseless. Imagine how you would feel if you were badly hurt and some jerk was poking and prodding you and saying things like, "My God, look at all that blood. Do you think he's going to die?" Talk to your friend, even if you don't know whether he can hear you. Try to be calm and tactful and to sound competent, whether or not you feel so. Tell him what you're doing, and tell him it might hurt. Don't tell him everything is all right. He knows everything *isn't* all right!

The nature of an examination will be determined to some extent by what you already know. If a person has become sick while you are stormbound in a tent, you will not be checking for broken bones, but beware of skipping steps because of unwarranted assumptions you may have made. If you have to treat someone you have found somewhere, the examination must be broader than with one of your companions whom you have been observing all along. It is primarily the latter case with which we're concerned. The kinds of problems that are likely to be encountered by a healthy person on a winter trip in the wilderness are fairly limited. They include a few special problems resulting from the cold environment, but consist mainly of traumatic injuries—those resulting from physical violence: cuts, broken bones, or internal injuries.

Circumstances resulting in trauma are obvious: falls, collisions with trees, and so on. When the victim is reached, the would-be rescuer should first check his breathing, a requirement often satisfied by the emanation of colorful language from the subject. After a cursory check for major bleeding, some effort should be made to make the patient comfortable before proceeding. Several sleeping pads may be slipped under him for insulation from the snow, or clothing may be substituted if pads aren't available. Several people should be used to lift the injured person, and everyone should know what motions are to be made beforehand. If there is any danger of spinal or neck injury, particular care must be taken to move the whole spinal column as a unit. The patient should be gotten into a sleeping bag at the same time. All this can be accomplished smoothly and with little movement of the victim, if several people are available and their movements are well coordinated. The patient merely needs to be lifted a few inches from one side while someone slips the pads and sleeping bag into position from the other side. If, as is usually the case, injuries are on one side, this side should be on the zippered side of the sleeping bag, so that you can work on them while keeping the victim warm.

These actions to keep the patient warm need to be started quickly in the winter snow, even before a thorough examination has been made. In more clement surroundings this might be inadvisable, but in the cold and snow the always serious problem of shock is greatly exacerbated. The patient must be kept as warm as possible while further examination and treatment are carried out. If it is convenient when the patient is moved, the legs should rest above the head by six inches or a foot as further treatment for shock.

Examination of the accident victim usually starts at the head and proceeds to the feet. Breathing is checked first, and treatment for impaired breathing should be made immediately. Besides suffocation in water or snow, breathing difficulty could be caused by a head injury, by foreign matter lodged in the mouth and throat, or by a chest injury. Chest injuries and maintaining an airway with an unconscious victim are discussed below. Foreign matter such as snow or vomitus should obviously be removed from the airway. Artificial respiration must be administered immediately if breathing stops.

If the victim is unconscious, he should be examined for signs of a head injury. Bleeding or passage of a straw-colored fluid from the ears or nose may be significant, but bleeding may be due to local injury. Check the eyes. Are the pupils dilated and are they sensitive to light? Feel gently for signs of injury, and take care for a broken neck, movement of which could kill your patient.

If the person is conscious, talk with him. In addition to cheering him and obtaining information from him directly, a head injury may be indicated by confusion. Irrationality is also a symptom of several other problems, including severe and dangerous chilling. Anyone who has had a bump on the head sharp enough to have knocked him unconscious for a few minutes must be watched carefully for at least the next twenty-four hours for signs of brain injury. A blood clot developing under the skull can press on the brain and end in death.

Below the head, the examiner should go over the shoulders, arms, torso, pelvic area, legs, ankles, and feet, feeling gently but firmly to detect any wounds, tender spots, or broken bones. Pressure and twisting action from both ends of the major bones should detect most complete fractures, but it must be applied very carefully and stopped immediately at the first sign of pain. If you have good reason to suspect a fracture, assume that you have one, rather than risking more severe injury by testing the bone further. Sprains can be difficult to distinguish from fractures, especially after muscle spasm has stiffened the area.

The signs of fracture are usually easy to recognize except at the joints. Fractures and bad sprains of the knee, elbow, ankle, or wrist should be treated in about the same way anyhow, so there is not much difference for our purposes. Final diagnosis can wait for doctors with X rays. Particular care must be taken of these injuries, since pinching of the nerves in the area of a fracture due to improper handling can cause permanent damage.

Fractures are likely to cause swelling and extreme tenderness in the area around them, and unless there is only partial cracking, the victim probably (not always!) will be unable to put normal weight on the injured member. Deformities are sure signs of fractures, including the sometimes inconspicuous shortening of a limb. Shortening is easily detected by comparison with the uninjured member.

No attempt will be made here to describe an examination of a person who has become seriously ill on a trip without the intervention of an accident. Excellent descriptions of such techniques may be found in *Medicine for Mountaineering,* which has been mentioned before. It is worthwhile, however, to keep a written history of any illness, whether accidental or not. Paper and pencil should be included in the first-aid kit, and a thorough history should be taken as soon as circumstances permit. The history should include all the information you have obtained in your examination, and with a person who has become ill, it should at least include a description of his complaints, a record of his temperature every few hours, any symptoms you have noticed, and any medications that have been administered. The history should go with the patient. It may greatly simplify the work of the doctor. It will also enable you to think systematically and will thus give you a better chance of acting intelligently.

FRACTURES

Broken bones are the most common injury likely to be encountered on any wilderness trip, particularly one undertaken on skis. Most fractures are closed: There is no break in the skin. Treatment is simple in principle if not in practice. The fracture must be immobilized so that no further damage will be done by movement of the sharp ends of the bone. Unless imminent danger requires moving the victim immediately, the fracture should always be immobilized before he is transported.

Immobilization is usually accomplished by splinting, which consists of fastening the injured part to something that will restrain it from moving. As a general rule, proper splinting requires immobilizing both the joint below the fracture and the one above. In a break of the lower leg, for example, the foot and the knee must both be restrained.

Usually, the person giving aid should not attempt to straighten deformities, since this entails the danger of doing further damage to blood vessels or nerves, as well as general tissue. There may be exceptions to this rule, however, which will have to be decided in the best judgment of the person giving aid. If circulation to an extremity beyond the fracture seems to be impaired, this may be caused either by pressure on an artery, which may be relieved by straightening (or may be worsened), or it may be due to bleeding from an artery that has already been ripped by the bone ends, in which case straightening will bring about no improvement. Straightening may also be necessary in some cases to make the patient comfortable or to make splinting possible. If it *must* be done, straightening should be accomplished with tension on both ends of the break, with very slow, careful manipulation and attention to any pain experienced by the victim. Severe pain is a warning, and it should be heeded. Straightening a bone that has been partially immobilized by spasm in large muscles like those of the thigh is next to impossible, so if any manipulation is necessary, it should be done as soon as possible.

The fracture of any large bone damages a good deal of tissue, and thus causes quite a bit of blood loss. This may not be apparent to the person giving first aid, because the blood is not pouring out messily the way it does with a bad cut. It spreads out into the surrounding tissues instead, but in the conditions of the outdoors in winter there can be enough blood lost as a result of the fracture of any of the major bones to pose a grave threat of shock. The fracture of the thighbone, the pelvis, or a combination of smaller bones should alert the person giving aid to anticipate shock and to institute treatment for it, especially in cold conditions.

The difficulties of splinting are also greatly increased in the situations likely to be encountered by those touring in the snow country. Materials for making splints are likely to be scarce. Particular care must be taken both to keep the injured part of the body and the victim himself warm, and the danger that a splint may restrict circulation must be very carefully avoided. If any of these problems are ignored in a cold environment, the injured extremity is likely to become frostbitten in addition to the initial injury. Boots should be removed and replaced with soft, nonconstricting insulation, except when the boots are an essential part of the splint. Cutting a tight boot may be necessary to remove it without causing further injury.

Finding materials for splints requires quite a bit of ingenuity in wilderness situations. Many injuries can be splinted in whole or in part by using other parts of the victim's body. Arms can be bound to the body. A leg can be splinted partly by tying it to the other leg. A finger can be taped to its neighbor. These methods have the advantage of conserving warmth. Padding should be placed near all bony projections like knees, or the patient will be uncomfortable in a short length of time. Some cloth should separate any skin surface from another to prevent maceration. Air mattresses, sleeping pads, and pack frames all can be used to help improvise splints, but ski poles, skis, ice axes, and snowshoes should be used as a last resort, since they may be needed for other purposes. Available branches and sticks are obvious sources of rigidity when properly padded.

In your enthusiasm for engineering splints, try to remember your patient. Besides watching him for shock and cold, you need his advice to make a good splint. *He is the expert; he knows what hurts and what is relatively comfortable,* and this is the best guide to proper position in splinting. If you can make the patient comfortable, then you have found a good position for splinting him. The patient's comfort and immobilization of the injured area are the two main considerations. Don't assume that you know better than the injured person what position is best for him; you probably don't.

Any injured extremity must be well padded and insulated, but it should also be easy to get to. It must be checked frequently for signs of impaired circulation or frostbite, and this will be put off if it is made too difficult to gain access to the limb. Even a healthy person who is inactive is likely to become cold despite his wearing much more clothing than those around him. An injured person has much less heat-producing capacity, and any impairment of circulation to the feet or hands by the injury itself or by splints is likely to cause very rapid chilling and cold injury.

Fractures that are not disabling, such as those of fingers, arms, and so on, should be properly splinted, but unless they cause inordinate pain or there is evidence of nerve damage or impairment of circulation, they need not be considered as emergencies. There is no compelling need for the fracture to be set, and the party should plan a relaxed and organized retreat. Harrowing forced marches are particularly foolish in such cases.

A broken leg or pelvis will probably be disabling, but the major threats lie in possible complications. If shock and cold injury are warded off, there is no great danger in keeping the patient in a tent for a while until an orderly evacuation can be carried out. The poor fellow has suffered enough without his friends bouncing him out through the woods in the middle of the night.

WOUNDS

The major problem resulting from lacerations, cuts, and other flesh wounds has already been alluded to—the danger of major bleeding, especially in the event that an artery has been severed. Stopping bleeding is the first job of anyone giving first aid to an injured person. With bleeding under control the rescuer must anticipate the possibility of shock, which should be expected to follow any major injury, and treatment should be started as soon as possible. Shock is discussed below in more detail. Finally, treatment for flesh wounds must include any measures possible to promote healing and to prevent infection of the wound. Since the means of combating infection that are available on a backcountry trip are quite limited, the winter tourer is fortunate that his environment is relatively clean and free of bacteria.

Once bleeding has been controlled, the person giving first aid should clean the wound as much as possible, but without risking another incident of major bleeding. The hands should be thoroughly washed before working on the wound. Sterile swabs or pads from the first-aid kit should be used for cleaning out any foreign material. Sterile water should be used for washing the wound if possible. Melted new snow may have to be substituted if fuel supplies are inadequate for boiling water. The area around the wound can be washed with a solution of aqueous Zepharin or pHisohex, neither of which will damage the tissues or dye the surrounding skin red and thus mask developing signs of infection. If the wound was made by a protruding compound fracture, which does not seem to have been significantly contaminated, it is probably best to confine cleansing to the skin around the wound. If there is foreign matter on the bone end, it should be removed, but any contamination of the bone should be avoided with great care, since infection of the bone can be very dangerous. When the wound has been cleaned, it should be covered with a sterile dressing and then with a bandage. The same cautions about insulating fractured limbs and taking care not to impede circulation apply to limbs injured by flesh wounds.

In cases where severe arterial bleeding has occurred, particular care should be taken not to dislodge blood clots once they have formed. The additional bleeding that will result can probably not be tolerated by a patient who has already sustained considerable blood loss. For this reason, it is advisable to wait a few days before attempting transport of an accident victim with this type of cut, providing other considerations do not make immediate evacuation necessary.

Compound fractures—those that have a surface wound extending to the fracture—usually result from a sharp end of bone poking through the tissues and skin. The dangers, and hence the treatment, are those associated with both fractures and flesh wounds. Bleeding must be stopped first, of course, and the wound should then be dressed. If the bone is still protruding, it should not be withdrawn back into the skin unless this is absolutely imperative, since the possibility of dangerous infection will be greatly increased. The limb must be splinted like any other fracture before the victim is moved.

No attempts should be made to close a wound with sutures or other devices, since infection is far more likely to spread if the wound has been closed. Pus in a closed infected wound is forced into the tissues around the wound instead of draining.

If much time passes before the accident victim is evacuated, the dressing on the wound should be changed periodically, and both the wound and the surrounding area should be examined for signs of infection. An infected wound will become red around the edges and is likely to be swollen and to exude pus. If an infected wound closes over, it should be opened, preferably by dissolving the sealing matter with warm water before forcing the edges open. The wound should be thoroughly cleaned and should be probed with a sterile instrument to open any pockets of pus. A dressing should then be placed on the wound that will allow it to drain and not encourage closing. When possible, soaking infected wounds is helpful. Dressings must be changed after soaking.

All dressings from infected wounds should be handled very carefully to avoid spreading the infection with the tremendous number of bacteria present in the pus. The preferred method is to handle such dressings with forceps to be sterilized afterward. The dressings should be burned. Such procedures may or may not be possible in your situation, but they should be approximated to the greatest possible degree.

SPECIAL PROBLEMS

Head Injuries
Injuries of the head are particularly dangerous, because they threaten the brain, a vital and easily damaged organ. Luckily, this type of injury is rather unlikely in most wilderness situations in winter, with the exception of winter mountaineering. Participants in the latter activity should consider wearing hard hats for warmth and protection in case of falls.

With wounds of the face and scalp, considerable bleeding may be expected, since these areas are well supplied with blood. This bleeding can be readily controlled by pressure. Such wounds are particularly resistant to infection, but additional care should still be taken, since infection would be especially dangerous so near the brain and the eyes. Injuries to the eyes and eyelids themselves are quite uncommon, but they are very dangerous and should prompt evacuation as quickly as possible. The affected eye should be carefully bandaged after washing and the unaffected eye should be covered to prevent movement. In washing, foreign particles may be removed, but great care should be taken not to damage any blood clots or tissues of the eye itself. Broken bones in the face do not usually cause much serious trouble. Only the jawbone needs splinting, and this will reduce the victim to a liquid diet.

The most serious injuries to the head are those involving damage to the brain or the skull that protects it. Any blow to the head that is followed by unconsciousness has involved some damage to the brain: That is the reason the victim is unconscious. Usually, no complications follow if the person regains consciousness within fifteen minutes or so, but even someone who has been unconscious for a short time should be watched carefully during the next twenty-four hours. The reason is that after an injury, bruising, bleeding, and swelling can occur in the brain, just as in any other part of the body, but since the brain is enclosed in a rigid case, swelling will produce pressure inside the skull. Too much pressure will cause unconsciousness and finally death.

In examining a person who has received a blow on his head, you should be alert for signs of brain injury, whether he is unconscious or not. A scalp wound, bump, or tender spot may be associated with a skull fracture, but this will be difficult to determine, except in cases so obvious that they kill the victim. Signs of brain injury include: pupils that are of different size or are dilated and do not react to light; irrationality or confusion greater than would be expected from the circumstances; bleeding or leakage of yellowish, clear fluid from the nose or ears; a slow pulse rate; irregular breathing; nausea.

Depth of unconsciousness may give some indication of the seriousness of a coma. A person who still shows some reaction to stimuli—voices or other noises, touch, or pain—is in a relatively light coma, and there is some chance that he may regain consciousness and be able to walk out. A deeper coma is more likely to last a long time and require the victim to be carried out. In any case, there is no treatment possible for the brain injury outside of a hospital. Treatment must concentrate on care for other injuries and supportive care. It is particularly important that the patient's airway be kept open, since the muscles of a comatose patient may be so relaxed that his tongue will drop back into his throat and suffocate him. If possible, a record of pulse and breathing rates, together with any information of a deepening or lightening coma, will be of help to the physician when the patient reaches him.

Broken Back or Neck

A broken back or neck is a particularly dangerous fracture because of the danger to the spinal cord, the central nervous column that carries impulses between the brain and the body. Actual damage to or pressure on the spinal cord may cause lack of feeling and paralysis in those areas below the fractured vertebra. In less severe cases it may cause some loss of sensation in those parts, tingling, pain flowing around from back to front and down the arms and legs. When checking for loss of sensation or power of movement, always check both sides of the body, since only one side may be affected.

A fractured vertebra threatens damage to the spinal cord, but damage may not be sustained at the time of the injury. After any fall that might have broken the spinal column, it should be carefully checked for possible fractures. Any painful, sensitive, or swollen spot along the spine should be assumed to be a fracture, and the victim should be treated accordingly. A spinal fracture must be adequately splinted before the patient is moved at all. The splint should insure that no lateral or twisting movement can take place. Evacuation should normally be postponed until a wire basket stretcher can be brought in, though this may not be practical. Temporary splints are usually best made from packframes, skis, and snowshoes. With a fracture of the neck, the head must be padded and strapped so that it cannot move at all from side to side, with a small pad about the size of a fist under the nape of the neck. *A broken neck must not be flexed,* lest the victim be killed. For splinting the spine, a pad should rest under the small of the back.

Chest and Lung Injuries

Injuries of the chest and lungs pose the particular threat of interference with breathing, so they require some special attention. The most common chest injury is a broken rib, normally not a serious injury. Pain in the chest wall following a sharp impact may result from a broken rib or from simple bruising. If the pain becomes more intense when a large breath is taken, it is probably a broken rib. Except in rare cases, the rib will be adequately splinted by the surrounding muscles, and no special treatment is required. If the patient is suffering from too much pain, but he is not having difficulty getting enough air, the rib can be taped to make him more comfortable. Several strips of tape running from the spine to the center of the chest roughly along the line of the injured rib and applied after a breath has been expelled will make the patient more comfortable. Taping should not be attempted if the victim is having trouble getting enough air, since it will partially immobilize one side of the chest and will impair breathing. The tape should be removed after a couple of days.

Occasionally, considerably greater damage is done to the chest, and breathing may be impaired in one of several ways. A rib may be broken in such a fashion that the sharp end penetrates the thick layer of muscle surrounding it and actually perforates the lung. Symptoms are those of a normal broken rib, except that pain is more intense, the patient will have difficulty in breathing, and there will be at least some bleeding into the lung so that blood may be coughed up. This type of injury can be very dangerous, since pressure can build up in the injured side of the chest and interfere with breathing even in the good lung. Such pressure can also be created by bleeding into one side of the chest cavity. The chest should be taped on the injured side, and the patient should lie on the injured side, before and during transport. This serves a combined purpose: lying on the side helps to splint it; not so much air can get into the injured side, where it does no good anyhow; and blood will pool in the injured side and run out the windpipe, rather than flowing into the good lung and damaging it, too.

Another type of chest injury that will produce great difficulty in breathing is caused by a blow to the chest so massive as to fracture several ribs in a number of different places, destroying the rigidity of a section of the chest wall. When the victim tries to inhale, the injured section of the wall is sucked in, and when he tries to exhale, it puffs out. Thus, instead of moving air in and out of the chest, the diaphragm is merely moving the injured wall of the chest back and forth, and the patient may well be suffocating. This condition is known as flail chest. Immediate first aid is to roll the victim onto the injured side with the injured part of the chest resting on a wadded up jacket or similar object. The flailing section will then be immobilized so that the victim can breathe with his remaining lung capacity. The patient may also be transported in this position.

Finally, there is the possibility that an accident may occur that completely punctures the wall of the chest, creating what is known as a sucking chest wound. If the whole wall of the chest is actually perforated, the lung on that side will immediately collapse, as air rushes into the chest through the wound. Subsequent efforts by the victim to breathe will merely force air into and out of the wound, and since this air only goes into the pleural cavity and not into the lungs themselves, the victim gets no usable air and will suffocate in short order. A sucking chest wound demands immediate action on the part of the first aider. The wound must be stopped up without delay with the cleanest thing that can be grabbed quickly, even your bare hand. As soon as sterile dressings can be gotten out, they should be substituted for your first resort, but the transfer should be made carefully to avoid any air leaking through the wound. The dressing must then be thoroughly taped to prevent leaking, and the victim should be transported on his side as soon as possible. A clean plastic bag is a good emergency dressing for a chest wound of this type.

With any sort of chest injury, there is great danger of pneumonia developing, because the pooled fluids in the injured lung make an ideal medium for the growth of bacteria. Whenever possible the patient should be encouraged to cough in order to clear the lungs, even though it is painful. This is especially important with an injury like a normal broken rib, which does not appear to be incapacitating and may not even force abandonment of the trip. The victim will be likely to favor the injured chest and avoid coughing, so that conscious forcing of a cough is necessary. The more serious injuries will almost certainly develop bacterial infections without antibiotic therapy, so evacuation is essential, but if evacuation must be delayed, coughing should be encouraged as long as the patient seems strong enough and there is no puncture of the chest wall.

Internal Injuries and Emergencies

Internal injuries are not very likely to result from any accident that would occur on a winter trip, other than a long fall. A severe blow to any part of the trunk can cause one of the internal organs to rupture, and severe pain following such a blow should lead the examiner to suspect the worst. Immediate evacuation is essential. The same rule applies if someone begins to show symptoms of appendicitis—gradually increasing abdominal pain associated after a few hours with nausea and fever. Severe internal injuries produce internal bleeding and shock, as does peritonitis, the infection of the abdominal cavity that may follow internal injuries or rupture of the appendix.

SHOCK

After any severe injury, the rescuer should expect shock, a complicated syndrome resulting mainly from a loss of blood pressure. The most common cause of shock is severe bleeding, which rapidly reduces the amount of blood left in the circulatory system. The first reaction of the body is to contract the blood vessels in surface areas and extremities in order to make more blood available to the vital organs. The heart beats faster, so that the remaining blood is pumped around the body more quickly. As the body functions are depressed, shock begins to set in. The patient is likely to become irritable, confused, and then listless. He may be nauseated. The skin becomes pale and clammy, and then sweaty. The pulse is fast but weak, and respiration is shallow and may be irregular, with occasional deep and sighing breaths. The patient is thirsty because he wants to replace the liquid lost. He is likely to feel nauseated.

All these problems are intensified by the difficulties of a cold environment. Dehydration will predispose a person to shock, because his reserve of fluids is already low. Cold speeds up the general depression of the body's functions and increases the demands being made on an overtaxed system. Treatment for shock should be started after any injury outdoors in winter, since therapy is far more likely to be effective if it is begun before severe signs of shock appear. Shock will nearly always follow severe injuries and often fairly minor ones. Unless the patient has suffered a heart attack, a head injury, or breathing difficulty, his feet and legs should be elevated slightly. In cold weather, it is vital to try to keep him warm. It is not enough to wrap him in a sleeping bag, since he will not be able to produce enough heat to warm it up. Someone should get in with him. Heated objects may be used, but only with great care. Since circulation at the surface of the body is impaired during shock, the patient can be severely burned by temperatures that would not harm someone whose blood carries away excessive local heat. Also, because of depressed conditions and possible cold injury, the patient may not be aware he is being burned.

Whenever possible, the fluid losses suffered by the injured person should be replaced. Sips of water will help if he is not too nauseated. Put a pinch of salt in a cup of water. Warm liquids are all right, but they should not be hot, and they should be administered a little at a time.

Psychological factors are very important in the treatment of shock. Fear and pain are likely to greatly increase the patient's difficulties. A calm and helpful manner in giving first aid, together with care in handling the victim to avoid unnecessary pain, will do much to avoid the complications of shock.

COLD INJURIES

In cold weather, of course, the possibility of cold injury is always present, but it practically never bothers the healthy, well-clothed, and well-fed traveler. Even more than with other emergencies, the cure for cold injury is prevention. In fact, most cases of cold injury accompany other emergencies. In mountaineering, for example, frostbite rarely occurs on easily accomplished assaults. It happens on desperate, last-ditch retreats.

When the body becomes chilled, it begins to reduce circulation to the skin and to the extremities in order to maintain the proper temperature in the vital organs. Once circulation to the hands and feet has been reduced or stopped altogether, they will become progressively colder until they finally begin to freeze. No matter how well the extremities are insulated, they will not warm up again until the central core of the body is warmed. The body will sacrifice the hands and feet in order to preserve the organs that are essential to life. Chilling of the central core is known as hypothermia, or exposure, and it results in death if it proceeds too far. Its prevention is central to the prevention of cold injury, since frostbite generally follows hypothermia. The hands and feet will begin to freeze only when circulation to them is reduced. This may occur because of tight-fitting boots or because of an injury, but it is usually the result mainly of chilling of the body as a whole.

To prevent hypothermia, you must prevent your body from losing more heat than it is producing. If you continue to lose heat, your body temperature will continue to drop. Clearly, avoiding this progression involves a balancing operation. If the air gets colder or the wind stronger, you must either increase your insulation or your heat production. Most cases of hypothermia occur when something slightly out of the ordinary throws one of the factors in the heat equation far out of its normal value and there is no compensating reserve available. For example, cold rain soaks a person's clothing, and thus greatly reduces the insulation he has available, leaving him susceptible to temperatures and winds that would not otherwise have been much bother. Exhaustion or injury may greatly reduce the capacity of someone to produce heat, so that clothing that is quite adequate for those in good shape no longer protects him from the effects of the cold.

A person beginning to suffer from hypothermia will generally be awkward in his movements and judgment. He may be irritable and deny suffering any ill effects from the cold. He may shiver and complain of the cold. His nails and lips will be blue or pale. He will stumble if he is moving, and his speech will become slurred. He will forget things. The terminal stage of hypothermia often includes the pooling of liquid in the lungs, producing a bubbling sound in his breathing, and perhaps causing frothy sputum to be coughed up.

Under difficult circumstances, members of a party should watch each other carefully for signs of hypothermia. Action must be taken quickly to be successful, especially under the circumstances that are likely to prevail on winter trips. In early stages, the person suffering from the cold should be encouraged to increase his heat output. He should be given carbohydrates to eat, should be better protected from the cold, and his companions should help him to warm up. If the party is stopped, he should be encouraged to shiver or do isometric exercises. He should be insulated from the snow or ground. Someone can get into a sleeping bag with him to help him get warm. Hot drinks may help physically and psychologically.

If the victim is farther along, assistance to him in building up his supply of heat must be more vigorous, but exercise on his part is not a particularly good idea (he will probably be past being able to do much anyway). Food given to a patient suffering from severe hypothermia should probably be limited to sweet and salty warm drinks given slowly in small swallows. The blood supply available to the stomach at this stage is limited, so that heavier food cannot be digested. General treatment should be similar to that for shock. The person giving aid should expect signs of increased cold at various times during rewarming of the victim. Blood that has been trapped in the cold tissues in the extremities is returned to the heart and may produce sudden cooling of the central core. The victim should be supplied with as much heat as possible during such secondary chills, since these can overburden an already weakened system.

Frostbite is an injury resulting from freezing of the tissues, usually the hands, feet, or the extremities of the face. Frostbite is a serious injury that can be prevented with reasonable care. In addition to maintenance of the general warmth of the body, each person traveling in extremely cold weather must pay careful attention to his extremities, particularly the feet. Tight boots or footwear inadequate for the conditions can result in cold feet. Painfully cold feet must be attended to, not ignored until they become numb. Frostbite usually gives adequate warning: Extremely uncomfortable feet that suddenly cease to hurt must be taken care of immediately. It is better to stop and warm them even earlier, since the job is easier then. In conditions of cold wind, the party should pair off, with each person responsible for watching a companion's face. If the skin starts to become pale, a halt must be made for warming before serious freezing takes place.

Minor frostbite, where only the surface of the tissues has begun to freeze, should be rewarmed immediately against warm skin of the victim or of a companion. A vigorous burning sensation and subsequent minor blistering and peeling will be all the difficulties suffered. Deep frostbite with the flesh frozen solid is another matter altogether, and the decision on how to treat it can be very difficult indeed.

The proper treatment for true frostbite is rapid rewarming in a water bath maintained at a temperature between 108 and 112 degrees Fahrenheit. Temperatures must not be allowed to rise higher lest the rewarming be accomplished by cooking the frozen part. Rapid rewarming results in saving the maximum amount of damaged tissue, and where the choice can be made, it is far better to delay rewarming until it can be done properly, even if the delay lasts many hours. Rewarming should never be attempted until the patient can be cared for as a litter case. Walking or skiing out on a frozen foot will not do a great deal more damage, but once the extremity has been thawed, such abrasion will kill more tissue. Decisions about treatment of frostbite should be made with these considerations in mind, but many difficulties are likely to arise in applying them. For the small party without the manpower or equipment to evacuate an invalid, the decision would probably be to head back without rewarming, but the victim can obviously not be left out in the cold at night to prevent his foot from thawing. The only satisfactory solution is to avoid frostbite and situations from which it might result.

If rewarming is to be attempted, the frozen part should be suspended in a container so that it does not touch the sides. The larger the vessel the better, since water temperature will be difficult to maintain in a small container. Direct heat should never be applied to the rewarming vessel while the injury is in it, since burning the injured part is hardly likely to promote proper healing. Ideally, water at the proper temperature should be poured in from another container. The temperature must be checked constantly, preferably with a thermometer, but *never* with the injured part. If no vessel large enough for rewarming is available, the injury can be wrapped in cloths and the water poured over. Rapid rewarming is quite painful, by the way, and the victim should be prepared for an unpleasant experience.

After rewarming, the injured area must be propped in such a way that nothing rubs against it. If the patient is still under a first aider's care, the main rule of subsequent treatment is to soak the injury daily to keep it clean, and otherwise to leave it strictly alone. Frostbite injuries have a very unpleasant appearance, and both the victim and those caring for him should expect this, but no tissue should be touched or picked. Eventually, if infection is avoided, any dead tissue will fall off of its own accord, and any interference will merely result in much more damage being done. This is a rule for doctors dealing with frostbite, so it certainly applies to laymen.

It should go without saying that methods like rubbing a frostbitten area with snow belong to chambers of horrors rather than discussions of sensible treatment. No seriously frostbitten area should be rubbed at all, since this can only cause more damage to already injured tissues. Any warming that is done with the hands should be accomplished without rubbing.

Rules for Avoiding Cold Injury
To avoid cold injury, be certain that you adhere to the following rules at all times.

1. Carry clothing adequate for any weather you may encounter, including enough extra so that you will be able to keep an injured member of the party warm even though he is not exercising. Include wool or synthetic clothes, which will retain some insulating value even when wet. If rain might be expected, a *waterproof* shell layer must be carried. Getting wet in cold weather is not just uncomfortable; it is frequently fatal.

2. If you would be required to bivouac under emergency conditions, carry equipment to fashion a bivouac in the area in which you are traveling—a shovel for a snow hole, saw for fires and lean-to, and so on.

3. Carry enough food. Under normal circumstances your body can run on its own fat, but its heat-producing capacity and capacity for exercise are greatly reduced. Don't let your body's available sugar supplies drop. Have a snack or a piece of candy frequently.

4. Don't become dehydrated. Make sure you get adequate supplies of water and salt. Dehydration can contribute to exhaustion, hypothermia, frostbite, shock, and perhaps altitude sickness. Don't drink alcohol in really cold weather, and if there is danger of frostbite don't smoke. Alcohol, tobacco, and other drugs affect circulation.

5. Don't sweat. Evaporation of perspiration produces chilling; wet and salt-impregnated clothing loses its insulating value, and large quantities of hard-to-get liquid water are needed to prevent dehydration. Open your clothing or remove it when you are working hard, to avoid perspiring.

6. Put on clothing as soon as you start becoming chilled. If you wait, your body will have to burn a lot of extra food just to get you warm. It's better to use the heat that is produced as a side product of other muscular activity. As soon as you start to cool down at the top of the hill or lunch stop, start getting out the extra sweater.

7. Don't overexert in really cold weather. A great deal of body heat is lost in warming the cold air you breathe. If you are panting, you're warming a lot more air, and you may become chilled from the inside no matter how thick your down parka. Panting also increases fluids lost to evaporation, which loses more heat and contributes to dehydration.

8. Take care of your extremities, especially your feet, which may be in snow much colder than the air temperature. Wear footgear adequate for the temperatures you will encounter. Don't lace them too tight or wear so many socks that they are tight. Wear wool socks and change them when they become damp. Stop to warm your feet if they get cold. Don't touch metal objects with bare hands in very cold weather.

9. Watch yourself and your companions for signs of hypothermia and frostbite. Pale or white spots on the face indicate frostbite. Irritability, irrationality, stumbling, clumsiness, heavy speech, bluish lips, breathing difficulties, and dilated pupils warn of hypothermia.

10. *Bivouac early.* A well-prepared bivouac started while you are still in good condition will enable you to survive very difficult conditions. Going on too long is likely to result in a spiraling chain of difficulties for your party and for your body.

GETTING THE VICTIM OUT

The difficulties of transporting an injured person over snow-covered wilderness terrain are formidable, and they should not be taken lightly. Serious consideration should be given to going out for help, or at least for a sled or toboggan. If you have a large party and the victim's skis are available for the manufacture of an improvised sled, it may be best to try to get the victim out yourself, but the smaller the party, the more advisable it becomes to send someone out at least as far as the nearest rescue toboggan. If skis are not available for the manufacture of a sled, this is even more true.

If you are attempting to transport an injured person, his injuries *must* be adequately splinted to withstand the trip. He must be strapped on the sled, toboggan, or drag so that he is reasonably comfortable and so that he can brace himself against jolting, and he must be kept warm. The vehicle must obviously be arranged with enough safety lines so that any downhill sections of the trip will not result in the loss of the sled.

If someone is being sent for help, two should go whenever possible, in order to provide a reserve for possible additional accidents. When supplies are low, it may be best for all but the injured person and one companion to go out for help and supplies, leaving as much food and clothing as possible with the victim and his nurse.

RISKS, RESCUERS, AND RESPONSIBILITY

Because of the possibility of accidents and other emergencies, every small party in wilderness areas is dependent to some extent on outside help if it gets into trouble. It is a fine tradition in wilderness areas on this continent that help is freely given when it is needed. It is also traditional that this help has been pot luck, and that parties going into the wilderness have been expected to be basically self-reliant. Many thousands of man hours have been given by the U.S. Forest Service, the Park Service, various military services, state and local officials, privately organized rescue groups, and outdoorspeople who happen to be available to rescue those who have gotten into trouble in the wilderness, generally at no expense to those rescued.

The system that has developed has the important virtue of retaining the freedom for the individual that many of us prize as the most valuable aspect of the wilderness experience. The essential premise has been that anyone has a right to go into the woods and take what chances he chooses, whether he exercises common sense or acts the fool. The risks taken by rescuers to save even fools have been worthwhile because they have preserved a freedom that is valuable to us all.

With increasing numbers of people going into the wilderness every year, many of them inexperienced or willfully careless, it is inevitable that the number of accidents, lost parties, and so on should increase. In many cases, professionals like those of the Park Service and the Forest Service have an obligation to rescue those who get into trouble in their areas of jurisdiction. Rescue operations are expensive and risky, and it is understandable that those charged with the responsibility for wilderness areas want to keep the number of rescues that they have to perform at a minimum. The natural reaction, especially among bureaucrats, is to attempt to regulate those using wilderness areas, not only for purposes of land management but by attempting to establish definitions of who is competent, "for their own good."

This tendency for more and more regulations to appear is repugnant to me and to many others, since it limits the freedom of people to enjoy the wilderness on their own terms, a freedom that ought to be considered a right qualified only by the obligation not to spoil the land for others' use. Inevitably, the tendency toward regulation goes hand in hand with "improvement" of the land, with administrative procedures designed to make regulation easier and more practical, and with attempts to define and compartmentalize which sorts of wilderness experience you and I should have.

If the tendency toward regimentation is to be curbed, however, wilderness travelers, new and old, are going to have to take a hard look at themselves and their attitudes. The trend toward heavier use of wilderness areas is bound to continue, and if larger and larger numbers of people act irresponsibly, first getting into situations much more difficult than they are equipped to handle, and then expecting the rangers to come in and bail them out, officials will have plenty of excuses for writing more rule books.

Anyone has a right to risk his own neck if he wants to, but those going into a wilderness area have a responsibility toward those who may be called upon to help them. If you aren't leaving anyone at home who might call for help when you don't get back, and if you're not leaving your car in a place where it might attract attention, then by all means go off and break your leg on the nearest snowy peak if you want to, but if a couple of hundred people are going to have to drop their usual activities to come after you, you have some obligation to make their job as easy as possible.

You should tell some responsible person when you plan to go, when you expect to be back, and how much longer you are equipped to last without being in real trouble. You should leave a note on your car with the same information. Finally, you should follow reasonable safety rules and carry normal emergency equipment. In most cases, this will enable you to stay out of real trouble and to hold down the expense and difficulty of any necessary rescues. If you're adequately equipped and break your leg, you can sit out a storm with your companions. A couple of them can go out and get a toboggan and a couple of extra people and take you out without any great fanfare. On the other hand, if you don't have adequate food, clothing, or presence of mind, your rescue will be a survival ordeal for you and an expensive and risky operation for dozens of other people.

At the same time, it is inevitable that some people will get in trouble, and sometimes it will be their own fault. Getting them out of trouble is the friendly thing to do, a traditional obligation of the outdoorsperson in this country, and it is also the price that must be paid if we are to avoid expensive professional rescue groups and the regulation-writing bureaucrats who pay them. We have recently witnessed the attempted rescue by one agency of a couple of rock climbers who didn't want to be rescued, and we may be sure that the expense of the operation will be used as an excuse to further control other wilderness travelers. Backcountry travelers should form their own rescue groups to take on responsibilities for these operations as much as possible, and the users of wilderness areas should accept both the responsibility for their own safety and the limitations of existing rescue facilities. If you call in a helicopter to get you out, you are giving the helicopter owner some claim to need to regulate your right to go in. Wilderness use is best regulated by wilderness lovers and users, not by helicopter owners.

Finally, unless our public lands are simply to become copies of many other regimented and bureaucratic areas of our national life, those who love the outdoors must call a halt to excessive regulation of their activities in state and nationally owned wilderness and semi-wilderness areas. There are many legitimate needs for regulation as a conservation measure, some of which will be discussed in the last chapter. The necessity of this kind of control can only be eliminated by educating users of the land in its proper treatment. Other types of regulation are of a quite different kind, however. Winter travelers will find that many areas are closed to use in the winter, some for conservation reasons, but most "to protect the public." If you feel you are being protected by being barred from any place a ranger cannot conveniently watch you, that is your privilege. I don't. Wilderness travelers should insist that they be allowed to go where and when they wish on the public lands, provided conservation of the environment does not require its protection. If a government agency does not feel it can be responsible for the rescue of wilderness travelers, a sign disclaiming responsibility is quite adequate to warn those who insist on passing. At the same time, outdoorspeople should assume responsibility for their own safety, rather than taking unnecessary risks with the expectation that a rescue party will come in to pick up the pieces.

13 | The World of Winter

Some of the special attractions of the winter landscape have already been mentioned—the special beauty, sharp contrasts of color, and starkness of both calm and stormy weather. Everything in winter seems sharper than at other times of the year. The beauty is of a harsher and colder kind than during other seasons, and for most living things winter is a time of retreat, of dormancy, or of a struggle for survival. Gone, for most, are the periods of mating, raising young, or general frivolity. The rigors of simply staying alive are dominant.

The energy that supports life on the earth comes ultimately from the sun. It may be received directly by a particular organism, or it may pass through many intermediate steps before being used by some forms of life. However, regardless of the means of collection, all life depends on the sun for its maintenance. It follows that the amount of life that can be supported on the earth, or on an individual part of it, is intimately related to the amount of sunlight that falls on the land. During winter less sunlight, and hence less energy, is available for sustaining life, and this accounts for the more tenuous state of life in the winter world.

This energy deficit in winter is only temporary, of course, and is not at all detrimental to those species that have adapted well to the annual pattern. The interest for the observer lies in the fact that so much of the pattern of nature in the winter is related to the cycle of cold weather. Living species may be helped or hindered by the mantle of snow, but they are rarely unaffected.

THE INTERRELATIONSHIP OF THINGS

When you begin touring in the winter landscape, the combination of vigorous exercise, beautiful scenery, and personal challenge will probably be interesting enough. Unless you are already something of an amateur naturalist, you are likely to take only a casual interest in a fresh set of tracks or a passing bird. You are more apt to develop an

The oneness of things A snowshoer stands above a lake in front of three muskrat homes.

early interest in some of the larger natural phenomena like storms and avalanches, if only because they refuse to be ignored. The forms taken by snow crystals may attract your interest at first by their influence on your ski waxes or the depth to which your snowshoes sink, and the fascination with their infinite variety may follow from this pragmatic concern or from the more desperate one of predicting avalanche danger. Stars and trees are likely to be subjects mainly of aesthetic interest.

Eventually, though, most people who have developed a love for the woods and mountains in winter dress also become interested in the inhabitants of that world and in the many interlocking patterns that characterize their lives and that of the landscape around them. Whether your interest begins with a study of avalanches or of birds, you are liable to find eventually that each part of the world you are watching is connected to everything else. The avalanche watcher soon sees that a formerly safe slope that has been clear-cut by loggers or devastated by the avalanche of an exceptional year is now subject to sliding after every major storm. The topsoil that accumulated there over thousands of years is washed into the valley in a season, and the animal life supported by the trees will no longer be found there.

Anyone interested in the life of the larger mammals will soon find how much they are affected by the amount and kind of snow that falls. A deep and soft snow cover that falls in a short time is likely to trap deer in small yards, where they quickly consume most of the available food and condemn many members of the herd to starvation. The same deep snowfall will make fine insulation for the chipmunks hibernating below, many of which would die from cold in a year when the snowfall was unusually light.

Once you begin to learn about some part of the world surrounding your winter campsite, you are likely to be led step by step from one facet to another. You may find that your favorite bird prefers a certain kind of tree, or that moose are especially fond of some kinds of browse. The dependence of one part of the food chain on another will suddenly explain observations that seemed before to be merely capricious. Some pine trees produce cones only in a particular year, and birds that in other years migrate south to find food will stay to feed on the seeds that year. Nature is recalcitrant in her refusal to be bound by the categories we use to classify her. Each part interlocks with many others, and each relationship always turns out to be more complex than it seemed at first. Each cycle of life and death or building up and breaking down is linked with so many others that one can never know more than a fraction of them. The more one learns, the more questions are posed that remain unanswered. Yet the satisfactions of the small knowledge one wins are not dimmed by awareness of its limitations, because a knowledge of the many interrelationships in the winter world can give one a sense of belonging there oneself—a sense of kinship.

WATCHING IN WINTER

The serious naturalist, whether professional or amateur, must become interested in all the seasons, since one is as much a part of the various life cycles as another. On a more superficial level, however, each season is likely to present particular attractions and frustrations depending on the short- and long-term interests of the observer. The bird watcher, especially one living along one of the major flyways, will have a particular fondness for spring and fall when the great migrations occur, bringing species that only pass through and never stay long. Those with a special love for wildflowers are likely to be impatient of winter snow, even though they know that it is the watering pot for their favorite blossoms. Winter, too, has its special satisfactions and frustrations for the observer quite aside from its deeper meanings and implications.

The disadvantages of winter as a time for observing nature are fairly obvious. Deciduous plants have shed their leaves, leaving them harder to identify. With the leaves have gone those forms of life that used them for food. The mating season has passed and with it the bright colors and ostentatious manners that make so many species stand out. Most birds have followed the sun and the food supply south, and many of those that remain are quieter, their colors more nondescript. Insects may migrate, hibernate, or coordinate some dormant stage in their life cycle with the winter months, but in any case they disappear from view. Many mammals spend the winter in hibernation, and others sleep through most of the cold months, even though they may come out for short forays from time to time. There is little resemblance to the humming world of spring, with life going on everywhere at a furious pace.

Winter has its special compensations for the observer, however. In deciduous forests, those birds that remain are often much easier to see. The lack of foliage increases the range of visibility, and birds that are very difficult to pick out among summer leaves stand out readily on the stark branches of winter or on the background of the snow. Many more birds than one might expect stay in northern climes. There is a special advantage for the beginner also in the reduced number of species. He has fewer choices to make in the difficult first stage of identification. Spring may be a paradise for the experienced birder, who delights in picking out the single rare European visitor in a flock of varied spring shorebirds, but the recent convert from modern life who has yet to identify his first chickadee may find comfort in the less complicated catalog of winter. Even among the migrants, there are species that appear in temperate climes only in winter, when they retreat from their usual homes in the Arctic, or who are blown in from the sea by winter storms.

Despite the fact that many mammals either hibernate or sleep through most of the winter, it is often much easier to observe signs of mammal life in winter than in summer. The reason for this lies in the snow cover itself. Most mammals are nocturnal, so that they are rarely seen even in summer, but they do make tracks on soft surfaces, and the snows of winter provide a frequently renewed recording medium that shows the signs of many passersby. In summer, you may have to travel a long way to find a soft riverbank or sandhill that holds tracks of visitors, but in winter, you need only to go out on a walk to come upon many stories written in the snow. Visibility of mammals is also sometimes improved by the snow cover, lack of deciduous foliage, and the burying of small plants and other hiding places.

The tenuous nature of the winter food supply can also be a friend to the observer, precisely when it becomes a threat to the observed. The threat of starvation drives many animals out to search for food in spite of a caution that would prevail in the months when the food supply was more plentiful. A few species are unperturbed. Porcupines are as happy to eat your pack straps in winter as in summer, and their other tastes adjust easily to the season. They seem equally satisfied with canoe canvas or snowshoe webbing. Other animals are more easily attracted by an offer of food, however, whether voluntary or not. Chickadees will be happy to pick up your crumbs, and if any raccoons are still awake they will make sure that you are, too, first finishing off any leftovers in your pots and then throwing the pans at each other.

LEARNING WHAT'S WHAT

The field of natural history is so broad and has such a long and honorable past that more is known than any one person could possibly digest in a lifetime. At the same time, it is one of the few areas of science to which amateurs can still make significant contributions. More significantly, any wilderness traveler interested in the surrounding world can observe many things that are fascinating, quite apart from whether anything like it has been seen before or not.

Regardless of whether your interest lies in scientific study or not, identification remains the starting point for those who begin to try to understand the workings of the natural world. Some people are lucky enough to have acquired a basic repertoire of birds, flowers, trees, and animals painlessly in childhood or through some effort when they were older. They can delve fairly easily into whatever area they choose with no help from this book. Others have had a more urban upbringing or recalcitrant character and will have to start from a point close to that from which I began—I *could* tell a robin from a maple.

The modern beginner has at least one great advantage over those of a few years ago. He may have a poorer background, but he has some very good, inexpensive, and relatively painless guides to help him get started. Many modern guidebooks make the task of acquiring the initial knowledge of a subject much easier than was possible a few years ago. The first few trees or birds or tracks are always the most difficult. After that, patterns begin falling together, descriptions that once seemed obscure take on meaning and each additional species falls into place more readily than the last. Most older guidebooks were particularly difficult for the beginner to use, but that has been changed by the technology of modern methods of printing, together with the enterprise of a number of naturalists who have made special efforts to produce guidebooks that are made for easy use by the layman. Roger Tory Peterson deserves particular praise for his writing, drawing, and

The characteristic tracks of a cottontail Signs of many mammals are easiest to find in winter.

editorial work and for the inspiration he has provided for other authors and publishers.

By far the easiest way for the complete novice to acquire some of the basic information about any field of nature study is by having someone point things out. One weekend with a knowledgeable friend is worth half a dozen with a guidebook. Unfortunately, guidebooks are generally easier to come by than naturalist friends.

For those who are put off by the systematic and somewhat boring approach involved in the use of guidebooks, a good start can be made by reading the delightful works of a few naturalists. Some of the finest literature ever written in this country was created by lovers and observers of wild things. Though it is a less efficient way of accumulating information than more systematic methods, such reading is an enjoyable way to acquire some of the basic information about the intricacies of the natural world. A few titles are suggested in Appendix B.

CHOOSING GUIDEBOOKS

The guidebooks that are currently available would easily fill a small library, and an attempt to stuff them all into a rucksack would serve no useful purpose. You must be selective in your choice of guides both for the sake of your back and your sanity. At the beginning stage it is more important to become familiar with one guide, so that you can find things quickly, than it is to have numerous references to consult. Frequently the most convenient and thorough guides are those that cover a particular area or season. Because they need discuss a much more limited number of species, they are more compact and easier to search through, though their usefulness is limited by their self-imposed boundaries. More complete guides require a smaller investment, and they are useful on trips to different areas without requiring the purchase or study of a new key for each region you may visit. Your choice will depend on your preferences and the availability of special guides. These are usually more likely to be written for well-known areas like national parks.

Appendix B lists some of the useful general guides. Special guides limited to one area and perhaps one season as well are too numerous to mention, but quite a few are published at nominal prices by concerned government agencies. A booklet covering the trees of a national park or forest will be equally useful in the surrounding country.

WHERE TO BEGIN

The most obvious place to begin is at the place that most interests you, but those with catholic tastes may again end up with a rucksack full of guidebooks. You might also consider your temperament, the opportunities you will have for observation, and the things you can pick up at home. Trees, for example, are considerably easier to identify than birds. They stand still. They can be approached as closely as you like, and you can look at them as long as you please. They will still be there on the following weekend if you wish to return for another look. Birds, despite their other virtues, will do none of these things. The rank beginner with but a few weekends a year to spend in the wilderness might do better to stick to trees for a while and get over his initial bird-watching frustrations closer to home.

Animal tracks can be easier to identify than many trees or far more frustrating than the most difficult birds. Those who must have an answer to every question should stay away from them. Each set of tracks has a story to tell, but it is not always easy to read. Patterns of hunts and chases, of successful escapes and desperate ends are all traced in the snow, but even years of experience sometimes cannot decipher them. This is a good field for the amateur detective, from the easily recognized track of a rabbit to complex jumbles of trails. The observer of tracks must learn the habits of many animals he has never seen before he can be successful in reading the signs.

The star gazer is likely to be able to achieve satisfying results a bit more quickly and surely. He can learn the major constellations at home, eliminating the need to carry heavy guidebooks into the woods. He need not drive his companions mad with his enthusiastic side trips or persistent stopping. He can observe his field of inquiry from the comfort of a sleeping bag. He can even claim a useful purpose when scoffed at by his unimaginative friends, claiming that his knowledge may one day be needed for navigational purposes.

Of course these are only suggestions, and the possibilities for one interested in the world around him on a winter trip are practically unlimited. Certain practical subjects can occupy the attention for a lifetime. The study of snow and of weather are examples that have been mentioned in earlier chapters. The literature of natural history is tremendous, though that part of it devoted to winter is quite a bit smaller, leaving much room for investigation. With a whole world to observe there are many pleasures to be gained by both the dilettante and the serious student.

GADGETRY

The Englishmen who made the first ascents of the snowy summits of the Alps felt the need to carry many heavy scientific instruments with them, both to satisfy real scientific curiosity and to provide a legitimate justification for the otherwise useless pursuit of climbing mountains. Most of us who now venture into wilderness regions no longer feel the need to pretend a useful purpose, and this has lightened our loads considerably. Instruments are also much more compact these days, however, and those who wish to satisfy their curiosity can carry some of them without noticing much extra burden. I will leave advanced instrumentation to those who are interested in it, but there are a few small items that may be useful to the untutored amateur.

A thermometer with a metal case is very valuable to anyone interested in the study of avalanches in particular or the snow cover in general. A small Weston type, with a metal shaft and a dial reading, is the most useful. It may also be of some use in studying the weather and waxing skis. A pocket magnifier is necessary for studying snowflakes and helpful for looking at details of plants. The serious bird watcher will rarely be caught without binoculars, and several very light and compact models are now available. These may also be of interest to the star gazer, and their use in studying terrain provides an excuse to palliate weight-conscious companions.

Mountaineers and meteorologists may wish to indulge themselves with the purchase of an altimeter or barometer (the same instrument with different markings) to measure air pressure. Good ones are rather expensive. An avalanche student may want his compass to include a clinometer to enable him to accurately measure slope angles. Either can also be useful in navigation. Finally, a light wind-speed gauge may help to pass the time during storms, though you may be disillusioned to find that the wind isn't gusting to 150 mph, after all.

All things considered, it is pretty easy to get along without any gadgets except perhaps a guidebook and a camera. You may want some of them if you develop specialized interests, but for the generalist, they often tend to be more a nuisance than a convenience. If you take a camera, you can spend almost any amount of money you choose. The literature of photography is so extensive there seems little point in producing more here, but it might be worth mentioning that most heavy cameras end up buried in the pack, and are rarely available when you want to take a picture. There is much to be said in favor of sacrificing some optical quality for light weight and compactness.

14 | A Plea for Wild Places

A few years ago it was still possible for lovers of wild places to labor under the illusion that, despite man's previous ravages, some wilderness areas on this continent would remain inviolate, if only because nobody wanted them except for the native animals, Indians, and a few outdoorspeople. By now, that illusion would be too heavy a cross for the most confirmed optimist to bear. Loggers are rapidly finishing off the California redwoods and the forests of southeastern Alaska; oilmen are busy planning vast new Arctic Santa Barbaras; the roar of snowmobiles disturbs the peace of forests once almost inviolate in winter, and those areas that have not interested other exploiters now beckon recreational developers.

In addition to this catalog of well-known pressures, the sheer force of numbers is threatening many areas. Backwoods campgrounds that used to be visited only a few times a season are now trampled by hundreds each year. Wilderness areas that were once the preserve of a few are now invaded by thousands, and by every indication the crowds will continue to grow. Supplying the growing numbers of people who want to spend time outdoors has become big business. Part of the business has consisted of creating a demand for mechanized gadgets, and once the gadgets have been purchased, the new owners want the space and facilities to use their acquisitions.

Quite aside from those areas that have been bulldozed into housing projects or superhighways, many formerly pristine and still roadless areas are suffering from serious problems of pollution. The majority of still underdeveloped areas have remained undeveloped precisely because they are too precariously balanced to support much exploitation. Plant life in many high mountains resembles that of the Arctic: Seemingly meager size may represent years of growth. Alpine meadows take many years to recover from overuse. Many high-altitude lakes are becoming seriously polluted and are no longer safe to drink. Nearly all low-altitude lakes have been undrinkable for years. The time has come for those who love the unspoiled wilderness to band together against people who would "improve" it, and there is also a desperate need to educate the bands of newcomers to the mountains and woods. Before setting out on their crusades, however, many back-packers, ski tourers, snowshoers, and mountaineers need to take a hard look at their own practices.

Wilderness travelers are fond of making unkind comments about many polluters of modern industrial society, but, while most of this derision is merited, the practices of the critics in the wilderness of which they are so fond are often as shortsighted as those of industrial polluters. Chimney Pond on Maine's Katahdin was not polluted by a paper company, and the trash and pollution beginning to appear in some of the high lakes of the Sierra Nevada did not come from oilmen. No one spends time on the glaciers of Mount McKinley except mountaineers, yet some of the favorite glacier camps are littered with trash, and there is so much sewage scattered here and there in the snow that some who camp there are having difficulty finding a safe water supply.

Winter travelers and mountaineers are often the most radical conservationists at home, and yet some of them seem to feel that they have a special dispensation in the woods, just because they deliberately choose to brave the harshest natural environments. Thus, a rock climber who will rant and rail about an ordinary car camper who leaves trash lying about the campground feels no qualm about tossing a sardine can off a ledge when he is climbing.

Snow campers are often particular offenders in this respect. They bury trash in the snow that becomes litter on the ground in the spring. They give little if any thought to the location of their privy, leaving pollution and toilet paper as their contribution to other snow campers and to the spring thaw. Because they choose a harsh season, they often seem to feel that they have some special privilege to cut live trees or leave tin cans.

In fact, winter campers have the obligation to take more pains than their warm-weather brethren, not fewer. Since the snow cover in many areas is too deep to permit digging to the ground, anything that is left behind will be deposited on the surface of the ground when the snow melts. You should pick a site for your toilet facilities very carefully, and you should dig to the ground whenever possible. If you can reach dirt, dig a hole and fill it before you leave. Toilet paper ought to be burned if this is at all feasible. In places that receive particularly heavy use, such as ski huts, it is essential to build a properly designed outhouse with a winter access door.

Trash must be burned or carried out. If cooking is being done on stoves, this will mean carrying paper and garbage as well as tin cans, plastic, and so on. If you burn your trash, make sure it *all* burns; aluminum foil, orange peels, and many other things don't. If it doesn't burn, carry it out. Extra plastic bags will help keep your pack clean.

If you can carry a full container into the woods, you can certainly get the empty one out.

If you use the same area repeatedly, one alternative is to use caches not only for storing supplies but for refuse as well. You can walk in to your caches in the spring and pick up the trash. This applies only to legitimate caches, though. Nobody has a right to dump a few bags of garbage next to the trail in a national park, saying to himself that he'll drop by and pick it up in June.

There aren't too many places left where the cutting of live foliage is justifiable except in a dire emergency. You should depend on building fires only where plenty of genuinely dead wood is available. Deciduous trees shed their leaves in winter, which does not make them dead—until someone comes along with his little hatchet. Birch bark is a wonderful fire starter, but stripping a ring of it from a tree will kill the birch. Bark should be collected only from obviously dead trees. Beautiful snags should also be left alone for the next visitor to enjoy. The gnarled and tortured branches of timberline trees often take hundreds of years to grow—a lot more time than it takes to carry in a stove.

Of course, in a genuine emergency, some of these rules may have to be disregarded, but if you're having that kind of emergency every other trip, it's a phony and you are abusing the woods. If you make planned bivouacs, they should be the kind that don't wreck the area. Those bough beds and lean-tos shingled with live twigs that fill the imaginations of thousands of old Boy Scouts have no place in the areas that most weekend outdoorspeople can reach.

Notwithstanding the remarks just made on the necessity for wilderness lovers to get their own woods in order, the major threat to the remaining wild places in this country does not come from backpackers or ski tourers. It comes from the many people who feel that there are more worthwhile uses for such lands than leaving them in their wild state. Some see profits to be made in clear-cutting the timber from the slopes or strip-mining ore, while others pretend more compatible uses that would be just as destructive. Finally, there are those who feel that the scenic and recreational "potential" of an area must be developed, lest it lie fallow and not be enjoyed by a sufficient number of people (all of whom require various expensive and profitable services, of course).

The most obvious enemies of the wild places are also the most powerful. Oilmen and lumber companies have a great deal of money to use in conservation fights, and they have many well-placed friends in high places. Still, the issues in this type of battle are fairly clear-cut, despite the attempts at window dressing that have recently become the fashion in the public-relations departments of many large corporations. Protection of an area threatened by a lumber company or housing development may be difficult, but in principle it is simply a matter of putting together enough political muscle from those who want to preserve the area.

Recently, there has also been a growing awareness of the broader issues that will ultimately determine the fate not only of wildernesses and open spaces but of the environment as a whole, both in this country and in the world. There is not space here for discussion of these issues, but obviously wilderness and open space cannot survive the indefinite expansion of population, perpetually spiraling consumption of energy, or bloated and wasteful squandering of both renewable and nonrenewable resources. The wilderness lover has a special interest and obligation in these matters, both because those who use the backcountry are more likely to be aware of the issues and because wilderness is bound to be considered an expendable luxury in a real crisis. Despite this special place outdoorspeople may have as conservationists, however, the broader issues raised here affect everyone in this society and the world very directly, and they are complex enough to defy summary here. Instead, I would like to consider a few more specialized problems.

A DEFENSE OF WILDERNESS

The first of these problems is the rapidly diminishing area that can be called wilderness, even in a very loose way. Many outdoor wanderers would say that no true wilderness even exists in the United States, except for Alaska, and there is a good deal of truth in the contention. I will not be quite such a purist here, but the distinction must at least be made between wilderness and other open spaces and scenic spots. The distinction operates on many levels, and it is an important one. A carefully tended park may be beautiful, but it is not wild. Ski touring on a golf course can be a fine way to spend a Sunday morning, but one occasionally wants something more stimulating.

Of the wilderness that covered almost all of this continent a few centuries ago, we have little left, and that is concentrated in those areas that were formerly of no interest to exploiters. What is left should be saved as best we can save it. Our increasing need for wilderness is amply demonstrated by the growing pressures on what we have. We simply cannot afford to diminish the supply. That supply is every bit as short as those of other resources, and no plastic substitute will be found.

There are quite a few "practical" reasons to preserve the wilderness areas we have left, but there is little point in cataloging them here. The economic or environmental absurdity of a particular development project only sometimes prevails against the host of technological sophists willing to argue that it is the last best hope for man and General Motors. The hundreds of ecological disasters of which we have daily evidence have not cooled the ardor of those who automatically see an active bulldozer as a sign of progress, no matter what it's doing. The idea that there is a practical use in maintaining habitats and species that provide the planet's reservoir of adaptable life will never carry any weight on cost-benefit sheets. Like the rights of the Indians, it merits lip service among the bureaucrats and politicians only as long as nobody wants the land for any other use and as long as preservation costs nothing.

The need for proper homework on the practical aspects of particular issues and the preservation of particular areas is obvious, but this is a matter of politics, not philosophy. There is no hope at all of saving the woods or the mountains by convincing the resource-management types that this is the best use of the land. We will only end up with more multiple-use schemes and eight-lane scenic highways on which it is both illegal and suicidal to look at the scenery.

The interests of the lovers of "development" have been pandered to for decades. Billions of dollars and God knows how many lives are sacrificed to the internal-combustion engine every year, while it chokes our cities, paves our countryside, and pollutes our air, yet we are told by the developers that in order to be democratic, we must also build freeways through the national parks so that speeding vacationers can cram Yellowstone, Grand Canyon, and Half Dome into the same week.

The winter months have long provided the saving grace of quiet and privacy by sending the motorized tourists home, covering their trash and roads with snow, and sending their engines back to the commuting routes. All this is changing, too, with the increasing demand for and supply of all-weather roads and the locust plague of the snowmobile. The days of complacency for the skier who wants quiet slopes away from the lift lines are gone, and winter tourers will have to join ranks with other embattled wilderness lovers quickly if they want to save any quiet valleys from the howl of the two-cycle engine.

Before anyone accuses me of being secretly intolerant, let me admit to being very openly intolerant. Though I don't much like snowmobiles anywhere, I don't really care much about the rallies in parking lots and on drag strips or about Farmer John, who likes to whiz around his fields in the winter on his new snow machine. However, I don't believe that the snowmobile has any place in wilderness or semi-wilderness areas, and in many other publicly owned lands it should be confined to established roads when it is permitted at all. Like other motor vehicles—speedboats, jeeps, camper-pickups, trail bikes, dune buggies, and their ilk—snowmobiles are incompatible with either wilderness or with peace and quiet.

The reason for both my statements and my intolerance is fairly simple. Quite aside from the damage it does (and the snowmobile does quite a bit), any motorized vehicle just uses up too much space. In areas that depend for their nature and their appeal on a feeling of space and uncrowded open vistas, motor-vehicle operators use up a lot more than their share of ground. The faster a conveyance goes, the bigger the empty space around it must be to allow it to turn or stop, and this space is no longer available for you and me and the trees. This would be true even if such vehicles were quiet, which they most emphatically are not. The whine of a snowmobile engine carries for miles. The effect of snowmobiles and other motor vehicles is to produce crowding in even sparsely populated areas, a phenomenon that is becoming all too familiar even to many sedentary citizens. In an Alpine valley, several parties of ski tourers and snowshoers may coexist without even being aware of one another, and if they do know of each other's presence, they will still not feel crowded. Thus, thirty people can get away from the pressures of the city in that one valley, while producing little or no effect on the country or its permanent inhabitants. A single snowmobile driven up the same valley inescapably insists on its own presence. Anyone else in the valley is stuck with an awareness of that presence, whether he likes it or not, and so is the wildlife.

This phenomenon of crowding is not unique to the snowmobile, of course. Lakes that are peaceful and undisturbed by a couple of dozen canoes shink to tiny warrens of activity with only three or four speedboats. A stretch of beach that is lonely and vast even when occupied by scores of people and thousands of shorebirds becomes crowded and frenetic with only a couple of dune buggies or Ski-doos. Encounters with a few backpackers on a summer trail tend to be sociable and may even increase the feeling of peace and space that pervades the trail beyond. An encounter with a trail bike lasts much longer, since the noise precedes and follows the vehicle, and it is a good deal less sociable, whether the rider tries to run you down or shout a greeting over the noise of his engine. Instead of being a minor social occasion, such a meeting tends merely to raise the specter of bile and crowding that you are trying to exorcise by heading for the hills in the first place.

Still another reason for my prejudice against motor vehicles in the backcountry is likely to seem snobbish, or flavored with sour grapes, though, of course, I think it is neither. It stems from the excessive ease with which the operator of a motor vehicle gets to his destination, or at least tries to get there. I think that one's attitude toward one's environment is always inextricably related to the effort and speed and personal involvement one has in traveling through it. Sticky snow to a ski tourer is likely to be challenging in the way of a friend with difficult idiosyncrasies; to a snowmobiler it is more often a nuisance for which he has no affection. The change in attitude is reflected in the piles of trash that are found in the backcountry: They seem to pile up in proportion to the aid that people have getting in. A motorized traveler can often carry no more garbage than one on foot, but he is more willing to leave it at the end of the trail. I don't really think that this is due to the inherent virtue of the traveler on foot, but rather to the feeling that you acquire for the land by direct contact with it. Felt through engine, treads, and gears, the land is an impersonal antagonist, which may be defiled at will.

Beyond the immediate annoyances and ravages of the motorized tourist, he must also be considered as a representative of a pressure group. Many of the individual operators of snowmobiles, trail bikes, and the like are more to be pitied than condemned. They have discovered only recently that there are pleasures and relaxations to be found in distant campgrounds that cannot be matched at home, but a sharp salesperson has conned them into believing that the discovery can be enjoyed only with the aid of a ton of expensive and not very durable equipment. In the end, instead of escaping the world of the machine, though perhaps with the aid of some of its advantages, he ends with merely another expensive mechanized amusement park, for which the passport must be renewed annually with a greater number of horsepower and new sleek design.

As part of its advertising campaign for new converts, the pleasure-machine companies must spend money lobbying for more facilities in which their product may be used, and this sort of campaign has the welcome advantage of being useful for the enlistment of new enthusiasts at the same time. If another hundred thousand snow machines are to be sold, the purchasers must have trails on which to ride, and what better place to create those trails than the national forests and parks, where no land need be paid for, where the scenic virtues are ready-made for the cameras of weekend publicity photographers, and where the actual cutting of the trails and safety of the users can be left to public servants already on the taxpayers' payroll and on a budget that is even supported by conservationists. There is money to be made in this enterprise, and it is being made.

One of the necessary ingredients of the snowmobile-trail-bike-all-terrain-vehicle-dune-buggy business is the lobbying for more facilities for the use of "recreational vehicles." The need for such facilities, and the others that inevitably follow them, is dictated both by the nature of the vehicles and the need for advertising that accompanies their promotion and subsequent exploitation. Lobbying for such facilities helps enlist the loyalty and community feeling of the machine owners and would-be owners. The facilities provide a place for them to meet and instill in one another the need to buy bigger and better machines, as well as convincing them of the justification for having bought the old ones.

Hence, once there are enough of the "go-anywhere" vehicles in an area, there must be trails on which they can go anywhere. Then there must be emergency facilities and rescue groups to take care of those who can go anywhere but can't get back again, and so on to the popcorn stands at five-mile intervals. Even when trails are not demanded by the owners of the vehicles themselves, they are soon necessitated by the problems of minimizing damage to trees, refuse disposal, and the "safety of the public." The problem becomes compounded by the dynamics of regulators requiring that snowmobilers stay on trails (partly to protect the countryside and partly to make the rangers' job of finding them easier) and the snowmobilers' demands for protection from a hostile environment. (While they ruin trees, they demand safety and complete freedom at the same time; rangers should be either out cutting trails for Ski-doos or rescuing their stranded owners.) The regulations resulting from this symbiosis carry over to other forms of activity, and soon the ski tourer who knows the region like the back of his hand is told by the brand-new ranger that he must stay on the new track cut for the snowmobiler. On his next visit the ski tourer doesn't bother to stop and see the ranger, thus complicating a rescue on the rare occasions when it is needed. This sort of ridiculous escalation seems common to most of the heavily used public areas these days, though such frictions are an absurd and unnecessary transfer of city problems to the woods.

As a modest contribution, I would like to make a few suggestions for administration of those areas that are still free from large-scale development. I make no pretensions to having definitive answers, but there are some points of emphasis that I think are important for conservationists concerned with wilderness preservation.

SAVING WHAT WE HAVE

Despite the depressing rapidity with which developers are making inroads on the remaining hinterland, there is also a new awareness by the public that there just might be something more worthwhile about a mountain than its possibilities as an ore heap, highway route, or ski development. There are tentative feelings to be found everywhere that the ravaging of natural areas and processes has gone far enough. The feelings are incoherent, but they are there, and therefore there is now a real possibility of tapping some of these feelings and converting them to political power in defense of threatened areas that should be preserved. It is testimony to this possibility that some of the richest and most destructive polluters in the country are spending vast sums of money to convince the public that their major corporate purpose is to preserve our forests and avoid disturbing the fish. At the same time, even the biggest pork-barrelers in Congress, who have never bridled at the destruction of great tracts of land by projects that might result in a few big campaign contributions, now feel it necessary to pay at least lip service to the cause of the environment.

Obviously, there is a possibility that the public will be taken in by the cheap tricks of the public-relations people, just as there is a strong chance that the widespread interest in conservation and reclamation of natural resources will prove to be merely dilettantish and will never develop the seriousness that will be necessary to really accomplish very much. The fact remains, however, that environmentalists of all kinds now have a starting point and a lever that simply did not exist a few years ago. Even in the mid-sixties, it was quite possible for a conservationist group to prove to nearly everyone's satisfaction that a particular development project would wreak tremendous environmental damage, as well as being economically foolish and profitable mainly to one private interest. The proof might then rate a three-inch summary on page sixty of the local paper. The problem was that nobody cared. Politicians, with a few honorable exceptions, felt little need to pay attention to the rumblings of conservationists because they were well aware that the issue was rarely one that would capture the imagination of a very large segment of the public.

Things have changed a good deal in the past few years. Environmental considerations from air quality to wilderness values now have legislative recognition as important factors in decision making, even though they are often ignored in practice. Wilderness areas that have been designated by Congress now have some protection under the 1964 Wilderness Act. The progress made already is only a beginning, however, and the pressures on the remaining wilderness can be expected to grow exponentially along with the economic and political pressures resulting from our habit of wasting resources, especially fossil fuels. Even as this is being written, the U.S. Forest Service is proposing the approval of oil and gas leases on areas presumably protected by the Wilderness Act, and there is enormous pressure for headlong development of western energy sources with no associated movement toward either energy conservation or mitigation of the destruction that will be associated with this type of exploitation. If any of our remaining wilderness is to be saved during the difficulties of the next few decades, environmentalists will have to become far more effective in their efforts.

One of the first things that conservationists ought to decide in their own minds is what sort of objectives they believe in, quite aside from those that they think are politically possible. Since everyone is now a self-proclaimed conservationist, the battle lines are no longer being drawn by the enemy. The current tactic of the logger who wants to wipe out a forest is to churn out reams of elegant tracts purporting to demonstrate that the true conservationist course lies in intelligent forest management and that the lumber comapny's proposed use would result in much nicer forests than those that would grow if they were left alone.

The point here is that it is in the interest of those who wish to continue to despoil our common heritage to cloud issues, to muddle distinctions, and generally to appeal to the instincts of reasonable people to avoid foolish and precipitate action. It is also in their interest to separate issues as much as possible, to use multiple jurisdictions and the proliferation of government agencies as an advantageous shell game, and to keep conservationists busy with red herrings and multiple fronts.

It is not possible to combat these tactics without a fairly clear idea of one's own objectives. Compromises are obviously unavoidable, as in every other aspect of life, but parties to a compromise who have no firm conception of their own goals are always the losers. This is particularly true in the conflicts with which conservationists concern themselves. A superhighway can be built or a redwood cut this year, next year, or ten years from now. It takes a great deal longer to go the other way. Conservationists are always fighting a holding operation; they can never advance. It takes minutes to cut a thousand-year-old tree, but it still takes a thousand years to grow another if you change your mind later about the wisdom of the operation.

For these reasons, environmentalists and conservationists must of necessity be reactionary in their attitude toward many types of development. There is plenty of room for creativity in rebuilding the central cities, setting up intelligent transportation systems, cleaning up our air and water, but those areas that remain in a relatively natural state should be left that way, with creative management taking a back seat to modest efforts of preservation. The obvious fact that this will not *always* be possible does not change its utility as a general principle. Our attitude in the past has generally been that those areas that need to be preserved from development were the exception, and that special justification was needed to divert the onrushing tide of progress. A change in emphasis is basic to a successful campaign to preserve the remaining wilderness in America. The nation as a whole is more ready to recognize such a goal than it ever has been before, and it is up to conservationists to emphasize the need for the shift in attitude. We must learn that the destruction of a wild area is irrevocable except in terms of geological time and that we can afford to wait before deciding that a particular form of exploitation really justifies the loss.

The change in emphasis—shifting the burden of proof to the developer—is a difficult change to effect, but the need for it is considerable. For one thing, it is a change that would represent a real shift toward a conservationist attitude—one of a decent respect for natural processes and an intelligent reluctance to interfere massively with their operation. Such a shift is also a strategic necessity in view of the money and power possessed by those who profit from destructive exploitation of the land. As long as conservationists are always compelled to present overwhelming cases for preservation on short notice to forestall the destruction of vast areas, they can expect to be in a continuous state of tactical retreat. The problem is always one of hundreds of fine areas being threatened at the same time, with the necessity of apportioning limited funds and energy. We have been faced again and again with decisions such as whether the Grand Canyon or the North Cascades is more important to save. We need to turn the tables so that instead of the saving of either requiring a major and desperate effort, the diminution or degradation of an existing wild area will require a long-term, public, and exhaustive study.

The current crisis in energy use (usually presented falsely as a crisis in supply) is already being used as an excuse for a broad-scale rape of the western part of the U.S. It is crucial that environmentalists make the point that the crisis should teach us just the opposite lesson—that nonrenewable resources are precious commodities that should be used wisely and with forethought, rather than being squandered at the maximum rate possible. In those rare instances where protecting a wilderness area would in fact "lock up" an exploitable deposit for a few years until a rational choice was made to tap it, the savings should be applauded. The idea of saving a few barrels of oil and a few cubic feet of natural gas for our children to dispose of is neither selfish nor shortsighted. It is not essential that we burn the last drop of oil available before beginning to deal with reality.

WILD PLACES AND OPEN SPACES

Naturally, the first interest of most of us who love wilderness is the preservation of the mountains, rivers, desert, marsh, or shore that we love. The importance of these areas is self-evident to those whose lives are entwined with them, but it is equally necessary for the same people to concern themselves with more civilized regions—with parks, cities fit to live in, outdoor recreation areas, and the proper use of many open spaces that could not be classified as wilderness by the most generous and citified observer. One reason we need to interest ourselves in such problems is the obvious one that they are vital public issues that concern us all, just as do the larger problems of pollution, overpopulation, and perverse waste of resources.

Wilderness lovers must also concern themselves with open spaces close to home for a more self-serving and parochial reason. The members of the population as a whole, or at least those segments of it who have acquired the basic privileges of the society, are turning to the outdoors as a relief from the pressures of their normal lives. They want the relief of open country, unpolluted water, and forested hills. It is important to try to counteract the influence of those who are trying rather successfully to convince these people that they can only enjoy the outdoors with the help of several thousand dollars' worth of mechanical garbage. Even if they are convinced that little equipment is needed to enjoy the outdoors, however, there are fortunately a lot of people who have no interest in enjoying the wilderness on its own terms. They want to get out in the country, admire the scenery, go swimming and perhaps camping. Many would be perfectly happy with rather tame woods and beaches and campgrounds close to home, but unless these are provided, and unless they offer at least a taste of challenge and adventure, the national parks and other places that *ought* to be reserved for headier and more Spartan joys will be converted to paved pabulum for people who haven't the slightest interest in a wilderness experience.

Those who wish to retain a little of the spice of independence and wildness in areas like the national parks will have to help provide tamer pleasures closer to home. Clearly, even in these more civilized areas, there are great problems of overcrowding, some of which could be reduced by eliminating excessive mechanization. The imagination needed to design many kinds of areas for outdoor recreation is obvious and should provide a challenge that is urgent. One of the major difficulties involved is in teaching people that the best way to escape the pressures of the machine is to get away from it, not to bring it with them.

There has also been a class bias quite evident in most of the conservation groups of the past, which has got to be eliminated if we are to have much hope for the future. This has been the case from national parks to city parks, and it is evident to anyone inspecting the park system in almost any city in the country. Where are all the nice parks?

In the "nice" part of town, of course. Small wonder that with urban decay and the spread of slums of displaced and alienated people, the parks that are in the path of the expanding slums become jungles in which it is not safe to walk at night. Why should a person without even a local patch of greenery to enjoy give a tinker's damn what happens to Yosemite Valley or some arches in the desert?

An interest in recreational open spaces in and around the cities on the part of wilderness conservationists is therefore necessary for several reasons. Places must be available for people to pursue a host of interests and tastes without "developing" genuine wilderness areas. These same areas can also serve as an introduction to the appreciation of the outdoors for many people who are just becoming interested in the pleasures and skills that are needed to travel comfortably in the backcountry. People who are stuck in the cities have even more need for parks to walk in, rivers and lakes to swim in, and open space to look at than do those fortunate enough to live where all these luxuries are more readily available. Finally, if the residents of the rotting cores of our cities, black and white, have no chance to enjoy any of the pleasures of decent open spaces, they can hardly be expected to be tolerant later on when they or their representatives are asked to join in efforts to preserve a distant mountain range. The preservation is more likely to seem to them a frivolous request redolent of privilege. As poverty in this country becomes increasingly an urban problem, conservationists will make a grave error if they allow wilderness preservation to become an issue of interest only to the wealthier classes.

Creation of decent recreation areas should not be at the expense of existing wild areas, both because of the distance from population centers and because of the need to save all the wild spots we have. With intelligent land use and reclamation, it is perfectly possible to create opportunities for recreation where they are most needed. Millions of people make exhausting drives to distant beaches, using up fuel and contributing to air pollution, because the bodies of water within walking distance of their homes are polluted or access to them is prevented by buildings. Cleaning up the river near home is a far better answer to the Sunday traffic than building a new freeway to a beach ninety miles away. A bit of thought and minor expense and effort could create hundreds of miles of ski-touring trails near any of our urban areas that receive adequate snowfall in the winter, and the same tracks could easily double as running trails or bicycle paths in milder seasons. The possibilities for humane use of the environment are innumerable, and attention to them is vital for wilderness preservation. Such possibilities also present one of the strongest means of creating pressures for further improvement of conservation methods. Who can get very interested in an oil spill on a polluted river fronted by a row of factories and warehouses? If the local residents spend their summers on a beach along the shore of the same river, they will not view the same oil spill very tolerantly.

While open spaces around the city call for better use and administration, the wild places that remain are often *over*administered. Policies tend either to total neglect, including a neglect of enforcement of legitimate restrictions on use, or toward a self-serving promotion of what Edward Abbey calls "industrial tourism." For advocates of this latter type of development, the national parks and other wilderness areas become mere tourist attractions, and the success of their administration is measured in the number of people that can be shoved through the gates. Many national parks are falling into syndromes characterized by more roads, more facilities, more rules, and finally citizen campaigns to protect the hurrying tourists against the few remaining pieces of scenery they might accidentally bump against or fall off.

Conservationists are going to have to lend strength to those beleaguered members of the government bureaucracies who are trying to preserve some of the lands entrusted to them. There are many working rangers and administrators in the various federal and state services responsible for parks, forests, and other public wild lands who know and appreciate and love the wilds, but they are often at the mercy of myopic administrators or of members of the public who want nothing more from them than a scenic rest stop on the highway, amply supplied with bars and immaculate toilets. The intelligent civil servants desperately need the support of conservationists and wilderness lovers to reverse the trend of overdevelopment of parks and wilderness areas.

There is a desperate need to reverse the programs of road building in the national parks and in roadless areas in the national forests and in other publicly owned wilderness. In most national parks, problems of overcrowding would be readily solved by elimination of motor vehicles from the parks. For winter travelers, a particularly urgent battle is now being waged in many parks over the issue of whether snowmobiles are to be permitted. My own position is pretty obvious, as is the importance of this particular issue to those who love the quiet spaces in winter. This is only one part of the more general problem of motor vehicles in the parks, however. Conservationists spend tremendous amounts of money and effort in the battle for the creation of a national park or the designation of a wilderness area, but the value thus derived is almost as easily frittered away after designation as before. Each of the agencies responsible for administering public lands is subject to many pressures for development, not the least of which is the bureaucrat's desire to increase the size of his department. Conservationists need to understand these pressures and to either create counter-pressures or work to change the administrative structures that enable the pressures to exist.

We will have to start holding public servants responsible for some of the appalling practices in areas for which they are supposed to be responsible. A lot of hard work is required, however, not just indignation. The existing conservation organizations have much of the political knowledge necessary to put pressure in the right places, and they desperately need and deserve support. A check is not enough. Those seriously interested in preserving our remaining wilderness are going to have to exert some pressure of their own—on both legislators and executive agencies. Pressure points and organizational characteristics have to be learned. The U.S. Forest Service, for example, is structured in such a way that it is particularly prone to local pressures, good and bad. Other agencies are more responsive to national pressure. All of them listen to Congressional delegations.

We need to stop making our national parks into amusement parks instead of wilderness preserves, and we need to stop making the rangers into traffic cops and office time servers. Quite a few parks, forests, and wilderness areas are going in the right direction because of really creative administration. These should be recognized and held up as sterling examples. Don't take them for granted: There are people who have been fighting tooth and nail to keep your favorite mountain in decent shape, and you'd better give them some help. Picking one random example from many that could be chosen, I would like to congratulate the administrators and rangers of Baxter State Park in Maine, site of Mount Katahdin. Despite the greatly increased population pressures, they have done a beautiful job of maintaining the character of the park. Many things could be improved, especially the regulations on winter travel, but they have maintained the park, and that in itself ranks as a fine accomplishment. Rules can be changed at any time, but the wilderness character of much of the park would take years to retrieve if it were once given up.

A FINAL NOTE

As noted earlier in this chapter, I have not been too fastidious in my use of the term *wilderness* while discussing the need for preservation. Many areas to which I have referred have already been greatly influenced by modern civilization even when the impacts are not obvious. The great forests of white pine that once stood in the eastern part of the continent are gone. Areas that have experienced less direct contact are still affected. The elimination of many predators has affected ecosystems in places that hunters have never reached. Still, we have to start where we are standing now; we have no control over yesterday's loggers, sheepherders, or campers. If we take "wilderness" as meaning a place where people still have only very slight influence on the current life of the land, aside from past interventions, there is still a good deal of country with a stable life of its own, worth saving and deserving to be left alone.

The value of such land for recreation is obvious, but it has intrinsic value which should govern recreational use. Human influence should remain peripheral, and administrative involvement with the environment itself should be concerned mainly with controlling the effects of human beings—fire control, for example. "Game management" is a more difficult problem, and conservationists have occasionally allowed themselves to be oversentimental, leaving themselves open to the sneers of the hunting lobby. By and large, however, the sneerers have shown themselves either ignorant or disingenuous.

The fact that many game animals would experience excessive population growth without hunting pressures is not due to sentimental bird watchers, but rather to the elimination of useful predators by stupid people, with guns and poisons and traps. Nor need the conservationist pay much attention to pious claims that hunters never do anything but good to non-predatory game species. Numerous harmless species in this country have been exterminated by hunters, and many others were saved only by "sentimentalists." Shorebird populations, for example, have still to recover from hunting pressures exerted many years ago, quite aside from the reduction in available habitat. Many game species are no longer controlled by predators, and hunting may frequently be a useful way to control populations. Similarly, hunting licenses may produce needed revenues for preservation of woods, and the hunters may then help lobby to preserve those woods, but conservationists need to take long hard looks at all the desires of such lobbies. Maximum production of game species is not always the sign of a healthy ecological balance.

Conservationists do not need to take any back seat to howling gun lobbyists. Everyone makes mistakes, but preservationists (that's the current dirty word for conservationists among loggers and some hunters) have made fewer ecological mistakes than those whose only outdoor interest is "harvesting" game. Hunting is often legitimate, whether it suits your taste or not, but it is also an activity that *requires* strict regulation by its very nature, unlike hiking, mountain climbing, and similar activities. We cannot be free predators anymore. When we took up agriculture and animal husbandry, we increased our population to an extent that cannot be supported by predation.

In any case, the most urgent need in the administration of most wilderness areas is for a style of treatment that respects the balances that already exist and that maintains a healthy conservatism concerning schemes of major intervention. The ancient Greeks used the word *hubris* to describe the overbearing pride and presumption against the laws of nature and the gods that preceded an inevitable and disastrous fall. *Hubris* is perhaps the most applicable term for technological civilization's attitude toward the natural system of which human beings are a part. There seems always to be an arrogant presumption that any well-intentioned intervention by people in complex natural processes will be for the good. The irresponsible exploiter who cares not a whit for what he destroys is bad enough, but sometimes the well-meaning interventionist can do even more damage. If you doubt this, go back and take a look at some of the statements and reviews that followed Rachel Carson's *Silent Spring,* a book that now seems a model of understatement.

We need to save what we have left of the wild spaces of this country and continent not only because they are nice places to ski tour, but because we have already fouled up more than enough of our land. We should feel extremely lucky to have some left to preserve and very jealous of those in a hurry to either exploit or "improve" what we have left. Uses of the wilderness that remains should be of a character that has only minimal effect on the environment, a character that is very much compatible with the cleansing of people's souls. Preserve the wilderness, and you'll have somewhere to go to renew yourself. More important, you'll have saved a little bit of the larger world of life that surrounds us and from which we came. Good touring!

Appendices

Appendix A: How to Make Your Own Equipment

A few years ago, suppliers of equipment for lightweight winter travel were few and their offerings necessarily rather limited. With the great interest shown recently in the outdoors, this is no longer true. Shops specializing in lightweight equipment are opening everywhere, many making some equipment themselves. There are several major manufacturers of high-quality equipment for lightweight wilderness travel. It is rarely necessary these days to go to the expense of having equipment custom made, since satisfactory gear for most purposes can be found in any one of a couple of dozen catalogs.

Though one of the major incentives for making one's own equipment—the unavailability of a ready-made substitute—is gone, there are still several reasons for going to the trouble of doing it yourself. The most common one is money—or the lack thereof. Many of the operations in the manufacture of quality outdoor equipment require tedious hand work, but if you're willing to spend your own time doing it, you won't have to pay someone else to do it for you. If you're trying to get through the initial expensive phase of acquiring good equipment on a limited budget, making some of your own gear can allow you to get much more satisfactory items. There are several other reasons for making your own outfit. There's an inherent satisfaction in using something you've made yourself. Very often it is possible to make a piece of equipment that is better suited to your needs than anything available from a supplier: You can incorporate special features ranging from pockets for particular items to special multiple-use arrangements. You may also be able to improve on currently available designs. Most good outdoor gear is still developed from the personal experience and ideas of the people who make the equipment, their friends, and their customers. You can do the same thing with your own equipment. Finally, making a few pieces of your own is one of the best ways to become an expert in evaluating the quality of equipment made by others.

FROM KITS OR FROM SCRATCH

Once you decide to make some of your own gear there remains the question of how to manage the project. There are several possible choices. If you're a rank beginner at sewing and you're not interested in designing your own gear, just in saving some money, your best bet for a first project may be a kit, especially if what you want to make is a difficult piece of down gear, like a sleeping bag or a down jacket. With the kits the planning has been done for you. You receive detailed instructions, precut materials, and down prepacked in the right quantities for each compartment. You do only the hand labor. Some of the advantages of this method are obvious, particularly the fact that you avoid all the pitfalls of designing and cutting. Less obviously, you may save money on materials. Cutting fabric is the cheapest part of the operation in making a good piece of gear, and since an outfitter is making many items, he not only can buy materials in quantity, but he can also cut with much less waste then someone making only one or two items—an extra scrap of cloth can always be used for an odd piece on another garment. Kits are to be highly recommended for a beginner who wants to slip into making equipment gradually, but no more need be said about how to make them, since all instructions are included.

However, many of the advantages of making your own equipment are lost if you rely exclusively on kits. Selection is much more limited than even the regular manufactured lines, and you may not be able to find a kit that suits your needs. The wise and patient cold-weather slogger can also save a good deal of money over the cost of even the kits by purchasing fabric and other necessities in the right way. You can't save much by buying just new material in small amounts, but several methods are suggested below which can cut your costs way down. Finally, of course, using kits robs you of both the interest and advantages of designing your own equipment.

Aside from kits, you are still left with several choices in making a particular piece of gear. You may find a pattern in this or some other book and follow it; you may design your own piece of gear from scratch; or you may mix these two methods, modifying an existing pattern to suit your own needs or whims. One other technique which is useful for some items is to modify or copy another piece of gear. Many items in surplus stores are suitable for wilderness use with a few modifications, for example. Or you may have a favorite old parka with a design that seems nearly perfect, but which has finally worn out— just rip out the seams and cut out exactly the same pattern from new material and sew it together, perhaps using the old hardware if it's still in good condition.

GETTING STARTED

Making your own gear successfully mainly requires that you plan things well. You don't have to be any kind of master with a needle to make fine equipment; outdoor equipment is generally rather baggy as a matter of choice and a few irregularities in the seams will not detract from either the usefulness or attractiveness of a finished garment. Proper care in sewing is necessary in outdoor gear, though, and good design is very important. A ripped-out parka seam in a bad storm is no joke.

For large pieces of equipment—sleeping bags, tents, and the like—a sewing machine is almost mandatory, but hand sewing is feasible on smaller items. A normal home sewing machine handles most outdoor equipment with little difficulty, though certain heavy or awkward spots may have to be sewn by hand, especially on packs. The little other special equipment that is needed is usually inexpensive. If snap fasteners or grommets are needed on a particular item, a set of dies is normally required to set them, but these are quite cheap and last indefinitely. A selection of needles with various curves will cost a dollar or so and will enable you to sew in hard-to-reach spots. For sewing very heavy fabric or leather, especially in packs, a sewing awl is hard to do without. This is essentially a hand sewing machine. It costs about $4.00 equipped with extra needles and plenty of thread.

You should plan the whole garment before going out and buying any material or equipment especially for it. The information provided in this chapter should be adequate for a start, but I believe that every lightweight winter traveler ought to get a copy of *Light Weight Camping Equipment and How to Make It* by Gerry Cunningham and Margaret Hansson (see Appendix B), even if he is not interested in making his own gear. This book has invaluable information on materials and design, including some excellent design ideas which are, unfortunately, not included in any commercially available gear.

If you are using a pattern, it will usually be presented as the ones in this book are: Either the shape is shown with dimensions or in more complicated designs the shapes are drawn out on a square grid, with each small square on the pattern representing a larger square of a particular size. You simply draw out a gird with the right size squares on big sheets of lightweight paper and transfer the pattern. This is easy to do freehand with the help of the squares, even if you have no drawing talent.

A few tips on using patterns:

1. Check the size of the person the pattern is to fit. If you are much larger or smaller, just enlarge or reduce the size of your squares to adjust the garment size. Remember, though, that most outdoor clothing should fit loosely, especially if it is to go over down garments.

2. Before you make up your paper pattern, decide on the fabric you will use, if possible, and cut the paper to the same width. If you do this, you can experiment with the most efficient way of fitting the pieces together to use the smallest amount of fabric.

3. When you cut out the paper pattern leave extra margins on the sides. Pinning paper takes more room than sewing cloth. Pin the paper pattern together and try it on. Make *sure* everything is all right before you even buy your material, or at least before you cut it. You'll regret it if you get six inches too little, which you may, if the person who made up the pattern didn't have your spectacular chest muscles or long, skinny legs.

4. If you are working with coated fabric, as in rainwear, there is an outside and an inside. Pay attention, when you are laying out the pieces, that everything is right. Mark each piece on one side of the paper or color it. Then, when you pin things together, all the outside surfaces should have the mark or the color. If they don't, you'll end up with a garment that is half shiny side out and half shiny side in.

5. If you're not sure about the fit, transfer the paper pattern to an old sheet or some other soft, dispensable piece of material, and sew it together (fast and sloppy—just enough to hold it). This gives you a mock garment to try on.

6. Once you've decided that the paper or cloth pattern is satisfactory, you can get your material and either pin or trace out the pieces for cutting. (Don't pin on coated fabric.) Pin together the cutout parts before sewing (use paperclips for coated fabrics) and check the fit. Decide what the best order will be for sewing the seams without getting in your own way. Write it down. Then put it together.

An even more satisfactory method than paper patterns is to use an existing garment. Old outdoor clothing is ideal, of course, but normal clothes will often serve, especially pants. The trick is to find something with a proper fit, which will usually be larger than your normal size. One good trick is to go down to your local thrift shop. The starving student and climber types will know where I mean; more affluent readers can look in the Yellow Pages for the Salvation Army or Goodwill store. Look around and find a good fit, ignoring the cuffs. Don't worry about worn seats or chartreuse checks—you're not going to wear this thing. Rip out the seams and, presto, you have a permanent pattern for some part of your anatomy, and if you have chosen wisely, it will have cost less than a dollar.

GETTING YOUR MATERIALS

Many outdoor suppliers carry materials, but they are naturally quite expensive. If you are in a hurry to make a piece of equipment, this is the source you will probably use, but there are a number of methods you can use to cut your costs if you make your own equipment regularly.

The makers of all sorts of outdoor clothing and equipment dispose of large quantities of fabric and other materials because of cosmetic flaws, color mismatches, discontinued items, and a host of other reasons having little to do with the serviceability of the goods. Backpacking outlets that make their own equipment often sell remnants at their retail outlets. The best bargains, however, can generally be purchased from factories that lack the facilities for selling retail. If you can locate such places, you can often get ideal materials for a song. The time, in this case, is spent mainly in searching the Yellow Pages and talking on the phone. When I find a good bargain in a particular fabric suitable for outdoor equipment, I buy enough to last for the next few years so that I usually have the materials I need when the time comes to make a new piece of equipment.

DESIGN CONSIDERATIONS

Many general considerations for equipment design have been discussed in the earlier sections of this book. Cunningham and Hansson also have excellent material that is worth many rereadings by people designing their own equipment. A few points will be made here, however, both concerning general design and specific pieces of equipment.

Fabrics
Many demands are made on any piece of equipment for lightweight winter use, and an actual design is inevitably a compromise. This fact is nowhere more evident than in the choice of fabrics. It is usually desirable that these be warm, light, strong, abrasion resistant, tear resistant, ravel-free, free breathing, waterproof, nonabsorbent, con-

densation-free, impervious to rot and mildew, fireproof, and possessed of several other incompatible qualities. The fabrics available today are pretty miraculous compared with what was available a few years ago, but they cannot now, and never will, fill all the requirements that a difficult environment imposes. The advantage to making your own gear is that you can choose the compromise that most precisely suits your own needs.

The materials useful for our purposes are fairly limited, both by design considerations and availability. The advantages of *wool* have been extensively discussed already. It is not a particularly strong fabric, is weaker when wet, is very heavy when tight woven for water and abrasion resistance, is itchy, is vulnerable to moths, and in most weaves is not easy to waterproof. It is still a very important fabric because of its unique characteristic of wicking moisture and drying first on the inside. Wool and the comparable synthetics are indispensable for some basic clothing wherever a survival situation may occur in both wet and cold conditions, and many recent accidents can be attributed to excessive dependence on down clothing to the neglect of wool. Because it is heavy when woven for even limited abrasion resistance and ability to turn wind and water, wool is usually best confined to underwear and to basic garments: socks, mitts, shirts, pants, and sweaters, which under winter conditions are worn under shell clothing. Providing it will not have to serve double purpose as outer wear, it is best in light, fluffy weaves. Pants that may be worn without wind pants should have a hard woven outer surface, however, both to prevent snagging and to keep snow from sticking to the outside. For outside garments and socks, a little nylon is often combined with the wool to improve wearing qualities, but light shell clothing of a different material is as good a solution. Virgin wool is warmer than reprocessed wool.

Cotton is generally an undesirable material for inner clothing. It is clammy when wet, and it dries slowly. However, it is still sometimes useful for shell clothing and tents, since it is cheaper than nylon and is easily made water resistant. With the exception of Gore-tex, a good quality, tightly woven cotton fabric is still the best water-resistant cloth made which also breathes adequately for use as a general shell garment. Since cotton is not nearly as strong as some of the synthetics, a more expensive nylon-cotton mixture is often used which is nearly as water resistant as cotton but which is stronger. The best cottons are made from Pima or Egyptian cotton, both of which have very long fibers. I have had good luck with an Oxford weave cotton fabric, but there are others that are also satisfactory.

Nylon has become the standard material for most fabrics used in outdoor clothing and equipment for the excellent reason that nylon cloth is stronger than any other fabric of the same weight. It can be made fairly wind resistant while still breathing well. It is nearly always used in covering down garments and sleeping bags, since nylon fabric strong enough for a satisfactory garment is still light enough to allow the down to loft well. The primary disadvantages of nylon for tents and clothing are that it is very difficult to waterproof without using an impermeable coating and that the smooth surface of the fibers tends to condense moisture more readily than cotton or wool. *Dacron* and *Orlon* are somewhat less strong than nylon, and they are satisfactory but not widely available for the uses being discussed here. An exception is fluffed Orlon, which is a slightly inferior substitute for wool, very useful for people who are allergic to wool.

Pile fabrics made from nylon or acrylics make excellent garments to be worn under shell clothing or as linings for jackets and the like. They are sold in fabric stores for fake fur, usually in sixty-inch bolts. Less important than the composition is the fluffiness of the pile side and the tightness of the backing. Backings are usually too loose to shed any wind or to wear very well. For outdoor purposes, the tighter the weave of the backing, the better. Pile retains a good deal of warmth when wet, dries faster than wool, and is quite warm. It does not shed wind or water at all, however, so a shell or an outer layer of tight fabric is essential.

Coated fabrics for quality lightweight equipment should always use nylon or Dacron for a base. The disadvantages of the synthetics are of no consequence in coated fabrics, since they are impermeable and waterproof as a result of the coating. The extra strength of the synthetics is important in coated fabrics, because the coating isolates any tearing force to a small area by gluing the fibers of the cloth together, and this action makes any coated fabric weaker than a corresponding uncoated one. Many types of coating have been developed, but no particular recommendations will be made here, since this is one of the most rapidly changing materials and since the home manufacturer will be limited to those coated fabrics available in small quantities. Most of the ones listed in the catalogs of mountaineering suppliers are quite good, with the weight per square yard giving a good indication of strength.

Laminates useful for outdoor gear use nylon for a backing fabric. A nylon fabric coated with urethane and laminated to a thin layer of foam has proven to be an excellent shell material for regions that receive heavy rain and works well in winter conditions too. The foam layer provides sufficient insulation to greatly reduce the condensation on the slick coated nylon. *Foamback* garments are made by Chouinard, but if you can obtain the fabric it makes fine shell garments. Gore-tex has been mentioned a number of times in the text. It is normally made in triple laminations, with nylon woven fabric on the outside, a light nonwoven fabric inside, and the Gore-tex film sandwiched between. The inner fabric can be eliminated on laminates that are intended for down garments or lined ones, where the inside will receive no abrasion. Gore-tex laminates are very expensive, and remnants are well worth searching out for the home sewer trying to save money.

Other materials are mostly pretty obvious, except perhaps for closures. Zippers, the handiest means to close and open long pairs of edges in garments and sleeping bags, used to cause some problems, especially in cold weather. They are, however, quite dependable if good quality, large nylon zippers are used. Good metal zippers are also adequate if rubbed with paraffin occasionally, but nylon is definitely preferred. Smooth operation is the main criterion: Don't use surplus zippers or buy any that don't operate perfectly smoothly. To avoid snagging edges, construction details around zippers must be examined closely. Buttons and snaps are occasionally used as main means of closure and often as backup closures which also hold storm flaps in place. Velcro, consisting of paired hook and mat strips, makes an excellent draftproof, snag free, easily opened, and easily installed method of closure, but it has certain disadvantages. The main one is that it is not self-aligning as are snaps, buttons, or zippers. For this reason Velcro is usually used either for backup closures or for quite short openings like pockets and cuffs. When using Velcro in spots where it might rub against the skin, install the hook side to face away from the skin—it's irritating.

Construction
It is important that the seams in equipment designed for lightweight outdoor use be strong and well made. Synthetic thread should be used throughout because of its extra strength. Nylon thread is excellent, but its stretchiness creates difficulties in some sewing machines by causing dropped stitches. This problem can usually be solved by reducing machine tension and perhaps using a larger needle. Textured nylon, nonstretch polyester, and cotton-wrapped synthetic threads are all satisfactory substitutes for regular nylon thread if the latter causes trouble with your sewing machine.
Nearly all seams in outdoor equipment should be finished seams; that is, the cut edges should be turned under so that they cannot ravel.

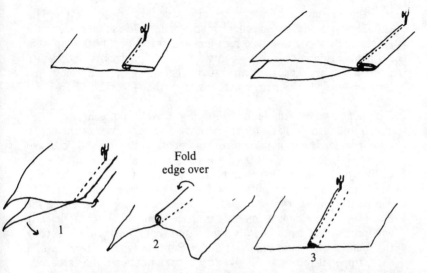

Good seams for outdoor equipment At the top are a simple finished hem and a finished hem seam; in both the cut edge is folded under to prevent raveling. The bottom row shows the steps in making a finished flat-felled seam, the main seam for tents and garments.

1. Lay the edges together, with the outsides facing out, and sew them together leaving the edges wide enough to fold back on themselves in the next two steps.

2. Fold one edge over the other and back on itself, so that the whole seam will form a shingle, *pointing downward in the final garment*.

3. Sew the shingled edge down.

Alternatively, they may be stitched in two lines to prevent raveling, but with the edge left rough. The only type of fabric that can normally be left safely with a single line of stitching is coated fabric, since the coating prevents raveling. All uncoated synthetic fabrics and webbing ravel very badly, and melting the edges will help prevent this, but melting does not substitute for finished seams.

Details of the more commonly used seams are shown in the illustration. Additional ones can be found in any sewing book, and many special suggestions are shown in detail in Cunningham and Hansson's book. Most clothing can be sewn with nothing more elaborate than flat felled and hem seams, however.

Shirts and pants can be made pretty easily if you get a pattern from an old piece of clothing, making necessary modifications such as cuffs, hoods, wear patches, and so on. However, because of the bounty of the surplus market for good wool clothing, I confine my activities to making a few modifications on surplus clothes. If you find the right suppliers you can get excellent ready-made cold-weather gear at a fraction of the cost you paid for them as a taxpayer. My favorite winter pants are air force flier's pants. They have knit cuffs, snap waist, padded seat and knees, a warm weave that doesn't pick up snow, and they cost me $3.95 a pair, much less than what I would have paid for the materials.

Shell clothing suitable for lightweight travel is not generally available in the surplus market, except for windpants, so parkas are a common item for home manufacture. Parkas for winter use should be cut *baggy,* so that you can wear your insulation under them. This is especially true if you use down clothing, since a tight shell over the down will compress it and nullify its value as insulation. It is desirable to use shell clothing over the down, so that wind will not penetrate the down layer. The light nylon used in these garments is not sufficiently windproof. Shell clothing for winter requires particular care in cutting sufficiently roomy arms and shoulders. Pullover types of parka with a short zipper at the neck will give adequate ventilation if they are made roomy enough with the bottom left wide, to be closed with a drawstring. Jacket styles are easier to ventilate, but they are more difficult to make and zipper failure is a slight worry in bad weather. Suit yourself.

Another question for the winter traveler to decide is how heavy to make a parka. Good all-purpose mountain parkas for summer and winter wear should be made of strong, fairly weatherproof cloth, perhaps cotton-nylon cloth weighing about four ounces per square yard. They should also be made double throughout. The winter traveler who is not planning on struggling up rock chimneys or summer bushwacking may elect to carry a light single-layer garment to break the wind and shed the snow. In cold weather when rain is likely, waterproof rain gear is desirable, so double layering the parka for rain protection is unnecessary. Gore-tex fabric is ideal if it can be found at a manageable price. Otherwise, a urethane-coated nylon is best. The pattern given for a cagoule can be shortened a bit and used for a very simple parka pattern, with a pocket sewn into the front closed by a Velcro taped flap. A good design for a more sophisticated parka is given in Cunningham and Hansson, but I recommend a hood that extends farther out than theirs for storm protection. Try sewing on a hemmed rim around the edge of the hood, containing a drawstring. Incidentally, drawstrings are better made of some material other than nylon, since nylon won't hold knots well. Try a round cotton boot lace. Alternatively, you can tack the drawstring down with stitching and use cord clamps instead of knots to tighten it.

Rainwear can be made very light, usually with a single layer of coated nylon. For heavier duty and longer wear, the garment can be made double throughout, with the coated sides facing in toward one another to prevent their rubbing off and to reduce the clammy feel of the coating. If a single layer is used, the coating should face in to prevent its being rubbed off. Rainwear should preferably be designed with as few seams on the shoulders as possible, and if the garment is made double, the seams on the inside and outside layers should not be sewn through or overlap, since the seams are the main leaking points of rainwear.

Take care in sewing rainwear to avoid mistakes—in most garments a bad seam can be ripped out with no harm done, but coated fabric is permanently punctured every time the needle goes through. After sewing, the seams of rain garments should be sealed with seam sealer. Renew the sealer once a year. All rainwear should fit very loosely to allow ventilation. The bottoms should open as wide as wind permits, and some sort of zipper or drawstring openings around the neck and cuffs are mandatory. With a long garment like the cagoule shown on page 315, the legs can be protected by rain chaps. Shorter tops require rain pants.

Tents are larger projects than most clothing, and more care is required in designing and sewing them. For use at high altitudes, in open spaces subject to severe storms, and for general use without fires, small closed tents are the most practical solution. The usual design for one or two people is a mountain tent, which may be designed with one high end or two. For more people the Logan design is more practical. The mountain tent is a refined pup tent, and the Logan a modified pyramid tent. Dome and quonset shapes are excellent, but they are difficult to design and get poles for, unless you purchase a kit. Many good suggestions will be found in Cunningham and Hansson, which is required reading for beginning tent makers, but probably the best preparation for anyone designing tents like these is to visit a good supplier and study the construction of his tents. Material for winter tents that may have to withstand high winds and snow loading should be strong. Waterproof material should be used for floors, but never for the upper parts of closed tents designed for winter use. Waterproof tents require very good ventilation, and in blizzard conditions such ventilation will insure a snow-filled tent. Double-layer tents with two canopies of nylon, the outer one coated, are generally the most practical for the home sewer.

The large areas of cloth supported by the seams and suspension points of tents require considerable attention to their strength. Make a number of drawings of your tent and think about the lines of stress. Well-made seams are strong, and they will reinforce lines of stress; nylon tape will serve the same function. All pullout tabs, stake loops, pole tubes, and suspension points must be reinforced to prevent their pulling out, especially in storms. Walls of tents will tend to bow in, especially under a load of snow, and they should be held out with pull-outs or wands. Pull-outs are easy to sew in, but they require additional staking points. Wands are a more difficult solution to construct, but they make pitching simpler. Light fiberglass rods are inserted in sleeves arranged so that they force the rods to bow out and hold the tent wall up. Wands must be carried with the tent. If you take ski poles, make sure to design any pole sleeves wide enough to allow the handle ends of the poles to go through; this eliminates the need to remove pole baskets in order to use ski poles to hold up the tent. (If this is done, pockets ought to be substituted for the standard grommets at the tent corners, to accommodate the handle ends of the ski poles.)

A frost liner is a worthwhile addition to any tent designed for use in very cold weather. It is generally made of very light nylon material which forms an inner tent wall suspended a couple of inches inside the outer one. Its purpose is to keep the tent warmer by channeling cold air blowing through the walls around the living space of the tent and to catch frost falling from the outside wall before it falls on your face. Liners require numerous suspension points to keep from sagging more than a few inches from the tent walls. Ties are commonly used, but I do not recommend them, since they can only be tied in the proper order. Snaps are better, since they can be fastened even when the whole liner is in, as can single ties on the tent wall which are knotted through small grommets in the liner.

A good first tent project is the mountain tent described in Cunningham and Hansson. Study it carefully and make any design modifications you think appropriate.

Sleeping bags and down clothing involve much more complicated problems of construction than other equipment, though they also present a good place for the poverty-stricken outdoors wanderer to save some money. Since materials are expensive, however, so are mistakes. If you want to make a down garment or sleeping bag as your first project, it is best to use a kit. The kits have the special advantage of prepacking the down in bags separated for each tube or pocket in the piece of equipment. If you start from scratch you will have to experiment to get just the right amount of down to fill each compartment; do it outdoors—you would not believe how elusive those bits of down can be when they get loose in the room, which they will surely do if you work indoors.

Proper design of down equipment requires that the down layer be held in compartments which are small enough to keep it from shifting and which exert as little compressive force on the down as possible.

The best designs have a large number of compartments and thus require less down fill, since extra down does not need to be added to compensate for shifting. The baffling that forms the inside walls of the compartments is best made from very lightweight nylon material—its only purpose is to prevent the down from moving about. The best designs will result in many compartments shaped to allow the down to expand them easily, but requiring as little fabric as possible. Such combinations require a great deal of thought.

One of the first principles of designing down equipment is to use a differential cut. All garments and most sleeping bags for lightweight camping must fit the body fairly closely. If the inside and the outside are cut to the same dimensions, then when you stretch around inside, you will stretch them both out to their maximum circumference, which will also push the inside and outside walls together and compress the down. By cutting the inside layers smaller, it is impossible for the body to push the inside wall against the outside one: You may still be cramped in your sleeping bag, but you won't be cold as well.

A differential cut is mandatory for thick down-filled parkas and for close-cut sleeping bags. Down jackets with sewn-through seams do not use a differential cut.

Several methods of down construction are shown in the illustrations in Chapter 3. The easiest method of construction uses *sewn-through* seams to block shifting of the down. The outer and inner shells are simply sewn together in a quilted or tubed pattern. This is a very satisfactory and simple method to use with supplementary down equipment like down vests and the light jackets. These are among the most useful pieces of down equipment you can have. They are very light and take up little space, but provide lots of extra warmth when it is needed. They are worn under shell parkas, so the sewn-through seams and light outside material do not detract from their value. Sewn-through seams provide a major heat leak, however, and can be used only in light garments. They must never be used in big down parkas or winter sleeping bags.

Sleeping bags and big down parkas must be designed to compartmentalize the down without using sewn-through seams. The simplest technique is to construct two sets of sewn-through tubes and then overlap them to eliminate cold seams. This is reasonably effective, but it is heavier and less efficient than other methods. Probably the most common method is box-type construction, in which baffles are sewn straight across between the two walls of the sleeping bag or garment. The triangular pattern shown in the illustration controls down shifting more effectively because of the smaller compartments and because the walls cannot be pulled together by having the inside shell turned with respect to the outer one. However, it also adds weight by requiring the use of additional baffling material.

The biggest complication in making down equipment comes from the closures. These require interruption of the pattern of the insulation, and they generally create cold seams. The most common solution is to install a zipper closure and to sew in a down tube behind it to stop drafts and heat leaks. Velcro can be used to advantage as an alternative means of closure, since it can be sewn to the clothing shells and used without collapsing the down tubes.

Again, much attention is due to *Light Weight Camping Equipment* for those seriously interested in making their own gear. A few other suggestions for making down gear: Include insulated, down-filled pockets for warming your hands; make your sleeping bag long enough to accommodate your boots at the bottom beyond your feet, and then put them in a plastic bag at the bottom of your sleeping bag; make some down booties as a cheap, light, welcome luxury; don't forget head protection in designing down equipment—that's the most important source of heat loss; plan your equipment so that your down gear is enclosed in a windproof shell.

Packs are easy to make for day use, since they require less sewing than many other pieces of equipment, the main trick being to make the pack large enough to prevent its becoming a hard little ball on your back. At the risk of being repetitious, I again refer the interested reader to Cunningham and Hansson, since there is little point in repeating their many useful points. The main difficulty in making bigger packs lies in fabricating the frames. For contour frames, the solution is simply to buy the frame and make your own packbag to fit it. Rucksack frames cannot be so readily purchased, but several of my friends have been reusing the same rucksack frame for years. When the old bag wears out, they rip out the seams, cut a new set of pieces from coated nylon pack fabric, and sew it together, using the same hardware and always having a ready-made pattern. I know a couple of people who like the design of the old army ski mountaineering packs (still available), and who have each put three or four new nylon sacks on the old frames.

Modern rucksacks with internal frames are more difficult to make. Some of the sewing can be tricky, and home machines will not always handle the reinforced seams in heavy material. It is quite possible to make your own internal-frame rucksack, but it is not a very good beginning project. A pattern can be worked out from a pack that fits your needs well, and hardware can be modified to use items that are readily available.

CAGOULE

You will need ten feet of coated nylon fabric or Gore-tex laminate forty-four to forty-six inches wide, nylon thread, something to sew with, four grommets and a setting tool, a few snaps, and a setting tool, about three yards of drawstring, and a zipper, open at one end, twelve or fourteen inches long.

First lay the pattern out on paper or scrap material, cut it out, put it together, and try it on. After making necessary modifications, lay it out on the fabric and cut it out. Sew the skirts B and C onto the bottoms of A, using finished fell seams lapped downward. Then sew the edges together from the bottom to the sleeve ends, again using finished fell seams, and leaving the bottom and the ends of the sleeves open.

Next, sew the three main pieces of the hood together. F goes between D and E, with the narrow end facing forward. Sew the hood into the opening in A, fitting it carefully first with paper clips. Piece G now fits around the front edge of the face opening, forming a visor and holding the drawstring. It is folded double with the wide part in the center above the forehead. Before sewing it on, punch holes on one side at each end and install grommets for the drawstring. Sew it on. Sew in the zipper. Velcro may be substituted for both the zipper and wrist snaps.

Put in grommets at the bottom front of the parka, just high enough for the hem to fold over them. Sew in a finished hem at the bottom and at each wrist. Install the drawstrings. A small safety pin is good for threading them through. Install snaps to close the wrists.

CAGOULE

Layout on material (45″ fabric)

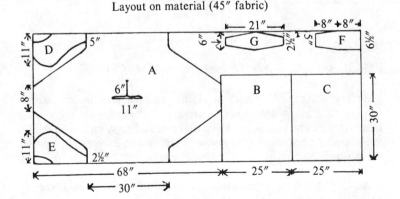

The size shown is a fairly versatile medium. To lengthen or shorten it, simply change the thirty-inch dimension of the skirts—room is left for this on the layout. An alternative wrist closure which I prefer is the friction tab shown in Cunningham and Hansson. An illustration of this cagoule will be found in the clothing chapter.

RAIN CHAPS

Rain chaps are very simple to make from coated nylon. All you need is the material, a little elastic or some snaps, and a little nylon tape for the tops. "A" is the length of the shortest loop of string or cloth that will fit easily over your boots, "B" is your inseam length to the floor, and "C" is the diameter around the top of your thigh with all your clothes on (measure loosely). Sew the two sides of each chap together with a finished fell seam, and hem the bottoms, either inserting elastics or installing snaps. Then hem the top edges and install belt loops with ties or snaps at the top corners.

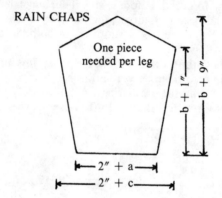

RAIN CHAPS

One piece
needed per leg

b + 1"   b + 9"

2" + a
2" + c

BIVOUAC SACK AND SLEEPING BAG COVER

Take two rectangular pieces of cloth, one of coated nylon and the other of light uncoated nylon or Gore-tex. Sew them together to form a bag open at one end, with the coated side of the nylon facing in and the seams finished. In the top install a hem with a drawstring. I prefer not to taper the bag, since the bottom provides space for my pack and gear. Grommets or snaps along the sides will allow you to make it into a half-size, double-layered footsack for use with the cagoule if the top layer is not made from Gore-tex.

Appendix B: Selected Reading

The books mentioned below should help the interested reader looking for additional information or different viewpoints on particular aspects of lightweight winter travel. It is also, in part, an expression of some of the debts incurred by the author, since many of my own ideas were derived from or modified by some of the books mentioned here. This list is not at all complete and is intended only to suggest a starting point for further reading.

GENERAL

Books on backpacking provide a good source of information on the basics of lightweight travel and living in the wilderness. The author's *America's Backpacking Book* is published by Scribners. For a somewhat different viewpoint, try Colin Fletcher's delightful *The New Complete Walker* (Knopf).

For winter techniques, even the snowshoer will find much useful information in the old Sierra Club *Manual of Ski Mountaineering*, edited by David Brower. The new paperback edition issued by Ballantine is largely unchanged, except for the excellent chapter on avalanches by LaChapelle. This book has become the standard guide for the subject, though the sections on technical climbing are now quite outdated. Because mountaineers generally backpack and often climb and camp on snow, mountaineering literature generally is of use to the winter tourist, even if he lives in Iowa. Two general books on mountaineering are the author's *Climbing: A Guide to Mountaineering* (Scribners) and one published by the Seattle Mountaineers, *Mountaineering: The Freedom of the Hills*, edited by Harvey Manning. A British handbook, published by Penguin, is Alan Blackshaw's *Mountaineering*. An older but still useful guide is Kenneth A. Henderson's

Handbook of American Mountaineering (Houghton Mifflin).

A very different point of view will be found among those whose experience derives mainly from the old north-woods type of camping for long periods in the great northern forests. Most such books are really not of too much use to the modern backpacker in heavily used wilderness areas. The major exception is Calvin Rutstrum, whose *New Way of the Wilderness* is a classic and a mine of useful information. His book on winter camping, *Paradise Below Zero,* is also good, but it is more anecdotal in style and does not add a great deal to the winter chapter of the earlier book. Both are published by Macmillan.

Also in this tradition are the many books written by those who have lived for months or years in the great northern wilderness. These are often entertaining and sometimes instructive. One of the best is John Rowlands's *Cache Lake Country* (Norton). From a different part of the country and in a different spirit, there is John Muir's *Mountains of California,* reissued in a paperback edition by Doubleday.

All the books just mentioned will give some advice on problems of clothing, camping, sleeping, and cooking.

FOOD AND COOKING

You will probably be able to develop your own recipes according to your preferences with only a minimum of practice, but if further advice is wanted Hasse Bunnuelle's *Food for Knapsackers* (Sierra Club) should provide ample food for thought.

Those going on reasonably short trips hardly need worry about nutritional problems, and can usually judge caloric values well enough by guesswork. Longer trips or stringent weight requirements demand a more precise approach. A very good discussion of nutritional needs and food characteristics can be found in the 1959 Yearbook of the U.S. Department of Agriculture, *Food,* available from the U.S. Superintendent of Documents in Washington, as is the very comprehensive list of food values, *Composition of Foods,* by Bernice Watt and Annabel Merrill.

SNOWSHOEING

The books by Rutstrum mentioned earlier contain much useful information on snowshoeing. On mountain snowshoeing the best summary of techniques and equipment modifications is Gene Prater's *Snowshoeing,* published by the Seattle Mountaineers.

SKIING

The Sierra Club *Manual of Ski Mountaineering* has already been mentioned, though it is now out of print and getting hard to find. The Sierra Club also publishes *Wilderness Skiing* by Lito Tejada-Flores and Allen Steck, which emphasizes alpine-style touring. A good book on basic touring and downhill technique on light skis is *Steve Rieschl's Ski Touring for the Fun of It* by Cortlandt Freeman (Little, Brown).

Books on downhill technique are innumerable, and quite a few of them are good. One comprehensive treatment is the *Official American Ski Technique* put out by the Professional Ski Instructors of America.

FINDING YOUR WAY

I think the best book on this subject is Calvin Rutstrum's *Wilderness Route Finder,* which includes some discussion of the sophisticated techniques needed for extended trips in extremely remote and featureless terrain. It is published by Macmillan. Robert Owendoff's *Better Ways of Pathfinding* (Stackpole) is good, and the makers of Silva compasses put out a book by Bjorn Kjellstrom called *Be an Expert with Map and Compass.*

STORMS, AVALANCHES, AND SNOW

Any textbook on meteorology will reward the outdoorsman with some insight, whether it helps his forecasting ability or not. A good layman's introduction is provided by the little Golden guide, *Weather,* by Paul Lehr, R. Will Burnett, and Herbert Zim. A very useful book on predicting the course of the weather is Alan Watts's *Instant Weathercasting* (Dodd, Mead), which, despite its rather misleading title, requires and deserves considerable study. With some practice, his crossed-winds rule is a great help in prediction.

Avalanches deserve all the study that can be afforded them by anyone going into the mountains in winter. The standard guide is the U.S. Department of Agriculture Handbook #489, *Avalanche Handbook,* by Ronald Perla and M. Martinelli, Jr. The best brief guide is Edward LaChapelle's booklet *ABC of Avalanche Safety,* published by Colorado Outdoor Sports. This booklet is reprinted with few changes as the avalanche chapter of the paperback edition of the *Manual of Ski Mountaineering.* LaChapelle's *Field Guide to Snow Crystals* and his chapter on "The Cycle of Snow" in *Mountaineering: The Freedom of the Hills* are also very worthwhile. The former is available in paper-back from the University of Washington Press.

Two narrative books contain a great deal of practical wisdom on avalanches: Colin Fraser's *The Avalanche Enigma* (Rand McNally) and Montgomery Atwater's *The Avalanche Hunters.*

Malcolm Mellor's *Avalanches* is recommended to the technically minded and to those looking for a comprehensive bibliography. It is published by the U.S. Army Matériel Command, Cold Regions Research & Engineering Laboratory, Hanover, New Hampshire. *The Snowy Torrents: Avalanche Accidents in the United States, 1910–1966,* edited by Dave Gallagher, is instructive. The latest in avalanche rescue technique is *Modern Avalanche Rescue* by Ronald Perla. Both are published by the Alta Avalanche Study Center. The pictures of avalanche terrain in *Snow Avalanches Along Colorado Mountain Highways* are educational. It is U.S. Forest Service Research Paper RM-7, from the Rocky Mountain Forest & Range Experiment Station, Fort Collins, Colorado.

STEEP SNOW

Aside from avalanches, the techniques for climbing on steep snow are discussed in the books on mountaineering already listed. For pictures of a master showing how it's done on *really* steep snow, see Gaston Rebuffat's *On Snow and Rock* from Oxford University Press.

EMERGENCIES

The standard book on first aid is, of course, the American Red Cross *Advanced First Aid and Emergency Care* (Doubleday), and this should be everyone's starting point. The *Ski Patrol Manual* published by the National Ski Association is good. Two books for ambulance personnel by Carl Young are worth studying: *Transportation of the Injured and First Aid and Resuscitation* (both C. C. Thomas). For summaries of first aid that can be carried in a pocket, check your local mountaineering store. Several good ones are available.

For advanced techniques going beyond first aid, the standard book is *Medicine for Mountaineering,* edited by James Wilkerson and published by the Mountaineers. The standard book on wilderness rescue methods is W. G. May's *Mountain Search and Rescue Techniques,* published by the Rocky Mountain Rescue Group in Boulder, Colorado. Also excellent is the booklet *Mountain Search and Rescue*

Operations put out by the Grand Teton National Park rescue group. Good discussions of many problems of wilderness first aid and medicine are contained in *Mountain Medicine Symposium,* available for $1.00 from the Appalachian Mountain Club in Boston. The best volume on frostbite is Bradford Washburn's booklet *Frostbite: What It Is and How to Prevent It,* published by the Museum of Science in Boston. Theodore Lathrop's booklet on *Hypothermia: Killer of the Unprepared,* put out by the Mazamas, is excellent.

NATURE AND WILDERNESS

Even a brief bibliography on this subject would take a book of its own, so only a few suggestions will be made here. Many general books of appreciation have been written by the great naturalists, and all of them contain a wealth of information. A few, selected at random, are: John Terres's *From Laurel Hill to Siler's Bog: The Walking Adventures of a Naturalist* (Knopf), Sigurd Olson's *Listening Point* (Knopf), Aldo Leopold's *A Sand County Almanac* (Oxford University Press), and Sally Carrighar's *Wild Heritage* (Houghton Mifflin).

Ann Morgan's *Field Book of Animals in Winter* (Putnam) is a good handbook for winter travelers. A brief guide is Margaret Buck's *Where They Go in Winter* (Abington). A wise and useful guide to the winter tourist's main animal signs is Olaus Murie's *Field Guide to Animal Tracks* (Houghton Mifflin). Another book on tracks is Ellsworth Jaeger's *Tracks and Trailcraft* (Macmillan). For four-footed animals, there is *A Field Guide to the Mammals* by William Burt and Richard Grossenheider (Houghton Mifflin).

For birds, a good introduction is Roger Tory Peterson's paperback *How to Know the Birds* (New American Library). I think the best field book is *Birds of North America* by Chandler Robbins, Bertel Bruun, and Herbert Zim (Golden), but the older standard Peterson guides are preferred by some. *A Field Guide to the Birds* (read "Eastern") and *A Field Guide to the Western Birds* are both published by Houghton Mifflin.

For trees, a good field book is C. Frank Brockman's *Trees of North America* (Golden). G. A. Petrides's *Field Guide to Trees and Shrubs* is excellent for winter use, but it covers only eastern trees. A fine set with much more information on trees than the field books is Donald Peattie's two volume (eastern and western) set, *A Natural History of the Trees.*

In addition to the many general books on photography, two that may be of special interest to the wilderness traveler are David Linton's

Photographing Nature (American Museum of Science paperback) and Russ Kinne's *The Complete Book of Nature Photography* (Chilton).

MAKING YOUR OWN GEAR

Lightweight Camping Equipment and How to Make It by Gerry Cunningham and Margaret Hansson is published by Scribners.

Appendix C: Where to Buy It

Lightweight winter gear is far more widely available now than it was when the *Complete Snow Camper's Guide* was first published, so the need for a comprehensive list of suppliers is not as great. All the companies listed publish catalogs, and a look at them should give the snow camper a good idea of current equipment for comparison.

Early Winters, Ltd., 110 Prefontaine Pl. South, Seattle, Wash. 98104 Makers of some of the best and most innovative equipment on the market.

EMS, Vose Farm Rd., Peterborough, N.H. 03458 An extensive catalog of their own and others' products, including useful comparison charts.

Forrest Mountaineering, Ltd., 1517 Platte St., Denver, Colo. 80202 Mountaineering gear, clothing, packs and bivouac sacks.

Frostline Kits, Frostline Circle, Denver, Colo. 80241 Kits for making outdoor gear.

Holubar Mountaineering, Ltd., P.O. Box 7, Boulder, Colo. 80306 A long time maker of good quality equipment.

Moor & Mountain, 63 Park St., Andover, Mass. 01810 A good selection of equipment with a northeastern emphasis.

North Face, P.O. Box 2399, Station A, Berkeley, Calif. 94702 Makers of high quality tents, clothing, sleeping bags, and packs.

Recreational Equipment, Inc., P.O. Box C-88125, Seattle, Wash. 98188 A co-op which gives its members rebates on their purchases at the end of the year. One of the most complete catalogs. Some of REI's prices are quite good, but their down gear is below standard.

Rivendell Mountain Works, P.O. Box 199, Victor, Idaho 83455 A small maker of excellent equipment.

Sierra Designs/Kelty, 247 Fourth St., Oakland, Calif. 94607 An amalgamation of two companies with a long and well-deserved reputation for making excellent equipment.

Ski Hut, P.O. Box 309, Berkeley, Calif. 94701 A good catalog. Manufacturers of the excellent Trailwise equipment.

Synergy Works, 255 Fourth St., Oakland, Calif. 94607 Innovative, well-made equipment.

United States Geological Survey, Distribution Center For maps east of the Mississippi, 1200 Eads St., Arlington, Va. 22202 For maps west of the Mississippi, Federal Center, Denver, Colo. 80225

Warmlite, R.F.D. 4, Box 398, Gilford, N.H. 03246 For many years the most original, the most copied, and the least acknowledged designers of lightweight outdoor equipment in the business.

Appendix D: Checklists of What to Take

The following checklists hopefully include everything that would be needed for tours lasting from a few hours to a couple of weeks. Not all the items are necessary on all trips. Rainwear is quite unnecessary in some areas at some times of year, for example. Quantities also clearly vary. More spare food and socks are required on a two-week mountain trip than on a weekend jaunt near home. Quantities are thus left for the reader to calculate, but the lists can serve as a memory aid if they are used systematically as the pack for the trip is made up.

Items generally needed even on day trips:

Underwear
Shirt
Pants
Sweater
Shell parka
Mittens or gloves with extra set of liners
Hat or balaclava
Socks with extra set
Boots or equivalent
Goggles or glasses
Watch
Food, including some extra
Emergency kit
Pack
Water bottle
Matches in waterproof container
Map in case or plastic bag, onionskin paper, pencil
Compass
Pocket knife
Flashlight or headlamp with lithium or alkaline batteries and extra
    bulb
Toilet paper
Chapstick
Sunburn goo
Gaiters or anklets

To which you may need to add, depending on conditions, means of transportation, and individual needs:

Rain gear
Extra wool clothes
Windpants
Face mask
Down clothing
Overboots
Bivouac sack
Foam pad for bivouacs
Avalanche beacon or cord
Avalanche probe
Saw
Shovel
Skis
Pole(s)
Snowshoes
Ice ax
Touring waxes with scraper or putty knife, waxing block, hand cleaner
Climbers (for skis)
Tethers for skis
Crampons
Ski or snowshoe crampons
Wands
Route markers (plastic strips)
Water purification tablets
Extra eyeglasses
Eyeglasses strap
Antifog compound for glasses
Camera
Film
Nature and area guides
Thermometer
Barometer or altimeter
Innersoles
Boot liners
Protractor
Fire starters
Can opener
Handkerchief(s) or facial tissue
Toothbrush and powder
Soap
Comb or brush
Sanitary napkins or tampons

For overnight camps and longer trips you'll need:

Tent with the necessary pitching equipment or tools for building an
    appropriate shelter
Sleeping bag
Sleeping pad
Eating utensils
Pans
Cup
Salt
Pepper and other desired seasonings
Stove
Stove accessories: funnel, pricker, windscreen, and so on
Fuel in can
More matches (in waterproof container)
Plastic bags for trash, and so on
Changes of some clothing like socks, undershorts, and such

To which you may want to add:

Bowl or plate
Sleeping bag cover
Large plastic bags
Extra batteries
Extra fuel containers
Pocket sharpening stone

EMERGENCY KIT

The contents of the emergency kit will vary depending on your prudence, equipment, plans, experience, and access to helpful doctors. Whether you carry them in one container or separately, it is essential to be able to give certain basic first aid and to repair some types of equipment failures whenever you are traveling far from the beaten track in winter. You will have to figure out some items for yourself—what tools you need for repairing and adjusting your ski bindings, for example. Locking pliers or a plier-wrench-screwdriver combination may be needed by skiers but not by snowshoers. An emergency ski tip is a good idea even for skiers with modern skis. Skiers should also carry a spare basket for poles and a spare bale for pin bindings. In general, one emergency kit is sufficient for a group that doesn't intend to break up, but some care must be taken that spare parts, ski tip sizes, and similar items are given consideration.

General repairs of equipment are facilitated by:

> Hank of parachute cord for laces, packs, tent ties, and so on
> Length of strong malleable wire for ski, binding, snowshoe, pole, pack repairs
> Needles and nylon thread for repairing rips
> Ripstop fabric tape for tent and clothing repairs
> Adhesive tape from first-aid supplies makes repairs if warmed to body temperature so that it sticks
> Pocketknife already carried
> Spare parts that may be needed for bindings, stove, pack, and so on
> Tools needed for installing the above
> Quick-set epoxy

In all cases, more elaborate repair kits are clearly advisable on more extended trips. A snowshoe repair adequate for getting you over a few miles will not do for a week of rough mountain travel. More spare parts are prudent for longer trips.

First-aid and medical supplies range from very small kits to the elaborate field hospitals of expeditions. For long trips in remote areas especially, I would advise consulting specialized books and a physician. Since this is a necessary step to get prescription drugs, none will be discussed here.

A basic first-aid kit is suggested:

> Waterproof container
> Summary of first-aid and emergency medicine (several are listed in the reading list)
> Large roll of two-inch-wide cloth adhesive tape—not waterproof—on cardboard roll which can be collapsed (can be ripped into narrower strips—warm near skin before using)
> At least ten 4 $\times$ 4" sterile gauze pads
> Ace bandage
> Moleskin
> Bandaids
> Triangular bandage
> Two single-edged razor blades in sterile packages
> One pair tweezers
> One pair scissors
> Thermometer
> Aspirin

PHisohex—small plastic bottle
Aqueous zepharin—clear antiseptic
Antacid tablets
Milk of Magnesia tablets
Tube of Vaseline

SAVING MONEY ON YOUR OUTFIT

The lists just given are likely to seem insurmountable obstacles for the impoverished beginning tourer, but winter camping really is a cheap recreation. Some of the principles of getting equipment have already been mentioned, the most important of which is to buy equipment in the order you will need it, especially if you are paying standard prices. Snow campers on a budget should get most of their wool clothing from attic trunks or the surplus market. Some other good surplus buys are mittens, bearpaw snowshoes, and army ski mountaineering rucksacks, which are not quite as good as some modern designs but will serve well at a quarter the price.

Another good source is the secondhand market. The bulletin boards of mountaineering shops are often productive. Haggle!

Mountaineering shops themselves generally have annual or semiannual sales of rental equipment, discontinued models, irregulars, and so on. Find out when the sales are, check the advance lists, if any, and go early, armed with a list of what you *really* need and how much you can get it for in the cheapest catalog. This is often the best way to get down gear, tents, parkas, and skis.

Finally, if you *have* to pay catalog prices, write for all the catalogs and compare—prices for identical items often vary considerably. Despite shipping costs, local sales taxes often make it cheaper to shop by mail. Some suppliers give quantity discounts—get together with friends. Prices and offerings change annually.

Index

Illustrations are indicated by *italics*.

Abbey, Edward, 294
Adidas, 143
Alaskan trail shoe, 117
alpine-style skiing, 130, *132*
altimeter, 280
Appalachian Mountain Club, 169
avalanche beacons, 234, 237–38
avalanche cord, 234
azimuth marks, 177

back, broken, 260
backpacks. *See* rucksacks
barometer, 280
barometric readings, 214
base lines, 181, *182*
base plates, 194
batteries, 105
bearings, 175, 176, 180, 243–44.
    See also compass bearings
bearpaw snowshoe, 118–21, *115,
    128*
bindings, ski, 140, *141*
    twin, 162
binoculars, 280
bivouac sack, instructions for
    making, 316
bleeding, stopping, 250–51, 257
blisters, treatment for, 101
booties, 142
boots
    climbing, 142
    cross-country racing, 143
    double, 142
    rubber, 124–25
    ski, 141–43
    touring, *143*
brain injury, 259
breath stoppage, 247–50
butane, 77

cagoule, instructions for making,
    314–15
camber, 136–38, 139
cameras, 109
Camp 7, 38, 43, 44, 45
carbohydrates, 80
chest injuries, 260–62
chilling, 249
chinooks, 230
climbers, 154–56, *155,* 160–61
clinometer, 280
closures, 22, 36–37
coated fabrics, 307, 309
Coleman, 77, 78, *78*
compass bearings, 181–86, *184–85,*
    187
compass card, 178, *179*
containers, 108–9
contour lines, 170–72, *171*
cotton fabric, 17, 306
couloirs, 228
crampons, 126, 198, 199, 200, 206,
    207–9
cross-country racing, 136

cross-country skiing, 130
cross-country snowshoeing, 118
cruiser compass, 178, *179*

Dacron, 307
declination, 186–88
  offsetting devices, 193–94
dehydration, 14, 63
depth hoar, 227
deviation, deliberate, *187*
Diet for a Small Planet (Lappé), 81
dishwashing, 85
double poling, 160
down, goose, 10–12, 18, 32–33, 37–38, 39, *39*
down clothing, instructions for making, 312–14
downhill technique, 161–62
dressings, wound, 258

Early Winters, 44, 58, 59, 104, 142
emergency equipment, 218–20
emergency kit, 108
emergency supplies, 84–85, 218
emergency treatment, 247–71
Ensolite, 47
epoxy, 130, 135
equipment, modern, 3, 4
Ethafoam, 47
eyeglasses, 106

fabrics, 305–8
falls, stopping, 201–2, 204
fiberglass equipment, 130, 135
field compass, 194
first aid, 247–71
  kit, 246
fishnet, as insulator, 18
flashlights, 105
flex pattern of skis, 136–38
foamback garments, 308
foam pads, 47–48

food, 80–82
  dried, 82–83
  emergency, 84–85
  planning, 84
  preparing, 82–83
Forrest Mountaineering, 104
fractures, bone, 254–56
frames, contoured, 102–3
frostbite, 123
  avoiding, 266–68
  treatment, 265–66
Frostline kits, 41
fuel, 84–85

gaiters, 28, *29*
gasoline, 109
glare, 106
glissading, 210
goose down. *See* down
Gore-tex, 13, 24, 26, 27, 42, 44, 58, 310
Green Mountain bearpaw, 121, 199
guidebooks, 278–79
gullies, 228

Harscheisen crampons, 200
hats, 20–21
head injuries, 258–59
headlamps, 105
herringbone step, 160
Hine Snowbridge, 104
hitches, tying, *122*
Hollofil, 18, 27, 38
Holubar, 38, 58, 59
  Trimlite, 43
hunting, 296
hypothermia, 49, 215–16
  avoiding, 266–68
  treating, 264–65

ice ax, 198, 199, 202–4, 206, 209–10, *203, 205*

igloos, 60–62, *61*, 220
  constructing, 64, 66, *67–68*
injuries
  internal, 262
  See also specific body areas

jackets, 18–20
Jensen pack, 104

Karrimor, 104
Kelty, A. I., 102–3
klisters, 150
knives, 107

laminates, 307–8
landmarks, 166–67
Lappé, Frances, 81
latrines, 74
lights, 105
*Light Weight Camping Equipment
  and How to Make It* (Cunningham and Hansson), 303,
  309, 310, 311, 312, 314
lithium cells, 105
Logan tents, 311

magnetic bearings, 175
magnetic declination, 175, *175*
magnetic field, 192–93
magnifier, pocket, 280
Maine snowshoe, *115*, 116, 117,
  119
maps, USGS, 168
markers, trail, 191–92
Marmot, 38, 42, 43
masks, face, 20–21
Medicine for Mountaineering
  (Wilkerson, ed.), 246, 254
metamorphosis, of snow cover, 225–
  26, 229
meteorology, regional, 213–14
Michigan snowshoe, 117
Millet, 104

mirrors, compass, 193
moccasin shoe pacs, 125
mohair strips, 139, 140
mountaineering boots, 125
mountaineering snowshoes, 126–27,
  127
Mountain Safety Research, *72*, 77–
  78
mountain snowshoes, *120*, 121

naphtha, 77
nature, observing, 274–76
nautical charts, 168
neck, broken, 260
nordic equipment, 130, *133*
North Face, 38, 43, 58, 59
novices, 4–5
nutritional requirements, 80–81
nylon, 28, 35–36, 307

olefin, 21
Optimus, 77
orientation, 188–89
orienting compasses, 178, *179*
Orlon, 307

pants, 20
  instructions for making, 309
parachute cord, 107
parkas, *19*, 25
  instructions for sewing, 310,
  313
peritonitis, 262
Peterson, Roger Tory, 276–77
Phisohex, 257
pickerel snowshoe, 117, 118
pile fabrics, 307
PolarGuard, 18, 27, 38, 40, 44, 45
pole brake, 162
poles, touring, 143–44
polyester fabrics, 33
potholders, 109
pullovers, 18–20

Ragg socks, 21
rain chaps, instructions for making,
    316
rainwear, 310–11
recreation areas, 293
Red Cross courses, 245
repair kits, 107–8
rescue teams, 235–37
resuscitation, 247–50
Rivendell Mountain Works, 104,
    142
rivers, crossing, 93–94
rucksacks, 103–5
    instructions for making, 314

self-arrest, 204–7, *205*
sewing, 303–16
shell clothing, 24–25, 310
shelters, in storms, 217–20
Sherpa snowshoes, 121, 123, 199
shirts, 18–20
    instructions for making, 309
shock, 252, 262–63
shovels, 71–72, *72*
sidestep, 160–61
Sierra Designs, 38, 43, 58, 59
sighting, 189, 193
Silent Spring (Carson), 297
skating, 159–60
skiing
    kick turns, 158, *158–59*
    turns, 157, *157–59*
skins, 154–56, *155*
ski poles, 126
skis
    racing, 139
    touring, 135, *134, 136,* 139
slab avalanches, 224–25, 226, 231
sleeping-bag cover, instructions for
    making, 316
sleeping bags, 26
    instructions for making, 312–14
slopes, avalanche, 227–29, 232–33

snow, judging conditions, 148–49
snow avalanches, 224
snow blindness, 106
snow bridge, 94, *95*
snowmobiles, 285–88
snowplow technique, *162*
snowshoes. *See* bearpaw snowshoe
snowshoeing, 98
socks, 21
Sokkets, 125
spikes, 199
splints, 254–56, 260
Stephenson, Jack. *See* Warmlite
stoves
    cartridge-type, 77
    high-capacity, 77
    pumped, 77–78
    self-pressurized, 77
suncups, *96*
sunglasses, 106
sun goggles, 106
sun protection, 105–6
suntan preparations, 106
Suunto compass, 193
Suverin, 143
sweaters, 18–20
Synergy Works, 104
synthetic materials, 17, 18, 33, 38,
    306, 309

Taslan, 24
telemark, 163–64, *163–64*
temperature-gradient
    metamorphism, 226
tents
    A-frame, 54–55, *55*
    dome, 55–59, *57*
    instructions for making, 311
    pitching, 59
    pyramid, 54–55, *56*
    quonset-shaped, 55–59
    snow, *69*
    in storm conditions, 217

thermometer, 280
Thinsulate, 18, 27
thread, for snow gear, 308
toilet articles, 106–7
tools, 107–8
Top Ramen, 82
tourniquets, 250–51
trails, marking, 191–92
Trailwise, 38
    Slimline, 43
Trapper Nelson, 102
trauma, 252–53
trench shelters, 70, *71*
Trima climbers, 154–55, *155*

unconsciousness, 259
underwear, 17–18
United States Forest Service, 289,
    295
United States Geological Survey,
    168
utensils, 108–9

vapor-barrier liners, 41–42
vests, 18–20
Vinersa, 155, *155*

waist belt, 102–3
Warmlite, 38, 40, 42, 58
water supplies, 72, 73, 79, 108

waterproofing, 97
waxes
    applying, 151–53
    base, 146, 147
    basic kits, 148
    binder, 146, 147
    choosing, 150–51
    cross-country, 144–45
    glider, 146
    problems with, 153–54
    running, 146, 147–48
    and snow conditions, 145–46,
        148–49, 150–51
    terminology, 146
    types, 146
waxless skis, 139–40
Weston thermometer, 280
Wilderness Act, 289–90
wilderness skiing, 132
Wilkie Bearing compass, 193
windchill chart, *11*
wind-speed gauge, 280
wool fabric, 17, 18, 206

Yukon trail shoe, 117, 118

Zepharin, 257
zinc oxide ointment, 106
zippers, 36, 308